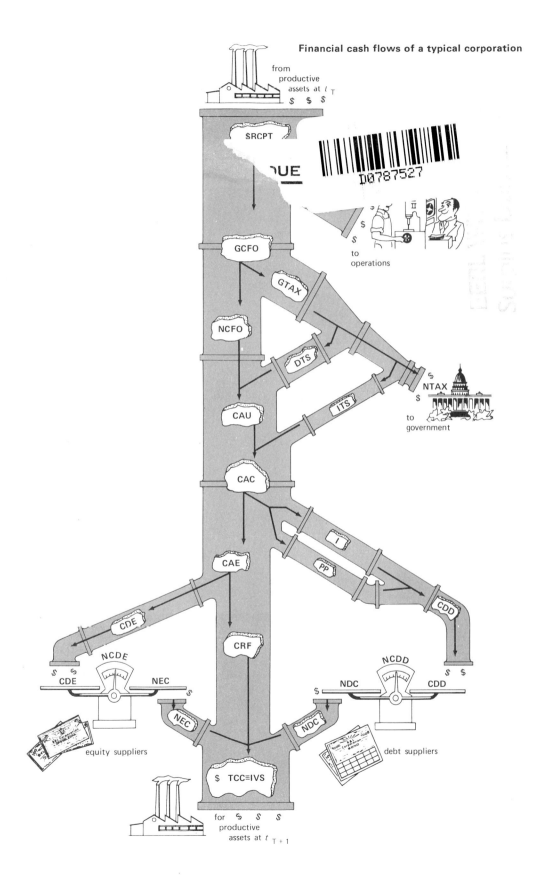

Financial cash flows of a typical corporation

from productive assets at t_T

$ $ $

$RCPT

UE

D0787527

$
$
to operations

GCFO

GTAX

NCFO

DTS

ITS

$
NTAX
$
to government

CAU

CAC

I

CAE

PP

CDD

CDE

CRF

NCDE

CDE   NEC $

NCDD

NDC   CDD
$ $

NEC

NDC

equity suppliers

debt suppliers

$ TCC≡IVS

for $ $ $
productive
assets at t_{T+1}

THE
BASIC THEORY
OF
CORPORATE FINANCE

Kenneth J. Boudreaux / Hugh W. Long

Tulane University

Prentice-Hall, Inc., Englewood Cliffs, New Jersey 07632

Library of Congress Cataloging in Publication Data

BOUDREAUX, KENNETH J (date)
    The basic theory of corporate finance.

    Includes bibliographical references and index.
    1. Corporations—Finance. I. Long, Hugh W.,
(date) joint author. II. Title.
HG4011.B65   658.1'5'01   76-42910
ISBN 0-13-069435-5

Printed in the United States of America

10 9 8 7 6 5 4 3 2 1

Prentice-Hall International, Inc., *London*
Prentice-Hall of Australia Pty. Limited, *Sydney*
Prentice-Hall of Canada, Ltd., *Toronto*
Prentice-Hall of India Private Limited, *New Delhi*
Prentice-Hall of Japan, Inc., *Tokyo*
Prentice-Hall of Southeast Asia Pte. Ltd., *Singapore*
Whitehall Books Limited, *Wellington, New Zealand*

Contents

Contents

Valuing Equity in a Typical Firm.
Overall Required Rates of Return and Capital Costs for a Typical Firm.
Overall Valuation of a Typical Firm.
Review of General Cash Flows and Formulas. Corporate Perpetuities.

PART TWO

THE THEORY OF CORPORATE FINANCIAL
DECISION MAKING

159

Contents

Preface

Most of us who teach others have heard the adage that the best way to learn a subject in depth is to teach it. As a case in point, *The Basic Theory of Corporate Finance* is perhaps best considered a history of our own education in finance during the five years that we have taught the MBA core finance course at Tulane University. We, like many finance instructors in the past decade, began our careers with the appropriate credentials, reasonable knowledge and skills in certain specialized areas of finance, and a grasp of the field's academic literature. As we faced our first classes, we had at our disposal a number of highly regarded textbooks and also some teaching experience from our doctoral education. What we did *not* have, however, was a clear, cohesive, straightforward, thoroughly integrated view of our field, with which we could communicate the ideas of corporate finance to our students. This book is meant to serve that need.

We were very fortunate in receiving the kind of support an effort like this needs, from a wide variety of sources. Colleagues were encouraging, students and alumni gave frank and forthright reactions and advice, and administrators allowed us much freedom and logistical back-up.

Associate Dean Eric W. Vetter boosted our early efforts with support from broad-purpose grants to Tulane from the Frost and Esso (now Exxon) Foundations. A classroom version of much of Sections I and II resulted, aided greatly by James E. Maurin, Daniel R. Gresham, and John W. Barter. We are also indebted to them for first urging us to write this book. Notwithstanding our comments about accounting, colleagues David W. Harvey and Stephen A. Zeff were also most helpful, as was James T.

Murphy. Doctoral student John Page gave us useful comments, Marcia Curtis compiled the index, and she with Chick Schoen made many improvements to the problem sets. Typing (and retyping our myriad changes) was faithfully performed by Gene Andrews with her usual careful attention to detail and quality, and Fred Johnson is owed much gratitude for his assistance in graphics. We are also grateful to Susan Anderson, our editor, for the battles she fought for and with us.

We were extremely fortunate to have had the manuscript read by an unusually large number of external reviewers (publishers are wary of texts like this) who provided valuable suggestions, corrections, and a surprising amount of encouragement. Those whose identities we know are: Stephen H. Archer, Willamette University; E. Eugene Carter, M.I.T.; Jack C. Francis, CUNY; Peter Goulet, University of Northern Iowa; Charles W. Haley, University of Washington; Michael Hopewell, University of Oregon; Pearson Hunt, University of Massachusetts; Stewart C. Myers, M.I.T.; Dennis J. O'Connor, California State University (Fullerton); Michael L. Rice, University of North Carolina; David F. Rush, University of Colorado; J. B. Silvers, Indiana University; William F. Sharpe, Stanford University; Ezra Solomon, Stanford University; Roger Stover, University of Minnesota; and David West, University of Missouri (Columbia).

With such a distinguished list of reviewers, we unsuccessfully resisted the temptation to paraphrase a classic disclaimer of disclaimers:

> Tradition requires that we absolve our critics from responsibility for all conceptual errors. Although we deeply respect all tradition as a matter of principle, we see no reason to absolve them. If we have committed blunders, one or another of these learned persons should have noticed; if they did not, then let them share the disgrace. As for separating them from our interpretations and bias, the usual disclaimer is unnecessary since no one in his or her right mind is likely to hold them responsible for either. (Following Eugene D. Genovese, *The World The Slaveholders Made: Two Essays in Interpretation.* New York: Pantheon Books, 1969, p. xii.)

To our families and friends who suffered the drafting with us, our apologies and thanks, especially to Carole and Patricia. And finally, to the students at the Graduate School of Business Administration, Tulane University, whose patience, interest, and frank feedback over the past few years was absolutely indispensable, we owe our largest debt.

KENNETH J. BOUDREAUX

HUGH W. LONG

New Orleans, 1977

Introduction

Social scientists continually strive to refine the conceptual frameworks within which they pursue their disciplines. In particular, a highly desired but often elusive goal is the development of theory surrounding a body of knowledge—theory which is internally consistent, respectable in its rigor, and rich in its applicability.

Academicians in the field of corporate finance made great strides in the 1950's and 1960's in developing such theory. As in most emerging fields, however, theoreticians pursued multiple paths of inquiry and wrote of their findings and speculations for an audience largely comprising only their colleagues. A student wishing to comprehend this material during its development had but one path open: to become highly literate in accounting, microeconomics, statistics, and calculus, and then to plow through seemingly endless articles in academic journals. The typical article usually displayed unique notation and point of view, and offered arguments distinctly in conflict with other references. Such articles tended to focus narrowly on the most current controversy—often in isolation from other issues—and, to be honest, frequently left us as students quite confused.

Within the past few years, corporate financial theory has matured to the extent that there now are texts which can accurately claim to cover the existing body of knowledge with consistency and rigor. Advanced finance students, to whom these texts are addressed, thus have a much more efficient means of learning financial theory than did those of us whose only recourse was the dissection of academic journal controversies. As purveyors of this body of knowledge, we are naturally pleased with this progress in our field and with the quality of material now available for advanced students of the subject.

This text also treats financial theory as a mature, cohesive whole. In doing so, however, it differs in a major and significant way from other theory texts: *Our treatment is directed particularly at early, indeed even beginning, students of finance.* (We regard this group as composed primarily of second-level finance undergraduates and first-level MBA's, with some membership from introductory undergraduate and second-level MBA students, depending upon the orientation of particular degree programs.)

We are convinced that an early, deep understanding of financial theory is of great value to finance students. With a solid appreciation of the theory, early finance students can much better comprehend, retain, and use the important financial techniques they are taught later in their studies, as well as better understand and function within the complex real markets and institutions that they will eventually encounter. Thus the study of theory need not be incompatible with the desire of professional business students to acquire managerial training in finance. Indeed, the *lack* of a solid theoretical background may leave the student or practitioner scant capability for evaluating either new financial techniques or changes in financial markets and institutions.

The texts currently being used in early finance courses do a fine job of presenting the descriptive detail and analytical techniques of finance. They also present some financial theory. Over the years, however, our students have succeeded in convincing us that these texts do not present the theory in a complete, understandable, and useful manner. A brief perusal of the widely-used early finance texts will show the main reasons why their theory does not work well: large, important segments in the logical progression of ideas are out of place or entirely omitted; the pros and cons of long-settled theoretical controversies are presented in all their unnecessary detail; and notational systems are confusing and overly complex, bearing little or no relation to the phenomena being described. What results as financial "theory" is a hodge-podge of ideas, individually good but loosely connected, interspersed with non-theoretical material, and having few common threads. It is small wonder that early finance students dislike theory.

We regard the lack of an understandable basic theory book in finance as unfortunate, since the material itself is inherently interesting and quite manageable by undergraduate and MBA students. This book is the result of our concern.

Instructors well-schooled in finance will recognize that the theory we present is, with only a few exceptions, the "received" or more mature theory of corporate finance. Because this book is aimed at early finance students and because it is intended to be innovative primarily in the pedagogical realm, we have concentrated on presenting the theory as it exists, and have left the expansion of the frontiers of finance to more advanced treatments. The progression of ideas follows the logical path of first describing financial market economics and exploring corporate valuation in those markets, and only then introducing the impact of the major internal corporate financial decisions on market valuations.

Compared with both more advanced *and* lower-level survey texts, this book is unique in a number of ways. First, and most important, there is a general emphasis throughout on consistency and cohesiveness of presentation; the chapters follow each other in a logical progression, building toward the construction of a complete theory of corporate finance. Further, the presentation of corporate financial activity is in a cash-flow format. This mode is both more accurate (in finance terms) and, perhaps surprisingly, more understandable than the less appropriate accounting model which still appears in most basic finance texts. In addition, the text introduces a unique system of financial terminology, using abbreviations, or "acronyms," that have easily recognizable relationships to the terms being represented. This system is used consistently across the whole spectrum of corporate financial theory and decision-making. (We have been pleasantly surprised by the success this simple tactic has achieved in the classroom. Evidently, notational confusion has been one of the major barriers to learning financial theory.)

We also introduce the risk dimension of corporate finance early, and do not relegate it to obscure appendixes. By developing capital market risk concepts gradually throughout the text, the Capital Asset Pricing Model can be used as a decision mechanism in a basic and non-threatening way.

Also, the presentation of the corporate dividend decision is in the context of a more general capital acquisition/disbursement decision, which recognizes that real corporations have more degrees of freedom in this financial decision than most theoretical treatments portray.

Extensive numerical illustrations are used and interconnected throughout, and each section is followed by detailed problems so that students can test their understanding of the theory.

This text can be used in a number of ways. We have had significant success in a full-semester course by combining it with the technique and descriptive chapters of James Van Horne's *Financial Management and Policy* (Prentice-Hall: Englewood Cliffs, N.J., 4th ed.), and several short case study discussions. Other survey texts would probably also be satisfactory. In a sixteen-week semester, we are hard pressed to complete Chapters 14-16, and have usually delayed that material until later in the finance curriculum. Although this deferral is consistent with most programs we have seen, we feel that it is suboptimal, and see two potential solutions, depending on a school's calendar. In the quarter system, a two-quarter sequence covering the same package of material described above would provide about twenty weeks and allow everything to be handled nicely.

In the semester system, we plan to incorporate Chapters 1-3 at the end of our required microeconomics course. This will allow us to retain the materials in Chapters 14-16 in our one-semester basic finance course.

Reviewers have also suggested that a good casebook in finance is all the material needed to supplement this text for an introductory course in which the instructor lectures on technique. Further, some business programs reserve a theory course for undergraduates; this text will serve well there, as it also will in an MBA theory course to which some outside readings are added.

Based on the four years of classroom experience we have accumulated in its use, we would predict an enthusiastic reception and excellent retention of concepts by students whether this book is used to provide the theory portion of an introductory finance course or as the cornerstone of a course in the theory of corporate finance. We hear regularly from alumni who indicate their pleasure at being able to deal successfully with new situations and market conditions which were never mentioned in the classroom, but which are nevertheless amenable to analysis within the theoretical framework presented here. For us, that is the essence of professional education, and we shall be most pleased if this text furthers that end.

Dedicated To:

Irving Fisher
John Burr Williams
Harry Markowitz
Franco Modigliani
Merton Miller
Jack Hirschlifer
Diran Bodenhorn
William Sharpe
John Lintner

We here recognize their significant contributions to the field of finance; we have chosen to forego detailed textual references to their work and that of other financial theorists in favor of this general acknowledgment.

THE THEORY OF FINANCIAL MARKETS AND CORPORATE VALUATION

This book is divided into two parts. In Part One we introduce some of the most basic and important ideas in financial theory. In Section I (Chapters 1–4) we describe how financial markets work and the functions they perform for individuals and corporations. At the same time we develop in some detail certain ideas that you may have already encountered, such as investment, present value, market prices, and risk. We include these ideas and others here because you probably have not seen how they all interrelate within the general context of a financial or capital market.

In Section II (Chapters 5–7) we discover how the unique characteristics of the corporate form affect (and are affected by) the basic financial ideas from Section I. Specifically, Section II is concerned with how corporations are valued in capital markets.

In general, this first part of the book sets the stage for Part Two, which deals with corporate financial decision making. Although corporate financial decision making is the major concern of students of finance, its study, as we shall see, is fruitless without the solid base of market awareness developed in Part One.

Introduction to Financial Markets and Investment

This section contains four chapters. In Chapter 1 we describe the fundamental characteristics of a financial market, how that market functions, and the services it provides for its participants. In Chapter 2 we introduce the idea of investment, discussing what it means to financial market participants and how they make decisions about investing. Chapters 3 and 4 ("Multiperiod Analysis" and "Introduction to Uncertainty and Capital Markets") expand the basic concepts of the first two chapters in preparation for Section II, in which our discussion of the financial market will be enlarged to deal with corporations.

Do not be surprised if at first some of the ideas in Section I seem extremely basic. At this stage we are only laying the foundation for corporate financial theory by demonstrating the common ideas that underlie all financial topics. The applicability and worth of these basic ideas should rapidly become clear to you.

Chapter 1

Financial Markets and Value

Certain basic financial ideas are used repeatedly in corporate financial theory. In this section we shall introduce a number of these ideas from the viewpoint of a participant in a financial market. This participant could be you as an individual, or a corporation, or any other entity that has financial decisions to make. Our method of presentation will be to build an example, simple in concept and simple numerically, which will illustrate the decision-making behavior of participants in a financial market.

As we shall discover, *finance* can be very appropriately considered as *economics extended into the dimensions of time and uncertainty.* We shall deal with the uncertainty dimension as it becomes necessary to advance our analysis. The time dimension, however, needs our immediate attention.

TIME Since time is so essential to the ideas and examples we shall develop, it is important that we invest some of ours right now to explain the way the concept of *time* works in this book. Figure 1.1 shows the two elements we shall use to measure and label time. We shall describe time by referring to time *points*, or *locations in* time, and time *periods*, or *durations of* time. To

FIGURE 1.1   **Time points and time periods**

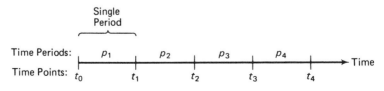

illustrate, our financial-market participants will make decisions at time points, and the effects of such decisions will occur through a number of subsequent time periods. If a participant makes a decision "now" having implications extending through two periods, we would say that the decision (1) was made at time point t_0; (2) has impact in time periods p_1 and p_2, passing through time point t_1; and (3) ends at time point t_2.

Note that time points are located at both ends and beginnings of time periods. Thus, t_2 is located both at the end of period p_2 and at the beginning of period p_3. Remember also that time points are only *locations* in time; they have no duration. Said another way, everything that happens at a time point occurs *instantaneously*. Indeed, even if several financial decisions are made at a single time point, we shall think of them as all having been made simultaneously, with neither any single decision, nor the group of decisions, having used up any time.

The examples of basic financial ideas that we develop in this section will be mostly *single-period* illustrations. A single-period situation is one that involves a single time period and two time points. If we think of time point t_0 as "now" and time point t_1 as "later," we have a single-period example running through time period p_1, which begins now and ends later. That is, we start at time point t_0, run through time period p_1, and end at time point t_1 (see Figure 1.1).

Of course, single-period examples are not very common in real financial markets. But we shall find that the simplicity of the one-period illustration helps us to present many ideas in a clear and straightforward manner. There will be occasions when more complicated time patterns will be required to demonstrate financial concepts. In such cases we shall fully explain these more sophisticated examples.

FINANCIAL MARKETS AND THEIR CHARACTER- ISTICS

The validity of the examples in this chapter depends very much on the existence of a financial market with certain characteristics. We define a *financial market* as *a place where market participants get together to exchange time-dependent assets among themselves.* You may think that we have made the market sound like a formidable place, and that the concept must therefore be terribly complicated. Actually, it is amazingly simple. A financial market is just a place where people come together to lend and borrow money.

For example, if you have some money now (t_0) and you can participate in a single-period financial market, you might choose (1) to spend (consume) all your money (resources) at t_0, or (2) to consume less than all your t_0 resources immediately and to make available to the financial market that part of your t_0 resources which you do not consume. The act of making resources available to the financial market is called *lending*. In return for your lending, the financial market will give you an asset (like an I.O.U.) at t_0 which promises to return to you later (t_1) the exact amount of resources that you made available (loaned) *plus* something called interest. *Interest* is simply a payment from the financial market which compensates for the use of your resources during the period between t_0 and t_1.

Alternatively, suppose that you want to consume more resources (spend more money) at t_0 than you have in hand. If you can participate in the financial market, it can make additional resources available to you at t_0. The act of acquiring resources from the financial market is called *borrowing*. In return for your borrowing, you must give the financial market an asset at t_0 that promises to return at t_1 the exact amount of resources which you borrowed *plus interest*, a payment to the financial market for your use of the borrowed resources for one period.

Even this simple introduction to a financial market shows that it is little more than a conduit or intermediary between all those market participants who might want to lend resources at a particular time point and all those who might want to borrow resources at the same time point. *Intermediation*, then, is the first characteristic function of a financial market.

The second basic function of a financial market is *setting the market interest rate*. We have already implied that interest is a payment by which the borrower compensates the lender through the financial market for the use of the lender's resources during a time period. The actual market interest rate that prevails during a time period can be thought of as "the price of time" in that period, and its numerical level will be the result of the interaction between market participants. In economic terms, the market interest rate will be some function of the demand for and the supply of resources in the financial market.

To understand this second financial market function, let us back up one step and ask several questions that may have occurred to you:

1. Why do we have to have interest at all?
2. Why must a lender be compensated for making resources available to the financial market?
3. Why is a borrower of those resources willing to pay interest?

The answers to all three questions are based on characteristics of financial market participants considered both as a group and as individuals.

First, why does interest exist? The most basic reason is that our financial-market participants get satisfaction from the *consumption* of resources, not from the holding of financial assets.[1] Furthermore, an increase

---

[1] We recognize that some people may get satisfaction from simply holding or manipulating financial assets. The reasons for such satisfaction may be distinct from the consumption such assets allow. For example, satisfaction might have a psychological or moral basis. But motivations such as these, when they exist, are most efficiently included as additions to a financial-market theory developed from purely consumption-based behavior. Therefore, we shall proceed to build our financial market independent of any nonconsumption satisfactions.

in consumption at any time point makes financial-market participants happier, provided that their consumption is not decreased at any other time point. And finally, the increases in happiness that participants get from higher consumption get smaller and smaller as the total amount of their consumption steadily increases. Appendix I.A demonstrates that these three characteristics of financial-market participants result in each having a time preference for consumption of resources. This means simply that each participant can decide which time pattern of resource consumption makes him most happy. If his time pattern of resource endowment is not the same as the time pattern of resource consumption that makes him most happy, he can go to the financial market and, by borrowing or lending resources, achieve his desired consumption time pattern. We shall illustrate the details of these transactions soon, but, for the moment, just remember that participants use the financial market to alter their consumption patterns across time so as to maximize their satisfaction.

When they go to this market, some participants will wish to alter their patterns by postponing some consumption to future time points. Others wish to use the market to increase their present consumption and lower their future consumption. The result of all these participants "coming to market" will be a supply and demand for lending and borrowing. The market finds a price for altering time patterns of consumption so that the total amount lent equals the total amount borrowed. That price is called the *market interest rate*.

Another characteristic of our financial market is that the interactions of participants' resource endowments and time preferences for consumption produce a *positive* market interest rate. This is actually a simplifying characteristic from the point of view of economic theory, but, fortunately, it is also realistic, since we almost always see positive rates of interest in real financial markets. The supply of dollars to be lent and the demand for dollars to be borrowed result in borrowers paying lenders an amount of compensation to bring enough lending dollars to the market to satisfy borrowers' time-pattern consumption preferences.

In answer to questions 2 and 3, we can now address the specific reasons why lenders must be compensated and borrowers must (and are willing to) compensate. With a positive market interest rate existing, the participant who lends money (resources) now (at t_0) to the financial market is giving up an amount of present (t_0) consumption and therefore happiness. He is foregoing the satisfaction he could have attained had he spent the money (consumed the resources) now (t_0), and in exchange, by lending, he is looking forward to future (t_1) consumption and satisfaction which will be higher than they would have otherwise been. While he has delayed the satisfaction associated with consuming the money (resources) lent until that money is repaid and he again has the option of spending it, he will also receive additional money (interest) which he can use to increase his consumption level (at t_1) and thus his overall happiness. This interest he receives in the future (t_1) is the inducement necessary for him to alter his consumption pattern in the particular way described by the act of lending. The interest is his compensation for having delayed his consumption through lending. In combination with his time preferences, the net result of decreased present (t_0) and increased future (t_1) consumption is an increase in his overall level of satisfaction.

Similarly, a borrower's time preferences tell us that she desires to raise her current (t_0) consumption level above what it would be in the absence of borrowing. Her future (t_1) consumption is decreased by both the amount she borrows (principal) *and* the required compensation through the financial market to the lender (interest). She is giving up additional future (t_1) consumption in exchange for increased present (t_0) consumption. The net effect of this change in her pattern of consumption is an increase in her overall level of happiness. Although she would naturally prefer not to pay compensation (interest) to lenders, she knows that the loan and her increased satisfaction would not be forthcoming were she unwilling to make such a payment. Thus, even though she pays interest, her time preferences for consumption indicate that she ends up happier by altering her time pattern and paying interest than she would be by not doing so.

We shall soon see that the market rate of interest has an important influence on the actions of lenders and borrowers. From our short introduction you can probably gather that the amount of resources or money that a lender will choose to make available to the financial market as well as the amount a borrower will choose to take from the market is heavily dependent on the consumption effects which accompany these transactions. And these consumption effects are themselves significantly influenced by the market interest rate.

Thus far, we have identified two functional, indeed definitional, characteristics of a financial market:

1. A financial market is a place that exists to allow market participants to exchange time-dependent assets (borrow and lend), thus performing as an *intermediary* among participants.
2. A financial market performs the function of *setting the market interest rate*. For convenience, we shall assume that the interaction between participants' time preferences for consumption and their resource endowments produces a *positive* market interest rate.

SIMPLIFYING CHARACTER-ISTICS

We shall now give our financial market some additional characteristics which will help to keep it a fairly uncomplicated place. Some real financial markets display certain of these characteristics and others do not. Realizing this, several of these simplifications will be discarded as we proceed further into the theory and try to understand how different real-world conditions affect our examples. But to begin, we shall simplify the operation of our financial markct by adopting the five characteristics in the following list, the first of which we discussed earlier in the section on Time. Simplifying characteristics 2 through 5 will be discussed below:

1. The financial market deals with a single time period beginning now (t_0) and ending later (t_1).
2. Conditions of certainty exist in the financial market.
3. Perfect competition exists among participants in the financial market.
4. The financial market performs its functions without "friction"; specifically:
   a. No transactions costs.
   b. Equal lending and borrowing interest rates.
5. There is no taxation of the financial market, its activities, or its participants.

Conditions of certainty mean that if a market participant lends money at t_0, he is certain to have returned to him at t_1 the amount he lent plus the agreed upon amount of interest. This implies that we know for certain that a borrower will repay all principal and interest amounts when due. In other words, default does not exist. This assumption is convenient for the moment because we wish to treat uncertainty only after we have dealt with market participants changing the timing of their consumption. As it happens, when uncertainty *is* present in the financial markets, it requires compensation in much the same way that the decreasing of present consumption requires compensation. In order to understand each form of compensation in and of itself, we shall wait and introduce uncertainty into our financial market at a later stage of our development.

The third simplifying characteristic which we attribute to our financial market is one that we shall maintain throughout this book. *Perfect competition among participants* means that no participant or group of participants is able to dominate the market. Said another way, no single decision to borrow or not to borrow, to lend or not to lend, will have any measurable effect on the market interest rate. The effect of such perfect competition is that all market participants are "price takers." They cannot bargain with the market for reduced or increased interest rates, owing to their large size or any other economic characteristic.

Fourth, we have assumed a *frictionless market*. Here the only amounts of money paid and received by participants within the market are the lent and borrowed amounts and their associated interest payments. There are no "transactions costs." Frictionless markets under the condition of certainty also imply that interest rates are the same for borrowers and lenders. Thus, a participant in our financial market pays the same interest rate to borrow money as he would receive if he lent money. That is, if the market interest rate is 8% between t_0 and t_1, a participant would receive \$8 in interest at t_1

for each \$100 he lent at t_0, and would have to pay \$8 of interest at t_1 for each \$100 he borrowed at t_0.

Real financial markets are, of course, influenced in no small degree by such frictions as specific transaction costs and spreads between lending and borrowing rates (bids and asks). However, their presence at this introductory stage of our discussion would only complicate our task. To the extent that such frictions are important in corporate financial theory, they will appear in later chapters.

Our last simplifying characteristic, *no taxation*, is made for reasons similar to those mentioned in the preceding paragraph. Taxation, specifically income taxation, will be introduced shortly and will be seen as a major factor in corporate financial theory. But to keep things simple at first, we shall begin our treatment with the unusual circumstance of a tax-free world.

This discussion of simplifying characteristics has been brief, but as we progress through this and later chapters, you will clearly see why these characteristics have been adopted here and when it will be appropriate to depart from them. Table 1.1 summarizes all the basic characteristics of our financial market and its participants.

TABLE 1.1 **Basic characteristics of our financial market and its participants**

A. The market—general characteristics
   1. A financial market is a place that exists to allow market participants to exchange time-dependent assets (borrow and lend), thus performing as an *intermediary* among participants.
   2. A financial market performs the function of *setting the market interest rate*. For convenience, we shall assume that the interaction between participants' time preferences for consumption and their resource endowments produces a *positive* market interest rate.
B. The participants—behavioral characteristics
   1. Participants get satisfaction only from the *consumption* of resources.
   2. Participants prefer more consumption to less consumption at each time point as long as there is no decrease in their consumption at any other time point.
   3. Although B2 is always true, each additional increment of consumption (measured, say, by a unit of money) gives a participant a smaller increase in satisfaction than did the immediately preceding (and equal) increment of consumption.
C. The market and its participants—simplifying characteristics
   1. The financial market deals with a single time period beginning now (t_0) and ending later (t_1).
   2. Conditions of certainty exist in the financial market.
   3. Perfect competition exists among participants in the financial market.
   4. The financial market performs its functions without friction; specifically:
      a. No transactions costs.
      b. Equal lending and borrowing interest rates.
   5. There is no taxation of the market, its activities, or its participants.

RESOURCE ALLOCATION ACROSS TIME

Now that we have outlined the definitional and simplifying characteristics of our financial market, we can begin to explore how it works. Let us assume that there is a financial market participant who has an initial resource endowment (cash inflow) of \$80.00 now (t_0) and \$75.60 in cash later (t_1). You may think of this resource endowment as coming from wages or salary, a gift from a rich relative, or even unemployment or disability insurance. Actually, the exact source does not matter; the important things are the *amount* of cash involved and the time point *when* each amount of money becomes available. (We are not now concerned with any questioning of the cash sources because, you will recall, we have characterized our market as certain. We know without doubt that the cash inflows at both t_0 and t_1 occur, regardless of their source.)

This participant's initial financial situation is shown graphically in Figure 1.2. In this display we measure dollars that occur at t_0 along the horizontal axis and dollars of t_1 money along the vertical axis. Thus, every point on the graph represents some unique combination of dollars at t_0 and dollars at t_1. In particular, point O is located even with the $80.00 mark along the t_0 axis and at $75.60 along the t_1 axis. That location precisely depicts the financial situation of our market participant in a convenient graphical way. A glance at point O in Figure 1.2 tells us all we need to know about his financial resources.

If our participant chose to consume the $80.00 of t_0 money at t_0 and the $75.60 of t_1 money at t_1, he would have no need for a financial market. But people often desire to consume resources in a pattern that is not perfectly matched to the pattern in which their resources become available. Our participant might well want to consume in a pattern different from $80.00 at t_0 and $75.60 at t_1. A financial market gives him the flexibility to alter his consumption pattern, *to reallocate resources across time.*

Suppose that forces of supply and demand have dictated a financial market interest rate of 8% for the period, and our participant has free access to the financial market in the form of borrowing and lending at that interest

FIGURE 1.2   Initial resource endowment

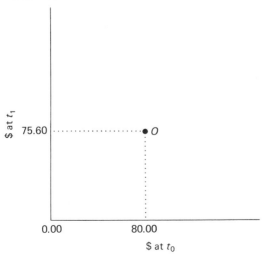

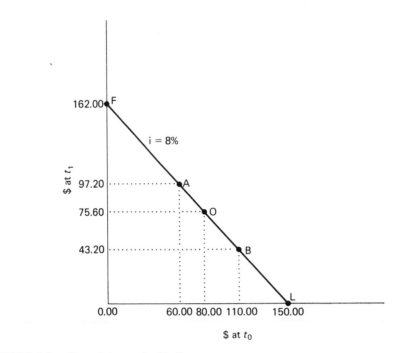

FIGURE 1.3   **Financial opportunity line**

rate. Figure 1.3 shows some of the opportunities he has to reallocate his resources across time. For example, if for some reason he decides to consume only $60.00 of his $80.00 t_0 resources, he can make the remaining $20.00 of t_0 money available to the financial market. With an interest rate of 8% his t_1 resources then become

$75.60   initial endowment at t_1
+20.00   return of principal lent at t_0
+ 1.60   interest on $20.00 for one period at 8%

$97.20   resources available at t_1

By lending $20.00 at t_0 to the financial market at 8%, our participant moves from his initial position at point O ($80.00, $75.60) to a new position at point A ($60.00, $97.20). He has decreased his t_0 resources by $20.00 and increased his t_1 resources by $21.60.

On the other hand, our participant might have chosen to increase rather than decrease his t_0 consumption. For example, at t_0 he might have borrowed $30.00 from the financial market, thereby raising his t_0 resources to $80.00 + $30.00 = $110.00. Then at t_1 his resources become

$75.60   initial endowment at t_1
−30.00   return of principal amount borrowed at t_0
− 2.40   interest payment on $30.00 at 8% for one period

$43.20   resources available at t_1

By borrowing $30.00 at 8% at t_0 he moves from point O ($80.00, $75.60) to point B ($110.00, $43.20). His t_0 resources are increased by $30.00 and his t_1 resources are decreased by $32.40.

If our participant were a real profligate, he might choose to consume as much as he could right now. This would amount to his $80.00 t_0 initial endowment plus whatever the financial market would lend him with the certain promise to pay a total in principal and interest at t_1 of $75.60, the amount that becomes available to him then.

From the earlier examples you may have noticed that the amount due in principal and interest at t_1 is equal to 1.08 (1 plus the interest rate expressed as a decimal) times the amount lent or borrowed at t_0. That is,

$$\text{total repayment} = (1.08)(\text{amount lent or borrowed})$$

Thus, our participant can calculate the maximum amount he could borrow at t_0 as

$$\$75.60 = (1.08)(\text{maximum } t_0 \text{ borrowing})$$

Therefore,

$$\text{maximum } t_0 \text{ borrowing} = \frac{\$75.60}{1.08}$$

and

$$\$70.00 = \text{maximum } t_0 \text{ borrowing}$$

By borrowing $70.00 at t_0, our participant then has, at t_1,

$75.60	initial endowment at t_1
-70.00	principal repayment of t_0 borrowing
$- 5.60$	interest on $70.00 at 8% for one period
$ 0.00	resources available at t_1

This consumption location is point L in Figure 1.3, showing a t_0 amount of $80.00 + $70.00 = $150.00 and a t_1 amount of $0.00.

Of course, our participant could instead choose to starve at t_0 and make all of his t_0 resources available to the financial market. Doing that would maximize his t_1 consumption:

$ 75.60	initial endowment
$+80.00$	return of principal lent at t_0
$+ 6.40$	interest on $80.00 at 8% for one period
$162.00	resources available at t_1

This consumption location is at point F in Figure 1.3, indicating t_0 resources of $0.00 and t_1 resources of $162.00.

In this example, we have so far shown two specific lending opportunities, shifting our participant from O to either A or F, and two specific borrowing opportunities, allowing movement from O to B or L. Our participant can, of course, choose to use any one of these if he desires.

FINANCIAL
OPPOR-
TUNITY
LINE

It should now be clear to you that with a market interest rate of 8%, *any* amount (up to a maximum of $70.00 as we calculated above) he borrows at t_0 will require a t_1 payment of 1.08 times the amount borrowed. Thus, the number of specific opportunities available to our participant far exceed the four specific cases, *A*, *B*, *F*, and *L*, that we have detailed. In fact, an unlimited number of possibilities exists. Graphically, *all of these allowable opportunities for lending and borrowing (or, equivalently, for differing combinations of t_0 and t_1 consumption) lie along a straight line.* This straight line is shown in Figure 1.3 running from point *F* through our participant's initial resource endowment at point *O* to point *L*. Of course, points *A* and *B* also lie on this straight line as particular examples of possible combinations. We shall call this line our market participant's *financial opportunity line* (FOL). He can attain *any* combination of t_0 and t_1 consumption which lies on his FOL by either (1) transferring t_0 resources to t_1 through the process of lending within the limit of his t_0 resources, or (2) transferring t_1 resources to t_0 by borrowing within the limit that the initial t_1 resources place on his ability to repay principal and interest.[2]

You may wish to test the validity of the FOL for yourself by choosing some amount for our market participant to borrow or lend other than those amounts we have already used. Calculate the new t_0 and t_1 resources which result from the transaction and see whether or not this new consumption combination seems to plot along the FOL. It will if you do the computations and plotting accurately.

Even from this simple introduction, it should be clear to you that the FOL looks the way it does mainly because of our participant's initial endowment, point *O*, and his ability to borrow and lend at the market interest rate. Those two things allow him to move up and down the FOL as he chooses. The price that he pays to increase his t_0 consumption (moving down the FOL from point *O*) is the market rate, 8%; the return he gets from decreasing his t_0 consumption (moving up the FOL from point *O*) is also the market rate, 8%. From the graph in Figure 1.3, you might be able to recognize that the price he pays or the return he gets is determined by the steepness, or *slope*, of the FOL. Therefore, it seems reasonable that the market interest rate and the slope of the FOL be related. This relationship is expressed as

$$\text{market interest rate} = -(1 + \text{FOL slope})$$

Let us illustrate this relationship by looking at the move from point *O* to point *A* in Figure 1.3. You will recall that this move was accomplished by our participant lending 20 of his 80 t_0 dollars to the financial market. The

---

[2]If our market participant really wanted to, he could attain a consumption combination lying not on the financial opportunity line but inside the triangle formed by that line and the horizontal and vertical axes. To do this, however, would require his lending at lower than the market rate of interest or borrowing at higher than the market rate of interest. Either action would hardly seem to be in his best interest (pun intended). Indeed, either action would violate the second characteristic of participants listed in Table 1.1.

slope of the FOL is the change (Δ) in t_1 dollars between O and A divided by the change (Δ) in t_0 dollars between O and A,[3] or

$$\text{FOL slope} = \frac{\Delta\$ \text{ at } t_1}{\Delta\$ \text{ at } t_0} = \frac{\$A \text{ at } t_1 - \$O \text{ at } t_1}{\$A \text{ at } t_0 - \$O \text{ at } t_0}$$

$$= \frac{97.20 - 75.60}{60.00 - 80.00}$$

$$= \frac{21.60}{-20.00} = -1.08 \text{ [4]}$$

Since we have calculated the FOL slope, we can now determine the market interest rate:

$$\text{market interest rate} = -(1 + \text{FOL slope})$$
$$= -[1 - (1.08)]$$
$$= -(-0.08)$$
$$= 0.08 \quad \text{or} \quad 8\%$$

This same rate, 8%, would be the result of a move from O to any other point on the FOL, or even between *any* two points on the FOL since it is a straight line and therefore has constant slope. If you think it would be worthwhile, you can convince yourself of this by repeating our O to A calculation for other sets of points.

PRESENT VALUE Our financial market has now been well enough developed so that we can introduce one of the most important concepts in finance: *present value*. Probably the best definition of this concept is: *The present value of a promise of present and future cash flows is that sum of money a person would need right now in order to duplicate the amounts and timing of those promised cash flows by participating in the financial market.* Further, it is the present amount a participant would be both *willing* and *able* to exchange for the promised flows.

We can illustrate the meaning of this by computing the present value of our market participant's initial resource endowment, which was $80.00 at t_0 and $75.60 at t_1. The $80.00 cash inflow at t_0 has a present value of $80.00 because t_0 is now or present in time. Our participant would require a payment of at least $80.00 for this t_0 portion of his endowment, and no reasonable person is likely to give him more than $80.00.

But what is the present value of the t_1 portion of the endowment, the $75.60 which is a cash inflow one period hence? Our participant surely will

---

[3]The slope of any straight line is constant and is given by choosing any two points on that line and taking the difference (change) between the vertical axis measurements of the two points and dividing it by the difference in the horizontal axis measurements of the same two points.

[4]Note that it makes no difference whether we subtract point O dollars from point A dollars, as we have done, or point A dollars from point O dollars, provided that we do it the same way in both the numerator and denominator of this fraction. We will get the same result: FOL slope is equal to -1.08 either way.

not accept an amount of money now in exchange for the $75.60 at t_1 unless the amount received now meets the following condition: It must be big enough so that, if it is lent to the financial market, it will produce *at least* $75.60 in total interest and principal payments at t_1.

Now consider a second person in our financial market. Suppose that she is interested in purchasing the t_1 portion of our participant's initial resource endowment. Surely participant 2 will be willing to offer participant 1 *no more* at t_0 than the amount which would produce total payments of $75.60 at t_1 by using the financial market. This is because the endowment she is buying returns only $75.60 at t_1. In other words, if our original participant demanded a t_0 payment for the endowment that was larger than the amount necessary to get $75.60 from the financial market at t_1, our second participant would turn him down cold. This is because she would be better off (have greater satisfaction) by *not* buying the promise of $75.60 at t_1 from participant 1. Rather, she would make her larger amount of dollars directly available to the financial market and, as a result, receive more than $75.60 at t_1.

Thus, the present value of $75.60 at t_1 must be exactly that amount of money which, if lent to the financial market at t_0, will produce $75.60 at t_1. Participant 1 will accept no less; participant 2 will provide no more. And what is that exact amount of t_0 dollars? Fortunately, we have already performed that calculation as part of finding point L for Figure 1.3. There, you recall, we discovered that $70.00 of t_0 money borrowed from the financial market at 8% required a t_1 payment of $75.60. Since the borrowing and lending rates are the same, $70.00 lent to the financial market at t_0 will return $75.60 at t_1. Therefore, $70.00 is the present value of $75.60 of t_1 money when the market rate is 8%.

Since the present value of the t_1 part of our first participant's initial endowment is $70.00 and the present value of his t_0 cash inflow is $80.00, the present value of his entire initial endowment is the total of the two parts: $150.00 of t_0 money. With $150.00 in hand right now, our participant could exactly reproduce the cash inflows of $80.00 at t_0 and $75.60 at t_1 (or any other consumption combination on the FOL) by using the financial market. We shall call the present value of someone's total financial resources his or her *present wealth.*

We have seen in the previous discussion of Figure 1.3 that our first participant can, by borrowing and lending at t_0, reallocate his financial resources across time along the FOL as he pleases. If you look at Figure 1.3 again, you will notice that one of his possible reallocations, point L, is, in fact, the present value of his entire endowment, $150.00, at t_0. You will note that point L is where the FOL intercepts the horizontal (t_0) axis. *It is generally true that the present value of any point on an FOL is the line's horizontal intercept.* [We, logically enough, call the FOL's vertical intercept—where the FOL intersects the vertical (t_1) axis—the "terminal value" of any point on an FOL.]

We have previously characterized point L as that consumption combination that places all of our participant's resources at t_0. This points up a convenient way of visualizing what your present wealth is: *the total t_0 dollars your present and future cash flows would add up to if you brought them all back to the present by using the financial market.* The process of calculating the present value of future dollars is called *discounting*. It tells us how many t_0 dollars we could accumulate in exchange for all present and future cash inflows if we did use the financial market. In Figure 1.3 point L is also the present or discounted value of our participant's initial time-dependent endowment of resources.

We have now identified two ways of finding a present value. The first of these is graphical—finding the horizontal intercept of the FOL; the second is numerical—discounting. We would caution you that the first method only works well in single-period examples such as the one we have been using. Discounting, however, is a numerical procedure that works, as we shall see later in this section, for both single- *and* multiple-period examples. Therefore, it is the more important way of finding a present value.

As a review of what we have done, here is the numerical procedure (or formula) for finding a present value in a single-period example using discounting:

$$\text{present value} = \$ \text{ at } t_0 + \frac{\$ \text{ at } t_1}{1 + \text{market interest rate}}$$

PRESENT VALUE AND MARKET VALUE

The idea of present value will have several important roles to play as we continue developing financial theory, but we can point out one of these applications already. *With the characteristics that we have given our financial market, present value is the same as market value.* *Market value* is the price that something sells for in a market. It is the number of dollars that a buyer and seller would agree upon for the buyer to give the seller in exchange for some market instrument (promise). Suppose that our first participant's initial resource endowment came from an I.O.U. or promissory note written (issued) by someone else. This I.O.U. pays \$80.00 at t_0 and \$75.60 at t_1, and we have seen that the present value of this instrument is \$150.00 of t_0 money. If our participant chose to sell the I.O.U. at t_0 before he received the first \$80.00 payment, he could expect to get \$150.00 for it, no more and no less. In our earlier discussion of present value we pointed out why he would insist on at least \$70.00 for the t_1 payment of \$75.60, so it seems reasonable that \$150.00 is a minimum asking price on our participant's part. Similarly, a maximum bid price by a buyer will be that amount which can just duplicate the promised cash flow stream by using the financial market. So \$150.00 will be the going market price of the I.O.U. at t_0 before any of its payments are made.

Suppose that you were also a participant in the financial market, had only t_0 resources of \$150.00, and wanted t_0 consumption of \$60.00 and t_1

consumption of $97.20. Would you be willing to pay $150.00 at t_0 for the I.O.U. described above, even though it promises a cash-flow stream that is different from the one you desire? The answer is yes. You can buy the I.O.U. for $150.00 and then lend $20.00 of the $80.00 you receive from the I.O.U. at t_0 to the financial market. That will yield your desired pattern. Or, of course, you could merely lend $90.00 of your $150.00 t_0 resources and not buy the I.O.U. That would also give you what you want. But even though you achieve what you want without buying the I.O.U., its $150.00 market price should seem perfectly reasonable to you and you should be indifferent between buying and not buying the I.O.U.[5]

PREFERRED ALLOCATION

So far our discussion of the financial market has been concerned mostly with describing the opportunities for resource allocation across time which are available to a participant in that market. But we have not yet discussed how he would *choose among* the available consumption opportunities, or stated graphically, where he would finally locate along his financial opportunity line.

The general answer is actually quite simple: He would choose the consumption pattern that makes him most happy. In financial theory, happiness or satisfaction is called *utility*. We make the rather reasonable assumption that financial market participants try to make themselves as happy as possible, or, in other words, are *utility maximizers*.

Without going to too much trouble, we can use the utility-maximization assumption to come up with something called an *indifference map* for our participant. This appears in Figure 1.4.[6] The lines with Roman numerals I–IV are *indifference curves*. They describe the way this particular participant gets satisfaction from consuming resources at t_0 and t_1.

Indifference curves work like this:

1. The participant gets the same amount of satisfaction or utility from all consumption combinations on any single indifference curve.

Look, for example, at indifference curve II in Figure 1.4. Points R and S each represent a consumption combination: (R_0, R_1) for R and (S_0, S_1) for S. Since R and S are both on indifference curve II, our participant gets the same amount of happiness from each. He is indifferent between the consumption choices represented by R and by S. Although indifference curve II contains a great number of combinations, they all give the single amount of utility represented by II. This brings us to the next step:

[5]You can now see why we have assumed no transactions costs. Buying the I.O.U. and then lending $20.00 at t_0 are two transactions, as compared to lending $90.00 at t_0 (one transaction). If there were a charge for each transaction, you would no longer be indifferent between buying and not buying the I.O.U.

[6]Since you already may have been exposed to microeconomics, we have placed the derivation of Figure 1.4 in Appendix I.A so you will not be delayed by something already familiar to you. If you have not run across this idea before, you will probably find Appendix I.A interesting.

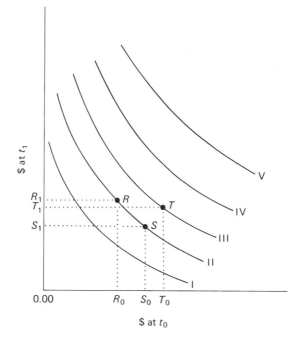

FIGURE 1.4 **Single-period indifference map**

2. The higher the number of the indifference curve, the higher is the participant's satisfaction.

Indifference curve numbers increase as we move in a northeasterly direction on the map. This means that the participant prefers any and all points on III to any and all points on II. For example, the combination for T, (T_0, T_1), makes him happier than that for either R or S. But T, of course, gives him the same amount of satisfaction as any other point on indifference curve III.

You can probably see now that our participant would like to get to the highest indifference curve he possibly can. This would maximize his utility. But there is a limit to the amount of utility he can get, which depends on his financial resources and the going rates for reallocating those resources across time.

The solution to his problem is shown in Figure 1.5. With his initial resource endowment ($80.00, $75.60) the highest indifference curve he can reach is III. That is the one just touching (tangent to) his financial opportunity line. He reaches III by moving to C, the point of tangency. As you can see, choosing C means that he must lend $8 of his t_0 money at the market rate of 8%. He therefore will consume $72.00 at t_0 and $84.24 at t_1. The market interest rate, his resources, and his preferences being what they are, there is no other course of action he could take that would make him happier.

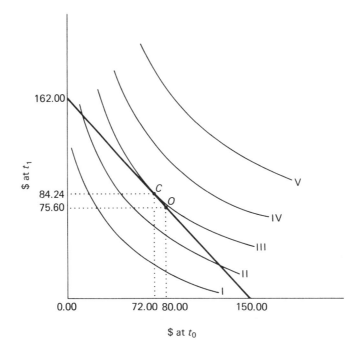

FIGURE 1.5 First participant's preferred allocation

Recognize also that the particular initial endowment of this participant is not necessary for him to finally arrive at *C*. *Any* initial endowment he might have on that particular FOL would always result in his choosing *C*. To say the same thing, with a market rate of 8 % and with resources having *present value* of $150.00, regardless of their time-specific amounts, he would always consume $72.00 at t_0 and $84.24 at t_1.

One strong word of caution about preference decisions in our financial market is in order here. Although all participants in the financial market are utility maximizers, they do not all have the same sets of indifference curves. Indifference curves can have a very wide range of shapes, and each individual's map may be quite different from everyone else's. For example, consider another participant in the financial market. Let us suppose that she has exactly the same initial resource endowment and FOL as our first participant but much prefers consumption at t_0 to consumption at t_1. This preference results in her having a set of indifference curves which, as you can see in Figure 1.6, are more vertical than our first participant's. Our second participant's utility map produces a tangency to her (and his) FOL at point *C′* ($95.00, $59.40) which is well down the FOL from point *C*. She is happiest consuming $23.00 more at t_0 and $24.84 less at t_1 than our first participant.

Thus, even though different participants may have resources with the same present value or market value (and hence the same FOL's), they would

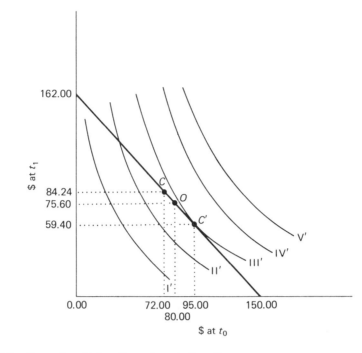

FIGURE 1.6   Second participant's preferred allocation

probably choose different combinations of t_0 and t_1 consumption because
their preferences would differ. You can probably recognize this fact from
observing real financial markets.

In addition to differing preferences, financial market participants might
not have financial resources with identical present or market values. Those
with larger values would have FOL's higher than our participant; those with
lesser, lower. But since the market interest rate is the same for everyone, all
FOL's would have the same slope (that is, be parallel to each other).

By now you should have a fairly good idea of (1) what a simple financial
market is, (2) the normal opportunities that exist there for reallocating resources across time, and (3) how financial market participants make their
decisions. Next we shall turn our attention to an additional set of possible
financial decisions which may exist totally apart from the financial market
we have seen so far.

Chapter 2

Investment

We have examined how financial market participants can make some very important financial decisions, lending and borrowing. But lending and borrowing through the financial market are not the only opportunities generally available to persons with financial resources. Another whole set of opportunities, called *investments*, exists. Although investments are separate from the financial market, the ability of persons to engage in investments is usually greatly aided if they are also financial market participants.

Suppose that a friend approaches our financial market participant and offers him the opportunity to take part in a venture she is organizing which she refers to as investment D. She advises him that to take part in investment D will cost $30.00 in cash at t_0 but that he can expect a return of $59.40 in cash at t_1 for certain (our certainty assumption is still in force). You can think of this venture as the manufacturing of a new product, the expansion of an existing production process, developing and marketing an invention, or the bringing together of some collection of assets in a productive way not previously known. In general, the venture can be any activity which has economic value and which is not yet widely known among persons with financial resources. Most commonly, involvement in such ventures requires an outlay of cash at one or more early time points with the promise of cash inflow(s) at one or more later time points. If our participant elects to take part in such a venture as that offered by his friend, we say that *he makes an investment*.

Should our market participant accept his friend's offer to participate

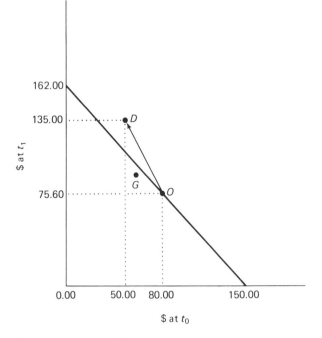

FIGURE 2.1   Investment opportunity

in *D*? Should he make the investment she proposes, or not? As in the case of his initial resource endowment, all that really matters in the consideration of the investment, given our financial market and no competing investments, is the amount and the timing of the cash flows, along with the fact that, in this example, those cash flows are certain. However, by analyzing this investment decision, we can introduce several additional important ideas in financial theory.

Figure 2.1 shows our market participant's initial resource endowment, point *O* ($80.00, $75.60), and what the effect on that position would be if he made the investment. He would give up $30.00 of t_0 money and get in return an additional $59.40 of t_1 money. This would move him from point *O* to point *D* in Figure 2.1. Point *D*, of course, represents $80.00 − $30.00 at t_0 and $75.60 + $59.40 at t_1, or ($50.00, $135.00). Would shifting from point *O* to point *D* be a good move or not? The answer, of course, must somehow depend on the satisfaction that our participant can obtain from the financial resources he would have *with* the investment versus those he would have *without* the investment. If he will be happier *with* the resources at point *D*, then he should make the investment; otherwise, he should decline his friend's offer.

It might seem logical, therefore, to compare the satisfaction our participant would get from point D with the satisfaction he would get by staying on his original FOL. Making only that comparison, however, would ignore another important opportunity available to him: Should he choose to do so, our participant could take advantage of the investment and also participate in the financial market. There is no rule against that. He could at t_0, for example, simultaneously take part in the investment and lend some of his remaining t_0 endowment at 8% in the financial market. Or he could invest and borrow simultaneously at t_0.

If we were to graph all such "invest to D and lend" and "invest to D and borrow" opportunities available to him, we would arrive at Figure 2.2. Notice that this would move our participant to a new financial opportunity line that lies outside (above and to the right of) his original FOL and is parallel to it. (It has the same slope because the market interest rate has not changed.) This shows that he now has available a whole new set of consumption combinations. But can we determine whether or not any one of these new consumption combinations will result in a higher level of satisfaction for our participant than any he was able to achieve along his old FOL? In fact, we can. Indeed, we can show he must have higher satisfaction. This is because his indifference curves must be shaped so that the new FOL, lying outside the

FIGURE 2.2   New financial opportunity line

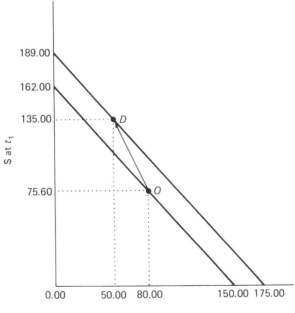

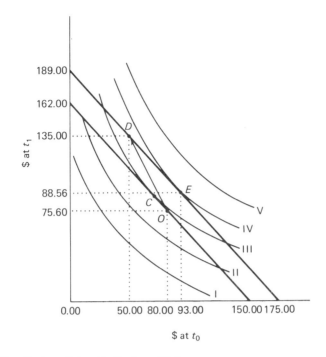

FIGURE 2.3   **First participant's final equilibrium**

old FOL as it does, allows him to use the financial market to reach a higher indifference curve.[1] And we have already seen that the higher the indifference curve, the more utility our participant has, and the happier he is. Notice also that his present wealth has increased (compare the horizontal axis intercept of the new FOL with that of the old FOL).

In Figure 2.3 we have superimposed our participant's indifference map on the investment and financing opportunities shown in Figure 2.2. This tells us exactly which actions he will take at t_0 to maximize his utility:

1. From his initial endowment (point O) he places $30.00 of his $80.00 t_0 endowment in the investment his friend offers. This $30.00 at t_0 returns $59.40 at t_1, which moves him to point D ($50.00, $135.00).

[1] Allowable shapes of indifference curves are discussed in Appendix I.A. From the following, you can see intuitively that he can use the financial market to reach a higher indifference curve. If we pick any point X on the old FOL in Figure 2.2, we can then pick points Y and Z on the new FOL such that Y represents the same number of t_0 dollars as does X, and Z represents the same number of t_1 dollars as does X. We then observe that *any* point on the new FOL between Y and Z represents more consumption at *both* t_0 and t_1 than does X. Thus, our participant is absolutely better off at both time points, and, given the assumptions about market participant behavior listed in Table 1.1, he is necessarily happier.

2. Then, still at t_0, he borrows \$43.00 from the financial market at 8 %
which he must pay back with accrued interest at t_1, resulting in

\$135.00	t_1 resources from initial endowment, \$75.60, plus investment return \$59.40
− 43.00	repayment of principal borrowed at t_0
− 3.44	interest on loan at 8 %
\$ 88.56	consumption at t_1

This moves him to point E (\$93.00, \$88.56), which is the tangency of
indifference curve IV and the new FOL. This is the location that maximizes
his satisfaction. It is the highest indifference curve he can reach on the new
FOL. We call this his *final equilibrium*. In getting to point E, he has made
both an investment decision (moving from point O to point D) and a financing
(borrowing) decision (moving from point D to point E).[2] Notice also that
point E is on a higher indifference curve than point C, the position that

FIGURE 2.4   Second participant's final equilibrium

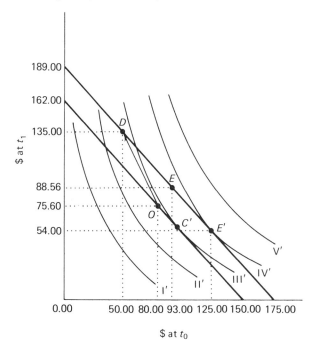

$ at t_0

---

[2]Our participant first made his investment and then borrowed. Point E could just as easily
have been reached, however, by first borrowing and then making the investment. Using
the latter order, our participant would first move down the old FOL to a point representing
(\$123.00, \$29.16). You may wish to verify this consumption combination and show that
making the investment from this point indeed results in moving to the same final equilibrium,
point E.

maximizes our participant's happiness in the absence of the investment opportunity.

We mentioned earlier that all financial market participants need not and do not have identically shaped indifference curves. Does this mean that some participants would have chosen not to take part in this investment? No. As long as the participants get more satisfaction from more consumption at both t_0 and t_1, they will all choose to make this investment. Consider again, for example, the other participant we analyzed in Figure 1.6. You will recall that she likes t_0 consumption somewhat more than our first participant. This preference resulted in her allocating her initial resource endowment (which, you recall, was identical to his) across time in a pattern different from the one that he preferred. In the case of investment D, we see a similar contrast. She, too, chooses to make the investment and to borrow, just as he did. But as shown in Figure 2.4, she borrows $32.00 more than the $43.00 which he took from the financial market. Her final equilibrium is at E' ($125.00, $54.00), the point on the new FOL tangent to her highest indifference curve and a point well down the new FOL from his final equilibrium at point E. Also notice her present wealth due to the investment.

INVESTMENT AND PRESENT WEALTH

We have discovered in this chapter that an outward shift in any participant's FOL means that participant's present wealth has increased. *An increase in present wealth will increase the satisfaction of any financial market participant.* This is because a higher FOL always allows any participant to reach a higher indifference curve. We cannot predict at exactly what point each participant will reach his or her final equilibrium along the higher FOL. This is because we do not know the exact shape of each individual's indifference curves. But we do know that anyone who accepts investment D will be happier. This is because no matter what the shape of his or her indifference map might be, provided only that it follows the rules stated earlier, making investment D will increase present wealth and allow the attainment of a higher indifference curve.

This characteristic of changes in present wealth will become very important when we begin to deal specifically with corporate finance. A corporation usually does not know what the indifference maps of its shareholders look like. But it can be pretty confident that as long as its actions increase the present wealth of its shareholders, they will be happier. The corporation can let the shareholders individually decide how to allocate their respective shares of that present wealth across time. This will prove to be a crucially important finding as we develop the theory of corporate financial decision making in Part Two.

Finally, just because investment D is a good one is no reason to think that all investments are. Look, for example, at point G in Figure 2.1. You can probably figure out for yourself that an investment G which moves the investor from point O to point G is no good. We shall discuss investment G later in more detail.

PRESENT WEALTH AND NET PRESENT VALUE

When our first participant decided to make the investment offered to him by his friend, he shifted his financial position from the old financial opportunity line to the new FOL. If you look at Figure 2.2 you can see that this increased the present value of his financial resources (his present wealth) from $150.00 (*without* the investment proposal at t_0) to $175.00 (*with* the investment proposal at t_0). In other words, an increase of $25.00 along the horizontal (t_0) axis was achieved. You will recall that, in this market, present value and market value are the same thing. Therefore, this increase of $25.00 in present value also means that our participant could now sell his initial resource endowment *plus* the investment opportunity for $175.00, its new market value. Clearly, the presence of the investment opportunity has caused this increase in his present wealth. But why $25.00? Why not some other amount?

The answer to these questions will introduce several important financial concepts. One is that of *net present value*. When we discuss investment opportunities, *net present value is the difference between the present value of all the cash outflows and the present value of all the cash inflows that occur as the result of making an investment. The net present value of an investment is also the change in the present wealth of any participant who decides to make that investment.* The change in the present wealth of our participants is $25.00 when either invests in D; therefore, $25.00 at t_0 must be the net present value of investment D.

To calculate net present value directly we need to discount or find the present value of the investment's cash outflows and cash inflows, and then find the difference between them. For investment D:

$$\text{net present value}_D = \text{present value of inflows}_D$$
$$- \text{present value of outflows}_D \qquad \textbf{[2.1]}$$
$$= \frac{\$59.40}{1.08} - \$30.00$$
$$= \$55.00 - \$30.00$$
$$\text{NPV}_D = \$25.00$$

There is a cash outflow for investment D of $30.00 at t_0 which does not need to be discounted, because it occurs now. The $59.40 inflow must be discounted back one period so that it is *time-comparable* with the $30.00 outflow. $59.40 at t_1 is worth $55.00 when we discount it back one period at the 8% market interest rate. The difference between the present values of the outflow and inflow for the investment is $25.00, its net present value (NPV_D).

Why do we discount the investment flows at 8%, the market interest rate? When we found the present value of our first participant's FOL, we discounted at the market rate. That told us how many dollars he needed at t_0 in order to move to any consumption combination along his FOL by lending some of that t_0 money. Similarly, by discounting the cash flows from the investment at the market interest rate, we are seeing how much money he would need to lend to the financial market at t_0 in order to have at t_1 the same amount of money as the investment returns at t_1. As it turns out, he needs

$25.00 of additional t_0 resources so as to (1) participate only in the financial market, (2) not invest in D, and (3) still do as well as if he had made the investment from his position on the old FOL.

You can see that calculating the net present value of an investment by discounting at the market interest rate is nothing more than comparing the investment to the alternative of lending in the financial market. This process of comparison introduces a very important idea. We call it the concept of opportunity cost. An *opportunity cost* is the cost you incur when you make a decision to take one action and not another. It is the amount of money you did not get from the thing you did not do. It is the *foregone* amount on the next-best alternative.

As difficult as this concept might sound, it is actually quite simple to work with. For example, reconsider investment D. It required a $30.00 outlay at t_0 and promised a $59.40 return at t_1. The next best alternative to D is the financial market rate of 8%. It would produce $32.40 for us at t_1 for the same outlay of $30.00 at t_0 [$32.40 = $30.00(1.08)]. The opportunity cost, then, of the $59.40 t_1 return from investment D is the $32.40 t_1 return that could have been earned in the financial market but was not. The difference between $59.40 and $32.40 is $27.00 in t_1 money. Now we could stop right there and say that the investment will return $27.00 more at t_1 than would the financial market. This is called comparing terminal values, and there is nothing wrong with making this comparison. But because we are also interested in *present* wealth levels and current market values (or soon will be), we prefer to move the $27.00 of t_1 money back to the present by discounting it at the market rate of interest (the opportunity rate):

$$\frac{\$27.00 \text{ at } t_1}{1.08} = \$25.00 \text{ at } t_0$$

$25.00 is the t_0 value of the amount ($27.00) by which the investment's return ($59.40) exceeds its opportunity cost ($32.40).[3]

So the reason we discount back to the present at the market interest rate is that the market rate is the appropriate opportunity rate which allows us to calculate the opportunity cost. If an investment has a positive net present value when discounted at the market rate, we know that the investment returns more than would the financial market. The present value of the excess cash return is the net present value.

MARKET VALUE OF AN INVESTMENT AND MARKET EFFICIENCY You might have noticed that when we introduced investment D we specified not only the amount, timing, and degree of uncertainty (none) of its cash flows, but also that not many people knew about it or had access to the idea. That might sound unnecessarily secretive, but the investment probably would not have worked the same way without that assumption. This is because of something called *market efficiency*.

[3] In economic terms you may have heard that the return in excess of opportunity cost is called *pure economic profit*. Net present value can be quite accurately considered the present value of pure economic profit.

Suppose a number of other market participants know that investment D is available and that it is only available once.[4] Now these other participants can only earn 8% on their t_0 dollars in the financial market. $30.00 lent to the financial market at t_0 returns them only $32.40 at t_1. But the same amount of money put into D would earn them $59.40 at t_1. D looks like a pretty good thing to them, too. In a competitive marketplace such as ours, a situation of this type would cause participants to begin bidding against each other to get D. This bidding would continue as long as D promises to return more than its next best alternative, which is the financial market. How high will the bidding go? Whatever the final bid is, the total dollars spent by the high bidder will return to him the same number of dollars as if he had lent the investment money to the financial market. If the return is more than that, someone else will bid higher; if the return is less, the bidder will have made a mistake because the financial market would have returned more to him.

The question then must be: How many dollars lent to the financial market at t_0 will return $59.40 at t_1?

$$(\$ \text{ lent at } t_0)(1.08) = \$59.40 \text{ at } t_1$$

$$\$ \text{ lent at } t_0 = \frac{\$59.40 \text{ at } t_1}{1.08} = \$55.00$$

Thus, a financial market participant would be willing to pay up to a total of $55.00 at t_0 to get D's $59.40 t_1 return. If D requires a cash outlay of $30.00 at t_0, he would be willing to pay up to $25.00 in addition to that outlay for the privilege of investing in D. The woman who originally told our participant about investment D is obviously a very good friend of his indeed. The friendship is clearly worth at least $25.00, the amount that the high bidder would be willing to pay for the information about D. Barring other compensation, our participant received a true gift.

The total *market price* of D in an efficient market would be $55.00 at t_0 (assuming that the $30.00 outlay has already been made). This value returns exactly the 8% financial market rate. At this price of $55.00, and recalling formula 2.1, note that D has a net present value of

$$\text{NPV}_D = \frac{\$59.40}{1.08} - \$55.00 = \$0.00$$

Once the price of D has adjusted to competitive conditions, its net present value disappears.[5]

The notion that a competitive or efficient market always stands ready to quote a t_0 price for some promised future financial return is one that will

---

[4] That is, the investment cannot be repeated. An example of this might be the purchase of a specific piece of real estate which would be a desirable location for a retail business establishment.

[5] This is consistent with market competition from basic economics. In a competitive market there is no pure economic profit. Since net present value is nothing more than discounted pure economic profit, we should not be surprised that NPV = $0 in economic equilibrium.

be very important as we continue to develop financial theory, especially corporate financial theory, in the next few chapters. Remember that in the example of investment D, its market price at t_0 is not $30.00, the cash outlay required for the investment, but, rather, is $55.00, the present value of future cash inflows.

INTERNAL RATE OF RETURN

We have seen that one way of analyzing an investment is to calculate the present value of its cash flows, its net present value. There is another method of judging investments, called the *internal rate of return* (IRR). The IRR indicates for an investment nearly the same thing that the interest rate indicates for borrowing and lending in a financial market: *The IRR is the average percentage rate per period that invested dollars are earning.* If we lend money in our financial market, we earn at the rate of 8% for the period. In effect, the internal rate of return on those dollars would be 8%. For a financial market transaction, 8% is the discount rate that equates the value of the t_1 amount to the t_0 amount. For example, if at t_0 our participant had lent $20.00 of his initial resource endowment to the financial market, he would have received $21.60 at t_1. Discounting that $21.60 at 8%, we have

$$\$ \text{ at } t_0 = \frac{\$21.60 \text{ at } t_1}{1.08}$$
$$= \$20.00$$

Thus, we may more precisely define the IRR as *that discount rate at which the present value of the cash inflows of an investment equals the present value of that investment's cash outlays.*

Said another way, if a person had a sum of money at t_0 equal in value to the investment's cash outlays, the IRR is the rate that would have to exist in a financial market in order for that person to duplicate the amounts and timing of the investment's promised cash flows by participating in that financial market. For investment D:

$$\$30.00 \text{ outlay at } t_0 = \frac{\$59.40 \text{ inflow at } t_1}{1 + \text{IRR}}$$
$$1 + \text{IRR} = \frac{\$59.40}{\$30.00} = 1.98$$
$$\text{IRR} = 0.98 \quad \text{or} \quad 98\%$$

Investment D's internal rate of return is 98%. The $30.00 t_0 outlay earns a rate of 98% for the period.

Our participant knows that the financial market returns only 8% for the period, so D is a quite nice alternative to the financial market. But suppose that D's outlay had been $55.00 at t_0 (the competitive market price):

$$\$55.00 \text{ outlay at } t_0 = \frac{\$59.40 \text{ inflow at } t_1}{1 + \text{IRR}}$$
$$1 + \text{IRR} = \frac{\$59.40}{\$55.00} = 1.08$$
$$\text{IRR} = 0.08 \quad \text{or} \quad 8\%$$

Here the participant would be earning the same rate on D as he could in the financial market. He would be indifferent between investing $55.00 and lending $55.00; he would not care which, if either, alternative he took.

Figure 2.1 (p. 23) can help you to visualize the internal rate of return of a one-period investment. When we originally discussed the FOL, we said that its slope or steepness was determined by the market interest rate. And, of course, the market interest rate *is* the earning rate or internal rate of return for a loan made in the financial market. So the slope of the FOL tells us the IRR for financial market transactions.

By the same reasoning and procedure, the slope of a line that connects point O with point D can tell us the internal rate of return for investment D. The steeper the slope of that line, the higher is D's internal rate of return; the more gradual the slope, the lower is the IRR. The slope of the line OD is steeper than the slope of the FOL. So D's internal rate of return is higher than 8%. Specifically, we can calculate IRR_D using the slope of the line OD as follows:

$$
\begin{aligned}
IRR_D &= -(1 + \text{slope of } OD) \\
&= -\left(1 + \frac{\$D \text{ at } t_1 - \$O \text{ at } t_1}{\$D \text{ at } t_0 - \$O \text{ at } t_0}\right) \\
&= -\left(1 + \frac{135.00 - 75.60}{50.00 - 80.00}\right) \\
&= -\left(1 + \frac{59.40}{-30.00}\right) \quad \text{the investment flows, of course} \\
&= -(1 - 1.98) \\
&= 0.98 \quad \text{or} \quad 98\%
\end{aligned}
$$

This calculation of an IRR only works for one-period examples, so we caution you not to expect it to be useful in more complicated situations. The discount-rate method that we first used to calculate IRR_D is a more general tool, and later in this section we shall cover the IRR solution for multiperiod cases. It is important now, however, that you do understand the above calculation and the graphical visualization it represents (as, for example, Figure 2.1). What we have demonstrated is that simply observing that the slope of OD is steeper than that of the FOL is sufficient to know that D earns at a greater rate than the financial market and therefore has an IRR greater than the market interest rate.

Notice that any investment having an internal rate of return greater than the market rate (the line joining it with O having a slope greater than the FOL) would also have a positive net present value. This is because the investment would result in a new FOL outside the old FOL and would increase the present wealth of a participant who undertook it. By way of contrast, you can observe in Figure 2.1 that a line joining points O and G (G being the outcome for a market participant at O undertaking investment G) indicates that G's IRR is less than the market interest rate. This means that our participant would be better off lending at the 8% market rate than he would be investing in *G*. An FOL through *G* would lie inside the original FOL, implying a decrease in present wealth.

Notice finally that the IRR of an investment is not affected by the initial resource endowment of the participant. A participant might be initially located elsewhere on the FOL in Figure 2.1, or even somewhere on an entirely different FOL. As long as *D* requires a \$30.00 t_0 outlay and yields a \$59.40 t_1 return, the slope of a line joining the initial and investment locations will be the same as that of *OD*. Therefore, its IRR will remain 98%.

From our discussions of internal rate of return and net present value you can see that they tell us very similar things about an investment. In order to judge the desirability of an investment, the internal rate of return shows the earning rate of the money invested. This can be compared to the opportunity rate existing in the financial market. Net present value discounts the cash flows of an investment back to the present at the same opportunity rate. This shows whether the inflows are worth more than the outflows. Both of these procedures do a good job of telling us whether or not an investment should be undertaken. Net present value goes a bit further to specify the increments to present wealth that will occur. This information is important to the financial-market participant because he gets satisfaction from consuming wealth or resources, not rates of return.

MULTIPLE INVESTMENT OPPORTU- NITIES

We have seen how our participant decides whether or not to undertake an investment. But suppose that not just one, but a number of investment opportunities are available to him, all at the same time point. How do we expect him to react to this?

First, let us consider the situation when our participant has several opportunities and can undertake as many or as few of these as he chooses. We will also specify that his decision to accept or reject any particular investment has no effect on the cash flows of any other investment. We call these *economically independent opportunities*. For example, the investment alternatives of purchasing on the New York Stock Exchange one share of the common stock of either American Telephone and Telegraph or General Motors (or both) are economically independent. That is, choosing to buy (or not to buy) the AT&T share will in no way affect future cash flows (price movements and dividends) associated with owning the share of GM. Most existing stocks and bonds being traded in active markets are good examples of economically independent opportunities.

Suppose that our participant is considering three economically independent opportunities, investment *D*, investment *G*, and one other investment, *H*. The cash flows of the investments are shown in Table 2.1. Figure 2.5 shows a graphical analysis of this situation. Investments *D* and *H* are both desirable. By accepting both of these investments, our participant would move to the highest possible FOL and thereby realize the largest possible increment to his present wealth. The present wealth of the highest FOL is \$192.50, an increase of \$42.50 from the \$150.00 of present wealth attributable to his

TABLE 2.1

Investment	Outlay at t_0	Inflow at t_1
D	$30.00	$59.40
G	$18.00	$13.50
H	$10.00	$29.70

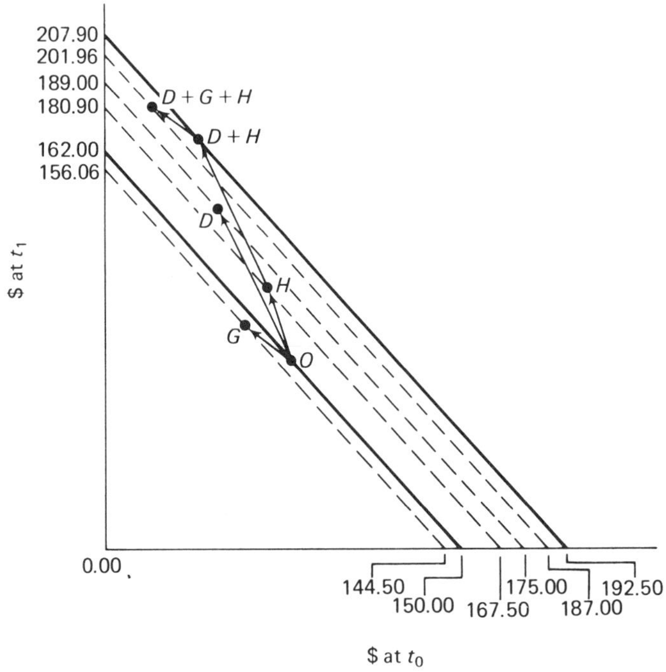

FIGURE 2.5   **Multiple opportunities**

original resource endowment. We have traced the path to point $D + H$ by stacking investment D's outflow and inflow on top of H's.

Investment G, as we have previously noted, is not so good. If he takes all three investments, including G, his present wealth would be only $187.00. This is less than he would have with only H and D. G results in a decrease of $5.50 in our participant's present wealth. This means that G must have a negative net present value of $5.50. As an exercise you might want to discount the cash flows of G to see if you get the same answer.[6] If you also

[6] G is obviously bad because it returns fewer dollars ($13.50) than it costs ($18.00). That was not a necessary condition for it to be bad, but it was convenient in order for G to show up well on the graph. Why don't you try another opportunity, say G', that has a positive return? For example, try a G' that requires a t_0 outlay of $18.00, the same as G, but which will return $18.90 at t_1, an amount not only greater than the t_1 inflow from G but also greater than the $18.00 outlay for the investment. Calculate the NPV, IRR, and present wealth effect of G'.

calculate the net present values for *H* and *D* you should be able to add those two figures to our participant's initial resource endowment and get $192.50.

By looking at Figure 2.5 you can see that the slopes of the lines for investment *H* and *D* are steeper than the FOL. This means, of course, that their IRR's exceed the market interest rate, and they are acceptable. The investment line for *G* has a slope less steep than the FOL. *G*'s IRR is less than the market rate. It is unacceptable.

We could also find our participant's final equilibrium by superimposing his indifference map on Figure 2.5 and finding its point of tangency with his highest FOL (PV = $192.50). If that point were different from the point *D* + *H*, our participant would then use the financial market to move himself to the final equilibrium. His complete decision rule would then be: accept investments *D* and *H*, reject investment *G*, and borrow or lend as appropriate. So, the rule for decision making is quite simple when available investment opportunities are independent of each other: A financial market participant will maximize his utility by accepting all investments with positive net present values, or, equivalently, with IRR's greater than the market interest rate.

Let us now look at the second situation in which our participant is faced with several investment opportunities. In this case, however, let us suppose that the investments are not independent of each other. There are, of course, degrees of dependence in which the acceptance of one investment opportunity affects the cash flows of the others. One type of nonindependence of investments is called *mutual exclusivity*. This means that if you accept one opportunity in the mutually excusive set, you cannot accept any others in that set.[7] For our consideration of nonindependence at this point, let us assume now that *D*, *G*, and *H* are a mutually exclusive set, that is, *D*, *G*, and *H* are now *investment alternatives*.

In this situation our participant, limited as he is to one investment, must choose the single best alternative among *D*, *G*, and *H*. As we know, the best investment will be the one that gives him the greatest present wealth, the one that places him on the FOL that is "farthest out." This will allow him to achieve maximum utility. By looking again at Figure 2.5 you can see that *D* yields a higher present wealth than any other single investment: $175.00 (*H* produces only $167.50, and *G* results in a miserable $144.50). Thus, both *G* and *H* are rejected in favor of *D*.

Ranking the alternatives by net present value gives us the same ordering as ranking by present wealth (Table 2.2). This should not be surprising since our participant's present wealth is simply his initial endowment's present value plus the net present value of the investment he accepts.

---

[7]A realistic example of mutual exclusivity would be proposals to build very different businesses on the same piece of real estate. *D* might be a day care center; *G*, an automobile service station; *H*, an apartment building. Building any one of these precludes our participant from building either of the others. As an example of dependence that is not mutual exclusivity, consider four investments, each of which is to build an automobile service station on one of the four corners of a major suburban intersection. However many you build, you will probably generate more total cash flow than had you built one fewer, but less cash flow per station. We will consider this type of situation again in Section V.

TABLE 2.2

Investment	NPV	Present wealth
D	$25.00	$175.00
H	$17.50	$167.50
G	$(5.50)	$144.50

But how about the internal rates of return of these alternatives? There seems to be some problem here. If you examine Figure 2.5 you will see that D's IRR is *not* the highest. The slope of H's investment line is steeper than D's. H's internal rate of return is greater than D's, but D is obviously the best investment. We have shown the truth of that by the present wealth comparison. What is going on? Has IRR made a mistake? Not really. It is simply an inappropriate criterion in this situation. Said more correctly, if our participant compared D and H on the basis of their IRR's and made his decision on that basis, *he* would make a mistake. He would choose H and get less present wealth and therefore less happiness than he would had he chosen D.

Why is the IRR an inappropriate criterion here? It still is doing what it always has done. It is telling us the rate at which the dollars invested in H and D (and G) are earning returns. But notice that there are a lot fewer dollars invested in H than in D. The answer is that though the money invested in H earns a higher *rate* of return than the money in D, the combination of D's earning rate and the relatively larger number of dollars involved causes D to have a higher net present value than H. The addition to our participant's present wealth is greater with D even though its rate of return or IRR is less than H's. This would be true for any participant regardless of financial resources. Again, a financial-market participant cannot consume rates of return; it is dollars that matter.

So our participant must be very careful when comparing mutually exclusive investments on the basis of their rates of return. There are ways he could adjust for the problem he has encountered here, but those are best left for books that are concerned with applied investment decision making.[8] Our main purpose in contrasting NPV and IRR here is the same as the objective sought through our other examples: explaining financial theory. In particular, this situation points out the overriding importance of present wealth levels in our financial market. Like love, the *consumption patterns* that people choose make the world go 'round.

The techniques of investment analysis that we have introduced are coming into continually wider use in corporate decision making. We feel that is a very encouraging development. We must caution you, however, that the coverage we provide in this book for investment decision making is not

---

[8]There are additional difficulties involved in the use of IRR as an investment criterion, particularly in multiperiod situations, which we shall discuss in Chapter 3.

intended to make you an expert investment analyst. The actual procedures necessary to perform an acceptable internal rate of return or net present value analysis are fairly complex and are well documented in other fine references, which we shall indicate later. Our purpose in introducing these concepts is to further our description of this basic theory of finance rather than provide you with a set of occupational tools. Because of that, we have presented just enough of the theory of NPV and IRR so that you could see generally how financial-market participants make decisions in our rather idealized market. We sincerely believe that seeing it first in this way will be an immeasurable aid in your future study of the detailed implementations of these techniques.

Chapter 3

Multiperiod Analysis

**MULTI-
PERIOD
CONSID-
ERATIONS**

By now, you have been introduced to a significant part of basic financial theory, even though we have used only a single-period model of a financial market. As we have seen, this model is simple, can be illustrated with graphs as well as demonstrated with numbers and formulas, and portrays the basic financial concepts with no sacrifice of theoretical accuracy. For these reasons, we shall continue throughout the book to use single-period examples to introduce additional financial ideas. But an understanding of the implications of financial events across multiple time periods is also important. This is especially true in corporate financial theory. So now we are going to show you how the financial market and investment concepts we have developed thus far apply to situations involving more than one time period.

Turn back to Figure 1.1 (p. 4), the time display. We have been working in time period p_1, which runs from t_0 to t_1. Now we shall expand our time coverage to multiple periods. For example, a four-period sequence would run from an initial time point, t_0, to its final time point, t_4, passing through t_1, t_2, and t_3. We can even design examples that do not have final time points. They have an infinite number of periods and extend forever into the future. We call such examples *perpetuities*. Their sequence of time points is usually shown as $t_0, t_1, t_2, \ldots, t_\infty$. We shall find occasional important uses for perpetuities as we continue.

All the financial ideas that we have covered so far work very similarly in multiperiod situations to the way they do within a single period. As we have noted, however, graphs generally cannot be drawn to represent these ideas in multiperiod cases. But by now you should be familiar enough with the concepts so as not to need graphs.

Recalling our first participant's initial situation in the one-period financial market, all of his actions and all of our analyses were really nothing more than shifting dollars around in time, either actually or conceptually. His resource allocation opportunities between t_0 and t_1 (depicted by his FOL) and our calculations of his present wealth, terminal value, and net present value were all instances of such shifting of dollars through time. For instance, our calculation of the present value of his initial resource endowment meant taking $75.60 of t_1 money and shifting it back to t_0. Because the market rate was 8%, 8% was also his opportunity cost and, therefore, the appropriate discount rate. Adding the t_0 $80.00 gave us the present value of his endowment, or his present wealth. Calculating the NPV of investment D involved much the same thing. We shifted D's $59.60 t_1 return back to the present by discounting it for one period to t_0 at 8%, and subtracted the $30.00 outlay which was already at t_0. Further, when our participant lent money in the financial market, it accrued outward in time at the 8% rate. The t_1 value was 1.08 times the t_0 value.

Each of these instances demonstrate that we can shift dollars out one period into the future by multiplying them by *1 + the appropriate % rate as a decimal* and we can shift them back one period in time by discounting or dividing by *1 + the appropriate % rate as a decimal*. This is just as true for multiperiod cases as it is for single-period cases. If there is a t_2 cash flow that we wish to shift back to t_0, we first discount it back one period to t_1. That gives us the t_1 value of the t_2 cash flow. Then we discount that t_1 value back one period to t_0. That gives us the t_0 value of the t_2 cash flow (and also the t_0 value of the t_1 value of the t_2 cash flow). A simple illustration might be worthwhile. Suppose that our participant will receive $181.50 at t_2 and the market rate for both time periods p_1 and p_2 is 10%. To find the present (t_0) value of the t_2 inflow we perform the following calculations:

1. Discount the $181.50 at t_2 back to t_1:

$$\$ \text{ at } t_1 = \frac{\$181.50 \text{ at } t_2}{1 + 0.10}$$
$$= \$165.00 \qquad \text{the } t_1 \text{ value of the } t_2 \text{ flow}$$

2. Discount the $165.00 at t_1 back to t_0:

$$\$ \text{ at } t_0 = \frac{\$165.00 \text{ at } t_1}{1 + 0.10}$$
$$= \$150.00 \qquad \begin{array}{l}\text{the present } (t_0) \text{ value of (the}\\ t_1 \text{ value of) the } \$181.50 \text{ at } t_2\end{array}$$

Thus, with the appropriate discount rate of 10%:

$$\xleftarrow{\text{discounting at a } 10\% \text{ rate}}$$
$$\$150.00 \text{ at } t_0 = \$165.00 \text{ at } t_1 = \$181.50 \text{ at } t_2$$
$$\xrightarrow{\text{compounding at a } 10\% \text{ rate}}$$

Mathematically what we have just done is the same as

$$\frac{\$181.50 \text{ at } t_2}{(1.10)(1.10)} = \$150.00 \text{ at } t_0$$

Given the market rate of 10%, $150.00 at t_0 *equals* $181.50 at t_2. That is a very important statement. In fact, we can make it even stronger: Not only are the two values equal, they are *equivalent*. That is the mathematician's way of saying that two things are exactly the same, totally substitutable, one for the other. With the existence of our financial market across any number of periods, a participant is absolutely indifferent between future and present sums of dollars related as $150.00 at t_0 and $181.50 at t_2 are by the market interest rate. Those two sums at their respective time points are indistinguishable from each other in that our participant could choose either one and achieve the same collection of possible consumption combinations (FOL's) across time. Viewed another way, $150.00 is the amount of cash that he would need at t_0 to acquire $181.50 at t_2 by lending the $150.00 for two periods at 10%. Equivalently, $181.50 is the amount of cash he would need at t_2 to repay a loan of $150.00 received at t_0 for two periods at 10%. The compounded (terminal) value of $150.00 at t_0 is $181.50 at t_2; the discounted (present) value of $181.50 at t_2 is $150.00 at t_0. *If we want to bring a future dollar amount all the way back to the present in one jump, all we need do is divide that dollar amount by the product of all the discount factors for every intervening period, where the discount factor for any period is equal to 1 + the discount rate as a decimal for that period.*

If the discount rates are the same in all future periods as is the case in this example, you can divide the future cash flow by *1 + the discount rate* raised to the power equal to the number of periods from now until the cash flow occurs:

$$\frac{\$181.50}{(1.10)^2} = \$150.00$$

But remember that this only works when the discount rate does not change across time. If it does change, then you must use the product of the discount factors as the denominator.

Suppose there are multiple cash flows, each occurring at different time points in the future. This presents no problem. We can discount them all back separately, or if the same rate applies to all flows at each time point, we can combine them. For example, if in addition to the $181.50 cash inflow at t_2 discussed above, our participant were to receive $76.70 at t_0, $109.23 at t_1, and $359.37 at t_3, and the market opportunity rate remained at 10% through the three periods, we could calculate his present wealth as follows:

$$\text{present wealth} = \$76.70 + \frac{\$109.23}{1.10} + \frac{\$181.50}{(1.10)(1.10)}$$
$$+ \frac{\$359.37}{(1.10)(1.10)(1.10)}$$

or, since the rate of discount is the same in each period, we could equivalently write:

$$\text{present wealth} = \$76.70 + \frac{\$109.23}{1.10} + \frac{\$181.50}{(1.10)^2} + \frac{\$359.37}{(1.10)^3}$$

Either way, we get

$$\text{present wealth} = \$76.70 + \$99.30 + \$150.00 + \$270.00$$
$$= \$596.00 \text{ at } t_0$$

Although the preceding calculations are straightforward and correct, there is an alternative method which we feel is both conceptually superior and, in current times, mechanically easier:[1]

	t_0	t_1	t_2	t_3
Cash inflows:	$ 76.70	$109.23	$181.50	$359.37

$+326.70 = t_2$ value of t_3 flow
$\$508.20 = t_2$ value of $t_2 + t_3$ flows

$+462.00 = t_1$ value of (t_2 value of) $t_2 + t_3$ flows
$\$571.23 = t_1$ value of $t_1 + t_2 + t_3$ flows

$+519.30 = t_0$ value of (t_1 value of) $t_1 + t_2 + t_3$ flows
$\$596.00 = t_0$ value of $t_0 + t_1 + t_2 + t_3$ flows

$* \div$ by 1.10

This multiperiod discounting process looks difficult at first, but as long as you keep your wits about you and learn to do it on your pocket calculator, you will find that it is really quite simple. You probably should work through a few problems of your own invention to get the feel of these calculations.

Let us now take our consideration of multiperiod flows to one higher step of complexity. What happens when we have such flows and the discount

---

[1] The advent of the electronic pocket calculator makes this procedure very simple. It can be performed on the most inexpensive models as a chain calculation, even if there is no capability for storing a constant. Begin by taking the cash flow at the time point furthest in the future. Next, divide it by *1 + the appropriate discount rate as a decimal*, the appropriate rate being that for the time period furthest in the future. Then, add this quotient to the next closest cash flow, divide the sum by the appropriate discount factor for that period, and so on all the way back to t_0 as shown. This procedure is actually quicker and easier than using present-value tables or other shortcuts, and has the additional advantage of providing useful intermediate figures in the process. Present-value tables can occasionally prove more efficient in a few limited applications (for example, annuity valuation). Such tables are found and explained in most applied finance texts.

The preceding calculation procedure is applicable to any set of future cash-flow expectations, including negative or zero expectations at any particular time point. (For example, a negative dollar cash-flow expectation would be deducted from the total being discounted through that time point from points further in the future.)

rates differ in future time periods? Suppose that we have exactly the same cash flows we just used. Now, however, we will assume that the market rate for period p_1 is 7%, for p_2 is 10%, and for p_3 is 8%. The basic calculation of present wealth now looks like this (rounded to the nearest cent):

$$\text{present wealth} = \$76.70 + \frac{\$109.23}{1.07} + \frac{\$181.50}{(1.07)(1.10)} + \frac{\$359.37}{(1.07)(1.10)(1.08)}$$

$$= \$76.70 + \$102.08 + \$154.21 + \$282.71$$

$$= \$615.70 \text{ at } t_0$$

Notice that with a variable discount rate we can no longer, in general, operate with discount factors raised to powers in the denominators. The same solution can also be achieved more quickly and easily with the multiperiod discounting process that we introduced earlier:

	t_0	t_1	t_2	t_3
Cash inflows:	$ 76.70	$109.23	$181.50	$359.37

$+332.75 = t_2$ value of t_3 flow *

$\$514.25 = t_2$ value of $t_2 + t_3$ flows

$+467.50 = t_1$ value of (t_2 value of) $t_2 + t_3$ flows †

$\$576.73 = t_1$ value of $t_1 + t_2 + t_3$ flows

$+539.00 = t_0$ value of (t_1 value of) $t_1 + t_2 + t_3$ flows ‡

$\$615.70 = t_0$ value of $t_0 + t_1 + t_2 + t_3$ flows

* ÷ by 1.08
† ÷ by 1.10
‡ ÷ by 1.07

Again, you may wish to work through some additional examples of your own invention to practice this technique on a pocket calculator.

MULTI-PERIOD PRESENT VALUE FORMULAS

In finance we often use a notational formula for present-value calculations in multiperiod examples. Although at first glance the formula looks like a very nasty one, all it does is instruct us to perform exactly the same calculations we just completed. Using the symbol V_A to represent value at time point t_A,

$$V_A = CF_A + \sum_{T=A+1}^{T} \frac{CF_T}{\prod_{P=A+1}^{T} (1 + k_P)} \qquad [3.1]$$

is the general multiperiod discounting formula. The other symbols we have used are as follows:

T number of the most distant future time point at which a cash flow occurs

A, P, and T   integer counters used to keep track of time, and used as subscripts to cash flows, discount rates, and values[2]

CF_T cash flow that occurs at time point t_T, just as CF_A is the cash flow occurring at t_A

k_P discount rate for the time period p_P (which ends with the time point t_P)

$\prod$ and $\sum$ instructions on how to do arithmetic, which will be explained below

Applying this notation to the last numerical example presented above, $T = 3$, $CF_2 = \$181.50$ and $k_3 = 0.08$ or 8%, and so on. In that example, we wished to calculate present value or V_0, so to obtain value at t_0, we let A $= 0$. The symbol $\prod_{P=A+1}^{T}$ is an instruction to perform a multiplication. It says to multiply together all the $(1 + k_P)$ discount factors from period p_{A+1} ($= p_1$ when A $= 0$) through period p_T. This product forms the denominator that discounts the future cash flow at t_T, CF_T, all the way back to t_0 in one jump. In our last numerical example, this part of formula 3.1 tells us to divide the $\$359.37$ cash flow at t_3 by the product $(1.07) \times (1.10) \times (1.08)$. The quotient is the t_0 value of the t_3 flow. In our formula, the symbol $\sum_{T=A+1}^{T}$ is an addition instruction that tells us to do the "one-jump" calculation for each and every cash flow beginning at t_1 (since A $= 0$) and then to add together all the t_0 values we get from those calculations. Finally, we add to all of this the amount of the initial (CF_A) cash flow. All of this is exactly what we did in our basic calculation of multiperiod present wealth before we had the formula.

Thus, the general formula 3.1 is nothing new. With A $= 0$, it is merely a shorthand way of instructing us to calculate the present value of a set of current and future cash flows when the discount rates for future time periods are not necessarily all the same. If they *are* all the same, you can still use formula 3.1, or you can use its simplified form, formula 3.2, which is what formula 3.1 looks like when k never changes:

$$V_A = \sum_{T=A}^{T} \frac{CF_T}{(1 + k)^{T-A}} \qquad [3.2]$$

Again, this is the formula for present value when A $= 0$.

---

[2]In general, when a cash flow or a discount rate is subscripted with either a number or a letter, the number or letter identifies the *timing* of the cash flow or discount rate. Cash flows and values occur at *time points*; discount rates apply to *time periods*. Thus, $\$205.00_3$ indicates a $\$205.00$ cash flow occurring at time point t_3. CF_T indicates a cash flow occurring at time point t_T, where the letter subscript T stands for some time-point number which is specified elsewhere, and k_P indicates a decimal discount rate k, applying to time period p_P; for example, $0.09_2 = k_P$ is a 9% discount rate applying to time period p_2. As shown in Figure 1.1, time point t_P is the end of time period p_P.

There is one final formula for value which is often useful. This is the formula for constant perpetuities. *Constant perpetuities* are sets of cash flows where the amount of each cash flow is the same at every time point, beginning now and continuing into the future. When dealing with such perpetuities we also assume that the discount rate remains unchanged forever. The value of such a set of constant, infinite cash flows is

$$V = CF + \frac{CF}{k} \qquad [3.3]^3$$

For example, $100 received now and at the end of each subsequent period forever at a constant discount rate of 10% has a present value of $1100. Notice that there are no subscripts in this perpetuity formula. Subscripts are not necessary because everything is constant across time. Formula 3.3 is simply formula 3.1 with CF_T and k_P constant for every T and P, and with T, the last time point, equal to infinity (∞). Note, too, that V is also constant, regardless of the time point A at which it is measured.

Formulas 3.1–3.3 provide us with a shorthand way of referring to the process of translating value backward through multiple time periods toward the present. We will occasionally use these formulas simply to indicate that a discounting or valuation process should occur. Since you will be familiar with what the formulas represent, our use of them as shorthand will help us develop our theory more quickly.

We can also translate value forward through multiple time periods. Although financial theory does not employ the forward process nearly as often as the techniques we have just discussed, you should be aware that there is a terminal-value counterpart to present value and that compounding is analogous to discounting. If we have a set of future cash flows given, we can move each flow forward through each time period by simply multiplying it by *1 plus the appropriate discount (compounding) rate* for each period. Suppose, for example, that we have a $400.00 cash flow at t_2 which will be lent or invested for two periods, the first period having a 6% rate and the second commanding $7\frac{1}{2}$%. Looking forward to t_4:

$$
\begin{aligned}
\$ \text{ at } t_4 &= (\$ \text{ at } t_2)(1 + k_3)(1 + k_4) \\
&= (\$400.00)(1.060)(1.075) \\
&= \$455.80
\end{aligned}
$$

We have compounded the $400.00 forward through two time periods to arrive at the terminal value of $455.80. What we have done is just the reverse of finding the t_2 value of $455.80 at t_4. Indeed, all the present-value calculating procedures we have developed, including our formulas, work perfectly well—although in reverse—for movements of value forward in time.

---

[3] If you have a friend who is a mathematician, he or she would undoubtedly be happy to show you the mathematical proof which allows us to use this formula: For any real number k greater than zero, the infinite summation over N, beginning with N = 0, of $(1 + k)^{-\text{N}}$ is equal to 1 plus the reciprocal of k.

MULTI-PERIOD NET PRESENT VALUE

Since the net present value (NPV) calculation is simply a particular use of discounting techniques, multiperiod NPV's present no problem. Outlays are entered as negative cash flows and inflows as positive cash flows in formula 3.1. For the k_p's, we use the relevant opportunity rates for each period. For example, suppose that our participant had the opportunity to invest $80.00 now for returns of $31.50 at t_1, $22.05 at t_2, and $92.61 at t_3. Assume that the opportunity rate is a constant 5% per period. Obeying the instructions of Formula 3.1,

$$\text{NPV} = \$-80.00 + \frac{\$31.50}{1.05} + \frac{\$22.05}{(1.05)(1.05)} + \frac{\$92.61}{(1.05)(1.05)(1.05)}$$
$$= \$50.00$$

or of Formula 3.2,

$$\text{NPV} = \$-80.00 + \frac{\$31.50}{1.05} + \frac{\$22.05}{(1.05)^2} + \frac{\$92.61}{(1.05)^3}$$
$$= \$50.00$$

MULTI-PERIOD INTERNAL RATE OF RETURN

The multiperiod internal rate-of-return calculation is more of a problem than multiperiod present values. What we must do is find the discount rate that equates the present value of the inflows with the present value of the outflows.[4] This involves, say for a five-period example, an equation that looks very complex:

$$\$0 = \text{CF}_0 + \frac{\text{CF}_1}{1 + \text{IRR}} + \frac{\text{CF}_2}{(1 + \text{IRR})^2} + \frac{\text{CF}_3}{(1 + \text{IRR})^3}$$
$$+ \frac{\text{CF}_4}{(1 + \text{IRR})^4} + \frac{\text{CF}_5}{(1 + \text{IRR})^5}$$

In fact, it *is* very complex. Although formulas exist for situations having fewer periods, mathematicians have shown that no general formula exists which will solve this (or any larger) multiperiod polynomial for IRR. One realistic way to approach this problem is to search for solutions to such equations by a trial-and-error method. What you do is simply try a discount rate that feels good. If, using that rate, the outflows turn out to be worth more than the inflows, you know you need to try a lower discount rate. If the value of the inflows turns out to be higher, try a higher rate.[5] Continue trying until you find the right discount rate. Usually, you will find that after two or three trys you will have bracketed the right rate and you can then simply close in on it from either side. Clearly, this search procedure becomes more difficult, or at least more time consuming, as the number of periods increases. Fortunately, high-speed electronic computers (including those that

[4]This says to modify formula 3.2 by letting $V_A = \$0$ and, in every time period, letting $k = $ IRR, the constant unknown discount rate. The equation is then solved for the value of IRR.

[5]This procedure assumes that the investment outflows generally occur earlier than the inflows. If the outflows occur farther in the future than the inflows, reverse the conditions for trying a higher or lower discount rate.

will fit in your pocket) can be programmed to use this same trial-and-error method to find a multiperiod IRR.

The IRR you determine will tell you the per-period earning rate of the invested dollars in a compounding sense. That is similar to a savings account where you leave interest paid you in the account to earn more interest. Keeping in mind that a passbook savings account is like our financial market, if a person had a sum of money equal in value to an investment's cash outlay(s), its IRR is the rate that would have to exist in a financial market in order for that person to duplicate the amounts and timing of the investment's promised cash flows by participating in that financial market.

You remember that in a single-period situation, it was possible for internal rate-of-return analysis to give incorrect signals to a decision maker judging mutually exclusive investments. Multiperiod IRR presents even *more* potential problems and needs even more careful use than single-period IRR. Before you attempt to perform an internal rate-of-return analysis of a real-asset investment, you should carefully review the usage prescriptions in a good applied investment or capital budgeting text.

Because of its application difficulties, IRR is not recommended as a real-asset-investment decision criterion. For this reason, and because the NPV criterion has none of IRR's shortcomings, we shall not treat IRR theory in greater detail here. We shall, however, find occasional use for the IRR concept in our further development of financial theory. That use, however, will not be of the type subject to the IRR application errors and conceptual weaknesses referred to above.

MULTI-PERIOD FINANCIAL DECISION MAKING

Now that we have seen how multiperiod considerations affect the calculations for shifting resources through time, discounting, and investment-choice techniques, we are ready to describe the way our participant behaves in a multiperiod situation. The financial market is exactly the same as we specified in Chapter 1, except that it now functions through several time periods. Our participant is still a utility maximizer. He still gets satisfaction only from consuming resources, but now he is concerned with several time points rather than just two. He also now has a multiperiod initial resource endowment which he can shift around in time by borrowing and lending in the financial market, and these transactions may extend across many time periods if he chooses. He still, of course, borrows and lends in order to get the time pattern of resource availabilities that allows him to maximize his satisfaction from resource consumption.

He may also have multiperiod investment opportunities. By performing appropriate net present-value analyses he can tell which to take and which to avoid. The net present value of a multiperiod investment is still the change in present wealth of the person who undertakes it. And market prices are caused by the same things that caused them in the single-period model.

Although graphs generally do not work in multiperiod cases, they can be used in *two-period situations*. We shall describe in words what such a display would look like for our participant. This might help you to get a better feel for the multiperiod case. The two-period picture is a three-dimensional graph with one dimension assigned to each time point. Our participant has endowment at t_0, t_1, and t_2, which, interacting with the market rates for the two periods, gives him a *financial opportunity plane* (FOP) rather than an FOL. Each point on the plane is a resource location for t_0, t_1, and t_2 which he can reach by borrowing or lending amounts of his endowment. If he undertakes an investment with a positive net present value, the whole plane shifts outward parallel to the original position. The amount of shift along the $-at-$t_0$ axis will be equal to the NPV of the investment. The location on the $-at-$t_0$ axis will be his present wealth. His preferences for t_0, t_1, and t_2 consumption appear as *indifference surfaces* rather than indifference curves. The surfaces look rather like a set of smooth-bottomed saucers stacked on top of each other with their bottoms facing the origin and tops tilted away. Our participant's final equilibrium is the tangency of his FOP and the highest indifference surface. This tangency determines the $ at t_0, $ at t_1, and $ at t_2 which maximize his utility.

We can go even further and describe a conceptual graphing for a more-than-two-period situation. The description has to be only conceptual because a real graph is limited to three dimensions. If our participant has an *n*-period resource endowment, he will have to deal with $n + 1$ time points (*n* is any number greater than 2). This gives him an $(n + 1)$-dimensional *hyperplane* as the set of available multiperiod consumption choices. (A hyperplane is like a plane but with more dimensions than you can draw.) Any point on the hyperplane is a set of consumption amounts that he can get by borrowing and lending in the financial market. An investment with a positive net present value shifts his financial opportunity hyperplane outward just as it did for his FOL and FOP. His preferences for *n*-period consumption appear as $(n + 1)$-dimensional indifference surfaces. The tangency point of his highest attainable financial opportunity hyperplane and an indifference surface determines the multiperiod consumption pattern that maximizes his utility.

We hope that these descriptions of multiperiod financial decision making help you to get an even better feel for the theoretical power of our simple financial market model. The important thing to see is that the financial concepts we developed earlier work just as well in these more complicated decision situations. But if nothing else, the last few paragraphs probably should help you to understand why we did everything first with a one-period model.

MULTI-PERIOD RETURN *OF* AND *ON* CAPITAL

The following example illustrates several of the important ideas we have introduced thus far. It should aid you in becoming more comfortable with notions of financial markets, valuation, multiperiod considerations, investments, and the distinctions between return *of* and *on* capital.

Suppose that you are a participant in a multiperiod financial market. The market interest rate is 10% per period for all periods. You personally have no financial resources, but possess an idea, the productive characteristics of which will generate the following cash flows for certain:

Time point:	t_0	t_1	t_2	t_3
Outlays (O):	$900			
Inflows (I) :		$190	$735	$825

You have only two tasks. First, you must decide whether or not this is a good investment, and second, if it is desirable, you would need to find $900 of t_0 money in order to finance it.

Doing first things first, you perform a net present value analysis of the investment to test its desirability. Since the appropriate opportunity cost across time at this level of risk (none) is the financial market rate of 10%:

$$\text{NPV} = \$-900 + \frac{\$190}{1.10} + \frac{\$735}{(1.10)(1.10)} + \frac{\$825}{(1.10)(1.10)(1.10)}$$
$$= \$500$$

or

$$\text{NPV} = \$-900 + \frac{\$190}{1.10} + \frac{\$735}{(1.10)^2} + \frac{\$825}{(1.10)^3} = \$500$$

or, using the multiperiod discounting process we introduced earlier,

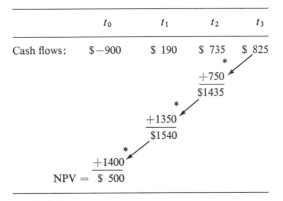

*÷ by 1.10

The net present value of the investment is $500, so you would like to undertake it. If you did, your present wealth would immediately increase from zero dollars to $500.

Perhaps you find the concept of NPV still a bit puzzling in concrete, realistic terms. The arithmetic you have done above is straightforward enough, but what really is the NPV number, this $500 figure you have calculated? It does not seem to be cash in your pocket; after all, you have not actually done anything yet. So what does it mean? What or where is this $500 of wealth?

To answer these questions, and also to help you develop a full appreciation for the power of the discounting process, let us first consider your remaining task—where do you get the $900 needed to undertake the investment?—and then we will trace *all* the real cash flows from both the investment and its financing to find out what NPV and discounting really mean in concrete terms.

Since you have no financial resources, where do you get the necessary $900 t_0 outlay for the investment? The answer is, in the financial market. The market will be happy to lend you money at 10% if you can make a certain promise to repay the principal and interest when due. If you use the cash flows from the investment to pay off the loan, you can do that easily. So you borrow $900 at t_0 at 10% per period from the financial market. But, to make the situation a bit more interesting, suppose that for some reason the particular lender you choose will require you to pay off the $900 principal amount of the loan in three equal installments of $300 at t_1, t_2, and t_3. Naturally, the interest due at each time point will be 10% of the principal amount outstanding during the immediately preceding time period. (You, for some reason, accept this deal, perhaps so as not to be forced to shop around anymore.) Your schedule of cash loan payments for the $900 cash inflow received at t_0 then appears as:

For the period ending at time point:	t_1	t_2	t_3
Principal outstanding:	$900	$600	$300
Payments:			
Principal	$300	$300	$300
Interest on principal outstanding at 10%	90	60	30
Total	$390	$360	$330

So for receiving $900 now you agree to pay $390 at t_1, $360 at t_2, and $330 at t_3 (You can check to see if this is indeed a 10% per period rate by discounting the payments at 10%. They should show a $900 t_0 value.)

Returning to the investment, let us now trace your cash flows through time. First, you receive a cash inflow of $900 from the loan and simultaneously outlay the $900 to undertake the investment at t_0. Then one period goes by. At t_1 your situation is:

$$
\begin{array}{rl}
\$\ 190 & \text{cash inflow from investment} \\
(300) & \text{principal due} \\
(\ 90) & \text{interest due} \\
\hline
\$(200) & \text{shortfall of cash at } t_1
\end{array}
$$

It seems you have another problem. You owe at t_1 $200 more than you have available. In order to pay the amount due, you must borrow an additional

$200 at t_1 from the financial market at 10%. But will the market lend you the money? Yes, it will. There is a $735 flow coming from the investment at t_2 which has only a $360 claim against it. There will be more than enough available at t_2 to cover the additional loan, so you borrow the $200 at t_1 for one period at 10%. Then, when you reach t_2:

$ 735	cash inflow from investment
(300)	principal payment on original loan
(60)	interest on outstanding principal of original loan
(200)	principal payment on t_1 loan
(20)	interest on t_1 loan
$ 155	

When t_2 rolls around, you make the necessary loan payments and have $155 left over. As you know, you can consume or lend any part of that $155, but for the sake of clarity, we will assume that at t_2 you lend it back to the financial market for one period at 10%.

At t_3 the following cash flows take place:

$ 825.00	cash inflow from investment
(300.00)	last principal payment on original loan
(30.00)	interest on outstanding principal of original loan
155.00	return *of* your $155 lent at t_2
15.50	interest to you (return) *on* $155 at 10% for one period
$ 665.50	amount of cash in hand at t_3

Notice that the $665.50 cash in hand at t_3 is what is left, not only after the investment has run its course, *but also after all the original and interim borrowings and lendings with the financial market have been settled.* (There has also been no interim consumption of any of the dollars associated with the project.)

Reexamine the detail of all the transactions at t_1, t_2, and t_3, and note that most of the cash flows represent interactions with the financial market through lending, borrowing, repayments of loans, and payment of interest. However, in finding the $500 NPV of this investment, you used only the *investment* cash flows:

	t_0	t_1	t_2	t_3
O	$900			
I		$190	$735	$825

These flows clearly *exclude* all principal payments (return *of* capital) and all interest payments (return *on* capital) as well as all the interim borrowing and lending transactions. When we *did* include all of these in our period-by-period analysis, we determined t_3 cash in hand of $665.50. Its t_0 value is $665.50/(1.10)^3 = $500.00.

Are you surprised by the fact that with a discount rate of 10%, the t_3 cash of \$665.50 is exactly the same as \$500.00 at t_0, the NPV of the investment? You should not be. All we did in finding the \$665.50 figure in this example was, instead of discounting cash flows backward in time, accrue them outward in time, subtracting opportunity costs (as interest payments) as we went along. The net terminal value (\$665.50 at t_3) is not only equal in value to, but *is actually the same money as*, the net present value (\$500.00 at t_0).

Why did not the necessity for borrowing an additional \$200 at t_1 detract from the value of the investment? The answer is simply that the interest rate paid was the same as the discount rate. Similarly, your lending of \$155 at t_2 did not increase the value of the investment since you lent at the market rate of interest. In multiperiod examples just as in our single-period case, *borrowing and lending in our financial market do not affect value*.

In all the borrowing and lending activity in this example you were, in essence, merely moving up and down the multiperiod equivalent of the financial opportunity line which is given by the investment decision. The present wealth and terminal-value intercepts of that conceptual figure are constant unless you change the investment decision, not the borrowing and lending amounts. You properly excluded all the interest and principal payments from your original NPV analysis and focused correctly on only the investment cash flows. This is because the mechanism of finding NPV by discounting pure investment flows at the market rate of interest *automatically* takes into account the return *of* the investment capital and the return *on* that capital (at the market rate) which are here represented by principal and interest payments, respectively. To have included any of the principal or interest payments with the investment cash flows to be discounted would have been double counting the investment costs (cash outlay cost and opportunity cost) and would have given you an erroneous NPV.

The discounting mechanism also automatically takes care of any necessity for interim borrowing or opportunities for interim lending during the life of the investment (all at the rate of return equal to the discount rate). Thus, the NPV figure is truly *net*—net of all costs, real and opportunity, associated with the investment.

If other financial-market participants concurred in your opinion of the cash flows from the investment, the market price of the investment (including the t_0 outlay) would be \$1400 at t_0. A financial-market participant would be willing to pay up to \$1400 at t_0 to receive a claim on certain cash flows of \$190 at t_1, \$735 at t_2, and \$825 at t_3 when the market rate is a constant 10%. (\$1400 is the present value of those flows at 10%.)

Suppose that you sold the investment to another participant for \$1400, with the agreement that you would make the \$900 outlay. Obviously your present wealth increases by \$500, the NPV of the investment. The entire NPV goes to you, as it should, for having discovered the investment. In a sense it is the return for your entrepreneurial effort. The buyer will get no NPV, he will achieve only his 10% return, which he is perfectly happy with, given the other available opportunities, namely the financial market.

We said that the buyer requires a 10% return on his invested $1400. Let us trace his cash flows through time. At t_0 he lays out the $1400. Then at t_1:

$ 190	inflow at t_1 from investment
(140)	required 10% return *on* $1400 outlay
$ 50	return *of* capital

During the first period he has $1400 invested and requires a 10% or $140 return. He gets $190, which means that the $50 left over can be considered a return *of* part of his $1400 investment. Therefore, during the second period he has only $1350 invested:

$ 735	inflow at t_2 from investment
(135)	required 10% return *on* $1350 remaining investment
$ 600	return *of* capital

Then, for the third period he has $750 invested ($1350–$600):

$ 825	inflow at t_3 from investment
(75)	return *on* remaining capital invested (10% of $750)
$ 750	return *of* capital

His full amount of invested capital is returned, as is the necessary 10%.

Why does everything work out so evenly? There is no magic here. We, again, merely accrued outward at 10% what we had discounted back previously at 10%. As a matter of fact, any set of cash flows will provide for the return *of* and *on* their present value if the required rate of return is the same as the discount rate.[6]

Finally, let us do a return *of* and *on* with the same t_1, t_2, and t_3 cash flows, but using your $900 t_0 outlay (Table 3.1). Once again, we have the $665.50 excess return (cash in hand) at t_3, the investment's net terminal value which, as we know, is equivalent to the NPV of $500.00.

TABLE 3.1

t_T	t_1	t_2	t_3
Investment cash inflow	$190	$735	$825.00
Return *on* capital	(90)	(80)	(14.50)
Return *of* capital	$100	$655	$810.50
Amount invested at t_{T-1}	$900	$800	$145.00
Return *of* capital at t_T	(100)	(655)	(810.50)
Amount invested at t_T	$800	$145	$(665.50)

[6]Occasionally you might find a negative return *of* capital at a time point if the required return *on* capital exceeds the cash flow. When this happens, the invested amount is increased by that amount because that much return was foregone and must be made up later "with interest."

Chapter 4

Introduction to Uncertainty
and Capital Markets

EXTENSIONS TO CORPORATE FINANCIAL THEORY

Believe it or not, we can arrive at a reasonably good basic theory of *corporate* finance merely by adding two extensions to the ideas that we have introduced in this section: (1) the complications caused by the corporate form of organizing a business (including some tax effects), and (2) uncertainty of future cash flows. Although these sound simple enough, it will take the rest of the book to complete this task.

Chapter 5 will address the first extension as we begin working with corporations rather than "just any participant." The second extension, the effects of uncertainty, will be introduced gradually throughout the rest of the book. We treat uncertainty of future cash flows like this because it is a fairly complex consideration, and if we tried to do it all at once, it might distract you from the other important ideas that we also must introduce along the way. The time has come, however, to begin to deal with the fact that we live in an uncertain world.

UNCERTAINTY AND CAPITAL MARKETS

The final bit of preparation we need for introducing corporate finance per se is a brief, general introduction to uncertainty. Remember that this is not a full treatment; it is just enough to let us proceed further.

Uncertainty of future cash flows means simply that we do not know the exact dollar amount that will actually occur when the time point at which we expect the cash flow finally arrives. Participants usually have *some* idea about future cash flows, but no one knows for sure how many dollars will actually occur. Uncertainty is a matter of degree. Some cash flows, as we shall see, are more uncertain than others, more *risky* than others.

We shall call a market where future claims on risky cash flows are exchanged a *capital market*. You recall that we used "financial market" to indicate a place where claims on *certain* (nonrisky) future cash flows are exchanged. Actually, we are merely expanding the notion of our financial market to include uncertain cash flows; or, more specifically, we are dropping the simplifying characteristic of certainty which has been maintained until now. This is such an important step that we recognize it by changing the name of our market from financial to capital. Those, of course, are merely our own labels that we use for the sake of convenience. Other references may use different names, but these work well enough for our purposes.[1]

Capital-market participants still have the three behavioral characteristics specified in Table 1.1 for financial-market participants. To those characteristics we must now add a fourth as a response to the removal of certainty from the market: *Capital-market participants dislike uncertainty*. Some may dislike it more than others, but everyone in our market is generally risk-averse. This means that if there are two promises of future cash flows that are identical in every way except that one is riskier than the other, a participant will always choose the less risky flow.

Uncertainty, of course, is always with us. In one degree or another it is unavoidable. Capital-market participants realize this and are willing to buy and sell promises of risky future cash flows. But since risk is undesirable, *participants require compensation for bearing risk*. This means that they are willing to pay less for the riskier of two promises even if the two are otherwise the same.[2]

We saw in our financial market that a participant required a return of at least the going market rate to lend or invest his resources. This was for future cash flows that were certain. It stands to reason, then, that capital-market participants will require not only the risk-free market rate but also a risk premium based on the uncertainty of the promise they are buying.

---

[1]Most common usage applies "financial market" as a generic term referring to all real markets in which securities or other promises of (claims on) future cash flows are traded. Since all such instruments involve risky or uncertain future cash flows, there is no need in practice to distinguish risky markets from certain markets. Rather, real financial markets have various names which characterize them along other dimensions. Examples of common names applied to real financial markets include:

1. The *primary market*—accommodates the initial purchase and sale of new claims.
2. The *secondary market*—trades already existing claims.
3. The *money market*—trades claims promising all cash flows in one year or less.
4. The *capital market*—trades claims promising some cash flows more than one year hence.
5. The *municipal market*—trades claims issued by state and local governments within the United States, the interest on which is not subject to federal income taxation.

Since the basic workings of all these markets are identical and interdependent from our theoretical perspective, we use the single term "capital market" to signify them all.

[2]The risk-aversion characteristic of capital market participants seems to be verified as representative of real participants. (See the references for Section I.)

Since capital-market participants are not all equally risk averse, some might be willing to pay more than others for a risky future cash flow. But in our capital market they need not. We assume that our capital market is always in equilibrium. This means that the bidding pressures from participants with different risk aversions have resolved themselves into a single market price for each promise. This results in kind of a "market-consensus risk aversion" that reflects to some extent the feelings of all participants about uncertainty. We shall discuss in detail in Section V exactly how this process of arriving at a market-consensus risk aversion takes place, reflecting participants' risk aversions and predictions about future cash flows. When the consensus occurs, however, equilibrium exists.

Even when cash-flow predictions or participants' preferences (risk aversions) change, the market adjusts the prices of the affected promises immediately in order to get back to equilibrium. When a market always fully reflects its participants' predictions and preferences about the promises or "securities" traded in it, we call it *efficient*. Our capital market is therefore efficient.[3]

Since discarding the simplifying characteristic of certain future cash flows, we have specified for our capital market two general characteristics and for its participants two behavioral characteristics in addition to the characteristics of financial market participants. These are all summarized in Table 4.1.

Suppose there is a wide range of "riskinesses" available in our capital market (from no risk to high risk) and the market behaves as we have described it. We can suggest what the implied equilibrium relationship between risk and participants' required rates of return might look like. One possible relationship is presented in Figure 4.1. Risk or uncertainty appears along the horizontal axis, and rates of return determined in the capital market appear on the vertical axis. The line that intersects the vertical axis and then continues upward is called a *security market line*, or SML. It describes the equilibrium relationship between risk and return that exists in the capital market.[4]

The SML in Figure 4.1 intersects the vertical axis at *i*. Since the horizontal-axis location of that intersection is at zero risk, the rate of return shown there is that required from riskless promises or securities. This is the

---

[3]You recall that in our financial market, the price of an investment changed to reflect its net present value only when other participants found out about it. What we are describing is exactly the same phenomenon, except that future cash flows are uncertain.

[4]We know that the relationship between risk and required rates of return is positive, based on the risk-averse characteristics of market participants. We have, for graphical convenience, chosen to depict the SML as a straight line and have not specified any particular measurement of risk. In Chapter 15 we will develop numerically a precise definition of this risk/return relationship. For now, it is sufficient to know that any SML must be positively sloped at all levels of risk, however measured.

TABLE 4.1   Basic characteristics of our capital market and its participants

A. The market—general characteristics
 1. A capital market is a place that exists to allow market participants to exchange time-dependent assets, and thus functions as an intermediary among participants.
 2. A capital market sets the *structure of share returns*, or decides the amount of compensation required for each amount of participant risk bearing. A corollary to this characteristic is that a capital market performs the function of setting the market price of the assets traded in the market.
B. The participant—behavioral characteristics
 1. Participants get satisfaction only from the consumption of resources.
 2. Participants prefer more consumption to less consumption at each time point as long as there is no decrease in their consumption at any other time point.
 3. Although B2 is always true, each additional increment of consumption (measured, say, by a unit of money) gives a participant a smaller increase in satisfaction than did the immediately preceding (and equal) increment of consumption.
 4. Capital-market participants are risk-averse (dislike uncertainty). Thus, given the choice between two future cash flows identical in all respects except risk, participants will always choose the less risky flow.
 5. Capital-market participants require compensation in the form of higher expected rates of return (lower market prices) for bearing the uncertainty (risk) associated with future cash flows.
C. The market and its participants—simplifying characteristics
 1. The interaction of participants' resource endowments and time preferences for consumption produces a positive risk-free market rate of return.
 2. The capital market is efficient, always fully reflecting its participants' predictions and preferences about the assets traded in the market, and instantaneously adjusting market prices to reflect changes in cash-flow predictions and participants' preferences.
 3. Perfect competition exists among participants in the capital market.
 4. The capital market performs its functions without friction; specifically:
  a. No transactions costs.
  b. "Bid" and "ask" prices for each asset traded in the capital market are equal; that is, there is no "spread."

same "market interest rate" that we used in our financial market, which was risk-free or perfectly certain. As we move up the SML, capital market participants require higher and higher rates of return as compensation for higher and higher amounts of risk. This should be no surprise from what we know about the risk aversions of participants. The relationship between risk and required rates of return in the capital market is often called the *structure of share returns*.

Let us do one very short numerical example to see how the capital market works. Suppose at t_0 we have a one-period security that is expected to pay $200.20 at t_1,[5] and the capital market assesses the risk of that security

[5]This *expectation* of $200.20 is not a certain amount of money to be received at t_1. Capital market participants realize that the actual cash flow at t_1 could be larger or smaller than $200.20. Were we to force these participants (the market) to come up with a single number ("best guess") to describe the uncertain cash flow to occur at t_1, they would say "$200.20"; we call this number the "expected" cash flow. This idea will be elaborated upon in Chapter 14, but until then, regarding expectations as "best guesses" will be quite sufficient.

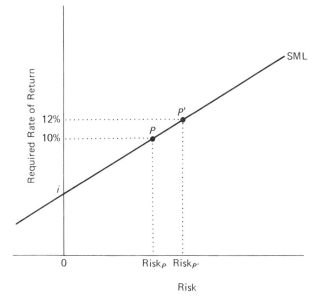

FIGURE 4.1   Structure of share returns

as requiring a 10% return. From our earlier discussions we know that its present value or market price must therefore be[6]

$$\text{present value or market price} = \frac{\$200.20 \text{ at } t_1}{1 + 0.10}$$
$$= \$182.00 \text{ at } t_0$$

This situation is shown as point P on the SML in Figure 4.1. The risk represented by P requires a 10% return in the capital market. For this $\$200.20$ expectation at t_1, the market price is therefore $\$182.00$ at t_0.

Now suppose the capital market discovers something about our one-period security that leads participants to believe it is more risky. $\$200.20$ is still the amount of t_1 dollars you expect to get, but you are just a bit more uncertain about it. This would move the horizontal-axis location of P outward from risk$_P$ to, say, risk$_{P'}$ (higher risk) and move P correspondingly up the SML to P'. The structure of share returns in the capital market indicates that the P' location requires a 12% rate of return. How is this 12% rate accomplished? The only thing a capital market directly impacts is *market price*. So the market price of our security must adjust so that the $\$200.20$ cash

---

[6]At this point we can offer a more sophisticated definition of present value: *The present value of a set of expected future cash flows is the amount of cash a person would need right now in order to duplicate the amounts, timing, and risks of those expected future cash flows by participating in the capital market.*

return is now providing a 12%, rather than a 10%, rate:

$$\text{market price} = \frac{\$200.20}{1 + 0.12}$$
$$= \$178.75 \text{ at } t_0$$

The increase in risk causes a decrease in the market price of our security from $182.00 to $178.75, all instantaneously at t_0. The reason why price falls is that the increased risk causes the capital market to require an increased rate of return. The only way the capital market can increase the rate of return is by lowering the market price. Changes in market price and required rates of return are inversely related. This means that a decrease in our security's risk would cause an increased t_0 price (a lower required return).

Changes in cash-flow expected amounts are, naturally, positively related to changes in market price. If a security's risk remains unchanged but its expected dollar return increases, its t_0 price goes up, and vice versa for a decrease in expected cash flow.[7]

You probably have noticed that although we have defined risk, we have not told how to measure it. Right now we are not going to. The reason is not that it is so difficult; the calculations are quite simple. The problem is that the reasoning behind the risk measure is fairly lengthy and really unnecessary for what we will be doing in the next three sections. When it does become necessary we shall present it. Before then it would only delay us in pursuing our primary goal of discussing corporate financial theory as soon as we reasonably can.

Consideration of risk or uncertainty of future cash flows has introduced the idea of a capital market where securities or claims on risky future cash flows are traded. The characteristics of participants cause higher risks to require higher rates of return in the capital market. The adjustments that the market makes to information about securities occurs in terms of the securities, prices. Higher required rates mean lower prices, and vice versa. At the same risk and required rate, a higher expected cash flow means a higher price.

It may seem that for a book about corporate finance we have spent an inordinate amount of time describing a capital or securities market. As we shall see very soon, however, capital markets and corporate financial theory are very closely related. The corporate form of organizing a business usually means that securities of the company are traded in capital markets. One of the major ways that the owners of a corporation get benefits from their ownership is through the capital market's changing the price of their securities. *The capital market is continuously watching the corporation's financial decisions.* When the market perceives a change of some sort, the prices of the company's securities may change and so, therefore, may the present wealth

[7]Changes in participants' preferences would affect prices by shifting the SML.

of its shareholders. A capital market is a most important component in the development of a reasonable theory of corporate finance. The capital market makes the final decision as to the value of the company's financial decisions, as we shall see in the following chapters.

Conclusion to Section I

We have covered quite a bit of ground in this section in order to prepare for our consideration of corporate financial theory that begins in the next section. Before you can feel comfortable with the material to come, you should have a good grasp of the following ideas:

1. A financial market and the opportunities it makes available to a participant: borrowing and lending, resource reallocation across time.
2. Present value, net present value, and internal rates of return.
3. The relationship between satisfaction or utility and present wealth.
4. Market prices and market efficiency.
5. Multiperiod discounting procedures, internal rates of return, market values, and returns *of* and *on* capital.
6. A capital market, the effect of uncertainty on required rates of return, and market price adjustments to information about security risks and returns.

The problems that follow Appendix I.A should help to test your understanding of these topics. Appendix I.A is the theoretical derivation of an indifference map for a participant in a single-period financial market.

Appendix I.A: Utility and Indifference Curves

This appendix will derive the indifference curves for single-period, two-time-point consumption which were presented without derivation in Figure 1.4. We assume two things about the way our financial market participant gets satisfaction or utility from consumption in any period. Specifically, our participant displays insatiability and decreasing marginal utility. The first of these assumptions means that he always reaches a higher level of satisfaction by consuming more. There is no level of consumption after which the next additional bit of consumption will make him less happy or leave him only as happy as he was. He is never "full" or satiated with consumption. The graphical depiction of this appears in Figure I.A.1, where the curve showing

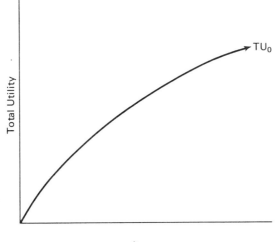

FIGURE I.A.1   Single-time-point utility curve

the relationship between t_0 consumption and total utility is always positively sloped. It never reaches a peak.

The decreasing marginal utility characteristic means that each additional dollar's worth of consumption at each time point gives him less of an increase in satisfaction than did the immediately preceding dollar's worth. At low levels of consumption he gets relatively large increases in satisfaction for each additional dollar of consumption. But at higher levels of consumption the incremental dollar means relatively little increase in satisfaction. This characteristic is also shown graphically in Figure I.A.1. It means that the total utility (TU) curve, although always positively sloped, has a continually decreasing slope or is concave downward.

So the way consumption at a time point affects utility for a participant can be seen in Figure I.A.1. As consumption increases, satisfaction also increases, but at an ever-decreasing rate. Figure I.A.1 is drawn for t_0 consumption, but the general shape of the TU curve would apply for any time point's consumption. Planned consumption at t_1 would generate utility for the participant at t_0 according to a relationship of the general form of the TU curve in Figure I.A.1. The curve would be positive, decreasingly sloped, and would show the relationship between (certain) planned t_1 consumption and t_0 utility.

In a single-period situation, we can consider simultaneously the effect of both t_0 and t_1 consumption on our participant's satisfaction level. We need to show the amount of utility that a participant obtains at t_0 from consuming a dollar amount at t_0 and knowing for certain that he will consume another dollar amount at t_1. Figure I.A.2 demonstrates this.

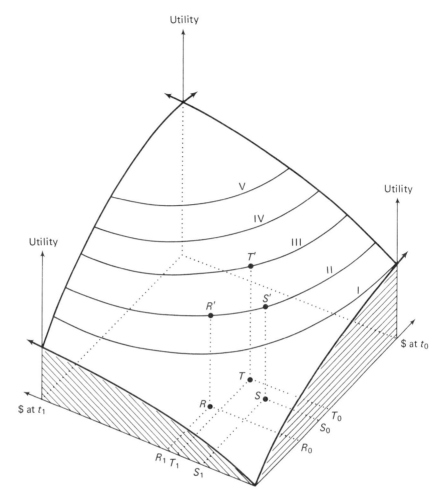

FIGURE I.A.2   **Single-period utility surface**

Figure I.A.2 is a three-dimensional graph that allows us to plot simultaneously a (t_0, t_1) consumption combination in dollars and the utility which that combination generates. The "$-at-$t_0$" and "$-at-t_1" axes are on the "floor" of the graph and utility is measured on the vertical axis. Suppose that our participant were consuming R_0 at t_0 and R_1 at t_1. This would place him at R on the floor of the graph. To find his satisfaction level we move up vertically from R to R', which lies on the curved, three-dimensional surface shown in the figure. The vertical distance from R to R' represents the amount of satisfaction he obtains from consuming (R_0, R_1) or R.

You can see by this example that the upper "roof" of the figure is a *utility surface*. The vertical distance from any point on the floor to the roof represents the utility our participant gets from that particular combination of (t_0, t_1) consumption. The utility surface touches the floor right at the origin and continuously increases in height (at a decreasing rate) as we move outward by increasing consumption at either t_0 or t_1 or at both. The shape of the surface reflects this particular individual's relative preferences for consumption at t_0 vis-à-vis t_1. Another individual might not have this particular utility surface, but the description of the general shape (increasing forever at a decreasing rate) would still apply. It might help you to visualize the construction of the surface by noticing that when there are zero dollars of t_1 consumption, we have a "surface" that is merely the TU_0 curve from Figure I.A.1.

Now, if you can, visualize yourself standing at the origin of Figure I.A.2. Pass a horizontal plane through the utility surface parallel to the floor but at the level of R'. The intersection of this plane and the utility surface appears as line II on the utility surface. Since II is horizontal, every point on it is the same distance from the floor as point R'. II is what a surveyor or mapmaker would call a *contour line*, representing a constant elevation around the side of a hill, for example. Therefore, every point on II gives our participant the same amount of utility as R' does. He is *indifferent* between R' and any other point on II (any other t_0 and t_1 consumption combination on the floor vertically below II). II then must be an indifference curve. Since S' also lies on II, the vertical distance $R'R$ must equal the vertical distance $S'S$ and our participant is indifferent between R' and S', between R and S, and between ($\$R_0$, $\$R_1$) and ($\$S_0$, $\$S_1$).

Now look at point T'. The utility of T' is represented by the vertical distance $T'T$. $T'T$ is longer than $R'R$ and $S'S$; it gives more satisfaction. Now pass another horizontal plane through the utility surface, this one at the level of T'. Its intersection with the surface appears as III. This also is an indifference curve, representing more utility than II. Our participant is indifferent among all points on III and prefers any such points to any point on II. Line III lies higher on the surface than does II.

In Figure I.A.2 we have drawn five indifference curves on the utility surface. You can see, however, that we could have drawn as many indifference curves as we wanted. There are an infinite number of indifference curves on a utility surface (and an infinite number between any two of them). This means simply that our participant's preferences are fully specified. Every possible consumption combination, down to differences of only a fraction of a penny, has its assigned utility.

In summary, indifference curves are nothing more than horizontal lines drawn on a single-period utility surface. Think of yourself as suspended directly above Figure I.A.2, looking down at it. If you were far enough above it and centered just right you would see Figure 1.4 (p. 19). This is the indifference map for t_0 and t_1 consumption for our participant.

If you have read the chapter on multiperiod considerations in Section I you know that we can also have multiperiod utility functions and indifference statements, but a graphical presentation is prevented by the necessity for more than three dimensions of space. If you can conceptualize an *n*-dimensional utility surface, a "constant-utility" section of that surface would give us an $(n - 1)$-dimensional indifference figure. Although we cannot show this graphically, the ideas involved are the same as in the single-period model that we have just discussed.

Problems for Section I

1. Suppose that your endowment is

$$\$ \text{ at } t_0 = \$7000$$
$$\$ \text{ at } t_1 = \$8800$$

You are a financial-market participant and these flows are certain. The market rate is 10%; t_0 is now.

(a) Determine the present value of your endowment and graph a general version of it.

(b) Demonstrate the attainability of the two consumption patterns ($8000, $7700) and ($6000, $9900) to you, and calculate their present values. Show them graphically.

(c) What rate of return (IRR) would you need on an invested $1000 at t_0 in order to change your present wealth to $18,000?

(d) If the investment is accepted you might wish to consume exactly $11,000 at t_1. Show graphically and numerically how you would accomplish this.

(e) Should you accept the investment? Why?

2. Assume the same endowment situation as in Problem 1 ($7000, $8800). Suppose that you accept the investment opportunity mentioned in Problem 1 but wish t_0 consumption of $4000. ($i = 10\%$.)

(a) Demonstrate how you would accomplish this.

(b) After all the necessary financial market transactions have been developed, show the effect on your present wealth compared to that for the Problem 1 investment.

(c) How could you be happier with this pattern of consumption than Problem 1's?

(d) Numerically account for the return *of* and *on* capital for your investment and financial transactions. What is the present value of the pure economic profit from the investment?

3. Suppose that the endowment mentioned in Problems 1 and 2 was, in fact, your salary expectations at t_0 and t_1. Totally unexpectedly comes an offer from a competing firm for a managerial position in the same type of work

at a salary increment for t_1 of \$4400 over that currently expected. (It should be noted that you work only for a salary; own no stock in the firm; are a well-known, experienced, and competent manager; and the nonsalary benefits offered by the competing firm are deemed comparable to the current benefits.) Your boss (the sole owner of the company's stock) agrees to match that offer by selling you stock at a price of \$1000 now (t_0), for which he promises a distribution (with certainty) at t_1 of \$5000 in addition to next year's salary of \$8800. The market interest rate is still 10%.

(a) Regardless of your utility choice for consumption this year vis-à-vis next year, would you prefer the competitive offer or the counteroffer? Demonstrate, either graphically or numerically, the rationality of your argument.

(b) Suppose that your choice of consumption patterns before the offer was exactly consistent with the expected salary (\$7000, \$8800) but that after the offer it changes to current (t_0) consumption of \$10,000 (you want a boat, your spouse wants a new fur coat, and your child wants a car). Would the fundamental decision change? Why? Show how the new consumption pattern can be effected. Also show that you would be worse off with the unacceptable decision, given a desire for t_0 consumption of \$10,000.

4. Again assume that your currently expected income pattern consists of \$7000 at t_0 and \$8800 at t_1. Rather than the job offers discussed above, assume that you are advised of two investment opportunities. The first promises to return \$2530 at t_1 for a t_0 investment of \$500; the second promises to return \$4400 at t_1 for an investment at t_0 of \$1000.

(a) If these are mutually exclusive investments, which would you select? Why?

(b) If both may be accepted, what is your decision? Why? For both (a) and (b) demonstrate the rationality of your decision, either numerically or graphically.

(c) For either investment case given in (a) and (b), what is the proper division between current consumption and next year's consumption?

5. A distant relative recently passed away and remembered you in her will. In keeping with this relative's personality, the will is rather strange. In it, you must choose one of two alternative ways of receiving your inheritance. The first gives you \$26,000 now, \$11,000 one year from now, and \$16,000 two years from now. The second method specifies only \$10,000 immediately, but \$14,000 one year from now, and \$32,000 two years from now. Assume that you have access to the financial market for both borrowing and lending at a rate of 10% per year, and that this is a world of certainty.

(a) Which method of receiving your inheritance would you choose? Demonstrate why.

(b) The probate lawyer next calls to your attention a clause or condition of the will that you must have completed the erection of a monument to this deceased relative exactly one year from now. The payment, which must come out of your pocket, is due upon completion of the monument, and is $14,000.

(1) Would this condition cause you to change your decision as to the method of receiving your inheritance? Demonstrate why or why not.

(2) If compliance with the terms of the will will require you to engage in any financial market transactions, specify those in detail.

(c) As is often the situation, your inheritance causes relatives and associates to offer congratulations and suggestions as how best to invest your money. Two proposals in particular have caught your attention. The first, made by your Uncle Joe, is to buy out his doubloon manufacturing business for $10,000 right now; he will continue running the business so that with no further effort on your part you will receive $5500 one year from now and $7400 at the end of the following year. At that time the business will fold and will be worth nothing in salvage value. The second opportunity, being proferred by "Turnover Tom" Trumble, your friendly stockbroker, is to buy $10,000 worth of shares of the P. U. Skunk Farm Corp. now, which will return a single payment of $12,000 at the end of two years and then be worth nothing.

(1) Using both IRR and NPV techniques, specify which opportunity you would choose. (Assume that they are mutually exclusive.)

(2) For the opportunity you chose, calculate the return *of* and *on* capital.

(3) Suppose that an efficient market were valuing your chosen investment. Recalculate its return *of* and *on* capital.

6. Your endowment as a financial-market participant is, with certainty, as follows:

t_0	t_1	t_2	t_3	t_4
$500	$1000	$2000	$3000	$4000

You expect the following market interest rates to apply:

p_1	p_2	p_3	p_4
9%	11%	14%	10%

You feel that you must consume $2100 at each time point t_0 through t_4, in order to maintain the lifestyle to which you are accustomed.

(a) With your endowment as it stands, demonstrate your ability (or lack thereof) to consume as you desire.

(b) Suppose that an investment requiring a t_1 outlay of $1500 and returning certain flows of $1000 at t_2 and $2000 at t_3 is available. Should you accept it? If so, show how you would transact to reach your goal.

References for Section I

Many of the ideas presented in this section, especially those having to do with resource allocation across time, derive from the Fisherian analytical model, which can be found in: Irving Fisher, *The Theory of Interest* (New York: Augustus Kelley, 1965), reprint from the 1930 edition. For a more extensive graphical development of these ideas, see: Jack Hirschlifer, "On the Theory of Optimal Investment Decision," *The Journal of Political Economy* (August 1958).

In various contexts it was suggested that you refer to good applied corporate finance or capital budgeting texts. A representative but by no means exclusive list might include: James C. Van Horne, *Financial Management and Policy*, 4th ed. (Englewood Cliffs, N.J.: Prentice-Hall, Inc., 1977); J. Fred Weston and Eugene F. Brigham, *Managerial Finance*, 4th ed. (Hinsdale, Ill.: The Dryden Press, 1972); and Harold Bierman, Jr., and Seymour Smidt, *The Capital Budgeting Decision*, 4th ed. (New York: Macmillan Publishing Co., Inc., 1975).

That the risk-aversion assumption introduced in Chapter 4 is reasonable may be verified by examining evidence as to how the capital market sets prices on risky claims, as in: Eugene Fama and James McBeth, "Risk, Return and Equilibrium: Empirical Tests," *Journal of Political Economy* (May–June 1973), or by reference to individual investors: R. C. Lease, W. G. Lewellen, and G. G. Schlarbaum, "The Individual Investor: Attributes and Attitudes," *Journal of Finance* (May 1974).

Corporate Financial Cash Flows and Valuation

In this section, Chapter 5 introduces the notions of corporate form and corporate cash flows. Chapter 6 presents a basic discussion of corporate valuation, which is extended to more realistic situations in Chapter 7.

The financial ideas that we have developed in Section I apply in general terms to corporations as well as to the individual financial- or capital-market participant. For example, we shall see that expectations about future cash flows along with appropriate opportunity costs or discount rates are as important in valuing corporations as they are in finding individual participants' present wealth levels. But corporations also have certain special characteristics that make it worthwhile to consider them separately. Mostly these characteristics are things the legal or regulatory environment allows (or forces) corporations to do. To the extent that such licenses, prescriptions, or proscriptions affect corporate cash flows, it follows that these impacts will also be reflected in how corporations are valued. And that is what we are primarily concerned about in this section: corporate valuation.

Chapter 5

Corporate Cash Flows

CORPORATE CHARACTERISTICS We can think of corporations as a special type of capital-market participant. The first and most important characteristic of this special participant is that *a corporation invests in and operates real productive assets.*[1] Across time, the corporation makes cash outlays in order to acquire assets (such as machines, plant, real estate, and so on), hires the necessary labor and management talent to use the assets productively, and generates cash flows from the sales of its products or services to consumers. But a corporation also must acquire cash from some place to buy assets to keep itself running. It does this by issuing *capital claims* on the future cash flows from operating its assets. One of the important reasons why capital-market participants are willing to buy these capital claims is because this allows them partial participation. This means that they can be involved in the investments the corporation is making without having individually to come up with the huge amounts of cash necessary to initiate many of these productive ventures. Corporations offer a very convenient way for many individual capital-market participants to pool their resources and thus take part in investments which they could not otherwise afford.

EQUITY AND DEBT CLAIMS Another of the most important characteristics of the corporate form is that a corporation, in raising capital, can issue different types of capital claims on its future cash flows. One option that a corporation has for the acquisition

---

[1]Some persons distinguish between nonfinancial and financial corporations. Although we are not terribly concerned about theoretical differences between the two, our definition most closely approximates that of a nonfinancial corporation.

of cash to invest is to issue *debt capital claims*. These claims promise to return specified numbers of dollars at various time points in the future to the suppliers of the debt capital. Corporations can also issue *equity capital claims*. These claims do not promise specific amounts and timing of cash flows to the capital supplier. Equity provides a *residual claim* on the resources of a corporation. In other words, equity suppliers, in exchange for providing cash to the corporation, get a claim on whatever future cash flows are available after all other capital claims (such as those of debt suppliers) are made good.

The fact that equity is a residual claim implies that there is a hierarchy or *priority* of claims on the cash flows of a corporation. In the simple case where there are only the two types of capital claims we have mentioned, debt has priority over equity when it is time to distribute available cash to capital suppliers. Debt gets its return first, and then, if there is any cash left, equity has the claim on the entire remains. Even though the corporation's management may choose not to distribute all (or any) of the residual cash to equity suppliers, those suppliers do own it. We can view the residual cash as potentially *available* to equity suppliers.

The characteristic of priorities of payments to various suppliers of capital allows a corporation to issue many types of capital claims. For example, it may issue some debt with a first-priority claim, other debt with a next-to-first-priority claim, and so forth, continuing down to equity with a residual claim. Although there are some interesting theoretical situations that arise in corporate finance when several different priorities of claims are issued, *we shall deal here only with first-priority debt claims and residual equity claims*. The other cases can be analyzed by elaborations of the development in this section but do not add enough theoretical substance to merit treatment in a basic text such as this. Thus, we shall limit our corporations to issuing first-priority debt claims and last-priority equity claims for the purpose of raising cash to invest in productive assets.

The priority relationship between these two kinds of claims tells us something about their *relative risks*. The future cash flows a corporation will generate with its productive assets are uncertain. No one knows exactly what dollar amounts will occur at what times. And it is these uncertain cash flows that will be used to provide all returns to all capital suppliers.

Debt suppliers have a claim on a specific number of dollars at a specific time point. Once they get their return, equity has a claim on whatever is left. Since the availability of cash for equity suppliers is contingent on debt suppliers receiving their promised returns, the residual cash for equity is riskier than the first-priority cash for debt. In a sense, whatever risk is present in the corporation's overall cash flows from assets is shouldered more by equity than by debt suppliers. The priority system of capital claims apportions overall risk unequally between debt and equity: less for debt, more for equity.

Debt suppliers get first crack at the risky cash flow, so their risk is less than that of equity suppliers, who are last in line and may find no cash remaining after the servicing of the debt suppliers' claims.[2]

We should insert a word of caution here to be clear about what we are and are not saying. In pointing out that debt claims are less risky than equity claims for any particular corporation, we are not saying that debt claims are riskless. Although it might not be impossible for a riskless claim to exist against a corporation's cash flows, it certainly is not the usual case. Debt *is* risky. Further, we are not saying that the overall cash-flow risks, the debt risks, or the equity risks are at any particular level. They might be high, low, or intermediate. All we are saying is that, whatever the riskinesses of the various capital claims are, equity will be riskier than debt because of the lower priority of the equity claim.

We have already seen in Chapter 4 that a capital-market participant requires a higher rate of return for taking on higher risk. It stands to reason, then, that an equity supplier will require a higher rate of return than will a debt supplier because of the increased risk equity bears. Look at Figure 5.1, where we have reproduced the security market line from Figure 4.1. Suppose there is a corporation whose productive assets are expected to yield cash

FIGURE 5.1   Risk and required return for equity, debt, and overall corporate cash flows

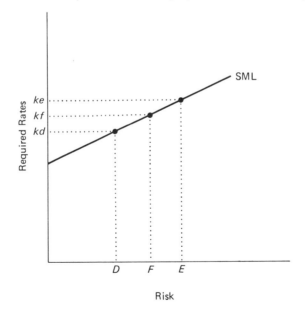

flows with risk equal to F on the horizontal axis. According to the SML, the capital market would require a return of kf on a capital claim that promises just the overall cash-flow stream of the corporation.[3] Suppose also that the corporation had issued some debt and some equity. We can be reasonably sure that the required returns on debt and equity would tend to look something like kd and ke, respectively, in Figure 5.1. The risk of debt is less than that of the overall stream, and the risk of equity is more than that of the overall corporate stream. Therefore, debt's required return, kd, lies below the corporate overall required rate kf; and equity's ke lies above kf. The reason for these relationships is simply the hierarchy of payment priorities for the capital claims.

We have introduced the idea of a relationship between required returns on equity and debt capital claims to convince you that, for a corporation, equity's return must be more than debt's. This has been the entire purpose of our discussion about these different types of capital claims. If a corporation has both debt and equity capital claims outstanding, debt will require a lower return than equity, because of the claim priorities. In Section III we shall return to the question of required returns on debt and equity. There we shall look much more closely at this relationship than was necessary here.

TAXATION The third characteristic of corporations that we must consider is their treatment under corporate income tax laws. Corporations must, like all of us, pay taxes on their income. In the United States, corporate income tax rates are about 50% for most large companies. Clearly taxation questions can be very important to a corporation and its capital suppliers since government's tax rules can have huge effects on corporate cash flows. Anything government gets in taxes is, of course, unavailable to the firm for satisfying claims of capital suppliers. The higher the tax, the lower the available cash, and vice versa. A corporation, in its attempt to please its capital suppliers, tries to minimize the tax claims against its cash.

In this regard there are some things a corporation does which are extremely important to our theoretical development. The taxes a firm pays are based on taxable income. As we shall see shortly, this "income" or "earnings" or "profit" figure is a peculiar sort of accounting number that is of relatively little use to us except for the fact that government looks at it to calculate a corporation's tax liability. Taxable income or profit before taxes in accounting usage may have little if any relationship to the real bases for value, corporate financial cash flows.[4] But this income is what gets taxed. So if a company can lower taxable income without also lowering the cash avail-

---

[3]There is such a claim possible. It is merely the equity of a firm that has no debt. Such a firm is often referred to as an "unlevered" corporation.

[4]Nor is there any particular relationship between the corporate cash flows and the accounting concepts of *net* (after-tax) income, earnings, or profit.

able to capital suppliers, government will get *less* tax, and *more* cash will be available to service capital claims.

In what ways can this happen? There are two very common mechanisms available to corporations to accomplish this. First, government allows corporations to deduct from before-tax income or earnings another peculiar accounting number called *depreciation expense*. Like income, depreciation expense is also not a cash flow. By various (law-specified) formulas a company can, across time, charge off the original costs of its real assets against taxable income. This serves to decrease a corporation's cash flow to government: income tax. Stranger still is the second mechanism: Government also allows corporations to deduct from before-tax income something called *interest expense*. Interest is, of course, a cash payment to the debt suppliers of a corporation. As such, it is a disbursement to certain capital suppliers that is wholly unrelated to the ongoing business of the firm. As a matter of policy, however, government has decided that before taxes are computed, income may be reduced by an amount (called "interest expense") equal to the cash amount of the interest payment. This also serves to decrease the total amount of cash going to government in the form of taxes.

We shall continue to discuss these tax effects on the corporate firm in this and following chapters as they become important to our theoretical progress. But for now it is enough to remember that *neither depreciation expense nor interest expense is really an operating cash flow.* Each is merely a legal accounting number that can be used to reduce taxable income and hence income tax. Depreciation is not a cash flow at all. Interest is a nonoperating cash payment to a capital supplier, and although its dollar amount is the same as that of interest expense, the former is actual cash that goes from a company to debt suppliers, whereas the latter is merely a number on a piece of paper called an "income statement" by accountants.

CORPORATE FINANCIAL CASH FLOWS

Now that we have introduced the corporate financial form, we can begin the study of corporate valuation. In essence the valuation of capital claims on corporations is no different than the simple market pricing examples we developed in Section I. The value of a corporation's debt claims is simply the expectation of future cash flows to debt suppliers, appropriately discounted back to the present at the required rates of return existing for the debt of that corporation in the capital market. Similarly, the value of equity is the present value of future cash flows to equity suppliers. And the value of the corporation as a whole is simply the sum of the values of its equity and debt claims. When the capital market sets a price on a company's stock and/or bonds, the market is doing exactly what we did in Section I: finding the present value of expected future cash flows.

So our job for the rest of this section should be fairly easy. All we need do is discover how to calculate the cash flows to each class of corporate capital supplier, find the rates of return required by each class, and calculate present values. Our job is even easier when you remember that present-value relationships have already been developed in Section I. Furthermore, for the purposes of this section, we shall identify the relevant corporate cash flows, allow the capital market to examine the risks of these flows, and assign required rates of return for each.[5] Really, then, all we need is the cash flows themselves. We shall devote all of the rest of this chapter to the question of corporate financial cash-flow definitions and relationships. Once we are familiar with the cash flows, valuing them amounts only to applying techniques that we already know.

The best way to introduce corporate financial cash flows is to present a straightforward numerical example. The first corporation we construct may not seem very realistic. But as we continue through the section we will gradually make our companies more and more like normal firms. You probably recognize that this follows our system of presentation in Section I. We begin with the all-important basic ideas, and then add the more complex characteristics.

Suppose that we are now at t_0 and would like to find the value of a particular corporation. We shall list below six rather detailed things which are expected to result from the operations of this company. Our list may appear at first to be an overwhelming amount of information to consider all at once. But just read it over, making sure that you understand each of the parts, and then continue reading the explanations that follow. You will have no trouble with this when our cash-flow framework is developed.

For the company we wish to value, the capital market expects the following:

1. There will be cash sales at t_1 of $6250 and at t_2 of $7500 from the product that the firm sells. After t_2 there will be no more revenue from sales of the product.

2. These cash sales (receipts) will be supported by t_1 cash expenditures of $3976.50 and t_2 cash expenditures of $4800.75. These are cash payments by the firm for raw materials, labor, management, advertising, and supplies. After t_2 these cease also.

3. In addition to having equity claims outstanding, the company has debt capital suppliers who expect to receive interest payments of $36 at t_1 and $18 at t_2, and principal repayments of $225 at t_1 and $225 at t_2. The risk which the capital market sees in those cash flows indicates an appropriate required rate of return of 8% per period for the payments to debt suppliers.

---

[5]As we progress through later chapters, we shall gradually relieve the capital market of this task. By the time we finish, we shall be able to assign these rates ourselves.

4. The company is incorporated, and the corporate income tax rate is 52% of accounting income.

5. For income tax and reporting purposes, the company will fully depreciate its assets across periods p_1 and p_2, charging depreciation expenses of $1800 at t_1 and $900 at t_2. At t_2 the assets will have no accounting book value and also will be worth nothing, that is, have no salvage value.

6. The company pays out all available cash to equity capital suppliers as it becomes available. The capital market has judged the risk of those future cash flows to equity as requiring a 20% per period rate of return.

Essentially what we have is a corporation that will generate cash flows at t_1 and t_2 and then cease to exist. If we were to hire an accountant and ask him to produce an expected (pro forma) income statement for time t_1 for this company, it might look like that shown in Table 5.1.

TABLE 5.1   Income statement for period ended t_1 (pro forma)

Sales (receipts)	$6250.00
Operating expenditures	−3976.50
Earnings before depreciation, interest, and taxes	$2273.50
Depreciation expense	−1800.00
Earnings before interest and taxes	$ 473.50
Interest expense	− 36.00
Profit before tax (taxable income)	$ 437.50
Income taxes at 52%	− 227.50
Profit after tax	$ 210.00

Although this statement has more subtotal detail than do many income statements, its general format is a fairly standard way of reporting the operations of a corporation. The items in our company's income statement are about the same as you would see on most real corporate reports. The major difference is that the sales figure is an actual amount of cash received by the company at t_1 and the operating expenditures are actual cash outflows. Our company does *not* use "accruals." In our company, transactions are recognized (entered on the books) only when a cash flow occurs. Thus, for us, revenue from sales occurs only on the *receipt* of cash payments; operating expenses occur only when there is an *expenditure* (payment) of cash to a supplier of goods or services (not including suppliers of capital). For an income statement to be useful to us, revenues and expenses must appear on the statement for the time period in which the cash flows they represent actually occur. Further, they must represent real cash flows to and from external economic units other than suppliers of capital.

As a matter of convenience, we shall use the following terms throughout this book to mean the particular concept listed for each:

Receipts	All cash inflows received by the firm other than those contributed by capital suppliers[6]
Expenditures	All cash disbursements (other than payments to capital suppliers and income taxes to government) which can be subtracted from receipts in the current period for income tax purposes
Expenses	Charges that an accountant would make against income which either (1) represent a cash flow to a capital supplier (for example, interest expense representing interest payment) or (2) do not result from any current or anticipated cash flow (for example, depreciation expense)

This last definition for expense differs from accounting usage enough to warrant some further explanation. In a cash (nonaccrual) accounting system, all disbursements we have identified as expenditures would also be labeled expenses by an accountant. Because it is more descriptively accurate, we choose to use the term "expenditure" for these payments, limiting our use of the term "expense" to include only those nonexpenditure items which the accountant also calls expenses as he makes charges against income. Specifically, we shall refer only to interest expense and depreciation expense as expenses.

Thus, in order to arrive at a figure called "profit after tax," an income statement reduces receipts by (1) the amount of expenditures, (2) the amount of expenses in two categories (depreciation and interest), and (3) the amount of taxes. But remember, what *we* are trying to do is *identify the expected cash flows to capital suppliers.* Does the income statement help us to do this? Not really. How many dollars are expected to be available to capital suppliers at t_1? The $36 in interest? The $210 of "profit"? Who knows? We still do not have much information on the amounts we are really interested in.

Let us take a closer look at what is happening to the actual cash in the company. Figure 5.2 is a cash-flow schematic of the income statement we just discussed. Cash receipts (sales) enter at the top of the diagram, and cash expenditures for operations flow out to the right side. Those expenditures decrease the cash holdings of the firm. Then notice that the accountant holds the expense charges for depreciation and interest out to the side. The corporate tax liability is calculated on what is left, profit before taxes; government takes its cash flow through taxation; and we are left with an accounting number called "profit after taxes." But there is obviously more cash available than

---

[6]This definition includes both operating cash inflows (from sales) and proceeds from the divestment of productive assets, which include fixed assets, inventories, and cash balances. In this section we shall not consider asset divestment and thereby maintain a degree of parallelism with standard accounting statements. Section V will deal with asset divestment in detail.

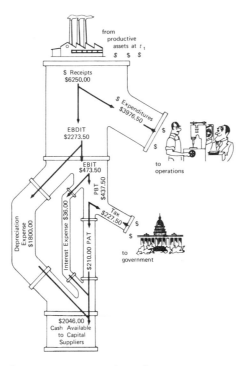

FIGURE 5.2   **Income statement schematic**

that. The two expenses, depreciation and interest, have not left the company
as cash outflows. *Those dollars are still available to capital suppliers.* They
were held out of the profit calculation so as to make taxes lower, but they
really were not operating cash outflows. So we must include them in any
reckoning of the total number of dollars of cash that capital suppliers can
claim.

We do this in Figure 5.2 by reuniting the depreciation and interest
expenses with the profit-after-tax amount. *The total amount of cash available
to capital suppliers, both equity and debt, is $2046.00 at t_1, a figure that never
appears on the income statement.*[7]

The standard accounting income statement does not seem to be very
well suited for keeping track of the actual cash flows of a corporation. Specifically, it mixes together some cash flows with some noncash flows, as well as
commingling operating cash outflows with nonoperating flows designated to
go to capital suppliers. We have used the standard accounting income state-

[7]Some people in reading this might be tempted to claim that this figure is nothing more
than the much maligned and misused cash-flow number occasionally reported by firms in
an attempt to inflate earnings unduly. In fact, the cash-available amount that we use is
something quite different in both intent and method of calculation. This will become clear
as we continue.

ment to this point because it is so widely accepted, and many people are familiar with its terms and definitions. But the shortcomings of the statement in depicting financial cash flows are severe. It serves quite nicely for reporting income to government for tax purposes, but it is much too cumbersome to be very useful in helping us to meet our objectives.

Therefore, we are now going to propose a different sort of system for examining corporate financial cash flows. In it we will attempt to concentrate on cash flows and the things that influence them. By doing that we should be able to reach a much clearer understanding of the bases of corporate valuation.

In the same manner that the accountant presented his income statement for our corporation, we now present, in Table 5.2, its financial cash-flow statement for t_1. The schematic of the financial cash-flow (FCF) statement appears in Figure 5.3. There are some terms in our statement that you probably have not run across before which we will begin explaining immediately. Again, remember that we are only interested in cash flows and the things that influence them.

TABLE 5.2 Financial cash flows for period ended t_1 (pro forma)

Sales ($ receipts)	$6250.00
$ Expenditures	−3976.50
Gross cash from operations	$2273.50
Gross income tax at 52%	−1182.22
Net cash from operations	$1091.28
Depreciation tax subsidy	+ 936.00
Cash available to an unlevered firm	$2027.28
Interest tax subsidy	+ 18.72
Cash available to all capital suppliers	$2046.00

Proceeding down the first three items either on the statement or in Figure 5.3, we encounter the same amounts as in the income statement. Cash receipts are $6250.00, cash expenditures $3976.50, and the difference between them is $2273.50. Accountants often call this amount "operating income." We prefer the more accurately descriptive *gross cash from operations*. Beyond this point on the FCF statement, we depart from the standard income statement, not only in terminology, but also in dollar amounts.

The next entry on our FCF statement is called *gross tax*. You can see this amount flowing off to the right in Figure 5.3. It is simply the corporate income tax rate applied to gross cash from operations. Fifty-two per cent of $2273.50 is $1182.22, the gross tax. Why perform this calculation? In the absence of any deductions other than cash expenditures for operations, $1182.22 is the amount of cash that government would collect as taxes. Gross tax is the tax rate times the amount of operating cash left after paying

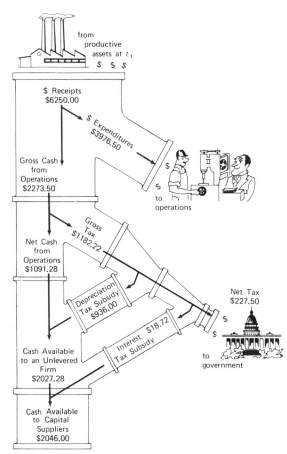

FIGURE 5.3   **Corporate financial cash-flow schematic**

operating expenditures for this period. We know, of course, that the corporation will not end up paying the entire amount of the gross tax to government, because we have not yet recognized the effect of depreciation expense and interest expense deductibilities. *But those effects are best thought of as reducing the tax liability of the corporation.* Gross tax is the cash amount the company would have to pay government if expenses were not deductible. By separating the cash-flow streams like this, we shall be able to glance at our FCF statement and immediately see the dollar effects of depreciation and interest deductibility. We could not do that with the accounting income statement.

This may not seem like a terribly valuable benefit right now because there is nothing we can do about the dollar amounts that appear in our statement. They are "givens." But in the following chapters we shall be very interested in how various corporate financial decisions affect things like interest and depreciation deductibility. Our cash-flow statement can show such effects quite easily, as we shall see.

Returning to the FCF statement itself, gross tax has flowed off to the side; we are left with $1091.28, which we call *net cash from operations*. It is merely gross cash from operations less gross tax. It is the amount of cash the corporation would be left with if government kept the entire gross tax (which it would if certain noncash and nonoperating expenses were not deductible).

**GOVERN-
MENTAL
TAX
SUBSIDY
EFFECTS**

But such expenses *are* deductible for tax purposes, and we must recognize that in our statement. This we accomplish with the *depreciation tax subsidy* and the *interest tax subsidy* cash flows. You can see by looking at Figure 5.3 that the two governmental subsidies reduce gross tax to net tax of $227.50, the same amount which appeared as tax on the income statement. But what is the particular significance of the $936.00 depreciation tax subsidy and the $18.72 interest tax subsidy? Why those dollar amounts? And what in their determination causes the net tax to be the correct net cash flow to government?

First, let us deal with the depreciation tax subsidy. Suppose government suddenly decides that depreciation is no longer deductible for tax purposes. The accounting income statement of our corporation is then as given in Table 5.3. To obtain the total amount of cash available to all capital suppliers (CAC) we add to the negative $726 PAT the $36 nonexpenditure interest expense and the $1800 noncash depreciation expense. The resulting CAC is $1110.

TABLE 5.3   Income statement for period ended t_1 (no depreciation deductibility; pro forma)

Sales (receipts)	$6250.00
Expenditures	−3976.50
Earnings before depreciation, interest, and taxes	$2273.50
Interest expense	− 36.00
Taxable income	$2237.50
Depreciation expense	−1800.00
Profit before tax (PBT)	$ 437.50
Income taxes (52% of taxable income)	−1163.50
Profit after tax (PAT)	$(726.00)

Comparing this revised income statement with the original situation where depreciation was deductible, we see that the profit after tax decreases from $210 to a negative $726 at t_1, and the total cash available to capital suppliers decreases from $2046 to $1110. The amount of cash going to government (tax) increases from $227.50 to $1163.50. Government gets $936.00 more and therefore $936.00 less is available to capital suppliers than there was when depreciation expense was deductible. In effect, by allowing the depreciation deduction, government is *subsidizing* the corporation in the amount of $936.00. For this reason we call the amount of cash government chose *not* to take, a depreciation tax subsidy. If that subsidy were not granted, cash available would be $936.00 less.

This is shown more directly in the financial cash flow (FCF) statement, Table 5.4, with depreciation not deductible. Here you can see that the loss of depreciation deductibility simply causes the depreciation tax subsidy to decrease from $936.00 to zero. Cash available, of course, drops by the same amount. The FCF statement isolates the impact of the depreciation deduction and identifies the exact effect it has on cash flow.

TABLE 5.4   Financial cash flows for period ended t_1 (no depreciation deductibility; pro forma)

Sales ($ receipts)	$6250.00
$ Expenditures	−3976.50
Gross cash from operations	$2273.50
Gross tax at 52%	−1182.22
Net cash from operations	$1091.28
Depreciation tax subsidy	0.00
Cash available to an unlevered firm	$1091.28
Interest tax subsidy	+ 18.72
Cash available to capital suppliers (CAC)	$1110.00

It would appear thus far that our calculation of the depreciation tax subsidy was made by comparing two accounting income statements (with and without depreciation deductibility). That is a valid enough procedure, but if we had to do that each time we wanted to find a tax subsidy, it would be very time consuming. Fortunately, there is a way of arriving at the depreciation tax subsidy directly. It does not require income statement comparisons. *If you multiply the depreciation expense by the tax rate,*

$$\$1800 \times 0.52 = \$936,$$

the result is the depreciation tax subsidy. It is as simple as that. After we discuss the interest tax subsidy we shall return to a more detailed consideration of this calculation.

The *interest tax subsidy* is conceptually identical to the depreciation tax subsidy. Suppose that interest expense is no longer deductible. The t_1 income statement then becomes as given in Table 5.5. The cash available to capital suppliers is now $2027.28, which is the sum of the $191.28 PAT, the $1800.00 noncash depreciation expense, and the $36.00 nonexpenditure interest expense. Thus, PAT has decreased from $210.00 originally to $191.28, and CAC has decreased from $2046.00 to $2027.28. Government gets $18.72 more, and that much less is available to capital suppliers because interest expense is not deductible.

TABLE 5.5   Income statement for period ended t_1 (no interest deductibility; pro forma)

Sales (receipts)	$6250.00
Expenditures	−3976.50
Earnings before depreciation, interest, and taxes	$2273.50
Depreciation expense	−1800.00
Taxable income	$ 473.50
Interest expense	− 36.00
PBT	$ 437.50
Taxes (52% of taxable income)	− 246.22
PAT	$ 191.28

The FCF statement for this situation is given in Table 5.6. Here the interest tax subsidy merely disappears, showing clearly the cause of the $18.72 decrease (from $2046.00 to $2027.28) in the cash available to capital suppliers.

TABLE 5.6   Financial cash flows for period ended t_1 (no interest deductibility; pro forma)

$ Receipts ($ RCPT)	$6250.00
$ Expenditures ($ EXPT)	−3976.50
Gross cash from operations	$2273.50
Gross tax at 52%	−1182.22
Net cash from operations	$1091.28
Depreciation tax subsidy	+ 936.00
Cash available to an unlevered firm	$2027.28
Interest tax subsidy	0.00
CAC	$2027.28

Like the depreciation tax subsidy, the interest tax subsidy can be calculated as simply the interest expense times the tax rate:

$$\$36.00 \times 0.52 = \$18.72$$

Government is, in effect, subsidizing our corporation in the amount of $18.72 in cash by allowing interest deductibility.

Between the depreciation and interest tax subsidies on our FCF statement is a subtotal labeled *cash available to an unlevered firm*. This is the only item that we have not yet discussed. You saw both in the FCF statements and in Figure 5.3 that cash available to all capital suppliers (CAC) is equal to the sum of the cash available to an unlevered firm (CAU) plus the interest tax subsidy. When a company is unlevered it has no debt capital claims outstanding. So the cash available to the capital suppliers of such a firm would include no interest tax subsidy, because the firm pays no interest. This means that the amount of cash available to an unlevered firm (CAU) which you see in our FCF statement is the amount of cash that would be available to the capital suppliers of any corporation engaged in precisely this business, provided that corporation had no debt claims outstanding.[8] CAC would be less by the amount of the interest tax subsidy, which results in our CAU cash amount. This figure will be very useful when we begin studying the theory of capital structure in Section III. For now you can regard it as merely a "subtotal" kind of cash availability before the interest tax subsidy is added.

In later chapters we shall occasionally refer to the CAU amount as the corporation's *operating* cash flow. This will be in contrast to our understanding of CAC as the corporation's *overall* cash flow. Although these terminologies are not particularly important to our discussion of valuation in this section, they will be very helpful in clarifying a number of points that we shall be making about the theory in subsequent sections.

ACRONYMS   Before going further (to include explaining why tax subsidies are calculated as they are), we need to adopt a shorthand way of referring to the items in our FCF statement so that we can save space in our presentations. Like the symbol FCF, we are going to employ abbreviations which we shall call "acronyms" to stand for the names of the various FCF statement items. From now on:

\$RCPT	stands for	receipts (cash from operations and/or divestment of productive assets)
\$EXPT	stands for	expenditures (cash) for operations
GCFO	stands for	gross cash from operations
GTAX	stands for	gross tax
NCFO	stands for	net cash from operations
DTS	stands for	depreciation tax subsidy
CAU	stands for	cash available to an unlevered firm (operating cash flow)
ITS	stands for	interest tax subsidy
CAC	stands for	cash available to all capital suppliers (overall cash flow)

and τ (Greek lowercase tau) will represent the corporate tax rate; for example, for our corporation, $\tau = 0.52$. Figure 5.3 is reproduced in acronymic form as Figure 5.4.

Also, for the discussion immediately following, we need from the accountant's income statement: EBDIT, to stand for earnings before depre-

---

[8]We make the assumption here that the capital structure of the firm has no impact or influence on its ongoing business operation. For example, we would argue that no one chooses to buy or not buy the goods or services offered for sale by a firm on the basis that it does or does not have debt in its capital structure. We shall maintain this assumption throughout the book.

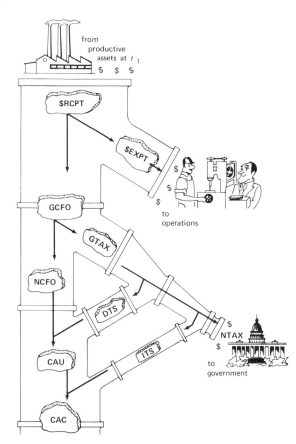

FIGURE 5.4   **Financial cash flows**

ciation, interest, and taxes; and NTAX, to stand for income taxes actually calculated and paid to government (net tax).

DTS AND ITS   Now let us return to our discussion of ITS and DTS, which, you will recall, can simply be calculated by multiplying the amount of the associated deductible expense (on the income statement) by the corporate tax rate, τ.

The total cash that capital suppliers can claim is whatever remains after cash expenditures are made and after the government gets its taxes. Cash expenditures reduce the cash available:

$$\text{\$RCPT} - \text{\$EXPT} = \text{GCFO}$$

GCFO dollars remain after receipts are reduced by expenditures. Remember that GCFO and EBDIT from the income statement are the same thing in our current discussion. When both depreciation and interest expenses are deductible for tax purposes, accountants and government figure the amount of tax the corporation owes by the following formula:

income tax = tax rate times profit before tax

or

$$NTAX = \tau(PBT)$$

and since

$$PBT = EBDIT - \text{depreciation expense}$$
$$- \text{interest expense}$$

then

$$NTAX = \tau(EBDIT - \text{depreciation expense}$$
$$- \text{interest expense})$$

So the total cash available to capital suppliers is

$$CAC = GCFO - NTAX$$
$$= GCFO - \tau(EBDIT - \text{depreciation expense}$$
$$- \text{interest expense})$$

But we just recalled that EBDIT equals GFCO, so

$$CAC = GCFO - \tau(GCFO - \text{depreciation expense}$$
$$- \text{interest expense})$$

Multiplying out,

$$CAC = GCFO - \tau(GCFO) + \tau(\text{depreciation expense})$$
$$+ \tau(\text{interest expense})$$

Look what we have here: $\tau(GCFO)$ is nothing more than our gross tax, GTAX from the FCF statement, so

$$CAC = GCFO - GTAX + \tau(\text{depreciation expense})$$
$$+ \tau(\text{interest expense})$$

Let us examine the formula directly above. GCFO is the number of dollars left in the corporation after cash expenditures for operations. And CAC is the number of dollars available for all capital suppliers. From the FCF in Figure 5.4, you can see that the only net cash outflow between GCFO and CAC is what goes to government in taxes. From the formulas above, the net amount going to government is

$$NTAX = GTAX - \tau(\text{depreciation expense})$$
$$- \tau(\text{interest expense})$$

This tells us that government's tax *in the absence of depreciation and interest deductibility* would be GTAX. (Depreciation and interest would not be deductible expenses and therefore would not appear in the formula above.) But because depreciation *is* deductible, GTAX is reduced by τ(depreciation expense). And because interest *is* deductible, GTAX is further reduced by τ(interest expense). In a real sense, by allowing these reductions in tax, government is subsidizing the operations of the corporation by the cash amounts τ(depreciation expense) and τ(interest expense). Because of this, we designate these cash flows as *tax subsidies*, where

$$\text{DTS} = \tau(\text{depreciation expense})$$

and

$$\text{ITS} = \tau(\text{interest expense})$$

Substituting these definitions in the same formula for CAC, we arrive at

$$\text{CAC} = \text{GCFO} - \text{GTAX} + \text{DTS} + \text{ITS}$$

which is nothing more than our financial cash-flow statement written horizontally rather than vertically.

Look again at Figure 5.4. You will see that the GTAX cash-flow channel branches to allow the depreciation tax subsidy to flow back into the net cash from operations, NCFO. The sum of DTS and NCFO ($1091.28 + $936.00) is the total amount of cash available before the interest tax subsidy is received. That sum (CAU) is, as we mentioned before, the amount of cash our corporation would have available if it had no debt claims outstanding (was unlevered). The CAU is $2027.28.

Then the interest tax subsidy also splits from the GTAX channel and flows in from government. Adding that $18.72 to the CAU of $2027.28 we get the cash available to capital suppliers, CAC, of $2046.00. If this were an unlevered firm, CAC would equal CAU because there would be no ITS.

By treating the tax subsidies this way we can see directly the effect of depreciation and interest deductibility, without the need for including non-expenditure accounting numbers in our FCF statement. This ability will prove very convenient in our further developments of corporate financial theory.

One of the main lessons we learned in the first section is that the expectation of cash flows is the basis of value in financial and capital markets. Our recasting of the traditional accounting income statement into a financial cash-flow statement allows us to concentrate on these important value determinants for a corporation. There is no time-consuming or distracting need to first subtract out and then add back noncash and/or nonoperating expenses, which are irrelevant to corporate valuation. By recognizing only real financial cash flows, we limit our study to the same things that the capital market will be interested in when the time comes to value our corporation.

We have developed our corporate cash-flow ideas with our company's flows at t_1. Future cash flows, of course, will occur at more than just one future time point. Our firm has another set which occurs at t_2, and it could conceivably have financial cash flows at each time point indeterminately far into the future. Before we worry about those longer-term situations, however, let us complete the two-period corporate valuation at hand.

To review what we have done and what yet remains, we are in the process of trying to set values for the debt and equity capital claims on our corporation. Our theoretical development in Section I tells us that these values will be simply the expectation of future cash flows to these capital suppliers appropriately discounted back to t_0 at risk-adjusted rates determined in the capital market. So far we have made major progress toward our goal. We have discovered how to calculate the expected total amounts of cash available to all capital suppliers of a corporation. We have done this by introducing the corporate financial cash-flow statement. This has allowed us to avoid the noncash, nonoperating expense, and tax-effect ambiguities of the accounting income statement. And this concentration on cash flows will continue to serve us well as we proceed in developing corporate financial theory.

So we can estimate the *total* amount of cash that capital suppliers can claim from our firm. As a review of our abilities, we can calculate the company's FCF statement for the period ending at t_2. This is displayed next to the t_1 statement in Table 5.7. The t_2 cash flows should be easy for you to recognize. Remember that the t_2 depreciation expense is $900.00, so DTS at t_2 is $(0.52)(\$900.00) = \$468.00$. Interest expense at t_2 is expected to be $18.00. ITS_2 must then be $(0.52)(\$18.00)$, or $9.36. The total amount of cash available to capital suppliers at t_2 is expected to be $1773.00. After that, no more cash will be available from the firm at future time points.

TABLE 5.7 **Financial cash-flow statements (pro forma)**

Period ending:	t_1	t_2
$RCPT	$6250.00	$7500.00
$EXPT	−3976.50	−4800.75
GCFO	$2273.50	$2699.25
GTAX	−1182.22	−1403.61
NCFO	$1091.28	$1295.64
DTS*	+ 936.00	+ 468.00
CAU	$2027.28	$1763.64
ITS†	+ 18.72	+ 9.36
CAC	$2046.00	$1773.00
*Depreciation expense	$1800.00	$ 900.00
†Interest expense	$ 36.00	$ 18.00

CASH FLOWS TO CAPITAL SUPPLIERS We have filtered the operational and taxation information about the firm through the FCF statement and discovered that $2046.00 cash is expected to be available to capital suppliers at t_1 and $1773.00 at t_2. These are the total amounts of cash available to both debt and equity suppliers. But in order to value the capital claims we must know how much of the total is expected to go to each separately. Fortunately, we already have enough information to solve that problem. We know the exact cash-flow amounts expected by debt suppliers. And since equity, as the residual claimant, will have available whatever is left after debt claims are paid, the difference between the total expectation and the debt suppliers' expectation will be the expected cash available to equity suppliers.

Debt suppliers expect to be paid $225 in principal and $36 in interest at t_1, and $225 of principal and $18 of interest at t_2. So the total expected flows to debt suppliers are $261 (= $225 + $36) at t_1 and $243 (= $225 + $18) at t_2. In keeping with our acronymic style, we shall call expected principal payments PP, and expected interest payments I. So $PP_1 = $225, $PP_2 = $225, $I_1 = $36, and $I_2 = $18. The sum of interest and principal will be called CDD, the expected *cash distribution to debt* suppliers. $CDD_1 = $261 and $CDD_2 = $243.

There is a total of $2046 cash available to capital suppliers at t_1; $CAC_1 = $2046. The expected amount of cash, then, available to equity must be $CAC_1 - CDD_1$, the difference between the total and what debt gets. CAE, naturally enough, is the *cash available to equity*, so $CAE_1 = CAC_1 - CDD_1 = $2046 - $261 = $1785. And $CAE_2 = CAC_2 - CDD_2 = $1773 - $243 = $1530. Equity suppliers expect to have $1785 available to them at t_1 and $1530 at t_2.

You remember that, for this particular corporation, we assume that equity suppliers will have the entire amount of cash available actually distributed to them. So, for our firm the expected *cash distribution to equity* suppliers, CDE, is the same as CAE, the expected cash available to equity suppliers. Those amounts, for our company, are the same. But this is not necessarily the case for all corporations. The entire amount of CAE may not actually be paid out to equity suppliers. Some of it may be *retained* within the firm for future use. If we had any of this, we would call it the *cash retention of the firm*, or CRF. The amount of the distribution then would be equal to the amount available to equity less the amount of the retention, or $CDE = CAE - CRF$.[9]

We probably should pause here to take stock of where we are. The purpose of this section is to show how available cash is split among capital claims. All we have really done is taken the total available cash, seen what debt's expectation is, and given equity the rest. Figure 5.5 and Table 5.8 should help to clarify this.

Figure 5.5 is similar to Figures 5.3 and 5.4 but with the cash flows to capital suppliers added on the bottom. There, the CAC flow splits into two parts, cash distribution to debt suppliers, CDD (= I + PP), and CAE, cash available to equity suppliers. Notice that CDD is expected to flow to the debt suppliers. CAE, however, has the potential of being split into two parts: CDE, the expected cash distribution to equity suppliers, and CRF, the

---

[9]Do not confuse cash retention of the firm (CRF) with the accounting number "retained earnings." We have discussed earnings enough to know that the two amounts *may* be quite different, and, in general, *are* quite different. For our purposes retained earnings are irrelevant.

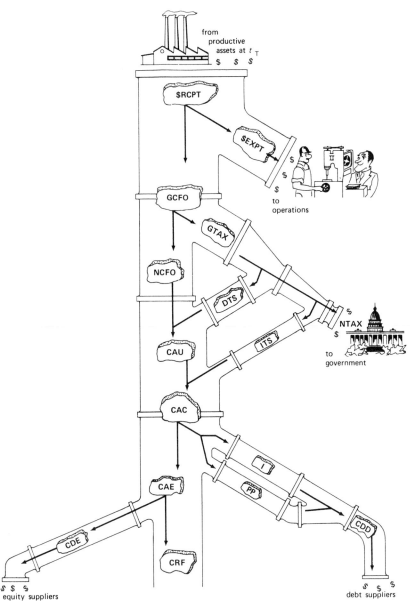

FIGURE 5.5   Financial cash flows, including those to capital suppliers

expected cash retention of the firm. Since the firm we are now considering does not retain cash, CRF = $0.00, and CDE = CAE.

Table 5.8 is the numerical statement of the diagram in Figure 5.5. It also includes the cash flows at t_2. Again, for both t_1 and t_2, the CAC's are split into two parts, CDD going to debt suppliers (in the form of I and PP),

TABLE 5.8 Complete financial cash flows at times t_1 and t_2 (including those to capital suppliers)

	t_1	t_2
$RCPT	$6250.00	$7500.00
$EXPT	−3976.50	−4800.75
GCFO	$2273.50	$2699.25
GTAX	−1182.22	−1403.61
NCFO	$1091.28	$1295.64
DTS	+ 936.00	+ 468.00
CAU	$2027.28	$1763.64
ITS	+ 18.72	+ 9.36
CAC	$2046.00	$1773.00
I	$ 36.00	$ 18.00
PP	+ 225.00	+ 225.00
CDD	$ 261.00	$ 243.00
CAE	$1785.00	$1530.00
CRF	− 0.00	− 0.00
CDE	$1785.00	$1530.00

and CAE, the remainder, being available to equity. Since no cash is retained by the firm, $CRF = \$0.00$ and $CDE = CAE$.

Before we proceed to Chapter 6 and the task of valuing these cash flows, we shall conclude this chapter by reviewing those characteristics of our analysis which are particularly important. First, our diagrams of the financial cash flows of a firm are drawn showing only one time point's flows. In fact, as Table 5.8 illustrates, there are two sets of financial cash flows (one each at t_1 and t_2), both of which are important in our corporation. And in general there will be a set of financial cash flows to be analyzed for each future time point through which a company is expected to pass. If there are ten future time periods when the firm will be operating, we need to analyze the cash flows occurring at each of the ten future time points concluding those operating periods.

Second, remember that, as in Section I, all financial cash flows at the same time point occur simultaneously. Even though we draw and speak of a sequence of cash flows from $RCPT through CDE taking place at each time point, we must regard all these flows as occurring at the same time. Points in time, you remember, have no duration. This condition might seem silly to you at first, but think about what could happen if it were not true. Suppose that some cash flow, say CAC_1, happened at t_1 and CDD_1 then took place at t_1 plus one day. From our discussion in Chapter 1 of the time value of money, you know that the present worth of a CDD_1 flow at t_1 would be different from the present worth of that same dollar flow occurring one day later. So we must be careful to remember that even though we are talking of our corporation as if it were a realistic company, we must strictly obey all the characteristics and conditions we have laid out for our capital market in order to keep our development intact. We cannot allow even small variations in timing when demonstrating how valuation works.

Third, we should constantly remind ourselves that the financial cash-flow dollars that we are working with are *expectations* of actual numbers to occur in the future. Since we are uncertain about what the *actual* numbers of dollars will turn out to be, we use estimates (best guesses) of those numbers. But we realize that the actual cash flows that finally occur may not be the same as the figures which appear in our expectational cash flow statements.

Finally, there is one more characteristic of the financial cash-flow analysis that involves both time location and uncertainty considerations. The financial cash-flow expectations that we have recorded for our firm for t_1 and t_2 are as seen from our present time location at t_0. There is no guarantee that when we get to t_1, our expectations about t_2 cash flows will be the same as they are now at t_0. Something could happen during period p_1 that would force us to reestimate the t_2 cash flows when we arrive at t_1. So any valuation statements we make on the basis of the t_1 and t_2 financial cash flows we have developed hold only as of our t_0 estimating point. We can compute values (or market prices) for t_0. We can also compute values expected for t_1, values based on t_0 expectations. But by the time we actually get to t_1, we might have a new set of expected cash flows for t_2 and beyond, which would result in an actual t_1 value different from that expected at t_0. The phenomenon of changing of future cash-flow expectations is one important reason why real security prices change across time. The price of a share of stock at each time point is based on a set of future expected cash flows to that share of stock. A change in price of that stock may mean the market has revised its expectations about either future cash flows or opportunity costs.[10]

With these characteristics in mind, we are now ready to consider the process of valuing corporate capital claims.

[10]Stock prices can also change even without changes in expectations. This is possible when the stock market experiences a shift in underlying utility or preference functions for cash flows. Another reason for stock price changes across time under these conditions will be developed in Section IV.

Chapter 6

Valuation of Corporate Capital Claims—I

VALUATION OF CAPITAL CLAIMS Now that we have seen the basic ideas of corporate cash flows, we can proceed to the final goal, placing values on the capital claims of the corporation. Because of our efforts up to this point, the task should not be difficult. We already know the mechanical procedures involved in valuation from Section I, and have in the previous chapter identified the appropriate cash flows expected by the capital suppliers for our two-period firm. These are the bases for value. All that remains to be done is to determine what the t_0 values of those expected t_1 and t_2 cash flows would be in an efficient capital market.

DEBT CLAIM VALUE First we shall value the debt claim. The expectation of cash flows to the debt suppliers (see Table 5.8, p. 89) are for a total of $261 CDD at t_1 and $243 CDD at t_2 ($I_1 = \$36$, $PP_1 = \$225$; and $I_2 = \$18$, $PP_2 = \$225$). When we described the characteristics of the company, we said that the capital market considers the riskiness of those expected future cash flows to debt suppliers and requires an 8% rate of return per period. This means that the appropriate opportunity cost for debt capital suppliers is 8% in period p_1 and also 8% in period p_2.

For notational purposes we will call the *rate of return required by debt capital suppliers in period* P, kd_P. So the suppliers of debt to our company have $kd_1 = kd_2 = 8\%$, or 0.08. Since in this example the rate is constant across time, we can drop the time subscript and say simply that $kd = 0.08$, the rate of return required by debt suppliers.

Valuing the debt claim is a simple matter of discounting the expected t_1 and t_2 cash flows to debt suppliers at 8% per period. If we use the symbol VD_0 to represent the value of the debt claim at t_0, then VD_0 equals the sum of the appropriately discounted CDD_1 and CDD_2 flows:

$$VD_0 = \frac{CDD_1}{1 + kd_1} + \frac{CDD_2}{(1 + kd_1)(1 + kd_2)}$$

or, since $kd_1 = kd_2 = kd$,

$$VD_0 = \frac{CDD_1}{1 + kd} + \frac{CDD_2}{(1 + kd)^2}$$

Substituting the appropriate amounts,

$$VD_0 = \frac{\$261}{1.08} + \frac{\$243}{(1.08)^2}$$
$$= \$450$$

The t_0 value of the debt claim is $450; in an efficient capital market the holder of that claim could sell it for $450 at t_0.

To exercise your memory of Section I, we point out that the t_1 value (VD_1) of the $243 expected t_2 cash flow to debt is $225,[1] and the t_0 value of the t_2 flow is $208\frac{1}{3}$. The t_0 value of the $261 expected t_1 cash flow to debt is $241\frac{2}{3}$. The sum of the t_0 values of the t_1 and t_2 cash flows is, hence, $241\frac{2}{3} + \$208\frac{1}{3} = \$450$, the value of debt.

So the debt of our company at t_0 is worth $450, the present value of the expectations of future cash flows to debt suppliers. We arrive at that dollar figure by discounting the expected CDD's at kd.

EQUITY VALUE In valuing the equity claim, we use exactly the same procedure as in valuing the debt claim. We already know the expected cash flows to equity suppliers: $CDE_1 = \$1785$ and $CDE_2 = \$1530$. And the capital market, you remember, has informed us that it finds the risk inherent in those cash flows to require a 20% rate of return per period. We shall note the *rate of return required by equity suppliers in period* P *as* ke_P. So $ke_1 = ke_2 = 20\%$, or 0.20.

Continuing along now-familiar lines, the value of equity at t_0, VE_0, must be the appropriately discounted CDE's:

$$VE_0 = \frac{CDE_1}{1 + ke_1} + \frac{CDE_2}{(1 + ke_1)(1 + ke_2)}$$

or, since $ke_1 = ke_2 = ke$,

$$VE_0 = \frac{CDE_1}{1 + ke} + \frac{CDE_2}{(1 + ke)^2}$$

---

[1] Remember that the t_1 value of the t_2 cash flow is based on expectations held as of t_0. By the time you actually arrive at t_1 the expected t_2 flow may have changed, as would, therefore, its t_1 value have changed from that expected on the basis of t_0 expectations.

In general, when we are regarding now as t_0, and are discussing market values of capital claims for future time points (VD_1, VE_4, and so on), those values are, naturally, market values expected for the future time points, *based on what the market believes at t_0 about future cash flows.* Similarly, if t_1 is now, capital claim values expected for future time points begin at t_2, and so on.

Substituting the numbers, we get

$$VE_0 = \frac{\$1785}{1.20} + \frac{\$1530}{(1.20)^2}$$
$$= \$2550$$

The value of the equity claim on our corporation at t_0 equals $2550. If the company had only one share of common stock (equity) outstanding, it would be selling for $2550 in our capital market. If there were 100 shares outstanding, they would be selling for $25.50 apiece.

Again from Section I, the t_1 value of the $1530 t_2 cash flow is $1275 and its t_0 value is $1062\frac{1}{2}$.[2] The $1785 expected cash flow at t_1 is worth $1487\frac{1}{2}$ at t_0. The sum of the t_0 values of the t_1 and t_2 cash flows, $1062\frac{1}{2}$ and $1487\frac{1}{2}$, is $2550, or VE_0. The value of equity is found by discounting the expected CDE's at *ke*.

VALUE OF THE FIRM The value of the equity claim on our corporation is $2550 at t_0; $VE_0 = \$2550$. The value of the debt claim at t_0 is $450; $VD_0 = \$450$. The value of the corporation as a whole, the value of all the claims on its future cash flows, must then be the sum of the values of the equity and debt claims. VF_0, the value of the firm at t_0, is

$$VF_0 = VD_0 + VE_0$$
$$= \$450 + \$2550$$
$$= \$3000$$

The value of our company at t_0 is $3000. If you owned all the debt and all the equity, your securities, in total, would be worth $3000 in the capital market.

COST OF DEBT CAPITAL Now that we have covered the basic ideas of corporate valuation, we can look at a few other closely related concepts which will build on our valuation knowledge. The first thing we shall consider is the *cost* of debt capital, as opposed to the rate of return required by debt capital suppliers. You remember that the return required by debt suppliers is noted as kd_p. That is the rate of return that debt suppliers expect to receive on the value of their capital claim.[3]

---

[2]We shall occasionally refer to the CDE cash flow from the corporation to equity suppliers as a "dividend." This is generally in keeping with common usage, although taxation rules (for example, Internal Revenue Service regulations in the U.S.) may regard part of such a flow as a return of capital for tax purposes. Nevertheless, we shall regard CDE and "dividend" as synonymous.

Stock market enthusiasts might recognize the $1275 t_1 value of the CDE_2 cash flow as the expected t_1 *ex dividend* stock price, based, of course, on t_0 expectations.

[3]Appendix II.D compares our usage and definitions of debt-related cash flows and rates of return with those which appear conventionally in real capital markets. For example, our kd_p, the rate of return required by debt suppliers, is distinguished from the commonly used yield-to-maturity rate of return on a bond.

For example, in our corporation, $VD_0 = \$450$. If $kd_1 = 8\%$, debt capital suppliers expect to receive VD_0 times kd_1, or I_1, as their interest payment (cash return) *on* capital at t_1. Substituting the numbers,

$$I_1 = VD_0(kd_1)$$
$$= \$450(0.08)$$
$$= \$36$$

$36 is the amount of cash "return *on* capital" that debt suppliers expect to to receive at t_1.[4] The required rate of return is 8%, the required cash return is $36. But are those the same as "costs" of debt capital to the corporation? The answer is no. A cost to the corporation is the amount of cash or rate of return that it actually expects to pay. It is true that debt suppliers expect to *receive* 8%, or $36, and the corporation also expects debt suppliers to receive that amount. But the corporation does not expect to pay all of it. How can this be? Who makes up the difference?

The answer is government. Let us look at our t_1 cash flows and see how the role of government affects the cost of debt capital for our corporation. The interest payment at t_1 is expected to be $36.00. But government supplies $18.72 of that in the form of the interest tax subsidy at t_1. So the corporation must only come up with ($36.00 − $18.72), or $17.28 of cash at t_1 from its own resources in order to pay debt suppliers. The cash *cost* of debt to the corporation at t_1 is only $17.28. In general, the cash cost of debt at time point T is

$$\text{cash cost of debt}_T = I_T - ITS_T$$

Interest deductibility means that corporate debt costs are always less than the returns required by debt suppliers. Required cash return is I_T; cash cost is $I_T - ITS_T$.

In the same way that the cash cost of debt is less than the cash return required, the cost of debt expressed as a rate is less than the rate of return required by debt suppliers. The latter, kd_p, we know is 8% per period for our corporation. We shall designate the *cost of debt capital as a rate* or simply the *cost of debt* as kd_p^*. Measurement of the cost of debt, kd_p^*, is quite simple. Earlier we saw that the expected interest payment or cash return required by debt suppliers at t_1 is

$$I_1 = VD_0(kd_1)$$

so

$$kd_1 = \frac{I_1}{VD_0}$$

The return required by debt suppliers during period p_1, kd_1, is the required

---

[4]On the basis of t_0 expectations, $VD_1 = \$225$. Since $I_2 = VD_1(kd_2)$, expected $I_2 = \$225(0.08) = \$18$.

cash return *on* capital at t_1, I_1, divided by market value of the debt claims at t_0, VD_0. The same relationship holds for kd_p^*. The cost of debt, kd_1^*, is equal to the cash cost to the corporation $(I_1 - ITS_1)$ at t_1 divided by the debt's market value at t_0:

$$kd_1^* = \frac{I_1 - ITS_1}{VD_0}$$

We can simplify this formula quite a bit. Since ITS_1 is equal to $I_1(\tau)$, substituting we get

$$kd_1^* = \frac{I_1 - I_1(\tau)}{VD_0}$$

Factoring,

$$kd_1^* = \frac{I_1(1 - \tau)}{VD_0}$$

But $I_1/VD_0 = kd_1$, so

$$kd_1^* = kd_1(1 - \tau)$$

kd^*, the cost of debt, is equal to the required return to debt suppliers, kd, times 1 minus the tax rate.

For our company, $kd = 8\%$ and $\tau = 0.52$, so

$$kd^* = (0.08)(1 - 0.52)$$
$$= 0.0384 \quad \text{or} \quad 3.84\%$$

Notice that for our firm, kd_p^* is constant at 3.84% for both periods p_1 and p_2. Since kd_p and τ are constant, kd_p^* must also be the same across time.

If interest payments were not deductible for tax purposes, the cost of debt, kd^*, would be the same as the required return to debt suppliers, kd, because no interest tax subsidies would be available. So you can see that interest deductibility can have a large effect on the cost of debt to the corporation, depending on the size of τ, the tax rate. A τ of 50%, for example, would mean that kd^* would be only half of kd.

Later in this section we shall find that it is worthwhile to know that for a two-period firm such as ours,

$$VD_0 = \frac{CDD_1 - ITS_1}{1 + kd_1^*} + \frac{CDD_2 - ITS_2}{(1 + kd_1^*)(1 + kd_2^*)}$$

or that the value of the debt claim can also be calculated by discounting the total net cash payments by the company (excluding the part paid by government, ITS) to the debt suppliers by kd^*, the cost of debt capital. You remember that our original calculation for VD_0 was made with the entire receipts of the debt suppliers, CDD, discounted by kd. That calculation is the one made, in effect, by the capital market. The market is interested in the total cash to be received, and its riskiness. It is not concerned about ITS's and kd^*'s. But the corporation is, because the higher the ITS, the lower the cost of debt to the company. The alternative way of calculating VD_0 (by subtracting ITS_T from CDD_T in the numerator and discounting the difference at kd_P^*) can be thought of as a debt valuation from the point of view of the company, not the capital market. The value of debt is the same in any case. But by using a lower cash payment (less by the amount of ITS) and a lower discount rate (debt cost rather than the return required by debt), the alternative calculation recognizes cash flows and valuation from the firm's viewpoint of what that capital claim costs. We could offer a simple algebraic proof that the two valuation formulas are the same, but it would not add much to the intuitive truth you have just recognized. You can, of course, verify with your calculator or by hand that, for our two-period firm, you get the same numerical values for the debt claim by using either the original formulation or the alternative just introduced. The important thing to remember, however, is that the original valuation procedure for debt recognizes the interest tax subsidy effect in the cash flows (numerators), whereas the second valuation procedure recognizes the interest tax subsidy effect in the discount rate or capital cost (denominators). For right now you should just store this idea somewhere. We shall return to it again shortly, and it will be especially useful when we look at the theory of capital structure in Section III.

REQUIRED RETURN, COST OF CAPITAL, AND VALUATION FOR THE FIRM AS A WHOLE

For our two-period corporation, we have completed all the cash-flow and valuation analysis that the capital market would do. We have estimated cash flows to each type of capital supplier, discovered the returns that the market would require, and valued the capital claims. As a matter of fact, we have even gone a bit further to discuss the cost of debt capital, kd^*, an idea that the capital market itself does not need for valuation purposes but which is useful to the firm. In the same vein, we are now going to introduce a few more concepts which are not directly considered by the capital market but which are most important to corporate financial theory and are closely related to the valuation ideas we have already presented. These are valuation and capital required returns and costs *for the firm as a whole*, rather than as separated into equity and debt. We shall find use for these ideas in Section III and also in Section V, the theory of asset acquisition and divestment, which is commonly known as *capital budgeting*. Indeed, concepts embodying the firm as a whole form a basic framework for corporate financial decision making. The firm's management will find it most efficient, as we shall discover, to consider the firm as an unified entity when making financial decisions.

OVERALL CORPORATE RETURN

We can now take an additional step to develop a view of the firm more from the perspective of management. We are not going to forget about the more specific focuses of the capital market, but, rather, broaden our horizons a bit. Think of the firm giving a total amount of cash at each future time point to all the suppliers of capital. For example, we expect our firm to distribute cash in the amount of CDD_1 plus CDE_1 at t_1, and CDD_2 plus CDE_2 at t_2. The flows in each period, of course, sum to CAC_1 and CAC_2.[5]

The company is expected to distribute CAC_1 and CAC_2 to the capital market, and this results in a value of the firm as a whole of VF_0, the sum of VD_0 and VE_0. Although the capital market never really performs such a calculation, we can think of the CAC_1 and CAC_2 cash flows being discounted back to the present at some required rate of return in order to equal VF_0. We shall designate that discount rate as kf_p and call it the *overall required rate of return for the firm*, where

$$VF_0 = \frac{CDE_1 + CDD_1}{1 + kf_1} + \frac{CDE_2 + CDD_2}{(1 + kf_1)(1 + kf_2)}$$

or

$$VF_0 = \frac{CAC_1}{1 + kf_1} + \frac{CAC_2}{(1 + kf_1)(1 + kf_2)}$$

We can think of the kf_p's as the *discount rates which, when applied to the expected cash distributions to all capital suppliers, result in a market value of the firm equal to the sum of the values of all capital claims.*

In calculating kf_p we could attempt to solve the formulas above. But unless we assume that kf is constant in both periods, we cannot solve the formulas to get a single set of values. There are many combinations of numbers for kf_1 and kf_2 that would give us VF_0. So we must come up with a better way of calculating kf_p.

Think back to our discussion of the cash return *on* capital required by debt suppliers at any particular time point. We showed, for example, that at t_1 debt suppliers expected

$$I_1 = VD_0(kd_1)$$
$$\$36 = \$450(0.08)$$

By the same token, equity suppliers have a required cash return *on* capital equal to $VE_0(ke_1)$ at t_1. We can think of the sum of debt and equity suppliers' required cash returns as the required return *on* capital for the overall firm. That, then, must be $VF_0(kf_1)$, the market value of the firm times the overall required return,

$$(kf_1)VF_0 = (kd_1)VD_0 + (ke_1)VE_0$$

Solving for kf_1,

$$kf_1 = kd_1\frac{VD_0}{VF_0} + ke_1\frac{VE_0}{VF_0}$$

The overall required rate of return for a corporation is the market-value weighted average of the required rates of return for the separate capital claims.

[5]Remember that our company retains no cash; $CRF = \$0.00$. If this were not true, $CDD + CDE$ would not equal CAC (check Figure 5.5). We shall discuss the situation in which CRF is not equal to zero before the end of this section.

A "market-value weight" means simply that, for example, debt's weight in the calculation is the ratio of debt's market value to the total value of the firm, VD_0/VF_0. Equity's weight is VE_0/VF_0. To find kf_1, we simply multiply each claim's required return for the period by its weight, and add. The answer is kf_1.

For our company, kf_1 is

$$kf_1 = \frac{VD_0}{VF_0}kd_1 + \frac{VE_0}{VF_0}ke_1$$

$$= \frac{\$450}{\$3000}(0.08) + \frac{\$2550}{\$3000}(0.20)$$

$$= (0.15)(0.08) + (0.85)(0.20)$$

$$= 0.182 \quad \text{or} \quad 18.2\%$$

The formula for the first period (p_1) can be generalized to

$$kf_P = \frac{VD_{T-1}}{VF_{T-1}}kd_P + \frac{VE_{T-1}}{VF_{T-1}}ke_P \qquad \text{where P = T}$$

Any period's overall required rate of return for the firm (kf) is debt's and equity's required rates in that period "weighted" by the market values of debt and equity relative to that of the firm, all taken at the beginning of the period. For that reason, kf may also be called the "weighted-average required rate of return for the firm."

Our corporation's overall required rate for the second period, kf_2, is thus

$$kf_2 = \frac{VD_1}{VF_1}kd_2 + \frac{VE_1}{VF_1}ke_2$$

We already know that kd_2 and ke_2 are the same as the first-period rates. The equity, debt, and firm values are those we would expect at t_1 on the basis of t_0 expectations:

$$VD_1 = \frac{\$243}{1.08} = \$225$$

and

$$VE_1 = \frac{\$1530}{1.20} = \$1275$$

so

$$VF_1 = VD_1 + VE_1 = \$1500$$

The market weights for the second period are the same as those for the first:

$$\frac{VD_1}{VF_1} = \frac{\$225}{\$1500} = 0.15$$

$$\frac{VE_1}{VF_1} = \frac{\$1275}{\$1500} = 0.85$$

So the weighted-average required rate for the second period, p_2, for our company is the same as for the first:

$$kf_2 = (0.15)(0.08) + (0.85)(0.20)$$
$$= 0.182 \quad \text{or} \quad 18.2\%$$

Our firm's kf, like its ke and kd, is also constant across time.[6]

We can validate our kf calculations by substituting the numbers in the overall valuation formula for this particular corporation:

$$VF_0 = \frac{CDE_1 + CDD_1}{1 + kf} + \frac{CDE_2 + CDD_2}{(1 + kf)^2}$$

or

$$VF_0 = \frac{CAC_1}{1 + kf} + \frac{CAC_2}{(1 + kf)^2}$$
$$= \frac{\$2046}{1.182} + \frac{\$1773}{(1.182)^2}$$
$$= \$3000$$

which we know is correct because $VE_0 = \$2550$ and $VD_0 = \$450$ from the basic capital claim valuations.

So the overall or weighted average required rate of return for the firm is the rate which the capital market would be applying to the overall cash flows to get VF_0, *if* it did such a thing. kf_p, however, as we have said, is never actually used by the capital market.[7] But it will be a very handy tool as we continue developing corporate financial theory.

OVERALL COST OF CAPITAL In the same sense that the required return for debt, kd, differed from the cost of debt, kd^*, *we make a distinction between the overall required rate of return for the firm, kf, and the overall or weighted average cost of capital, kf^*,* when interest payments are deductible for tax purposes. Remember, in our capital market only interest payments on debt capital are deductible; returns *of* capital and returns *on* equity capital do not reduce the corporation's tax bill. That means the tax effect will only appear in the debt part of the weighted average cost of capital calculation. Since the development of kf^* is the same as that for kf except that we use kd^* instead of kd, we will present only the final formula:

$$kf_P^* = \frac{VD_{t-1}}{VF_{T-1}} kd_P^* + \frac{VE_{t-1}}{VF_{T-1}} ke_P \qquad \text{where P} = \text{T}$$

[6]kf_P's, like ke_P's and kd_P's, need not be constant across time. Indeed, kf may change even if kd and ke do not. The general formula for calculating kf_P as a weighted average of kd_P and ke_P, however, is always the correct way of determining the firm's required rate of return, regardless of the behavior of these rates across time.

[7]When a corporation has no outstanding debt claims (that is, has only equity), kf and ke are the same thing. But the capital market would still say it is interested only in ke, the rate for the specific claim being priced.

For our t_1 flows,

$$kf_1^* = \frac{\$450}{\$3000}(0.0384) + \frac{\$2550}{\$3000}(0.20)$$

$$= 0.17576 \quad \text{or} \quad 17.576\%$$

The weighted-average cost of capital for p_1 is 17.576%. This is less than the weighted-average required rate of 18.2% because we use kd^* rather than kd in the calculation. The economic reason is, of course, because government subsidizes interest payments to debt suppliers in the amount of ITS = $I(\tau)$ dollars. That makes the overall cost of all capital claims, kf^*, less than the overall rate that those claims require, kf. kf_2^* is the same as kf_1^* since, for our firm, all rates and weights are constant during the two periods as we have already seen.

Recall that we were able to arrive at the value of debt, VD_0, by applying kd^* to the cash flows to debt minus the interest tax subsidies. This discounted the expected net cash costs of debt at the cost of debt capital. We can do the same thing for the firm as a whole. By subtracting the interest tax subsidies from the overall cash flow to capital suppliers, we arrive at the appropriate amounts which, when discounted at kf^*, result in VF_0. This is the overall valuation formula for our firm again, but using kf^* and ITS-adjusted cash flows:

$$VF_0 = \frac{CDE_1 + CDD_1 - ITS_1}{1 + kf^*} + \frac{CDE_2 + CDD_2 - ITS_2}{(1 + kf^*)^2}$$

or

$$VF_0 = \frac{CAC_1 - ITS_1}{1 + kf^*} + \frac{CAC_2 - ITS_2}{(1 + kf^*)^2}$$

or

$$VF_0 = \frac{CAU_1}{1 + kf^*} + \frac{CAU_2}{(1 + kf^*)^2}$$

The first two formulas are identical to those we saw earlier except that we use kf^* as the discount rate and subtract ITS from the cash flows. The third form recognizes that $CAU_\tau = CAC_\tau - ITS_\tau$. Substituting the numbers from the example,

$$VF_0 = \frac{\$1785.00 + \$261.00 - \$18.72}{1.17576} + \frac{\$1530.00 + \$243.00 - \$9.36}{(1.17576)^2}$$

$$= \frac{\$2046.00 - \$18.72}{1.17576} + \frac{\$1773.00 - \$9.36}{(1.17576)^2}$$

$$= \frac{\$2027.28}{1.17576} + \frac{\$1763.64}{(1.17576)^2}$$

$$= \$3000$$

The three numerical formulas above correspond to the three algebraic ones that we discussed immediately before. The overall or weighted average cost of capital, kf^*, is appropriate for discounting the "net-of-ITS" operating cash flows for our company.

Overall or weighted-average required rates of return and capital costs are, as we said, of no interest to the capital market. That market is in the business of pricing actual individual capital claims on the basis of expected future cash flows to those claims. kf and kf^* are associated with no *single* capital claim but with *all* the claims of a firm. In a valid sense, kf and kf^* capture in one number several pieces of information about the financial characteristics of a corporation: its operating risks, the separate risks for debt and equity, and the proportionate contribution of each to overall required rates or costs. Further, by examining kf and kf^*, we can, as we shall see in the next section, gain valuable information about the tax effects of various financing strategies. Even though the capital market may not be terribly interested in kf and kf^*, we, and all potential corporate financial managers, should be.

Chapter 7

Valuation of Corporate Capital Claims—II

OF THE
TYPICAL
FIRM

The two-period example of corporate financial cash flows that was the subject of Chapter 6 has allowed us to discover some very important ideas about the way firms are valued in capital markets. It has been rich in concepts of tax subsidies, cash distributions to capital suppliers, required rates of return, capital costs, and capital claim valuation. These ideas, in turn, proceeded in a straightforward conceptual form from our basic financial and capital market developments in Section I. We have come a fair distance toward a reasonable theoretical structure for corporate finance. But more remains to be done.

The characteristics that we gave to our corporation were not terribly unrealistic. It was subject to uncertainty, it had both debt and equity claims outstanding, it had to pay corporate income taxes, and it did plan to make cash distributions to capital suppliers from money generated by operating its assets productively. All these characteristics are common to real companies. But we did impose a few less-than-realistic characteristics on our company. We did this to keep the illustrations as simple as possible without sacrificing any of the important basic valuation ideas we wanted to introduce. Now that those ideas have been developed, we can begin to study corporations that are more realistic.

The less-than-realistic aspects of our two-period corporation are illustrated by the following characteristics:

1. It was not necessary for the company to make cash outlays for "renewal" investments to keep its assets operating efficiently.
2. The company did not invest in any "new" productive assets, nor did it sell for cash any old ones.

3. The company raised no additional cash from capital suppliers. There were no new debt or equity claims issued, nor were any existing claims refinanced.

4. All cash was paid out to capital suppliers as it became available. The company retained no cash.

5. The company planned to terminate operations at t_2, two periods from the present.

We would not be terribly surprised to hear that corporations such as ours really occur now and then. Real-world corporations exist for many different purposes. For example, we have heard of mining companies which have known some time in advance that the veins of ore they were digging would be exhausted at a particular future time point, and the company liquidated. Some firms even have expectational characteristics substantially stranger than that. But most do not. So to be complete, our theory must grow to include characteristics more representative of real firms. We must address questions such as asset acquisition and divestment, financing of operations, cash distribution policies, and operating plans extending far, even indeterminately, into the future. Of course, we shall not do all of these at once. In keeping with our now familiar strategy, we shall gradually introduce these conditions during the rest of the book. Even then, you will be comforted to know, the very basic ideas of value and markets that we illustrated in Section I extend very nicely to these more complex conditions.

You will remember that the purpose of this section is to develop the theory of corporate valuation. We have reached the point now where we can be very specific as to what that means in our theory. Corporate financial managers have the opportunity to make several types of financial decisions that can affect the values of their firms. These include changing the financing plans in terms of capital sources, altering the existing operational assets of the firm and hence their cash-flow expectations, and changing the time pattern of cash disbursements to capital suppliers. These actions are intimately related to corporate valuation theory.

So far we have introduced the idea of valuing an existing set of corporate cash-flow expectations. But the financial decisions described above imply changing the cash-flow expectations of a corporation. To analyze such financial decisions will of course require us also to value the altered cash flows. Unless we have developed a very deep understanding of corporate valuation, we cannot expect to be successful in studying and evaluating corporate financial decision making.

The remainder of this section will expand the theory we have developed so far to include just about everything you need to know about valuing an existing set of expectations for a firm engaging in the entire range of corporate financial activities. Sections III–V will, with our complete valuation model in hand, go on to consider the implications of financial decisions such as those we just mentioned, those which change the existing set of expectations for a corporation.

CASH FLOWS FOR TYPICAL FIRMS

As with our initial study of corporate valuation, we shall study the more typical firm by using a numerical example. Before we introduce our new corporation in specific numerical detail, we should say a few words about how its cash flows differ from those of our original company. Actually the cash flows for the firm include all those we have already seen, plus a few more to describe the possibility of raising new capital and making investment cash outlays. We must deal with the retention of cash, new debt capital cash contributions, new equity capital inflows, and investment cash outlays. Rather than discuss these in verbal abstraction, we present in Figure 7.1 a diagram of the complete financial cash flows at one time point for a corporation.

The upper part of Figure 7.1 should be quite familiar. $RCPT enters from productive assets at a time point, and $EXPT flows to meet operating expenditures, leaving GCFO.[1] Government claims GTAX of this, but returns DTS dollars because of the deductibility of depreciation expenses and ITS because of interest deductibility. NCFO and CAU are subtotal amounts of cash before DTS and ITS, respectively, resulting in CAC dollars that capital suppliers can claim. This amount is divided into CDD, which heads toward debt suppliers, and CAE, which may flow to equity.

This is about the point at which our original corporation's cash flows stopped. Since no new capital was raised and no cash was retained, debt expected to get CDD and equity expected to receive CAE ($=$ CDE). These cash amounts were the basis for capital valuation in our original example.

The cash flows for a more typical firm, however, continue past the point of distributions to capital suppliers, as shown in Figure 7.1. Notice that cash available to equity (CAE) may be split into two parts: cash retention of the firm (CRF) and cash distribution to equity (CDE). The cash retention of the firm will become part of the investment in productive assets for future periods. The decision that a financial manager makes as to how much of CAE is to be retained and how much to be distributed is called the *dividend decision*. We shall consider the questions involved with this decision in Section IV. But we will be able to value an *existing* set of these decisions in the present chapter.

From the viewpoint of equity suppliers, CRF dollars could be distributed to them but are not. Obviously, the amount of CRF_τ cannot enter into the dollars that equity suppliers can consume at time τ. But you can be

---

[1]We might take the opportunity here to mention again that the $RCPT flow includes not only sales of goods or services the company produces but also any cash that may come from liquidating productive assets. This, of course, includes the drawing down of cash balances.

FIGURE 7.1 Financial cash flows of a typical corporation

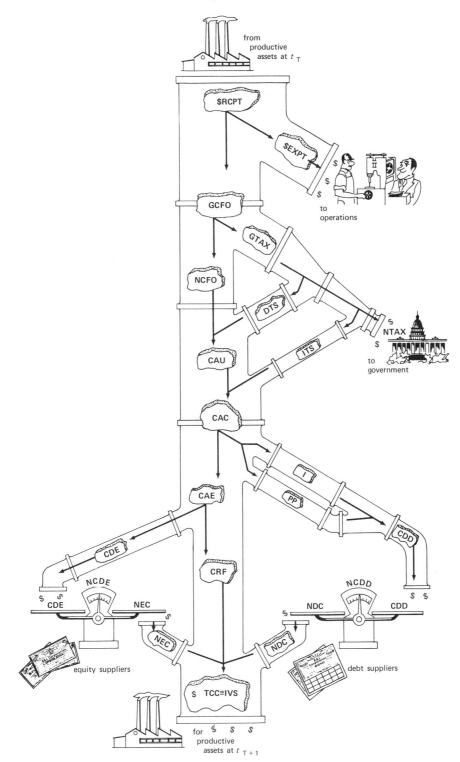

from
productive
assets at t_T

$RCPT

$EXPT

$
$
$

to
operations

GCFO

GTAX

NCFO

DTS

NTAX

ITS

CAU

to
government

CAC

T

CAE

PP

CDD

CDE

CRF

$ $
CDE

NCDE

NEC

NCDD

NDC

CDD

$ $

CDE

NEC

NDC

CDD

equity suppliers

debt suppliers

$ TCC≡IVS

for $ $ $
productive
assets at t_{T+1}

sure that they are expecting some increase in their present wealth by fore-going the CRF dollars at T. More on this in Section V.

The CDE amount, then, is the distribution to equity suppliers. Simul-taneously, however, the corporation may raise *new equity capital* (NEC). At this point the firm would, in essence, be giving out CDE with one hand and taking back NEC with the other. As far as the equity suppliers in aggregate are concerned, their cash-flow receipts at T are the *net* of CDE_T and NEC_T, or *net cash distribution to equity suppliers*, $NCDE_T$. Remember that it is the expectation of cash flows that generates value in capital markets. The cash flow that equity suppliers finally end up with at T, that which they can *consume*, is $NCDE_T$, not CDE_T. So expected *net* cash distribution to equity suppliers is the cash-flow basis for equity valuation in a typical firm.[2] This was also true in our original corporation because, although we did not call it NCDE, CDE was the same as NCDE, since no new capital was raised.

Figure 7.1 indicates (by the balance) that NCDE may flow out from the firm or back into the firm. We represent NCDE that way because it is entirely possible that at any particular time point, equity suppliers may be contributing more to the firm in NEC dollars than they are extracting in CDE dollars. *NCDE could be a negative amount.* As a matter of fact, it is not at all unusual for a new equity flotation by a corporation to exceed that period's dividend. The result is, of course, a net flow at that time point *from* equity suppliers *to* the firm. Again the net-cash-flow expectation is the basis for value.

Now let us shift over to the debt side of Figure 7.1. As before, CDD, the sum of expected interest and principal payments to debt capital suppliers, flows to them. But here again, as in the equity discussion, new capital may be raised from debt suppliers at the same time as payments are made to them. NCDD, the *net cash distribution to debt suppliers*, is the difference between CDD and NDC, *new debt capital*. The *net* distributions of cash to debt capital suppliers are the basis for valuation of debt claims, just as NCDE is for equity.[3]

Moving farther down the diagram in Figure 7.1, new equity capital, cash retention of the firm, and new debt capital combine to form the *total capital contribution*, TCC. This amount of cash will be used for investment in productive assets for future periods.

[2]The intuitive appeal of this argument is greatest when NEC is raised from the existing equity capital suppliers. The statement holds just as accurately, however, even when NEC is raised from different people entirely. This will be shown in Appendix II.A.

[3]We need to attach one condition here: Any new debt claims issued must have the same priority as existing debt claims. A moment's thought about the relationship between risk and required rates shows the necessity for this. We have seen already that the priority difference between debt and equity causes their required rates of return to differ; it should be clear from this that similar priority differences among debt claims would produce similar rate-of-return differences. Although our theory can be extended to handle multiple-priority debt, we shall allow more elaborate texts to treat that situation.

Before we discuss the investment cash flow, however, we should point out that the corporate financial cash flows in Figure 7.1 from CAC through TCC constitute two very important financial decisions made by the corporation. These are (1) the *capital structure decision*, the amount of corporate value claimed by debt versus equity suppliers, and (2) the *capital acquisition/disbursement decision*, the pattern of cash distributions *to* and cash contributions *from* capital suppliers. Section III deals with the capital structure decision, and Section IV addresses the capital acquisition/disbursement decision.

For the moment, however, we are concerned with the capital cash flows themselves rather than the financial decisions that generate them. Returning to Figure 7.1, the total capital contribution, TCC_T, becomes the dollars of investment in productive assets at T, IVS_T. The equivalence sign, $\equiv$, between the two in Figure 7.1 indicates that the total capital contribution must, by definition, equal the investment in productive assets.[4]

The dollars of IVS_T constitute a company's *investment cash flow* at time T. The number of dollars of IVS_T is determined by the company's time T *investment decision*. We shall deal with the theory of that decision in Section V; in this chapter we will focus on valuing an existing set of investment expectations.

NUMERICAL ILLUSTRA-TION

We have now completed our general discussion of the full set of cash flows for the typical firm and are ready to move from the conceptual diagram of Figure 7.1 to a specific numerical analysis of a new corporation. This new corporation will differ from our original corporation in the following ways:

1. In order to generate cash receipts from operations, the company must not only make cash expenditures but must also regularly invest cash in its operating assets so as to keep them running efficiently.
2. The company may, for the investment purpose noted above, retain cash that is available for distribution to capital suppliers.
3. The company may raise new debt and equity capital from the capital market to be used as part of its investment outlay.

[4]Even if a company leaves cash lying around doing nothing, that cash balance is a "productive" asset. It just would not have a very good return, and capital suppliers whose present wealth might be less as a result would not be very happy. We hasten to add, however, that every company needs some level of cash balance, if only to allow it to carry on normal business transactions, and such cash balances are clearly "productive" in that they facilitate such transactions. Whatever the productivity of cash balances, any increase in such a balance is an IVS cash flow, just as any decrease therein is a $RCPT cash flow.

Most generally, the IVS_T flow can be defined as all cash disbursed by the company at time point T *other than*:

1. Payments to capital suppliers
2. Income taxes to government
3. Disbursements which qualify under income tax rules as tax-deductible expenses at time T.

With these additional characteristics, the new corporation looks very much like one we would expect to find in real capital markets. The only limiting characteristic that we will maintain is a terminal point for operations. Our new company will have a five-period operating life and will then cease to exist. Later in this chapter we shall consider corporations with no terminal characteristic, but for the moment that is unnecessary and could detract from the important new ideas we want to show you in this section.

The specific numerical characteristics of our new corporation are given below. As with our initial example, the conditions at first seem terribly intricate, but as we work through the example, you will have little difficulty in becoming familiar with the numbers. We shall discuss the FCF statements for the company following this enumeration of our expectations for its five-period future:

1. We expect that the company will have $RCPT figures from t_1 through t_5 of \$4814.81, \$4930.56, \$4583.33, \$5005.78, and \$4577.87. In order to get these \$RCPT amounts, the company is expected to incur $EXPT_T of 55% of $RCPT_T. Also, to generate the expected $RCPT flows, it will be necessary for the company to make cash investments at t_1 through t_4. These investment outlays are designed to acquire operating assets which are intended to maintain the firm's productivity.[5] Historically, these renewal investments have been \$500 per period, with the real useful life of each increment being four periods. In anticipation of the termination of the business at t_5, \$500 of renewal investment with four-period life will be made at t_1, \$375 with three-period life at t_2, \$250 with two-period life at t_3, and \$125 at t_4 to renew productive assets through the last period only.

2. The corporate income tax rate is 52% of accounting income ($\tau = 0.52$).

3. Depreciation expectations for the firm are shown in Table 7.1. The only accounting depreciation expenses for the firm are those for the renewal investments. All other assets' book values have already been fully depreciated. \$500-per-period renewal investments have been going on for quite some time (at least since t_{-3}). With a four-period life and use of the straight-line depreciation method, the annual depreciation charge has been \$500 per period. This will remain constant at times t_3, t_4, and t_5 since the investments at t_2, t_3, and t_4 will be scaled downward in proportion to the remaining life of the company, and since the straight-line depreciation method will continue to be used. The depreciation tax subsidy figures for each time point are given at the bottom of Table 7.1.

---

[5] We recognize that it is to the real firm's advantage to write off as expenses as many expenditures for maintaining the future productivity of operating assets as are allowed by tax regulations. Such cash renewal outlays that may be "expensed" would appear in the $EXPT of the FCF statement so as to receive the desired tax treatment. In this example, however, we assume that the renewal outlays are not of that variety, and must be "capitalized"; thus they appear as IVS.

TABLE 7.1 Depreciation expenses and tax subsidies for our five-period corporation ($\tau = 0.52$; straight-line method)

Depreciation charge at: Based on Investment amount	At	t_1	t_2	t_3	t_4	t_5
$500	t_{-3}	$125.00	$ 0.00	$ 0.00	$ 0.00	$ 0.00
$500	t_{-2}	125.00	125.00	0.00	0.00	0.00
$500	t_{-1}	125.00	125.00	125.00	0.00	0.00
$500	t_0	125.00	125.00	125.00	125.00	0.00
$500	t_1	0.00	125.00	125.00	125.00	125.00
$375	t_2	0.00	0.00	125.00	125.00	125.00
$250	t_3	0.00	0.00	0.00	125.00	125.00
$125	t_4	0.00	0.00	0.00	0.00	125.00
Total depreciation expense		$500.00	$500.00	$500.00	$500.00	$500.00
DTS at $\tau = 0.52$		$260.00	$260.00	$260.00	$260.00	$260.00

4. The interest and principal payment expectations of the firm are shown in Table 7.2, rows I and PP. Note that the *total* cash distributions to debt, CDD, are not all the same as the *net* distributions, NCDD, since we expect the company to raise $100 of NDC at t_2 and $125 at t_4. The capital market, in appraising the risk of the NCDD stream, has assigned a kd of 6% per period for all five periods.

TABLE 7.2 Complete financial cash flows for our five-period firm

Time points:	t_1	t_2	t_3	t_4	t_5
$RCPT	$4814.81	$4930.56	$4583.33	$5005.78	$4577.87
$EXPT	2648.15	2711.81	2520.83	2753.18	2517.83
GCFO	2166.66	2218.75	2062.50	2252.60	2060.04
GTAX	1126.66	1153.75	1072.50	1171.35	1071.22
NCFO	1040.00	1065.00	990.00	1081.25	988.82
DTS	260.00	260.00	260.00	260.00	260.00
CAU	1300.00	1325.00	1250.00	1341.25	1248.82
ITS	41.06	37.71	31.94	24.62	13.42
CAC	1341.06	1362.71	1281.94	1365.87	1262.24
I	78.96	72.51	61.43	47.35	25.80
PP	107.44	284.80	234.64	484.04	430.07
CDD	186.40	357.31	296.07	531.39	455.87
NDC	0.00	100.00	0.00	125.00	0.00
NCDD	186.40	257.31	296.07	406.39	455.87
CAE	1154.66	1005.40	985.87	834.48	806.37
CRF	323.32	175.00	250.00	0.00	0.00
CDE	831.34	830.40	735.87	834.48	806.37
NEC	176.68	100.00	0.00	0.00	0.00
NCDE	654.66	730.40	735.87	834.48	806.37
TCC $\equiv$ IVS	500.00	375.00	250.00	125.00	0.00

5. Equity capital suppliers expect NCDE's at each time point as shown in the appropriate row of Table 7.2. These cash flows are the total cash that equity could receive (CAE) less the amount retained by the firm (CRF) and less the new equity capital contributions (NEC). In terms of our cash-flow arithmetic,

$$CDE_T = CAE_T - CRF_T$$

and

$$NCDE_T = CDE_T - NEC_T$$

The capital market, in appraising the riskiness of the expected NCDE's, has assigned a required return to equity, ke, of 25% for all periods.

6. By choosing certain combinations of cash distributions, cash retentions, and capital raising activities (which are all indicated in Table 7.2), the company comes up with the necessary dollars at t_1, t_2, t_3, and t_4 for the investments intended to renew productive assets. These, in turn, generate the $RCPT and $EXPT expectations for t_2, t_3, t_4, and t_5.[6]

Table 7.2 presents the cash-flow expectations (rounded to the nearest cent) which result from the characteristics of the five-period firm that we have just outlined. To acquaint you even better with these cash flows, we have placed those for t_2 in a cash-flow diagram, Figure 7.2. In Figure 7.2, $RCPT$_2$ of $4930.56 is expected to be generated by the productive assets as renewed by the previous IVS's and $EXPT$_2$ of $2711.81. $RCPT$_2$ − $EXPT$_2$ is GCFO$_2$ of $2218.75. The previous IVS's of renewal investment occur at the ends of the earlier periods, so even though $RCPT$_2$ depends on them, they do not enter directly into the GCFO$_2$ calculation. GTAX$_2$ of (0.52)(GCFO$_2$), or $1153.75, then heads toward government, leaving NCFO$_2$ of $1065.00.

DTS$_2$ then flows back from government. It equals the depreciation expense (see Table 7.1) times τ, or ($500) (0.52) = $260. This, with NCFO$_2$, gives a CAU$_2$ of $1325.00. The interest tax subsidy for t_2 also flows in from government in the amount of I times τ, or ($72.51)(0.52) = $37.71. Added to CAU$_2$, we get a CAC$_2$ of $1362.71. CAC$_2$ then splits into CDD$_2 = I_2 + PP_2$, or $72.51 + $284.80 = $357.31 to debt suppliers, and CAE$_2 = $ CAC$_2$ − CDD$_2$, or $1362.71 − $357.31 = $1005.40, which is available to equity suppliers. The debt suppliers accept the CDD$_2$ of $357.31 with one hand, and with the other contribute $100 of NDC$_2$ to the corporation. Their net receipts are then expected to be NCDD$_2$ of $257.31.

Of the $1005.40 of CAE$_2$, the company retains $175.00 (CRF$_2$) and distributes $830.40 of CDE$_2$ to equity suppliers. They accept this, and gra-

---

[6]Sooner or later the astute reader will see that in both the two-period and five-period companies, we have designed the various cash retentions and distributions and the raising of new capital so as to avoid a valuation complexity, which we prefer to deal with in Section III. What we are now admitting to is keeping the mix of debt and equity value unchanged across time, while promising that our further development in Chapter 8 will allow us to consider the implications of doing away with this simplification.

FIGURE 7.2 t_2 cash flows for our five-period firm

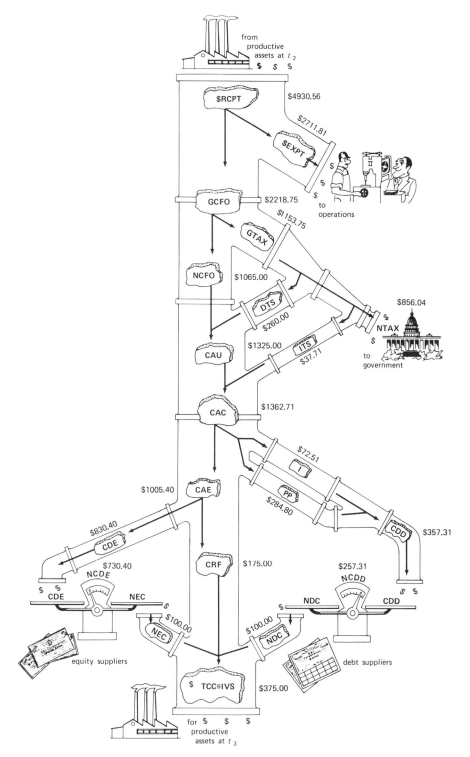

from productive assets at t_2

\$RCPT   \$4930.56

\$2711.81

\$EXPT

\$ \$ \$ to operations

GCFO   \$2218.75

\$1153.75

GTAX

NCFO   \$1065.00

DTS   \$856.04
\$260.00   NTAX

\$1325.00   ITS
\$37.71   to government

CAU

CAC   \$1362.71

\$72.51

I

\$1005.40   CAE   PP
\$284.80

CDD   \$357.31

\$830.40   CDE

\$730.40   NCDE
\$ \$ \$257.31   NCDD

CDE   NEC   CRF   \$175.00   NDC   CDD

\$100.00   \$100.00
NEC   NDC

equity suppliers   debt suppliers

\$ TCC≡IVS   \$375.00

for \$ \$ \$ productive assets at t_3

ciously provide $100.00 of NEC_2 to the company. The equity suppliers at t_2 then end up with $NCDE_2$ of $730.40 as the net of their transactions with the firm. NEC_2 and CRF_2 flow together with NDC_2 from debt suppliers to result in the needed $375 of TCC_2. TCC_2 is then used to renew the productive assets and appears as IVS_2 of $375. The IVS_2 dollars will allow the later $RCPT and $EXPT expectations to result.

The purpose of this rather long walk through the FCF diagram of this time point for our five-period company is to give you a "feel" for the way cash flows really work in a typical firm. The word "typical" should begin to have some recognizable meaning to you now. The interactions across time of investments, capital contributions, and cash flows to capital suppliers will continue to reveal themselves as we build our theory. But even this introduction to the typical firm's cash flows and their interdependencies should help you to anticipate the theoretical questions that we are going to ask:

Why that much debt capital?
Why that much equity capital?
Does the amount of each affect value?
Is there a best combination?
Why the retained cash amounts?
Do they matter?
Is there a best amount?
How did we decide on $375 of IVS?
Were there any alternatives?
How would others affect value?
How are the present wealth levels of capital suppliers affected by the financial decisions we have mentioned?

In one way or another, all these questions are important to the theory of corporate finance. Sections III, IV, and V will help us to discover the answers that the theory can supply.

But the financial cash flows of a typical firm are what concern us at the moment. And they *are* a bit complicated when you see them laid out for the first time. You might find it worth the effort to go back to another time point's cash flows for our new company and trace through them the way we have done with those for t_2. You will be surprised how quickly they become familiar and fit together. Keep in mind that all the cash must go somewhere. Some goes to $EXPT, some to government, some to capital suppliers, and the rest to investment. It is simply a matter of deciding who gets what.

Remember also as you are studying these cash flows that our present purpose is only to value an existing set of cash-flow expectations. We shall see that once the cash flows are specified, this is a very easy task. The set of existing cash-flow expectations for this firm comes from the assumptions that we have made about its specific characteristics. Once the operational, taxation, capital disbursement, capital acquisition, and investment expectations are known, the complete cash-flow statement is a matter of simple arithmetic. And if capital-market assessments of the riskiness of those cash flows are also known, the valuation of the firm is equally straightforward. Fortunately, all this information, in this instance, is at hand.

Section I taught us the lesson that value in capital markets is generated by capital claimants or participants applying appropriate opportunity costs or discount rates to future cash-flow expectations. This is just as true for our complex firm and its outstanding capital claims as it was for our simple one-period examples in Section I. The values of debt and equity claims are the appropriately discounted expectations of cash flows to those claims. In the typical firm, as we have seen, the cash flows of importance are the *net* cash distributions to capital suppliers, $NCDD_T$ and $NCDE_T$.

VALUE OF DEBT IN A TYPICAL FIRM

Let us value the debt claim of our firm. The value of debt is the stream of net cash distributions to debt suppliers, $NCDD_T$'s, discounted back to the present at the rates of return required by those suppliers:

$$VD_0 = \frac{NCDD_1}{1 + kd_1} + \frac{NCDD_2}{(1 + kd_1)(1 + kd_2)}$$
$$+ \frac{NCDD_3}{(1 + kd_1)(1 + kd_2)(1 + kd_3)}$$
$$+ \frac{NCDD_4}{(1 + kd_1)(1 + kd_2)(1 + kd_3)(1 + kd_4)}$$
$$+ \frac{NCDD_5}{(1 + kd_1)(1 + kd_2)(1 + kd_3)(1 + kd_4)(1 + kd_5)}$$

or, since $kd_1 = kd_2 = kd_3 = kd_4 = kd_5$,

$$VD_0 = \frac{NCDD_1}{1 + kd} + \frac{NCDD_2}{(1 + kd)^2} + \frac{NCDD_3}{(1 + kd)^3} + \frac{NCDD_4}{(1 + kd)^4}$$
$$+ \frac{NCDD_5}{(1 + kd)^5}$$

Substituting the numbers from our example,

$$VD_0 = \frac{\$186.40}{1.06} + \frac{\$257.31}{(1.06)^2} + \frac{\$296.07}{(1.06)^3} + \frac{\$406.39}{(1.06)^4} + \frac{\$455.87}{(1.06)^5}$$
$$= \$1315.99$$

The value of the debt claim at t_0 is $1315.99.

The first formula (with varying discount rates) in the preceding paragraph could have been written according to the shorthand notation for discounting that we used in Chapter 3 (p. 42):

$$VD_0 = \sum_{T=1}^{5} \frac{NCDD_T}{\prod_{P=1}^{T} (1 + kd_P)}$$

As we said before, the particular corporation that we are using here differs from the most general examples only in that it terminates operations at t_5.[7] Most companies have cash-flow expectations extending indeterminately into the future. The most general formula for debt claim valuation, applicable to any company, terminating or not, is then

$$VD_0 = \sum_{\scriptscriptstyle T=1}^{T} \frac{NCDD_{\scriptscriptstyle T}}{\prod_{\scriptscriptstyle P=1}^{\scriptscriptstyle T} (1 + kd_{\scriptscriptstyle P})} \qquad\qquad \textbf{[7.1]}$$

The capital T stands for the termination time point, which may be indeterminately far into the future.[8]

For our particular firm, since the kd's are all equal across time,

$$VD_0 = \sum_{\scriptscriptstyle T=1}^{T} \frac{NCDD_{\scriptscriptstyle T}}{(1 + kd)^{\scriptscriptstyle T}} \qquad\qquad \textbf{[7.1a]}$$

The value of debt is simply the net cash flows to debt capital suppliers discounted at their required rates of return.

You remember that in our two-period corporation we were also able to find the value of the debt claim by discounting at the kd^* rate the cash flows to debt suppliers minus the interest tax subsidies. The same thing is allowable here (with the knowledge that *net* cash flows, NCDD's, are the appropriate ones). Since

$$kd_{\scriptscriptstyle P}^* = kd_{\scriptscriptstyle P}(1 - \tau) \qquad\qquad \textbf{[7.2]}$$

the value of debt may also be calculated as

$$VD_0 = \sum_{\scriptscriptstyle T=1}^{T} \frac{NCDD_{\scriptscriptstyle T} - ITS_{\scriptscriptstyle T}}{\prod_{\scriptscriptstyle P=1}^{\scriptscriptstyle T} (1 + kd_{\scriptscriptstyle P}^*)} \qquad\qquad \textbf{[7.3]}$$

or, if the cost of debt capital, $kd_{\scriptscriptstyle P}^*$, is constant across time,

$$VD_0 = \sum_{\scriptscriptstyle T=1}^{T} \frac{NCDD_{\scriptscriptstyle T} - ITS_{\scriptscriptstyle T}}{(1 + kd^*)^{\scriptscriptstyle T}} \qquad\qquad \textbf{[7.3a]}$$

[7]One might argue that this firm is also atypical in that it makes only renewal investments as opposed to acquiring new and/or different productive assets across time. As we shall see in Part Two, for valuation purposes there is no distinction between these two kinds of investments.

[8]The valuation formulas we use for the corporation, since they begin with t_1 rather than t_0 cash flows, are *after*, and therefore do not include, any t_0 cash disbursements, and are also after, and therefore *do* include, any t_0 capital contributions. In this respect, our corporation valuation formulas differ from the general valuation given in formula 3.1, where for A = 0, V_0 included the value of the t_0 cash flow, CF_0. Here in Section II, and for the rest of the book, we shall focus on t_0 value measured *after* all t_0 flows (that is, using only the summation term of formula 3.1). This corresponds to the real capital market practice of *ex dividend* pricing of common stocks, for example.

Corporate valuation formulas completely consistent with formula 3.1 are also possible, but the formulas we develop in this chapter will serve us better as we illustrate financial decision making in Sections III–V.

Performing the debt-valuation calculation on the basis of debt costs for our firm ($kd* = 0.0288$),

$$VD_0 = \frac{\$186.40 - \$41.06}{1.0288} + \frac{\$257.31 - \$37.71}{(1.0288)^2}$$
$$+ \frac{\$296.07 - \$31.94}{(1.0288)^3} + \frac{\$406.39 - \$24.62}{(1.0288)^4}$$
$$+ \frac{\$455.87 - \$13.42}{(1.0288)^5}$$
$$= \$1315.99$$

the same value as found by discounting $NCDD_T$ at kd.

You can see that the valuation of debt for a typical firm is not much different in concept from the valuation of the debt of a corporation that makes no new or renewal investment and raises no new capital. Actually, since for a firm that raises no new debt capital, $NCDD_T = CDD_T$, the general formulas for debt valuation that we have just given work equally well for companies such as the one described in our original example. You can check this by simply applying the general debt formulas to the cash flows of our original two-period corporation. The values should not change.

We can also use the general debt-valuation formulas to discover the values expected for the debt claims at future time points, on the basis of t_0 expectations. For example, to find VD_2,

$$VD_2 = \sum_{T=3}^{T} \frac{NCDD_T}{\prod_{P=3}^{T}(1 + kd_P)}$$

or

$$= \sum_{T=3}^{T} \frac{NCDD_T - ITS_T}{\prod_{P=3}^{T}(1 + kd_P^*)}$$

or, if kd_P is constant,

$$VD_2 = \sum_{T=3}^{T} \frac{NCDD_T}{(1 + kd)^{T-2}}$$

or

$$= \sum_{T=3}^{T} \frac{NCDD_T - ITS_T}{(1 + kd^*)^{T-2}}$$

and similarly for other VD_T's. Remember that the future values calculated this way reflect only the expectations as held at t_0. If expectations change as time passes, the odds are that present and expected future values will also change.

Should you by any chance be interested, the set of future value expectations for debt on the basis of t_0 beliefs are

$$VD_1 = \$1208.55$$
$$VD_2 = \$1023.75$$
$$VD_3 = \$789.11$$
$$VD_4 = \$430.07$$

You might find it worthwhile to review these calculations yourself.

Notice, finally, that the company expects to issue "new" debt claims at t_2 and t_4 (see Table 7.2). How are these claims valued in our theory? Will our cash flows be confused by the existence of more than one debt claim? *The debt values which we have been calculating and which are indicated in the general formulas 7.1, 7.1a, 7.3, and 7.3a are for the total market value of all debt claims outstanding, both "new" and "old."*[9] If we choose to, it is a relatively simple matter to separate the formula values into new and old claims (t_2 and thereafter, when both kinds are expected to exist). But they follow all the rules that we have set down already and do not add much to our theoretical progress. Therefore, we have relegated those calculations to Appendix II.A.

VALUING EQUITY IN A TYPICAL FIRM   Valuation of the equity claims on a typical firm proceeds very much like the valuation of debt claims. The value of equity must be the appropriately discounted expectations of future cash flows to equity suppliers. Equity opportunity costs or required rates, ke_P, are the appropriate discount rates. And net cash distributions to equity suppliers, $NCDE_T$, are the appropriate cash flows. From our discussions of debt valuation you should feel comfortable with the general formula for equity valuation:

$$VE_0 = \sum_{T=1}^{T} \frac{NCDE_T}{\prod_{P=1}^{T} (1 + ke_P)} \qquad [7.4]$$

And for the case of constant discount rates,

$$VE_0 = \sum_{T=1}^{T} \frac{NCDE_T}{(1 + ke)^T} \qquad [7.4a]$$

The equity value at t_0 in our firm must then be, from formula 7.4a,

$$VE_0 = \frac{\$654.66}{1.25} + \frac{\$730.40}{(1.25)^2} + \frac{\$735.87}{(1.25)^3} + \frac{\$834.48}{(1.25)^4} + \frac{\$806.37}{(1.25)^5}$$

$$= \$1973.98$$

The value of the equity of the corporation at t_0 is \$1973.98. That would be the total market value of all its shares of common stock. It is the amount of money that you, as a rational capital market participant having the expectations of Table 7.2, would be willing to pay as a maximum at t_0 for all the

---

[9]Remember the assumption that all debt claims have the same priority in our examples.

company's stock. By the same token, it is the minimum amount of t_0 dollars that you as the holder of all the stock would accept from a bid to purchase it.

So the values of equity claims in a competitive capital market are simply the expected future net cash distributions to equity suppliers discounted at their required rates of return. This is as true for our five-period firm as it was for our original two-period example. As a matter of fact, the formulas for equity valuation, 7.4 and 7.4a, apply to both kinds of firms because the original two-period firm's $NCDE_T$ is the same as its CDE_T. Firms that do not invest, retain, or raise capital are merely special cases of the typical firm. The full FCF model applies equally well to either type. For the unusual case mentioned above, CAE_T flows untouched to equity claimants as $NCDE_T$, and CDD_T *is* $NCDD_T$. The t_5 cash flows of our typical firm (its terminating flows) illustrate generally what the complete FCF statement of our original two-period example would have looked like had we included the entire capital/investment flows section of the FCF statement.

As we did for debt, we can use the equity-valuation formulas to find *future* value expectations on the basis of t_0 beliefs. The value expected for equity at t_3, for example, is

$$VE_3 = \sum_{T=4}^{T} \frac{NCDE_T}{\prod_{P=4}^{T} (1 + ke_P)}$$

or, if applicable,

$$VE_3 = \sum_{T=4}^{T} \frac{NCDE_T}{(1 + ke)^{T-3}}$$

for constant required rates. The future value expectations for our example are

$$VE_1 = \$1812.82$$
$$VE_2 = \$1535.62$$
$$VE_3 = \$1183.66$$
$$VE_4 = \$645.10$$

You might find it a valuable exercise to calculate these numbers yourself.

You probably have noticed that, unlike the debt-valuation formulas, there is no alternative method of equity valuation. We do not attempt to specify a procedure for equity valuation like the discounting of $NCDD_T -$ ITS_T at kd^* for debt valuation. The reason is simple. No part of the cash distributions to equity suppliers is deductible for tax purposes. *Therefore, the return required by equity suppliers is the same as the cost of equity capital to the firm.* Discounting $NCDE_T$ at ke_P is the only valuation mechanism for equity.

Finally, you saw in Table 7.2 that new equity capital was raised at t_1 and t_2. How are these claims valued? Similar to our debt discussion, *the equity values calculated by formulas 7.4 and 7.4a are the total value of all equity claims outstanding.* Appendix II.A will illustrate how "new" and "old" claims' values may be separated. Naturally, all equity claims, being residual, have the same priority regardless of the time point of their issuance. It is entirely possible, for example, that the VE_0 value we calculate is composed of several claims issued at different times before t_0.

OVERALL REQUIRED RATES OF RETURN AND CAPITAL COSTS FOR A TYPICAL FIRM

The previous section showed us that valuing the capital claims of a typical firm is, once cash-flow expectations are known, very similar to valuing the debt and equity of our original corporation. The same holds true for the overall required rates of return and capital costs. Once the cash flows are adjusted to be net amounts, the analyses proceed identically.

The overall or weighted-average required rate of return for a typical firm is

$$kf_{\text{P}} = \left(\frac{VD_{\text{T}-1}}{VF_{\text{T}-1}}\right) kd_{\text{P}} + \left(\frac{VE_{\text{T}-1}}{VF_{\text{T}-1}}\right) ke_{\text{P}} \qquad \text{where P = T} \qquad \textbf{[7.5]}$$

and, similarly, *the overall or weighted-average cost of capital is*

$$kf_{\text{P}}^* = \left(\frac{VD_{\text{T}-1}}{VF_{\text{T}-1}}\right) kd_{\text{P}}^* + \left(\frac{VE_{\text{T}-1}}{VF_{\text{T}-1}}\right) ke_{\text{P}} \qquad \text{where P = T} \qquad \textbf{[7.6]}$$

VF_{T}, of course, is

$$VF_{\text{T}} = VD_{\text{T}} + VE_{\text{T}} \qquad \textbf{[7.7]}$$

Since the rationales for calculating kf, kf^*, and VF are exactly the same as those we used in the two-period example, we shall not waste time and space by repeating those rationales here.

For our five-period firm $VF_0 = VE_0 + VD_0 = \$1315.99 + \$1973.98 = \$3289.97$. The actual rates for p_1 according to formulas 7.5 and 7.6 are

$$kf_1 = \frac{1315.99}{3289.97}(0.06) + \frac{1973.98}{3289.97}(0.25)$$
$$= 0.174 \quad \text{or} \quad 17.4\%$$

and

$$kf_1^* = \frac{1315.99}{3289.97}(0.0288) + \frac{1973.98}{3289.97}(0.25)$$
$$= 0.16152 \quad \text{or} \quad 16.152\%$$

The weighted-average required rate of return for p_1 is 17.4% and the cost of capital is 16.152%. kf^* is less than kf, you remember, because of interest deductibility and the resulting ITS.

The overall rates for time periods later than the first are calculated similarly, using formulas 7.5 and 7.6. If you were to do this, kf and kf^* would, for our firm, turn out to be the same for all periods.[10] You can check this assertion by calculating the overall rates using the expected future debt and equity values that we have provided.

---

[10]We mentioned earlier, in footnote 6, that we had designed this example to hold in abeyance a question to be raised in Section III. The design was to hold kf and kf^* constant by holding constant the separate debt and equity rates and the *ratio* $VD_{\text{T}}/VF_{\text{T}}$ or $VE_{\text{T}}/VF_{\text{T}}$. Section III will show why it was reasonable for us to do that.

OVERALL We know already that the capital market never actually calculates the over-
VALUATION all valuation of companies that have different types of capital claims out-
OF A standing. The capital market is interested in valuing only *actual* claims, not
TYPICAL hypothetical combinations. But we also made a case for being interested in
FIRM overall rates and valuation not only for what those ideas can do in advancing
our theory but because they provide important information for managerial
decision making. In the same sense as we did for our two-period corporation,
we can calculate overall corporate values for typical firms *as if* the capital
market were doing it. This, of course, involves applying appropriate overall
rates or costs to overall or operating cash-flow expectations.

When we introduced equity and debt valuation for the typical firm we
discovered that the appropriate cash flows to be discounted were the cash
distributions net of capital inflows, $NCDE_T$ and $NCDD_T$. The correct *overall* cash flows are, logically, merely the sum of these two amounts. The value
of the firm as a whole can be considered as

$$VF_0 = \sum_{T=1}^{T} \frac{NCDD_T + NCDE_T}{\prod_{P=1}^{T} (1 + kf_P)} \qquad [7.8]$$

or, if kf_P is constant,

$$VF_0 = \sum_{T=1}^{T} \frac{NCDD_T + NCDE_T}{(1 + kf)^T} \qquad [7.8a]$$

The overall value of the firm, if the capital market would ever choose to calculate it, *would be the sum of the net cash flows to capital suppliers discounted
at their overall required rate(s) of return.*

The calculation of VF_0 using the numbers from Table 7.2 and formula
7.8a is

$$
\begin{aligned}
VF_0 &= \frac{\$186.40 + \$654.66}{1.174} + \frac{\$257.31 + \$730.40}{(1.174)^2} \\
&\quad + \frac{\$296.07 + \$735.87}{(1.174)^3} + \frac{\$406.39 + \$834.48}{(1.174)^4} \\
&\quad + \frac{\$455.87 + \$806.37}{(1.174)^5} \\
&= \frac{\$841.06}{1.174} + \frac{\$987.71}{(1.174)^2} + \frac{\$1031.94}{(1.174)^3} + \frac{\$1240.87}{(1.174)^4} + \frac{\$1262.24}{(1.174)^5} \\
&= \$3289.97
\end{aligned}
$$

This is the same total corporate value at t_0 that we found by valuing debt and
equity separately and then adding them together.

There is an equivalent way of formulating the overall value of the firm
that, although at first glance not quite as intuitively appealing as summing
net cash distributions, may help us to understand corporate cash flows more
fully. Formulas 7.8 and 7.8a use $NCDD_T + NCDE_T$ as the cash-flow-
valuation basis. Let us look a bit more closely at that sum. NCDD, we know,

is CDD $-$ NDC. And NCDE is CAE $-$ CRF $-$ NEC. Adding those together we get

$$\text{NCDD} + \text{NCDE} = \text{CDD} - \text{NDC} + \text{CAE} - \text{CRF} - \text{NEC}$$

But CDD $+$ CAE is CAC. (You might wish to refer back to the FCF diagram in Figure 7.1 to refresh your memory.) So now we have

$$\text{NCDD} + \text{NCDE} = \text{CAC} - \text{NDC} - \text{CRF} - \text{NEC}$$

But NDC, NEC, and CRF, taken together, form TCC, which is the same as IVS, so, finally,

$$\text{NCDD} + \text{NCDE} = \text{CAC} - \text{IVS}$$

The sum of the net cash flows to capital suppliers at any time point is equal to the total cash available to all capital suppliers less the investment outlays at that time point. Looking back at our algebra, you probably could have seen this relationship as easily by just glancing at Figure 7.1. It shows clearly that once you arrive at CAC, all the cash that is not invested goes, net, to the capital market. The algebra reinforces this visual conclusion.

So we can substitute $\text{CAC}_\text{T} - \text{IVS}_\text{T}$ for $\text{NCDD}_\text{T} + \text{NCDE}_\text{T}$ in formulas 7.8 and 7.8a and get

$$\text{VF}_0 = \sum_{\text{T}=1}^{T} \frac{\text{CAC}_\text{T} - \text{IVS}_\text{T}}{\prod_{\text{P}=1}^{\text{T}} (1 + kf_\text{P})} \qquad \textbf{[7.9]}$$

and if kf is constant across time,

$$\text{VF}_0 = \sum_{\text{T}=1}^{T} \frac{\text{CAC}_\text{T} - \text{IVS}_\text{T}}{(1 + kf)^\text{T}} \qquad \textbf{[7.9a]}$$

For our company, the calculation based on formula 7.9a and the data from Table 7.2 is

$$
\begin{aligned}
\text{VF}_0 &= \frac{\$1341.06 - \$500.00}{1.174} + \frac{\$1362.71 - \$375.00}{(1.174)^2} \\
&\quad + \frac{\$1281.94 - \$250.00}{(1.174)^3} + \frac{\$1365.87 - \$125.00}{(1.174)^4} \\
&\quad + \frac{\$1262.24 - \$0.00}{(1.174)^5} \\
&= \frac{\$841.06}{1.174} + \frac{\$987.71}{(1.174)^2} + \frac{\$1031.94}{(1.174)^3} + \frac{\$1240.87}{(1.174)^4} + \frac{\$1262.24}{(1.174)^5} \\
&= \$3289.97
\end{aligned}
$$

Both the total firm value and the summed cash-flow step above it are identical to those we found by applying kf_T to $\text{NCDD}_\text{T} + \text{NCDE}_\text{T}$. In a sense, looking to $\text{CAC}_\text{T} - \text{IVS}_\text{T}$ as the overall cash-flow valuation basis emphasizes the operations of the firm as a whole rather than distributions to separate capital suppliers. Our cash-flow analysis, however, correctly tells us that the two approaches are equivalent.

Overall valuation calculations may also be performed using kf^* rather than kf. You remember from our two-period example that kf^*, the overall cost of capital, is itself adjusted for the lower cost of debt capital due to interest deductibility. Because the discount rate, kf^*, includes the deductibility of interest effect, we must exclude this effect from the cash flows being discounted. If we did not, we would be double counting the benefits of the interest tax subsidy. This means that the overall cash flows must be decreased by the amount of the ITS:

$$VF_0 = \sum_{\tau=1}^{T} \frac{NCDD_\tau + NCDE_\tau - ITS_\tau}{\prod_{P=1}^{\tau} (1 + kf_P^*)} \qquad [7.10]$$

If kf^* is constant across time, then

$$VF_0 = \sum_{\tau=1}^{T} \frac{NCDD_\tau + NCDE_\tau - ITS_\tau}{(1 + kf^*)^\tau} \qquad [7.10a]$$

Stepping into our previous numerical calculations after $NCDD_\tau + NCDE_\tau$ had been summed, and with kf^* constant at 16.152%, formula 7.10a gives us

$$
\begin{aligned}
VF_0 &= \frac{\$841.06 - \$41.06}{1.16152} + \frac{\$987.71 - \$37.71}{(1.16152)^2} \\
&\quad + \frac{\$1031.94 - \$31.94}{(1.16152)^3} + \frac{\$1240.87 - \$24.62}{(1.16152)^4} \\
&\quad + \frac{\$1262.24 - \$13.42}{(1.16152)^5} \\
&= \frac{\$800.00}{1.16152} + \frac{\$950.00}{(1.16152)^2} + \frac{\$1000.00}{(1.16152)^3} + \frac{\$1216.25}{(1.16152)^4} \\
&\quad + \frac{\$1248.82}{(1.16152)^5} \\
&= \$3289.97
\end{aligned}
$$

So, by *not* including the interest tax subsidy in the net cash flows, we can use kf^*, the weighted-average cost of capital, as the appropriate overall discount rate.

If this procedure is appropriate for the $NCDD_\tau + NCDE_\tau$ cash-flow specifications, it must also work for the $CAC_\tau - IVS_\tau$ formulas, which are numerically identical. So for $NCDD_\tau + NCDE_\tau - ITS_\tau$, we can substitute $CAC_\tau - IVS_\tau - ITS_\tau$. But wait a minute. We already have a cash flow that covers two of the three flows mentioned in $CAC_\tau - IVS_\tau - ITS_\tau$. Remember CAU_τ? It is equal to $CAC_\tau - ITS_\tau$. Figure 7.1 will refresh your memory. That means that we can substitute CAU_τ for $CAC_\tau - ITS_\tau$:

$$CAC_\tau - IVS_\tau - ITS_\tau = CAU_\tau - IVS_\tau$$

so our final pair of overall valuation formulas is

$$VF_0 = \sum_{T=1}^{T} \frac{CAU_T - IVS_T}{\prod_{P=1}^{T} (1 + kf_P^*)} \qquad\qquad [7.11]$$

or, if kf_P^* is constant across time,

$$VF_0 = \sum_{T=1}^{T} \frac{CAU_T - IVS_T}{(1 + kf^*)^T} \qquad\qquad [7.11a]^{11}$$

Using formula 7.11a in our example:

$$
\begin{aligned}
VF_0 &= \frac{\$1300.00 - \$500.00}{1.16152} + \frac{\$1325.00 - \$375.00}{(1.16152)^2} \\
&\quad + \frac{\$1250.00 - \$250.00}{(1.16152)^3} + \frac{\$1341.25 - \$125.00}{(1.16152)^4} \\
&\quad + \frac{\$1248.82 - \$0.00}{(1.16152)^5} \\
&= \frac{\$800.00}{1.16152} + \frac{\$950.00}{(1.16152)^2} + \frac{\$1000.00}{(1.16152)^3} + \frac{\$1216.25}{(1.16152)^4} \\
&\quad + \frac{\$1248.82}{(1.16152)^5} \\
&= \$3289.97
\end{aligned}
$$

This calculation gives the correct total firm value and, as it should, the same net cash flows as in the $NCDD_T + NCDE_T - ITS_T$ form.

Counting the constant discount rate forms, we now have no fewer than eight overall (VF_0) valuation formulas for the corporation (7.8, 7.8a, 7.9, 7.9a, 7.10, 7.10a, 7.11, and 7.11a). At this point we imagine you are tempted to throw down the book and stamp on it in frustration. Why in the world would anyone want to learn eight ways of thinking about overall corporate valuation, especially when the capital market itself could care less about VF_0? All it deals with are VE_0 and VD_0.

Since you have continued reading, we assume that you have either temporarily suppressed your frustration or have picked the book up off the floor. It is fortunate that you did, because the overall valuation formulas we have developed in this section will prove to be quite powerful tools as we continue to study the theory of corporate finance. This will be especially true in our study of the theories of financing, dividend, and investment decisions in later chapters. Actually, the various ways of formulating overall valuation are very similar to each other. Four of the eight are just constant discount rate forms of their nonconstant rate counterparts. The remaining differences are either in the way interest deductibility is handled (kf or kf^*), or in

---

[11] If you have ever studied applied corporate finance you might recognize formula 7.11a as being very similar to what most textbooks recommend for making corporate investment or capital budgeting decisions. With the addition of the t_0 cash flows, the formula is identical to an NPV calculation, as Section V will illustrate.

whether we recognize cash flows as net to the capital market ($NCDD_T +$ $NCDE_T$) or net from the firm (CAC_T or $CAU_T - IVS_T$).

REVIEW OF GENERAL CASH FLOWS AND FORMULAS

The fact remains that we have covered quite a lot of ground in extending our theory to include the typical corporation. It might be wise to pause a while to collect our thoughts and structure a review. Perhaps the most important thing to recognize about our theoretical development in this example is that *the cash-flow relationships and formulas that we provided are applicable to any corporation, regardless of whether it raises capital or not, invests or not, retains cash or not, or even whether it has a foreseeable termination date.*

Our firm operated for only five periods, doing all those things real firms do. For this particular example, the expected terminal time point was $T = t_5$. But the formulas and cash-flow analysis work just as well for $T = t_{10}$, $T = t_{50}$, or $T = t_{1000}$. As a matter of fact, in the next section of this chapter we shall look at ongoing corporations that are never expected to terminate, or $T = t_\infty$. We have tried to emphasize the broad applicability of these general corporate-valuation formulas by numbering them (7.1, 7.2, and so on). We did not do that for the formulas we used in the two-period example earlier in this section because those formulas were too specific. They would work only for that limited type of firm.

Since these cash-flow relationships and valuation formulas will continue to be useful as we study the remainder of basic corporate financial theory, we shall list them here again so that you will not be forced to thumb through the book looking for each separate one as we refer to it.

First, we have reproduced Figure 7.1 as Figure 7.3, the cash-flow relationships for a single generic time point. Diagrams such as this are useful in that they help us to understand general relationships, but they can also sometimes be ambiguous or even misleading. For example, by looking at Figure 7.3 you might get the impression that new capital will be raised at every time point, or that cash flows could never be equal to zero or even be negative. So we shall also provide the algebraic statements in Table 7.4 of what appears in the cash-flow diagram. Table 7.3 will refresh your memory of the cash-flow acronyms used in Table 7.4, and their definitions. (For convenient reference, we have reproduced Figure 7.3 and Tables 7.3 and 7.4 on the endpapers of the book.) Table 7.5 lists the important concepts involved in valuing a corporation, together with their definitions. Finally, Table 7.6 lists the valuation formulas generally applicable to corporations.

Tables 7.3–7.6 cover just about all the ideas of corporate financial theory that we have introduced so far. Those definitions and relationships constitute nearly a complete statement of what theory has to say about corporate valuation.[12] By now, the FCF statement probably does not seem as awesome and

[12]The only significant omission is the relationship defined in the capital market for estimating required rates of return based on risk expectations. This relationship was not necessary for the development of basic valuation models, so we have deferred our discussion of it until later in the book.

FIGURE 7.3   Financial cash flows of a typical corporation

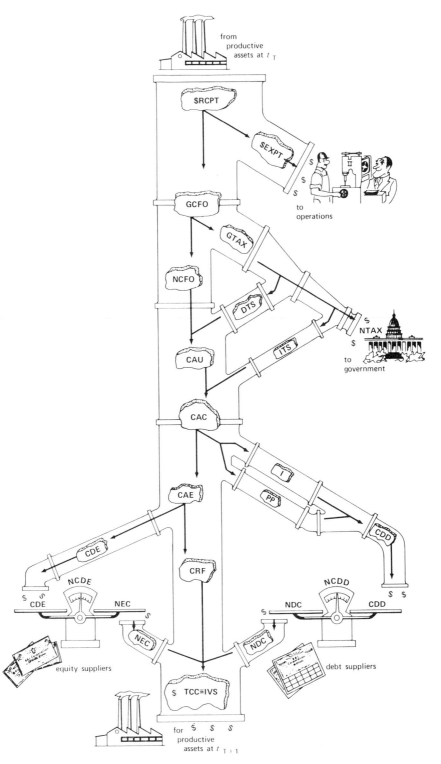

TABLE 7.3   Financial cash-flow definitions (all as expectations)

$\$RCPT_T$	= cash receipts from asset operations at time T
$\$EXPT_T$	= cash expenditures to asset operations at time T
$GCFO_T$	= gross cash from asset operations at time T
$GTAX_T$	= gross tax at time T
$NCFO_T$	= net cash from asset operations at time T
DTS_T	= depreciation tax subsidy at time T
CAU_T	= cash available to an unlevered firm at time T (operating cash flow)
ITS_T	= interest tax subsidy at time T
CAC_T	= cash available to all capital suppliers at time T (overall cash flow)
I_T	= interest to debt suppliers at time T
PP_T	= principal repayment to debt suppliers at time T
CDD_T	= cash distribution to debt suppliers at time T
NDC_T	= new debt capital at time T
$NCDD_T$	= net cash distribution to debt suppliers at time T
CAE_T	= cash available to equity suppliers at time T
CRF_T	= cash retention of the firm at time T
CDE_T	= cash distribution to equity suppliers at time T
NEC_T	= new equity capital at time T
$NCDE_T$	= net cash distribution to equity suppliers at time T
TCC_T	= total capital contribution at time T
IVS_T	= new and renewal investment at time T for asset operations at T + 1 and thereafter

Related definitions

τ	= corporate tax rate
$NTAX_T$	= net tax to government at time T

TABLE 7.4   Cash-flow relationships (all at time T)

1. GCFO $= \$RCPT - \$EXPT$
2. GTAX $= GCFO \times \tau$
3. NCFO $= GCFO - GTAX$
4. DTS $\quad=$ depreciation expense $\times \tau$
5. CAU $\quad= NCFO + DTS$
6. ITS $\quad\;= I \times \tau$
7. CAC $\quad= CAU + ITS$
8. CDD $\quad= I + PP$
9. NCDD $= CDD - NDC$
10. CAE $\quad= CAC - CDD$
11. CDE $\quad= CAE - CRF$
12. NCDE $= CDE - NEC$
13. TCC $\quad= CRF + NDC + NEC$
14. IVS $\quad\equiv TCC$

complicated as when you first saw it. And the more we work with it, the more familiar it will become. Before you finish the book, you may even find that financial cash-flow analysis makes more sense to you than standard accounting financial statements.

Although it may not seem so now, the same familiarization process will occur for the valuation relationships in Table 7.6 as it has for the FCF

TABLE 7.5   Valuation definitions

VE_T = value of all equity claims on a firm at time T
VD_T = value of all debt claims on a firm at time T
VF_T = value of all capital claims on a firm at time T
ke_P = required rate of return for equity suppliers for period P; also the cost of equity capital for period P
kd_P = required rate of return for debt suppliers for period P; also the cost of debt capital for period P when interest is not deductible
kf_P = overall or weighted-average required rate of return for the firm for period P; also the overall cost of capital for period P when interest is not deductible
kd_P^* = cost of debt capital for period P when interest is deductible
kf_P^* = overall or weighted average cost of capital for the firm for period P when interest is deductible

TABLE 7.6   Valuation relationships

Debt, by kd_P:

[7.1]
$$VD_0 = \sum_{T=1}^{T} \frac{NCDD_T}{\prod_{P=1}^{T}(1+kd_P)}$$

Debt, by constant kd_P:

[7.1a]
$$VD_0 = \sum_{T=1}^{T} \frac{NCDD_T}{(1+kd)^T}$$

Cost of debt capital, kd_P^*:

[7.2]
$$kd_P^* = kd_P(1-\tau)$$

Debt, by kd_P^*:

[7.3]
$$VD_0 = \sum_{T=1}^{T} \frac{NCDD_T - ITS_T}{\prod_{P=1}^{T}(1+kd_P^*)}$$

Debt, by constant kd_P^*:

[7.3a]
$$VD_0 = \sum_{T=1}^{T} \frac{NCDD_T - ITS_T}{(1+kd^*)^T}$$

Equity, by ke_P:

[7.4]
$$VE_0 = \sum_{T=1}^{T} \frac{NCDE_T}{\prod_{P=1}^{T}(1+ke_P)}$$

Equity, by constant ke_P:

[7.4a]
$$VE_0 = \sum_{T=1}^{T} \frac{NCDE_T}{(1+ke)^T}$$

Overall required rate, kf_P:

[7.5]
$$kf_P = \left(\frac{VD_{T-1}}{VF_{T-1}}\right)kd_P + \left(\frac{VE_{T-1}}{VF_{T-1}}\right)ke_P \qquad \text{where } P = T$$

Overall cost of capital, kf_P^*:

[7.6]
$$kf_P^* = \left(\frac{VD_{T-1}}{VF_{T-1}}\right)kd_P^* + \left(\frac{VE_{T-1}}{VF_{T-1}}\right)ke_P \qquad \text{where } P = T$$

Total value of capital claims, or value of the firm, VF_T:

[7.7]
$$VF_T = VD_T + VE_T$$

TABLE 7.6   **Valuation relationships (contd.)**

Overall valuation by kf_P, net cash distribution basis:

[7.8] $$VF_0 = \sum_{T=1}^{T} \frac{NCDD_T + NCDE_T}{\prod_{P=1}^{T} (1 + kf_P)}$$

Overall valuation, kf_P constant:

[7.8a] $$VF_0 = \sum_{T=1}^{T} \frac{NCDD_T + NCDE_T}{(1 + kf)^T}$$

Overall valuation, by kf_P, operations-investment basis:

[7.9] $$VF_0 = \sum_{T=1}^{T} \frac{CAC_T - IVS_T}{\prod_{P=1}^{T} (1 + kf_P)}$$

Overall valuation, kf_P constant:

[7.9a] $$VF_0 = \sum_{T=1}^{T} \frac{CAC_T - IVS_T}{(1 + kf)^T}$$

Overall valuation, by kf_P^*, net cash distribution basis:

[7.10] $$VF_0 = \sum_{T=1}^{T} \frac{NCDD_T + NCDE_T - ITS_T}{\prod_{P=1}^{T} (1 + kf_P^*)}$$

Overall valuation, kf_P^* constant:

[7.10a] $$VF_0 = \sum_{T=1}^{T} \frac{NCDD_T + NCDE_T - ITS_T}{(1 + kf^*)^T}$$

Overall valuation by kf_P^*, operations-investment basis:

[7.11] $$VF_0 = \sum_{T=1}^{T} \frac{CAU_T - IVS_T}{\prod_{P=1}^{T} (1 + kf_P^*)}$$

Overall valuation, kf_P^* constant:

[7.11a] $$VF_0 = \sum_{T=1}^{T} \frac{CAU_T - IVS_T}{(1 + kf^*)^T}$$

statement. Table 7.6 contains 18 formulas. These are the statement of our corporate financial theory to this point. But 18 is a deceptive number; there are only a few *ideas* which are repeated over and over. And most of those ideas were developed in the first section. *All the valuation formulas repeat the basic idea that value is generated by expectations of future cash flows.* That basic idea is said in so many ways in Table 7.6 only because (1) corporations are organized so that they can issue different types of capital claims, and (2) government views certain activities, which result in cash distributions companies make to their capital claimants, as worth encouraging through tax subsidies. Our basic approach to valuation from Section I has not been amended one bit. We have merely elaborated those ideas using the characteristics of the corporate financial form and its interactions with government.

CORPORATE PERPE- TUITIES

Our valuation theory and examples have until now dealt with corporations whose cash flows were expected to terminate at a specified future time point. Our original company ended at time t_2 and our more typical corporation's flows were expected to terminate at t_5. Actually, we expect most corporations to continue operating longer than that. And, as we have said, this causes no particular problems in our theory. A final operating period of $T = t_{10}$, $T = t_{50}$, $T = t_{1000}$, or even further into the future is handled exactly the same way for valuation purposes as are our two-period and five-period companies. There is a set of cash-flow expectations for each time point, and there is a set of required rates of return for each time period. However large these sets are, they enter our valuation formulas in exactly the same manner as the examples we have been studying. From a purely theoretical viewpoint, long-lived corporations are no different from those which terminate quickly.

But there are some reasons why we might wish to examine in a special way corporations that are expected to continue operating for many periods. First, most real companies have no specified expectation to ever terminate. Now we do not mean to imply that General Motors will necessarily operate forever. All we are saying is that at t_0, its termination point is not foreseeable. It is an ongoing corporation. And ongoing corporations present a practical problem in actually implementing our valuation formulas. This is because the indefinite future is a very long time and becomes increasingly difficult to predict as we consider more distant time periods. Even if cash-flow expectations were available for extended periods into the future, it can become quite a chore, difficult for even present-day data-handling capabilities, to grapple with the necessary valuation calculations. Given our estimating talents, some people also feel that to speak of particular dollar cash flows 100, 50, or even 15 years into the future is ridiculous.

All these considerations about long-lived firms have led to a great amount of reliance for real-world valuation on perpetuities. A *perpetuity* is, for our purposes, a series of cash flows that is expected to continue each period forever. You might justifiably ask here if we are not substituting one ridiculous cash-flow assumption for another. To that question there is no good theoretical retort. If estimating each future time point's cash flows as we have done so far is ridiculous, then from the viewpoint of valid estimating procedures, perpetuities are just as ridiculous, if not more so.

But there are also some counterarguments that can be made for using perpetuities. These are related to their mathematical simplicity. You will remember that back in Chapter 3 we introduced the idea of finding the present value of a cash-flow stream that continues forever. In Chapter 3 (formula 3.3) we included a cash flow at t_0. But, as we explained in footnote 8 in this chapter, t_0 corporate values are measured *after* t_0 flows. Hence, we need only look now at *future* cash flows. If the cash flow at each future time point is expected to be the same amount and if the discount rate is constant, then the present value of the stream is simply the constant cash-flow amount divided by the discount rate:

$$PV_0 = \frac{\text{cash flow per period}}{k}$$

If you expect to receive $150 at each future time point forever, and if your required rate of return is constant at 12% per period, the worth of those future flows to you now is

$$PV_0 = \frac{\$150}{0.12} = \$1250$$

$150 per period forever is a $150 perpetuity.

The simple fact that the discounting procedure for constant perpetuities is so easy has caused them, we believe, to be very popular as valuation devices. This simplicity, however, is both a strength and a weakness. In the midst of our delight about avoiding the drudgery of detailed period-by-period discounting, we run the danger of forgetting the very restrictive assumptions the perpetuity technique imposes on cash-flow and discount-rate behaviors across time. It is nice to be able to find values so simply, to just divide one number by another, but we must be careful that the quotient we get really tells us something. For example, you may be wondering why we have waited this long in this section on valuation to introduce such a commonly used technique. The reason is that many of the cash-flow relationships that we have dealt with in our numerical examples would have been ambiguous, hidden, or even impossible to demonstrate by the use of perpetuities. We shall presently illustrate these shortcomings in our numerical examples of perpetuities.

These cautions are probably strong enough to make you wonder whether it is worthwhile to bother at all with perpetuities. We are not trying to say that they should never be used. But when we do use them, we should be careful to recognize their limitations. If used correctly, perpetuities as valuation mechanisms can be convenient and time-saving.

With these observations in mind, we can investigate how perpetuities function in our theory. We begin by embarking from any valuation relationship that we already know well, say formula 7.4 for equity value:

$$VE_0 = \sum_{T=1}^{T} \frac{NCDE_T}{\prod_{P=1}^{T} (1 + ke_P)} \qquad \text{[7.4]}$$

The first thing we can do is recognize that cash flows for a perpetuity are expected to continue forever, or $T = t_\infty$. The formula then changes to

$$VE_0 = \sum_{T=1}^{\infty} \frac{NCDE_T}{\prod_{P=1}^{T} (1 + ke_P)}$$

Next we specify that ke_P is constant across all time periods:

$$VE_0 = \sum_{T=1}^{\infty} \frac{NCDE_T}{(1 + ke)^T}$$

and finally, if $NCDE_T$ is a constant per-period cash flow, we end up with

$$VE = \frac{NCDE}{ke}$$

Thus, the value of the equity claims on a corporation is simply the NCDE per period divided by *ke*, provided that NCDE is a constant perpetuity and *ke* remains constant forever. Note that no time subscripts are necessary because *all* the numbers, even value, are the same across time.

Since all other capital claims' valuation formulas are computationally the same as equity's, we can assert that, for constant perpetuities,

$$VD = \frac{NCDD}{kd} = \frac{NCDD - ITS}{kd^*}$$

$$VF = \frac{NCDD + NCDE}{kf} = \frac{CAC - IVS}{kf}$$

and

$$VF = \frac{NCDD + NCDE - ITS}{kf^*} = \frac{CAU - IVS}{kf^*}$$

kd^*, kf, and kf^* are calculated in the same way as they are when perpetuities are not present.

Recognize that the valuation formulas for perpetuities are derived from our general nonperpetuity valuation formulas previously developed. All we have done is rewrite those formulas, assuming constant periodic cash flows, and constant discount rates, both forever.

As an example of the perpetuity case, we show in Table 7.7 the financial cash flows for a constant-cash-flow perpetual corporation. As with our five-period firm, this new firm also experiences $EXPT which are 55% of $RCPT. Also in Table 7.7 we have listed the *ke*, *kd*, and tax-rate assumptions necessary to find all the required rates and capital costs for the company. Since it operates as a perpetuity, the company is expected to experience the cash flows shown in Table 7.7 at each time point forever. Notice that this company also fits our description of a typical firm in that it raises capital, retains cash, and invests.

The value of the equity of the company is simply figured as

$$VE = \frac{NCDE}{ke}$$
$$= \frac{\$1930.50}{0.27}$$
$$= \$7150.00$$

Debt valuation is

$$VD = \frac{NCDD}{kd}$$
$$= \frac{\$269.50}{0.07}$$
$$= \$3850.00$$

TABLE 7.7   Constant-cash-flow perpetual (ongoing)
corporation

	t_1 *through* t_∞
$RCPT	$11091.94
$EXPT	6100.57
GCFO	4991.37
GTAX	2595.51
NCFO	2395.86
DTS	364.00
CAU	2759.86
ITS	140.14
CAC	2900.00
I	269.50
PP	280.00
CDD	549.50
NDC	280.00
NCDD	269.50
CAE	2350.50
CRF	220.00
CDE	2130.50
NEC	200.00
NCDE	1930.50
TCC $\equiv$ IVS	700.00

$$ke = 0.27 \text{ per period}$$
$$kd = 0.07 \text{ per period}$$
$$\tau = 0.52$$

VD may also, you remember, be calculated using the cost of debt capital, kd^*:

$$kd^* = kd(1 - \tau) = 0.07(1 - 0.52) = 0.0336$$

and

$$VD = \frac{NCDD - ITS}{kd^*}$$
$$= \frac{\$269.50 - \$140.14}{0.0336} = \frac{\$129.36}{0.0336}$$
$$= \$3850.00$$

So the total value of the company is given by

$$VF = VD + VE$$
$$= \$3850 + \$7150$$
$$= \$11,000$$

In terms of the overall valuation calculations,

$$kf = \frac{VD}{VF} kd + \frac{VE}{VF} ke$$
$$= \frac{\$3850}{\$11,000} (0.07) + \frac{\$7150}{\$11,000} (0.27)$$
$$= 0.20$$

and

$$VF = \frac{NCDD + NCDE}{kf} \quad or \quad \frac{CAC - IVS}{kf}$$

$$= \frac{\$269.50 + \$1930.50}{0.20} \quad or \quad \frac{\$2900 - \$700}{0.20}$$

$$= \frac{\$2200}{0.20}$$

$$= \$11,000$$

And, finally, for overall valuation using kf^*:

$$kf^* = \frac{VD}{VF} kd^* + \frac{VE}{VF} ke$$

$$= \frac{\$3850}{\$11,000} (0.0336) + \frac{\$7150}{\$11,000} (0.27)$$

$$= 0.18726$$

and

$$VF = \frac{NCDD + NCDE - ITS}{kf^*} \quad or \quad \frac{CAU - IVS}{kf^*}$$

$$= \frac{\$269.50 + \$1930.50 - \$140.14}{0.18726} \quad or \quad \frac{\$2759.86 - \$700.00}{0.18726}$$

$$= \frac{\$2059.86}{0.18726}$$

$$= \$11,000.00$$

So the valuation of a company having constant, perpetual expectations proceeds more simply, but conceptually identically to finite-horizon or other ongoing firms.

Perpetuities may also be used as approximations for very long-lived and constant cash flows which do terminate. This is because, as T moves further from the present, the value of the cash flow quickly approaches the perpetuity value. The mathematical reason for this is that the far-into-the-future cash flows are being divided by very large numbers. Consider the NCDE of our perpetual company. Suppose that it was expected to terminate at t_{20} instead of t_{∞}:

$$VE_0 = \sum_{T=1}^{20} \frac{NCDE_T}{(1 + ke)^T}$$

$$= \sum_{T=1}^{20} \frac{\$1930.50}{(1.27)^T}$$

$$= \$7089.99$$

The last term of the summation adds only $16.20 to the total VE_0 of $7089.99, because the $1930.50 $NCDE_{20}$ is divided by a denominator value of $(1.27)^{20}$, which is equal to 119+. If we were to calculate VE_0 for $T = t_{30}$, $T = t_{40}$, and $T = t_{50}$, we would get

$$\begin{aligned} VE_0 &= \$7144.50 & T &= t_{30} \\ &= \$7149.50 & T &= t_{40} \\ &= \$7149.95 & T &= t_{50} \end{aligned}$$

You can see that we quickly approach the perpetuity value of $7150.00. Indeed, the additional 10 periods of $1930.50 NCDE flows *after* t_{40} add only 45 cents to the value of VE_0. In real corporate valuation exercises, where termination points are uncertain but expected to be at least several decades into the future, the perpetuity calculation may be a reasonable proxy for the actual expectation. But recognize that the perpetuity valuation is not substituting a general termination assumption for the specific ones in our formulas. Perpetuities specifically assume that $T = t_\infty$. The ease of calculation gained by that assumption should be weighed against the valuation error caused by using $T = t_\infty$, if it is not a good approximation of the true T.

We mentioned a bit earlier that perpetuities can obscure some of our cash-flow relationships. Take another look at the cash flows in Table 7.7. Notice that the principal repayment to debt suppliers, PP, is identical to the amount of capital raised from them, NDC. This *must* be the case in a constant perpetuity, because if PP were greater than NDC, debt capital would be quickly liquidated. If PP were less than NDC, the debt claim on the firm would become infinitely large. In a constant perpetuity, debt must just exactly refinance its principal repayments each period, or hold only perpetual bonds which never repay principal. A similar sort of "refinancing" is also going on for equity, but since it is not so obvious, we have a special discussion of it in Appendix B to this section.

If we had introduced you to cash flows through the use of perpetuities, our debt claims would have been rather restricted instruments. Again, you may be getting the feeling that perpetuities are not worth the effort. But, we repeat, they can be useful if applied carefully.

There is a special class of perpetuities called the "constant-growth perpetuity" or "constant-growth model" that often receives attention in corporate finance texts. Within our theoretical framework the constant-growth perpetuity looks as follows:

$$VE_0 = \frac{NCDE_1}{ke - g}$$

The term g is a one-period rate of growth in NCDE. It means that $NCDE_2$ is expected to be equal to $NCDE_1(1 + g)$, that $NCDE_3$ is expected to be $NCDE_2(1 + g)$, and so on. Mathematically,

$$VE_0 = \frac{NCDE_1}{ke - g} = \sum_{T=1}^{\infty} \frac{NCDE_1(1 + g)^{T-1}}{(1 + ke)^{T}}.$$

This formula assumes that NCDE increases each period forever at a compound growth rate, g. You can see that the higher the growth rate, the higher is VE_0.[13]

Constructions such as this constant-growth model have been presented as offering more realistic representations of corporate valuation than the usual perpetuity structure, since real companies do not display histories of unchanging cash flows. But, by the same token, neither do they show constant growth in their flows. The constant-growth perpetuities, like the constant perpetuities, merely substitute one specific set of cash-flow expectations for another. Unless that set is more representative of the expectations that we actually hold, the growth model is not an improvement. In and of itself, it adds little to our theory.

Another illustration of commonly used corporate valuation models is the popular *P/E* or *price–earnings ratio* often cited in stock market publications. When a company is said to have a P/E of 15 or 10 or whatever, attaching significance to this number actually implies a rather crude valuation theory.

Recalling the constant-perpetuity model,

$$VE_0 = \frac{NCDE_1}{ke}$$

VE_0 can be thought of as the price per share of a company's stock times the number of shares. So

$$price_0 \text{ per share} = \frac{NCDE_1 \text{ per share}}{ke}$$

If the company's NCDE is a constant proportion, C, of its accounting earnings (as it is in a constant perpetuity),

$$price_0 \text{ per share} = \frac{(earnings_1 \text{ per share})(C)}{ke}$$

and

$$\frac{price_0 \text{ per share}}{earnings_1 \text{ per share}} = \frac{1}{ke} \cdot C$$

The popular P/E ratio is simply a constant times the inverse (reciprocal) of the discount rate in a constant-perpetuity valuation model. Or if earnings are expected to grow at the rate of g per period as for the constant-growth perpetuity model,

$$\frac{P_0}{E_1} = \frac{1}{ke - g} \cdot C$$

Attaching importance to a P/E ratio per se or making comparisons among corporations on the basis of their P/E ratios implies that you are

---

[13]Until, of course, the point where $g = ke$, at which time $VE_0 = \$\infty$.

willing to agree with all the assumptions made in the perpetuity models and apply them equally to each corporation compared. If expectations of cash flows, especially those close to t_0, are not closely in accord with those cash-flow assumptions, then P/E ratios can be quite misleading.

Notice the two terms in the general valuation formula for equity which appear in boldface type:

$$\mathbf{VE_0} = \frac{\mathbf{NCDE_1}}{1 + ke_1} + \frac{NCDE_2}{(1 + ke_1)(1 + ke_2)}$$
$$+ \frac{NCDE_3}{(1 + ke_1)(1 + ke_2)(1 + ke_3)} + \sum_{T=4}^{T} \frac{NCDE_T}{\prod_{P=1}^{T} (1 + ke_P)}$$

Inasmuch as the P/E ratio dwells only on the pair of dollar amounts represented by the boldface terms (plus making an assumption about a relationship between $NCDE_1$ and accounting earnings), it obviously says little about the particular characteristics of the total set of cash flows and the risks of those flows other than at t_1. Two companies could have identical P/E ratios and t_1 cash flows to equity but have quite different future cash-flow and discount-rate expectations. And two other companies might have very similar characteristics past t_1 and quite different P/E ratios.

Perpetuities can be convenient shorthand techniques for working with corporate valuation theory. But they *are* simplifications of potentially much more complex cash-flow expectations. We should keep this in mind as we use them. And we should only depend on perpetuities when our general valuation formulas cannot do the same job as well.

Conclusion to Section II

The discussion of perpetuity valuation in Chapter 7 has introduced the notion that actual application of our theoretical model in real-market conditions could occasionally require amendments of some sort. We want to remind you here that this is a book on the *theory* of corporate finance. It is not intended to be a handbook of techniques for investors or corporate financial managers. We are trying to introduce you to the basic economic mechanisms that determine and change values in a capital market. There is a wealth of references on techniques. Some are excellent and some are not so good. We shall list several we like later in the book, but we make no pretentions toward competing with or substituting for those references. We merely propose that you are much more likely to be a successful user of the existing techniques if you appreciate the underlying market mechanisms that influence value.

IMPERFEC-
TIONS

On the other hand, we would be doing less than a complete job if we did not at least briefly discuss some of the questions that can be asked about our theory to this point. Since valuation has been our sole concern so far, the questions to be answered are those which address imperfections in using our market valuation mechanism to describe real markets.

First, we might ask about describing the market price formation process as a discounting procedure. You've probably known people who buy and sell stocks and bonds, and very few if any of those people actually attempt to estimate their future cash flow receipts, find opportunity rates appropriate to the riskiness of the flows, and discount back to the present to find a "bid" or "ask" price. If that is the case, how can we defend a theory that uses discounting as the primary description of the way a market sets prices?

The answer is that we are not trying to describe the actions of particular real individuals in the capital market and how they arrive at specific prices. We do know, however, that securities get bought and sold. And we know that the only benefit of those securities to their holders will be the cash flows they are expected to return. So market prices exist as values of securities which are really claims on future cash flows. The market is obviously going through *some* process to convert cash-flow expectations to market prices. We simply call whatever that process is, "discounting." We can further describe it in terms of opportunity costs or discount rates being applied, and the mechanics of present value computations being accomplished, but that is our own way of describing the valuation process. A rational, risk-averse capital market participant could value things that way, although a real capital market participant might not. Real capital markets price future cash-flow expectations by some mechanism that we choose to depict as a discounting process. Our theoretical model uses this process to value capital claims of corporations.[14]

"Well, OK," you might say, "discounting is probably as good a description of what capital markets do as anything else, but how about this business of market efficiency? You've got the capital market busily computing the valuations, and never making a mistake, or overlooking a future cash flow, or being too optimistic, and so on. Isn't that a pretty unrealistic picture of securities markets as we know them?" The answer to this last question is both yes and no. Capital markets make mistakes. They frequently misestimate future cash flows and their riskinesses and thereby set "wrong" prices. But

[14]Our description of the market valuation process is one of two acceptable ways to envision this mechanism, both of which use a discounting technique. We describe the market as discounting expected future cash flows using risk-adjusted discount rates. The alternative approach would describe the market as discounting risk-adjusted cash flows using risk-free market rates of return. This latter process is referred to as the *certainty-equivalent* approach. If used correctly the two approaches produce the same results in valuing capital claims.

Regardless of which approach is employed, there is more than just casual theorizing behind our valuation arguments. Careful empirical studies (cited in the references) have tended to show that market prices do react to changes in future cash-flow expectations in just the way our theory would predict.

our theoretical efficient market can do that, too. Remember, all we have said is that the market efficiently values a set of existing *expectations* of future cash flows. We never said those estimates are "correct" or "incorrect" in the sense that the *actual* cash flows which finally occur are the same or different from expectations. The market may well be valuing a completely incorrect set of cash-flow expectations. But it is doing this with the best t_0 information available to it. Unless someone else had access to actual future cash-flow information, they could not come up with a better price. And further, as soon as the market hears information that alters its existing cash-flow expectations, it changes market prices immediately to be in accord with the revised expectations. This description of capital markets applies well to both our theoretical market and real securities markets.[15]

So the capital market in reality is pretty close to being the way our theory describes it. The generating force behind that market is nothing more than a large collection of market participants buying and selling capital claims on corporations in order to maximize the participants' present wealths and allocate their financial resources over time. The pressure of all this competition forces the capital market to be efficient.

CONCLUSION This has been a rather long section. We needed a thorough introduction to valuation in the theory of corporate finance before we could tackle the theory of financial *decisions*, the things that can *change* corporate values. We have now achieved that thorough introduction. You will find the next three sections a good bit easier than they would have been without the work we have just done on valuation.

We shall not attempt to provide here a detailed summary of the rather large volume of material this section has introduced. If you have studied the section well, a summary is unnecessary anyway, since the ideas we have developed came in a straightforward way directly from Section I. There we studied how capital markets value future cash-flow expectations; here all we did was see how the market values expectations of cash flows to capital claimants of corporations.

The corporate financial form led us to develop a financial cash-flow statement that helps us keep track of who (among receivers of operational expenditures, government, and capital suppliers) gets what. The valuation processes are no different, once cash-flow expectations are known, from those in Section I. Remember that all the important diagrams, definitions, and formulas are contained in Figure 7.3 and Tables 7.3, 7.4, 7.5, and 7.6.

There are four appendixes to this section. Appendix II.A, as we promised, demonstrates how total market values may be separated into new and old capital claims. Appendix II.B discusses the refinancing question that we raised in our study of perpetuities. Appendix II.C argues that our multiperiod

---

[15]Empirical studies of real capital markets (cited in the references) tend to confirm this.

discounting valuation formulas are accurate economic statements of what a capital market does. Appendix II.D connects the theoretical characteristics of our debt claims with real contractual attributes of corporate bonds. These appendixes and the problems should expand your understanding of corporate valuation theory.

This section has provided us with a good introduction to corporate valuation. This preparation has readied us to begin in the following sections considering the theory of financial decisions—decisions that can *change* value.

Appendix II.A: Valuing New Capital Issues

The cash-flow analysis of our five-period firm in Chapter 7 indicated that the company issued new debt and equity claims during its lifetime. We also saw that our valuation formulas correctly yielded the total value of all existing capital claims at each time point, for old and new issues lumped together. The purpose of this appendix is to demonstrate the calculations of separate values for old and new claims.

As you must expect by now, valuing new issues separately from old issues follows all the valuation principles that we have already developed and requires no introduction of new concepts. All we need do is specify the cash-flow expectations for each claim and discount those at the appropriate required rates. The only reason that we reserve this for an appendix rather than include it in the body of the section is that it, for our purposes, is a minor theoretical question not really in the mainstream of important ideas discussed there. Nonetheless, the illustrations are interesting applications of our theory, and for that reason we include them here.

We have two types of capital issuances: debt and equity. Theoretically and in terms of the value calculations, they work the same way. We shall do the equity valuations here and leave the debt calculations as an exercise for you.

The only additional piece of information we must supply is that the market where new securities are sold (the primary issuance market for capital claims) is, like the capital market we have been working with, efficient and free of transaction costs. This tells us that suppliers of new capital dollars receive full value for their resources. These suppliers, of course, obtain a capital claim issued by the corporation. The initial market value of the new claim purchased by the capital supplier must be equal to the number of dollars paid for the claim (security). *Thus, the worth of the claim must be equal to its price at the time of issuance, if the primary market is efficient and frictionless.* If the new claim were worth less than the dollars being supplied, no one would be willing to give those dollars to the firm; if the new claim were worth more than the dollars being supplied, the new claimants would, as we shall see, be getting more than their proportionate share of future cash flows, something that would not be allowed by existing capital suppliers.

As a specific example, let us look back to our five-period corporation (p. 109). At t_1, the company raises $176.68 of NEC. We shall see that the capital claim that is issued at t_1 has a t_1 value of $176.68 based on its share of the future cash flows to equity suppliers. We know that the total VE_1 is expected to be $1812.82, so the new equity suppliers can claim $176.68/$1812.82 of the future equity cash flows if no more claims are issued. Under the same conditions the old equity suppliers henceforth claim an amount equal to ($1812.82 − $176.68)/ $1812.82 as their proportionate share of future equity flows.

This means that at t_2 the new suppliers at t_1 (call them E_1 suppliers) can claim $176.68/$1812.82 of the equity distribution, and the old suppliers, who have been around at least since t_0 (call them E_0 suppliers), can claim ($1812.82 − $176.68)/$1812.82 of the cash distribution to equity suppliers. Of course at t_1, the E_0 suppliers could claim the whole distribution because they were the only existing claimants then.[16]

At t_2, however, another new equity claim is issued to E_2 suppliers (for convenience we can think of them as another new group of people). These suppliers also must get their value-proportional claim on t_3, t_4, and t_5 equity cash distributions. At t_2 the total VE_2 is $1535.62, which includes the E_0, E_1, and E_2 values for capital claims. NEC_2 is $100.00, so the E_2 suppliers can claim $100.00/$1535.62 of future equity distributions if no more claims are issued. And the E_0 and E_1 suppliers can claim ($1535.62 − $100.00)/$1535.62 of future equity distribution under these conditions. But how much of that proportion goes to E_0 suppliers and how much to E_1 suppliers? The answer is conceptually simple, although the arithmetic might not look that way.

Going into p_2 we have the E_0 and E_1 proportional claims from t_1. Those same proportions apply to the remaining share that E_0 and E_1 together can claim at t_3. The E_1 suppliers can claim

$$\frac{\$176.68}{\$1812.82} \cdot \frac{\$1535.62 - \$100.00}{\$1535.62}$$

of the t_3 equity cash distribution. The E_0 suppliers can claim

$$\frac{\$1812.82 - \$176.68}{\$1812.82} \cdot \frac{\$1535.62 - \$100.00}{\$1535.62}$$

of the t_3 distribution.

All of this may seem very complicated. But bear in mind what we are doing. Our general rule is that the proportion of future cash flows to equity

---

[16]Remember that we have assumed *ex dividend* values, so the E_1 suppliers at t_1 get no dividend; it all goes to E_0 suppliers.

claimed by new equity suppliers is equal to their cash contribution to the firm at T (NEC_T) relative to the total equity value of the firm at T (VE_T—which includes NEC_T). As more new capital is raised, the existing claimants must relinquish part of their claim on future cash flows. Unless they are putting up the money themselves, this is only fair. And you can be sure that the capital market will value those claims accordingly. We should also recognize that the cash distributions to equity we have been talking about here are the CDE's, not the NCDE's. The new, not the existing suppliers are giving dollars to the firm. At t_1 the whole of CDE_1 goes to E_0 suppliers. E_1 suppliers give NEC_1 to the firm. E_0 suppliers provide none of NEC_1, so their net receipts at t_1 are CDE_1. E_1 suppliers have negative receipts of NEC_1 dollars, making the net receipts of all equity suppliers equal to $CDE_1 - NEC_1$ or $NCDE_1$ dollars, as we saw in the body of Chapter 7.

The same proportioning process would continue at t_3 if another new equity claim was issued for NEC_3. In our five-period example; NEC_3 was $0.00. Suppose, however, that it had been an amount larger than zero, say $X, coming from E_3 suppliers. Since VE_3 is $1183.66, E_3 suppliers could then claim

$$\frac{\$X}{\$1183.66}$$

of t_4 and t_5 cash flows to equity. E_2 suppliers' proportional claim becomes

$$\frac{\$100.00}{\$1535.62} \cdot \frac{\$1183.66 - \$X}{\$1183.66}$$

of t_4 and t_5 flows. E_1 suppliers get

$$\frac{\$176.68}{\$1812.82} \cdot \frac{\$1535.62 - \$100.00}{\$1535.62} \cdot \frac{\$1183.66 - \$X}{\$1183.66}$$

of t_4 and t_5 cash flows. And, finally, E_0 suppliers claim

$$\frac{\$1812.82 - \$176.68}{\$1812.82} \cdot \frac{\$1535.62 - \$100.00}{\$1535.62} \cdot \frac{\$1183.66 - \$X}{\$1183.66}$$

of the t_4 and t_5 cash distribution to equity suppliers.

Rather than continue to write out these long proportions, we can use a simple notation scheme. Let PK indicate a proportional claim on a cash flow. With the subscript T indicating the time point to which PK applies, and the superscript E_s indicating who holds the claim, we get $PK_T^{E_s}$ representing the claim by E_s suppliers on CDE_T. For example, $PK_2^{E_1}$ indicates the proportional claim of the E_1 equity suppliers on the t_2 equity distribution.

The array of proportional claims for each time point, calculated in the way we have just described for our original five-period example (in which $NEC_3 = \$0.00$), is shown in Table II.A.1. The proportions at each time point must, naturally, sum to 1. Notice that as each new capital claim is issued, proportional claims of the existing suppliers on future cash flows decrease.

TABLE II.A.1   Proportional equity claims on our five-period firm

	t_1	t_2	t_3	t_4	t_5
	$PK_1^{E_0} = 1.000$	$PK_2^{E_0} \simeq 0.903$	$PK_3^{E_0} \simeq 0.844$	$PK_4^{E_0} \simeq 0.844$	$PK_5^{E_0} \simeq 0.844$
	$PK_1^{E_1} = 0.000$	$PK_2^{E_1} \simeq 0.097$	$PK_3^{E_1} \simeq 0.091$	$PK_4^{E_1} \simeq 0.091$	$PK_5^{E_1} \simeq 0.091$
	$PK_1^{E_2} = 0.000$	$PK_2^{E_2} \simeq 0.000$	$PK_3^{E_2} \simeq 0.065$	$PK_4^{E_2} \simeq 0.065$	$PK_5^{E_2} \simeq 0.065$
	1.000	1.000	1.000	1.000	1.000

Table 7.2 (p. 109) tells us the total amounts of cash going to all equity suppliers. Thus, it is a simple matter of multiplying the correct proportions times the total cash amounts to find the cash receipts of each supplier at each time point. For example, the cash receipts of E_2 suppliers at t_3 are CDE_3 times $PK_3^{E_2}$, or ($735.87)(0.06512) $\simeq$ $47.92. Table II.A.2 shows each supplier's receipts at each time point rounded to the nearest cent. (The cash amounts are figured by the exact proportions and so may be as much as 40 cents different from the results you would get using the rounded proportions in Table II.A.1.)

TABLE II.A.2   Cash flows to equity suppliers of our five-period firm

		t_1	t_2	t_3	t_4	t_5
S	CDE_T	$831.34	$830.40	$735.87	$834.48	$806.37
U	E_0	831.34	749.47	620.90	704.11	680.39
P						
P						
L	E_1	(176.68)	80.93	67.05	76.03	73.47
I						
E						
R	E_2	0.00	(100.00)	47.92	54.34	52.51
S						
	$NCDE_T$	$654.66	$730.40	$735.87	$834.48	$806.37

Notice in Table II.A.2 that the cash contributions of equity suppliers enter as negative cash flows to them at the time points when the capital is raised. If those are combined with the positive receipts of existing equity suppliers (CDE's in total), we get the correct dollar amounts for NCDE's at each time point. The positive entries in each column (at each time point) sum to CDE_T, the negative one equals NEC_T, so their sum must be $NCDE_T$.

All that remains to be done is to value the expected cash flows shown in Table II.A.2. Since all existing equity claims at each time point have the same priority, they must be equally risky. Since *ke* for our five-period firm is 0.25, or 25%, per period, we know that this required rate of return must apply to all claims of this level of riskiness. Hence, *ke* = 0.25 applies to each separate equity supplier as well as to all as a group. To find the values of individual equity claims, we merely discount the cash flows expected to be received by each claim using $ke = 0.25$. For example, E_2 suppliers are expected to receive a t_3 flow of \$47.92, a t_4 flow of \$54.34, and a t_5 flow of \$52.51. So extending our notation to the value calculation,

$$VE_2^{E_2} = \frac{47.92}{1.25} + \frac{54.34}{(1.25)^2} + \frac{52.51}{(1.25)^3}$$
$$= \$100.00$$

Notice that the value of the E_2 suppliers' claim at t_2 is exactly equal to the cash they contribute to the firm at t_2. In an efficiently competitive capital market this equality must obtain.

Table II.A.3 shows the values at each time point of the capital claims computed by discounting their respective cash flows at ke. This is the separation of new and old issue values we have been working toward. Note that the values sum to the VE_T's that we calculated originally in this chapter. (Again, you may get slightly different results from your own calculations. One-cent differences are probably due to rounding errors.)[17] The negative cash flows to equity suppliers E_1 and E_2 are not included in these value calculations; hence, you can view each $VE_T^{E_s}$ as the *ex contribution* value at time T of expected future distributions to E_s suppliers. You can see that had we included the NEC contributions, the values of new equity claims would exactly equal zero at the point where the contribution is made. This merely says that the present value of the future claims is equal to the cash contribution. That, again, must be true in an efficient market.

TABLE II.A.3   **Values of equity claims on our five-period firm**

	t_0	t_1	t_2	t_3	t_4
$VE_T^{E_0}$	\$1973.99	\$1636.14	\$1295.71	\$ 998.74	\$544.31
$VE_T^{E_1}$	0.00	176.68	139.92	107.84	58.78
$VE_T^{E_2}$	0.00	0.00	100.00	77.08	42.01
VE_T	\$1973.99	\$1812.82	\$1535.63	\$1183.66	\$645.10

We remind you that all of the values, proportions, and cash flows we have been using are based on t_0 expectations. These are *expected* amounts, and are therefore uncertain and subject to change as time passes.

Finally, we leave the calculations for new debt issuances as an exercise for you. They work exactly the same way the equity valuations do but with different numbers. As a final point, if you are still unconvinced about these

[17]You might also notice that the separations of value could be calculated much more easily by using the NEC_T and VE_T (total equity values) directly. For example, $VE_2^{E_1} = (NEC_1/VE_1)(VE_2 - NEC_2)$. Knowing the cash flow and market efficiency logic, this solution is obvious. Unless the cash-flow determinations and separations are clearly understood, however, that solution would be arbitrary. Cash-flow expectations, again, are the bases of value.

value separations for new capital issues, think of how the calculations would work if the NEC amounts were raised from existing E_0 suppliers at t_1 and t_2. Their proportional claim would be a constant $PK^{E_0}_{1,2,3,4,5} = 1.0$, and their net cash receipts would be equal to the NCDE$_T$'s, since they are contributing the cash. The equity values at each time point would be the same as those we originally computed. The E_0 suppliers relinquish no claim on future cash flows, provided they are able to come up with the required NEC$_T$ dollars when they are needed. The t_0 value of their claim, however, is unaffected by whether or not they provide the NEC$_T$ dollars, since it costs them, in value terms, exactly the same amount that they gain. We shall return to this point in Section IV.

Appendix II.B: Refinancing, Liquidation, Expansion, Capital Gains, and Market-Value Changes Across Time

REFINANC-ING When we examined the financial cash flows of our constant-perpetuity corporation in Chapter 7, we observed that interest payments constituted the entire amount of NCDD and that any new debt capital raised was matched exactly by principal repayments to debt suppliers. We called this, you remember, a refinancing situation. Refinancing in our theory takes place when the net cash distributions to a capital supplier at any time point are equal to and only equal to the supplier's required cash return *on* the value of his claim.

In our constant perpetuity, the value of the debt claim was $3850, and at each time point the debt suppliers received $269.50 as a net cash distribution. The kd was constant at 7%, so debt suppliers' required cash return *on* the value of their claim was 7% times $3850, or $269.50, exactly their amount of expected NCDD. According to our definition, this constitutes a refinancing situation. If you check back to Table 7.7 (p. 131), where the perpetual cash flows are presented, you will find that the debt suppliers also received $280.00 of principal repayment each period. But debt suppliers also came up with the same amount, $280.00, of NDC at each time point. The net amount received remained at $269.50, the required cash return; the PP and NDC payments merely resulted in refinancing the debt. Even if no NDC or PP amounts were present, we would still maintain that debt was being refinanced, since NCDD is exactly equal to the required cash return *on* VD.

In the same sense, the equity claim on our constant perpetuity was also continually being refinanced. VE = $7150, $ke = 0.27$, so the required cash return was $1930.50 per period. But that is exactly what NCDE was at each time point. So, again, according to our definition, equity is also being refinanced. Note that equity suppliers actually received $2130.50 of CDE at each time point. So in a sense, $2130.50 − $1930.50 = $200.00 of their total cash receipts were in the nature of a "principal repayment to equity" or a return *of* capital. But notice also that they give back (supply) $200 at each time point in the form of NEC. The net, NCDE, is the $1930.50 required cash return. So equity is also continually being refinanced in our constant-perpetuity example.

In our original discussions of the constant perpetuity we said that exact refinancing of capital claims was a necessity [NDC = PP and NEC = CDE — (VE·ke)] in order to avoid liquidating a claim or otherwise upsetting the balance of existing capital claims. In a constant-perpetuity situation, refinancing is the rule. But you may have noticed that this refinancing argument bears close resemblance to certain ideas that we introduced in Chapter 3. There, you recall, we explored the return *of* and *on* capital. Perhaps the best way of investigating this refinancing phenomenon and its relation to the return *of* and *on* capital is to examine a situation where refinancing does *not* take place. Fortunately, we already have such an example at hand, our five-period typical firm.

LIQUIDATION   If refinancing occurs when capital suppliers' net cash receipts are expected to be exactly equal to their return *on* capital, then our five-period example is definitely not a refinancing situation. Let us begin our analysis of the five-period liquidating firm by examining the debt-related cash flows and values from Table 7.2 summarized in Table II.B.1.

TABLE II.B.1   **Five-period example: debt-related flows and values**

	t_1	t_2	t_3	t_4	t_5
VD_{T-1}	$1315.99	$1208.55	$1023.75	$789.11	$430.07
$RRD_T = I_T$	78.96	72.51	61.43	47.35	25.80
PP_T	107.44	284.80	234.64	484.04	430.07
CDD_T	186.40	357.31	296.07	531.39	455.87
NDC_T	0.00	100.00	0.00	125.00	0.00
$NCDD_T$	186.40	257.31	296.07	406.39	455.87
$NCDD_T - RRD_T$	107.44	184.80	234.64	359.04	430.07

The top row of Table II.B.1 is VD_{T-1}, the value on which a cash return is required. The required cash return, RRD_T, is equal to VD_{T-1} times kd, which is the expected interest payment, I_T. The principal repayment amount for each period is listed in the third row. Comparing the PP_T amounts to the NDC_T amounts, we can see that this is an example of liquidating debt. The capital is gradually being returned since PP_T exceeds NDC_T at each time point. More debt capital is being returned as PP_T than is being supplied (paid in) as NDC_T.

A glance at the $NCDD_T$ row of Table II.B.1 confirms this. The net cash being received by debt suppliers exceeds their required cash return *on* capital. The actual differences are shown in the final row, $NCDD_T - RRD_T$. Notice that the value of debt is expected to continually decrease by exactly $NCDD_T$ — RRD_T at the end of each period. The value of the capital claim decreases at time T by exactly the amount of the return *of* capital, $NCDD_T - RRD_T$. From what you learned in Chapter 3, this should be no surprise.

Note also that the NDC flotations of $100 at t_2 and $125 at t_4 are not enough to cause the NCDD's to be the same or less than the RRD_T's. If they did, debt values would hold steady or begin to increase. The $100 and $125 NDC flows can be thought of as partial refinancings of debt, but in order to be total refinancings, they would have to be equal to the PP's at the same time points.

A similar analysis can be performed on equity-related cash flows. These are presented in Table II.B.2. The first row of Table II.B.2 records the equity value of the previous period on which the required cash return for this period, RRE_T, is calculated by multiplying VE_{T-1} times *ke* (= 0.25). The expected total cash disbursement to equity is shown in the third row (CDE_T). Row four shows $CDE_T - RRE_T$. This amount is conceptually the same as a principal repayment, PP_T to debt. PP_T, you remember, was the amount by which CDD_T exceeded I_T. Since I_T is RRD_T, $CDE_T - RRE_T$ must be saying the same thing for equity as PP_T says for debt.

TABLE II.B.2 Five-period example: equity-related cash flows and values

	t_1	t_2	t_3	t_4	t_5
VE_{T-1}	$1973.98	$1812.82	$1535.62	$1183.66	$645.10
RRE_T	493.50	453.21	383.91	295.92	161.28
CDE_T	831.34	830.40	735.87	834.48	806.37
$CDE_T - RRE_T$	337.84	377.20	351.96	538.57	645.10
NEC_T	176.68	100.00	0.00	0.00	0.00
$NCDE_T$	654.66	730.40	735.87	834.48	806.37
$NCDE_T - RRE_T$	161.16	277.20	351.96	538.57	645.10

Comparing each period's $CDE_T - RRE_T$ to the NEC_T raised, you can see that the equity of this company is also being liquidated. Equity suppliers are consistently receiving more than their required cash return. The $NCDE_T - RRE_T$ row shows, numerically, exactly the same thing. Notice that the equity value at each time point is $NCDE_T - RRE_T$ less than at the previous time point, and that at t_5 the implication is that VE_5 = $0.00, because $NCDE_5 - RRE_5 = VE_4$ (rounding errors may cause one-cent differences).

Our assertion is that a capital supplier's expectation of receiving more than his required return *on* capital is a signal that his claim is being liquidated. With the negative connotation that usually goes with the word "liquidated," this assertion may leave you somewhat uncomfortable at first hearing. It seems to be saying something silly, like "receiving too much money is a bad thing." In fact, we are not saying anything quite so foolish with this liquidation assertion.

Remember, the value of a capital claim on a corporation is its expected NCDE or NCDD stream discounted back to the present at the required rates of return. And the required cash return *on* capital for any period is the value of that claim at the beginning of the period times the required rate of return for that period. To expect a capital claim to maintain a constant value across time even with unchanging expectations, it is also necessary to expect that net cash distributions will exactly equal the required cash returns *on* that capital claim. Our perpetuity example shows this as refinancing. If a capital claim is expected to receive more than its required return *on* capital at a time point, if its value at the beginning of the period has been calculated correctly, and if expectations have not changed, then for that period the claim will experience some liquidation (decrease in market value).

Similarly, if a net cash distribution is less than a required cash return *on* capital under the conditions we just mentioned, the capital claim will increase in market value. We can say the corporation is *expanding* that claim as opposed to liquidating it. *In a sense, the market value at the beginning of the period says that the capital is "owed" its required rate for that period, and will, somehow or another, receive it.* If the net cash distribution does not do it all, then a market price increase will make up the difference. That is an "expansion." If the net cash distribution exceeds the required return, the claim is getting more than it is "owed" and market price declines just enough to make up the difference. That is a "contraction" or liquidation. If the net cash distribution is exactly equal to the required return, no surpluses or deficits in return must be made up by the market and the price will remain constant, as was the case with our perpetuity.

The price changes of equity claims in Table II.B.2 should now have some greater meaning. Look at the t_1 column. The required cash return *on* capital is \$493.50. The $NCDE_1$ is \$654.66. That means that equity suppliers are receiving \$654.66 − \$493.50 = \$161.16 more than they are "owed." This must be made up by the capital market and *is* by a decrease in equity value of \$1973.98 − \$1812.82 = \$161.16 at the end of p_1. You can check to see that this same type of market-price adjustment continues at $t_{2,3,4}$ as the company is liquidated.

EXPANSION   Just so you will not get the impression that liquidation and perpetuities are the only suitable numerical examples our theory can handle, we provide the cash flows and valuation data for a four-period corporation that experiences an expansion. This appears in Table II.B.3. We shall, for the most part, leave this example for you to study and verify. However, we would like to mention two interesting points:

1. Notice that the value of all capital claims increases from t_0 to t_1; the firm is expanding during the first period.
2. Notice that, if you will accept our valuation figures, the required cash

return *on* capital at t_1, RRE_1 for equity, is VE_0 times ke, or $(\$4579.38)(0.15) = \$686.91$. But the net cash receipt at t_1, NCDE_1, for equity is only \$451.20. This means that the market "owes" the difference, $\$686.91 - \$451.20 = \$235.71$, to the equity supplier. And, as we would expect, the market provides it. The increase in the market value of equity from t_0 to t_1 is $\$4815.09 - \$4579.38 = \$235.71$.

TABLE II.B.3   Four-period company expanding for one period

A. Financial cash flows:

	t_1	t_2	t_3	t_4
CAU_T	\$ 1,500.00	\$ 3,500.00	\$10,000.00	\$ 1,000.00
ITS_T	372.07	391.23	358.13	32.83
CAC_T	1,872.07	3,891.23	10,358.13	1,032.83
I_T	715.53	752.36	688.71	63.13
PP_T	0.00	1,009.23	5,004.59	505.05
CDD_T	715.53	1,761.59	5,693.30	568.18
NDC_T	294.66	500.00	0.00	0.00
NCDD_T	420.87	1,261.59	5,693.30	568.18
CAE_T	1,156.54	2,129.64	4,664.83	464.65
CRF_T	356.54	629.64	0.00	0.00
CDE_T	800.00	1,500.00	4,664.83	464.65
NEC_T	348.80	370.36	0.00	0.00
NCDE_T	451.20	1,129.64	4,664.83	464.65
$\text{TCC}_T \equiv \text{IVS}_T$	1,000.00	1,500.00	0.00	0.00

B. Constant parameters:

$$\tau = 0.52 \qquad kd^* = 0.06$$
$$ke = 0.15 \qquad kf^* = 0.10$$
$$kd = 0.125 \qquad kf = 0.136111\ldots$$

C. Market values of capital claims:

	t_0	t_1	t_2	t_3
VE_T	\$ 4,579.38	\$ 4,815.09	\$ 4,407.72	\$ 404.04
VD_T	5,724.22	6,018.87	5,509.64	505.05
VF_T	10,303.60	10,833.96	9,917.36	909.09

We shall leave other comparisons to your ingenuity. You might want to work through the remaining periods for equity's returns, or for debt's. Or, you may find it worthwhile to return to Appendix II.A and separate the values of "new" and "old" capital claims and to perform this required return and price change analysis on the separated capital claim values. It works as well for them. This can be a very rich example, illustrating just about all of our theoretical valuation ideas.

CAPITAL GAINS   Finally, before we leave this numerical example, we would like to cover one additional idea that may have occurred to you already. You might have noticed that our market values are calculated on the basis of net cash flows between the corporation and the capital suppliers. In essence, for example, equity market prices are the discounted value of all net future dividends, to use stock market terminology.

But chances are you also have heard that people do not buy stocks just for their dividends; they buy expecting capital gains. A *capital gain* (or loss) in our model is the value change expected for a capital claim from one time point to another.

Let us see how the "capital gains versus dividends" argument works in our theory. Look back at our four-period corporation in Table II.B.3. If a person bought the equity of the firm at t_0, he would pay, rightly, \$4579.38 for the expectation of receiving the risky NCDE's for t_1, t_2, t_3, and t_4. But suppose he bought it instead for the expected capital gain. He can see that the market price of equity is expected to go up at t_1 and then decline thereafter. Why not buy at t_0 and sell at t_1?

Well, suppose he does just that. His cash returns at t_1 are then

$$\text{NCDE}_1 + \text{VE}_1 = \$451.20 + \$4815.09 = \$5266.29 \text{[18]}$$

and his gain is

$$\text{dividend} + \text{capital gain} = \text{NCDE}_1 + (\text{VE}_1 - \text{VE}_0)$$
$$= \$451.20 + \$235.71$$
$$= \$686.91$$

a nice piece of change. But is it really extraordinarily good? Has he cheated the market? You should know better than even to ask. The stock cost him \$4579.38 at t_0. The risk of the investment indicates a 15% required rate. So, to earn just that, he needs at t_1 a total of

$$\$4579.38(1.15) = \$5266.29$$

or a net gain of

$$\$4579.38(0.15) = \$686.91$$

which is exactly what he got. By taking the capital gain at t_1, he foregoes future NCDE$_\tau$'s having value exactly equal to the proceeds of his sale.[19]

So the argument about dividends versus capital gains for an investor is moot. If you get one, you miss the other. Your return, however, is the same for either course of action.[20] For the capital market as a whole, however,

---

[18]His cash return at t_1 is \$451.20 rather than the dividend of \$800 because the t_1 price of equity is both *ex dividend* and *post contribution*. (He gets the \$800 dividend and contributes \$348.80 NEC, then sells for \$4815.09.) If he does not contribute the NEC$_1$, he, as the E_0 supplier, could sell the equity at t_1 for only \$4466.29, but would receive the entire \$800 dividend at t_1, also netting \$5266.29.

[19]It was difficult until now to talk about capital gains because our corporations had only capital losses. Equity suppliers in those corporations obtained their required return in the form of cash receipts in excess of their requirements, with capital losses compensating for that excess.

[20]Remember that our individual capital-market participants are not subject to personal income taxes at this stage of our development, let alone differential taxes on dividends and capital gains (losses) which, in real markets can make the courses of action quite different in their impacts on present wealth. In Section IV we shall return to this question.

expcctations of nct cash distributions to capital suppliers are the *only* things that cause those claims to have any value. Capital gains are caused by expectations of future net cash disbursements, obviously. If no disbursements are expected, no capital gains or market value will be present. The common stock of a company that is expected never to pay a dividend, regardless of its "profitability," will have a market price of $0.00.

MARKET PRICE CHANGES ACROSS TIME

After studying these examples, one might be tempted to say, "Oh! Now I see why market prices change over time. It is nothing more than people receiving more or less than their required cash returns *on* capital." That is true in our examples. But you would be rather far off base if you concluded that that was the only reason market prices change. Indeed, that is only one factor in most real capital-market price changes across time. Remember: Our examples are working with a single set of cash-flow expectations as of a given time point, t_0. The price changes you see in our examples are expected ones based on that unchanging set of t_0-based cash-flow expectations. We are merely working our way through those expectations. *But real capital-market price changes over time are probably most importantly caused by changes in cash-flow expectations* rather than return *of* and *on* capital influences such as we have seen in these examples.

Recall our constant-perpetuity example. Its prices were never expected to change, because all flows were constant and all capital exactly refinanced. If a price change were to occur, it would of necessity be caused by a shift from one set of constant-perpetual cash-flow expectations to another.[21]

Appendix II.C: The Economics of Multiperiod Discounting

Our discussions of returns *of* and *on* capital as applied to corporate valuation questions (Chapter 3) allow us to clarify the economic basis for multiperiod discounting to an extent that was impossible in Section I. Applied to the valuation of corporate capital claims, we have the general discounting formula

$$\text{VCF}_\text{A} = \sum_{\text{T}=\text{A}+1}^{T} \frac{\text{CF}_\text{T}}{\prod_{\text{P}=\text{A}+1}^{\text{T}} (1 + k_\text{P})}$$

where CF_T and VCF_A designate cash flows and values of cash flows, respectively. The k_P's are one-period discount rates expected to apply during period P (these are sometimes called "forward rates").

To take a manageable multiperiod notational example, suppose that

[21]It might also reflect a shift in risk–return preferences in the capital market, or a combination of the two.

we are faced with a three-period situation. The formulas then become

$$VCF_0 = \frac{CF_1}{1 + k_1} + \frac{CF_2}{(1 + k_1)(1 + k_2)}$$
$$+ \frac{CF_3}{(1 + k_1)(1 + k_2)(1 + k_3)}$$
$$VCF_1 = \frac{CF_2}{1 + k_2} + \frac{CF_3}{(1 + k_2)(1 + k_3)}$$

and

$$VCF_2 = \frac{CF_3}{1 + k_3}$$

From our return *of* and *on* capital studies, we know that the required cash return *on* capital at t_1 is $VCF_0(k_1)$. By the same token, the required cash return *on* capital at t_2 is $VCF_1(k_2)$, and t_3's required cash return *on* capital is $VCF_2(k_3)$. This shows us that the correct economic interpretation of multiperiod forward discount rates is that they are the one-period required rates of return *on* the value of the capital claim during that particular period. The discounting procedures portrayed in our corporate valuation formulas are merely representations of the capital market applying required rates of return to market values. Discounting is nothing more than that idea applied in the reverse time direction to expected cash flows.

This view of one-period forward discount rates seems reasonable, but one aspect of the relationship deserves to be stressed. The particular future single-period discount rate for period P is *not* merely a function of the riskiness of time T's cash flows (P = T). It is related to the riskinesses of *all* future cash-flow expectations from T through T. You can see the rationale of this statement by remembering what k_P is. For P = T it is the one-period required rate of return on VCF_{T-1}. And VCF_{T-1} is determined by all cash-flow expectations from T through T and their riskinesses.

The idea, for example, of discounting CF_3 by $(1 + k_1)$, $(1 + k_2)$, and $(1 + k_3)$ to find its t_0 value now begins to have some intuitive appeal. In order to get CF_3 back to t_0 it must "pass through" three intervening required rates, k_1, k_2, and k_3, *all* of which are therefore affected by CF_3's riskiness. k_1 is a function of CF_1's, CF_2's, and CF_3's risks, because all three pass through period p_1 as they are discounted back to VCF_0. k_2, on the other hand, is affected only by the risks of CF_2 and CF_3 because (as you can see by our VCF formulas) k_2 never operates on CF_1 in any valuation form. The k_2 rate is the required one-period rate of return *on* VCF_1, which does not include the value of CF_1. Similarly, k_3 is solely a function of the terminal cash flow CF_3. k_3 never operates on CF_1 or CF_2. It applies only as the one-period required, rate *on* VCF_2, which is caused only by the expectation and risk of the CF_3 cash flow.

Multiperiod forward discount rates are one-period required rates of return *on* capital. Our valuation formulas are mechanistic representations of what the capital market is doing when it values a capital claim: applying risk-adjusted required rates of return to future cash-flow expectations, *all* future cash-flow expectations.

Appendix II.D: Financial Cash Flows and Corporate Debt Capital Claims

Our financial cash flows are intended to be representative of the cash-flow expectations held by participants in real capital markets. CDE_T, for example, is meant to represent the cash dividend expectation of stockholders of a company for time T. PP_T and I_T are, by the same token, meant to represent bondholders' principal repayment and interest cash-flow expectations for point T. The latter, however, could potentially cause some confusion if they are carelessly compared to commonly used terms with similar names in real bond markets. The problem is caused by the difference, under uncertainty, between *expected* and *promised* cash flows.

A debt claim in the form of a bond contract is written with promised interest and principal payments at specified future time points. From that viewpoint, these promised cash flows look very much like our I_T's and PP_T's. But in fact, they are not the same. To illustrate the potential differences, consider the following: a corporate bond of the B & L Corporation issued at t_0 has written in its contract with debt suppliers (indenture) that it promises to return 6% interest on its $1000 face value at each of the next two time points, and to return the $1000 face value at maturity, two periods from now. In other words, the bond promises interest payments of $60 at t_1 and $60 at t_2, and $1000 of principal at t_2. At t_1 the corporation's promise of $60 interest is a *maximum* amount that it will pay. Debt suppliers at t_1 can receive the $60 amount, or a lesser amount, but no more than $60, the promised amount.[22] Recall that we regard all future cash flows as being uncertain to a greater or lesser degree. Thus, there is some chance, however small, that the promised payment of $60 at t_1 will not actually occur, either with respect to amount or timing. (This is true even for the highest grade corporate bonds in real capital markets.)

With any chance at all (as we have just said there is) that the actual cash flow (t_1 interest payment) may be different from the promised payment written in the indenture, then, *that different actual t_1 interest payment must be less than the $60 t_1 promise.* Since $60 at t_1 is a maximum, the actual can only

---

[22]This assumes, of course, no prepayment of principal.

miss in one direction: down. We shall demonstrate in Section V that this means, under conditions of uncertainty, that the *expected* cash flow (t_1 interest payment) must be less than the *promised* t_1 interest payment. The I_1 expectation for our FCF statement is influenced by all possible t_1 interest outcomes and their respective likelihoods of occurring. The promised t_1 payment, on the other hand, is only one of many possible actual payments at t_1 and is the maximum of those. Since the I_1 expectation is influenced by all possible payments at t_1, not just the promised maximum, I_1 as an expectation must be less than the $60 promise. In other words, if the uncertain bond interest payment promise is $60 at t_1, our associated I_1 is less than $60.

Now consider the t_2 payments of interest and principal. If the bond contract has no provision for making up any shortfall of past actual interest payments vis-à-vis their promised amounts, the same arguments above apply to the t_2 expectation of interest, I_2, as applied in our discussion of I_1: I_2 will also be less than the $60 promise. And, of course, the PP_2 expectation will be less than the promised $1000 principal payment at t_2.

It happens, however, that bond indentures often allow past shortfalls to be recouped in future periods. Thus, I_2 may exceed the $60 promise if part of the I_2 expectation includes payment for past (t_1) shortfalls of actual versus promised interest. That portion of I_2 due exclusively to the original indenture promise of a t_2 interest payment will be less than $60, as we have argued above. But any addition to the t_2 expectation due to past shortfalls being recouped could cause total I_2 (as a sum of two parts) to exceed the $60 promise.

To generalize, the preceding discussion means that if you have a bond contract in hand, you can read it and ascertain the stream of promised interest and principal payments, which appears to be just like our I_τ's and PP_τ's. But if that debt claim is at all uncertain, there is no guarantee that our expectational cash-flow series will correspond to the indenture promises.

If there is no expectation that catch-up payments will be allowed or forthcoming to recoup shortfalls in earlier promised payments, then, with amounts of payments being uncertain, each of our I_τ and PP_τ expectations will be *less* than the corresponding promises. If catch-up payments (or principal prepayments) are also possible, then our I_τ and PP_τ expectations may be either less than or greater than the original time τ promises, as expectations of past shortfalls being recouped are included.

As a final note, this argument implies that our kd, the return required by debt suppliers, is not the same thing as the popular "yield to maturity" that is often mentioned in the financial press. The yield to maturity of a corporate bond is the rate that discounts the promised cash flows back to equal the market price of a bond. Our kd, however, is the rate(s) which discounts expected cash flows back to equal the market price of a bond. Since promised and expected flows are different, kd and the yield to maturity are also different. In fact, kd is less than the yield to maturity for any risky corporate bond. You can see this most clearly in the case of risky I_τ and PP_τ payments with no expectations of catch-up payments. Here all expectations are less than the associated promises. Since both series are being discounted back to the same market price, the kd, which applies to the lower I_τ and PP_τ expectational series, must be less than the yield to maturity, which applies to the higher promised payment series.[23] The only situation in which kd and yield to maturity are equal is when the debt claim is risk-free; there, the promises and the expectations are identical.

These arguments apply to all real capital claims that make specific cash-flow promises. Preferred stock is one other example. Common stock, however, has no contractual promise of any specific dollar cash flows or timing, so no similar caveats are necessary for equity claims.

Problems for Section II

1. Your family owns a corporation and is thinking of selling it. The company is expected to generate revenues of \$50,000 one period from now, \$35,000 two periods from now, and then cease to exist (no salvage value). Cash expenditures for productive operations will probably be \$26,000 one period from now and \$17,000 two periods from now. The company has \$10,000 in book-value assets, which it plans to depreciate by the straight-line method over the next two periods. There is also a debt issue outstanding which is expected to pay \$637.19 in interest and \$4946.87 in principal one period from now and \$290.91 in interest and \$4155.84 in principal two periods from now. The rate of return required by debt capital suppliers is 7% per period. The corporate tax rate is 40%; interest payments are deductible for tax purposes. Although there is no formal market in the shares of this company, a close appraisal of the risk of the equity claims seems to indicate that a rate of $13\frac{2}{9}\%$ is appropriate for valuation purposes. No investments are planned.

(a) Calculate the financial cash flows for this firm for each relevant point in time.
(b) What would you be willing to accept as a bid for the equity of this company now (t_0)?
(c) What is the value of debt of this company now (t_0)?
(d) Calculate kf and $kf*$.

[23]The kd is also less than yield to maturity when catch-up payments are allowed and expected. Some expectations will be less than the same time point's promise, and some may be greater. But as long as they are uncertain, each of the parts of any time point's expectation must be less than and/or later than its associated promise, so the same arguments hold.

2. The following financial statements belong to a two-period firm (points in time t_0, t_1, t_2):

Balance sheet t_0				Balance sheet t_1			
Assets		Liabilities and capital		Assets		Liabilities and capital	
P&E	$20,000	Debt	$10,000	P&E	$12,000	Debt	$ 5,000
		Equity	10,000			Equity	7,000
Total	$20,000	Total	$20,000	Total	$12,000	Total	$12,000

Income statement p_1	
Sales	$ 95,000
Cost of goods sold	35,000
Selling, administration, and general expense	5,000
Depreciation	8,000
Total expenses	48,000
EBIT	$ 47,000
Interest	700
PBT (taxable income)	$ 46,300
Tax at 40%	18,520
PAT	$ 27,780

You know the following information about the firm:

1. Sales, COGS, and SAGE are all cash flows.
2. At t_2 the firm will cease to operate and its assets will have no real or book value.
3. The equityholders of the firm require a 20% return per period.
4. Debt requires a 7% per period return (the balance-sheet figures for debt are market values).
5. At t_0 the equity of the company has a market value of $50,650.
6. Expenditures in the second period will be the same as in the first period.
7. No investment is foreseen.

Use your knowledge of our financial valuation model to:

(a) Calculate the financial cash flows at t_1.
(b) Deduce the financial cash flows at t_2.
(c) Construct the p_2 accounting income statement.
(d) Specify the value of the equity of the firm at t_2 (immediately before the cash available is disbursed and the firm liquidated).
(e) Specify the value of the equity of the firm at t_1 immediately before the cash from the first period is disbursed and immediately after the cash is disbursed.

3. Assume that you have the opportunity to undertake a business venture, for which the total outlay now (t_0) is \$10,000. You only have \$7201.90, so you must borrow the difference, \$2798.10, from the bank; the bank agrees to lend you that amount at 8% interest per period on the outstanding principal, this interest being deductible for tax purposes. Your expected principal-repayment schedule is as follows:

t_1	t_2	t_3	t_4	t_5
\$345.18	\$442.21	\$548.93	\$666.31	\$795.47

The best alternative use of your money involving the same amount of risk during the time of this investment would return you 12% per period and is generally available in the capital market. You intend to withdraw all cash as it becomes available to you and invest it (same risk) at 12% in the capital market. The venture promises dollar receipts (\$RCPT) of \$6000 starting at t_1 which you expect to grow by \$1000 at each time point thereafter to a final level of \$10,000 at t_5, at which time the opportunity will disappear and have no salvage value. All dollar costs (exclusive of depreciation and interest, of course) are expected to equal 50% of \$RCPT. You intend to use straight-line depreciation (\$2000 per period), and the government will levy a tax of 50% on the profits of the corporate venture.

Please calculate the following:

(a) The accounting income statements for each period.
(b) The financial cash-flow statements for each period.
(c) The present value of flows to the lender (VD_0).
(d) The present value of flows to you (VE_0).
(e) The appropriate discount rate to apply to the total cash flows to all capital suppliers (kf). [This problem has been designed so that all discount rates (required rates of return) are constant across time.]
(f) The present value of the total cash flows to all capital suppliers (VF_0). You should, of course, cross-check this to make certain it equals $VE_0 + VD_0$.
(g) Suppose that you wished to sell your equity in the firm immediately after you withdrew the cash available to you at t_2. How much do you think you could get for your equity right then, assuming an efficient capital market?
(h) What is the cost of debt capital to the firm (kd^*)?
(i) Use the cost of capital to the firm (kf^*) to calculate VF_0 and VF_2 by discounting the correct financial cash flows (assume the t_2 dividend has already been received).
(j) Calculate VD_0 and VD_2 using kd^*. Subtract VD_2 from VF_2 and compare with your answer to (g).
(k) Suppose that you personally (independently of the firm—i.e., the firm still borrows \$2798.10 at t_0) can borrow money at 12% per period,

and there is no personal income tax. What is the maximum amount of money that *you* could borrow at t_0 based solely on the strength of this investment? Demonstrate your ability to repay this loan.

(l) If you choose to do no personal borrowing, but instead accept the original premise to invest all cash you get from the firm in the capital market at 12% per period, what will be your terminal wealth at t_5? What is the present value of this to you at t_0? To what is this t_0 value equal? Why must this be so?

4. At t_0 the Sixper Corporation is expected to continue operating through the next six time periods. The capital market holds the following expectations about the Sixper Corporation:

1. At each time point for the next five, the following investment cash outlays (IVS flows) are expected:

t_1	t_2	t_3	t_4	t_5
$2136.20	$4736.05	$8023.17	$1003.92	$524.00

The investment amounts will be depreciated by the straight-line method over the remaining life of the corporation. (For example, the t_1 investment's contribution to each of t_2 through t_6 depreciation expenses is expected to be $2136.20/5 = $427.24, and so forth for the other investment outlays.) Depreciation expenses are deductible for tax purposes, and Sixper is subject to a corporate income tax rate of 52%. The corporation's assets have no book value at t_0, although its real assets at t_0 are still economically productive. At t_6 Sixper's real assets are expected to have no market value.

2. Sixper's existing t_0 assets, its investment outlays, and its operating expenditures are expected to generate cash receipts ($RCPT) at each time point for the next six as follows:

t_1	t_2	t_3	t_4	t_5	t_6
$89,763.28	$150,489.17	$22,987.66	$56,492.08	$68,550.94	$94,576.77

Cash operating expenditures ($EXPT) are expected to be 60% of cash receipts.

3. Sixper is expected to engage in the following financing actions: (a) new debt issues will be floated at t_1, t_2, and t_3 in the amounts of $1000.00, $2000.00, and $4000.00, respectively; (b) new equity issues will be floated at t_1 and t_3 in the amounts of $1000.00 and $4023.17, respectively; (c) the balance of financing needs will be made up by cash retentions, as necessary at each time point.

4. The interest and principal payment expectations (including new debt issues) at each time point are as follows:

	t_1	t_2	t_3	t_4	t_5	t_6
Interest (I)	$1525.75	$1335.57	$814.13	$1056.94	$ 873.94	$ 559.00
Principal (PP)	$3377.27	$8518.02	$964.81	$2287.50	$3936.83	$6987.47

Interest payments by Sixper are deductible for tax purposes. The capital market has examined the riskiness of the expected net cash flows to debt suppliers of Sixper, and has decided that a required rate of return of 8% is appropriate for all periods.

5. The capital market has also decided that the riskiness of equity suppliers' net cash-flow expectations deserves a required rate of 29% for all periods.

Please calculate the following:

(a) Financial cash-flow statements for each time point, t_1 through t_6.

(b) The values of debt and equity claims, and total corporate value at each time point, t_0 through t_5.

(c) $kd*$, kf, and $kf*$ for periods p_1 through p_6.

(d) To verify the above, total corporate value of Sixper using the weighted-average cost of capital, $kf*$, for each time point, t_0 through t_5.

(e) The value of debt at each time point, using the cost of debt, $kd*$.

(f) The returns *of* and *on* capital for both equity and debt suppliers, across the expected lifetime of Sixper.

(g) The values of the "new" and "old" debt suppliers' claims at each time point, t_0 through t_5, and the returns *of* and *on* capital for each across the expected life of Sixper.

(h) The same as (g), but for equity suppliers.

Please answer the following questions about Sixper:

(i) Suppose that Sixper were to make a mistake at t_2 and retain more cash than necessary for financing that time point's investment outlay. Would there be any effect on Sixper's value(s)? If so, what, and why?

(j) Suppose that Sixper intended using an accelerated depreciation technique such as sum-of-the-years' digits instead of straight line. Would you expect there to be any effect on Sixper's value(s)? If so, what, and why?

(k) Chances are that your calculations have shown Sixper's values as being expected to change from one time point to the next? Why is this? Suppose that Sixper was examined as time actually passed *between time points*, and we saw its values change between time points. Are the reasons the same? If not, discuss how the two situations differ.

5. The Perpetual Machine Corporation (PMC) expects to experience cash receipts ($RCPT) at the next time point of $207,698.64. PMC's cash expenditures ($EXPT) are expected always to constitute 50% of $RCPT. It is subject to a corporate income tax rate of 52%. Interest and depreciation

expenses are deductible for income tax purposes. PMC has no foreseeable termination date, and the market sees no reason to expect any period's operations to differ from any other's (as expectations). PMC has a debt claim outstanding which is expected to pay \$9113.51 interest (I) per period with no termination date, although PMC could retire any or all of the debt issue should it so choose. In order to generate the above expectations, PMC must plan to invest \$12,461.03 (IVS) in operating assets at each time point (it has been committing this amount of IVS per period for a very long time). Finally, the capital market has assigned required rates of 10% to PMC's debt and 26% to PMC's equity claims. These also are constant across future time periods.

(a) Calculate an expected FCF statement for PMC at the next time point.

(b) Comment on those for future time points.

(c) Calculate VF_0, VE_0, VD_0, kf, kf^*, and kd^* for PMC.

(d) Calculate VF_1, VE_1, and VD_1 for PMC, and comment.

(e) Return to your FCF statement in (a). Is that the only possible FCF statement that PMC could have? If there are any others, discuss what they could look like.

References for Section II

One of the predecessor discussions to the corporate cash-flow model of this chapter is found in: Diran Bodenhorn, "A Cash Flow Concept of Profit," *Journal of Finance* (March 1964); Bodenhorn addresses an all-equity situation and draws comparisons to the standard accounting model. Another elaboration of some of these concepts appears in: Robert K. Jaedicke and Robert T. Sprouse, *Accounting Flows: Income, Funds, and Cash* (Englewood Cliffs, N.J.: Prentice-Hall, Inc., 1965).

The main ideas behind the valuation of corporate claims were probably first stated in: John Burr Williams, *The Theory of Investment Value* (Cambridge, Mass.: Harvard University Press, 1938). For further discussions and extensions of the theory of corporate value, see: Charles Haley and Lawrence Schall, *The Theory of Financial Decisions* (New York: McGraw-Hill Book Company, 1973) and Eugene F. Fama and Merton H. Miller, *The Theory of Finance* (New York: Holt, Rinehart and Winston, Inc., 1972).

An excellent reference covering both the theoretical and empirical dimensions of capital market efficiency and pricing processes is: James Lorie and Richard Brealey, *Modern Developments in Investment Management* (New York: Praeger Publishers, Inc., 1972). See especially the article by Eugene Fama, "Efficient Capital Markets: A Review of Theory and Empirical Work" [originally published in *Journal of Finance* (May 1970)].

For some evidence on the effect of specific corporate factors on value, see: Burton G. Malkiel, "Equity Yields, Growth, and the Structure of Share Prices," *American Economic Review* (December 1963).

PART TWO

THE THEORY OF CORPORATE FINANCIAL DECISION MAKING

In Part One we studied the theory of financial and capital markets, corporate financial cash flows, and the theory of valuation in corporate finance. With these concepts as background, we are now ready to begin Part Two.

CORPORATE FINANCIAL DECISION MAKING

In Part One we saw that corporations and capital market participants may periodically make various decisions. They decide about their financial resource allocation or consumption patterns across time, about whether or not to take part in investments, about time patterns of cash disbursements to and cash acquisitions from capital suppliers, and about the proportions of capital claims held by various types of capital suppliers. When we studied corporate valuation in Section II, all these decisions had already been made by the companies we examined. They had raised capital, made investments, and planned for more investing, cash distribution amounts, and new capital flotations. All we wanted to do in Section II was value an existing set of future cash-flow expectations for a corporation. We did not really question the decisions that resulted in those cash-flow expectations. Now we shall begin to do so.

The very first step in studying the theory of corporate financial decisions must be to specify the purpose of those decisions. What should corporate financial managers be trying to do when they take financial actions of the type we have mentioned? We propose (and will assume) that *corporate financial decision making tries to maximize the present wealth of the company's current equity suppliers.* That is, when a corporation makes a financial decision at time point t_0, we know that the decision will probably affect cash flows well into the future. It may involve such things as making an investment at t_1, raising new capital at t_3, or even liquidating the company at some future time point. But, regardless of when the cash-flow effects are expected to take place, we assume that the guiding purpose behind the financial decisions made at t_0 is the maximization of the present wealth of the people who own the equity claims on the firm at t_0.

Why do we choose this as the purpose of financial decision making? Why not some other goal, such as increasing the total value of the company, or maximizing the salary of the financial decision maker, or even improving the public image of the corporation by undertaking socially desirable activities? Each of these alternatives is possible; we can find examples of each in real companies. Why do we reject them in favor of maximizing the present wealth of current shareholders?*

There are two basic reasons for choosing this as the goal of financial management in our theory. The first line of argument has an economic base, related to property rights. The second defends this particular goal in terms of actions which are sometimes taken by real-world financial managers and which seem to deviate from shareholder-wealth-maximization objectives.

First, present wealth maximization, as we saw in Section I, guarantees any capital-market participant the opportunity to maximize her or his satisfaction (utility) across time, regardless of that participant's unique preferences for time-specified consumption. If we wish to make any particular group of people as happy as possible, we should, logically, attempt to maximize their present wealths. But why currently existing shareholders? Why not debt suppliers? Or tax collectors? Or financial managers? The reason is that currently existing equity suppliers or shareholders are, in a legal sense, the *owners* of the corporation. All other parties, including suppliers of debt capital, must be given their contractual due before equity suppliers, as the residual claimants, gets whatever is left. So, short of breaking the law, servicing the interests of equity suppliers implies also having serviced all other operating and capital claims. The other claimants, however, have contracts and laws protecting them. Equity suppliers are similarly protected by the wealth maximization assumption. It is this normative standard that is the equity suppliers' "contract."

This brings us to our second line of argument. Do financial managers really attempt to maximize shareholder wealth, or rather, at the expense of shareholder wealth do they have other goals, such as maximizing their own

*The most direct—and technical—answer to these questions is that maximizing the present wealth of current equity suppliers is comparable to the profit-maximization assumption made by economists when they describe a company in microeconomic theory. Although we will not take the space here to demonstrate the point rigorously, you can probably intuit from your recollections of microeconomics that economic profit maximization is, for a single-time-point world under conditions of certainty, the equivalent of our shareholder wealth maximization.

wealth, or perhaps, as a matter of degree, shifting just a dollop of share-holder wealth to themselves?[†] And, if so, should we not recognize this in our theory?

Ideally, every corporate manager, including the financial manager, should have his or her performance judged by the company's board of directors, who, as the legal representatives of the currently existing shareholders, have the power to retain or terminate management personnel. Thus, in an ideal world, it is reasonable that managers would be concerned with keeping shareholders happy (by maximizing their wealth), because if management did not, it would be fired by the board. It can be argued, however, that in the real world, the separation of corporate control from equity ownership caused by the wide dispersal of those claims in large modern corporations changes decision-making priorities. Boards may be less responsive to a dispersed set of equity claimants. The absence of an effective representation of shareholders may decrease the pressure on managers to be guided by the interests of shareholders. And when the control of a company is insulated from its ownership, managers may be tempted to deviate from shareholder wealth maximization.

Academicians continue to study and debate the issue of managerial behavior in terms of shareholder interests, and have reached no resolution. Evidence can be cited to support several viewpoints. But we must remember that our purpose is to construct a basic theory of corporate finance (and financial management) that is realistic. Its realism must include the essential characteristics of actual markets, and at the same time be able to yield unambiguous, measurable predictions about the impacts of various financial decisions. The shareholder wealth maximization assumption, as we shall discover in this and following chapters, allows us to do that.

Specifically, this assumption will allow us to identify rather precisely the opportunity costs associated with financial decisions that deviate from shareholder wealth maximization as an objective. Further, should the future eventually resolve the question in favor of some other managerial goal, the wealth maximization-based theory could easily be modified and would serve as a valuable standard of comparison to other views of corporate finance.

In summary, therefore, we adopt the shareholder wealth maximization standard for corporate decision making for two basic reasons: First, it is an eco-

[†]In addition, there are a number of ways in which management may also act so as to decrease shareholder wealth without necessarily increasing its own wealth. These would include various amenities and perquisites (for example, company aircraft and plush boardrooms) which increase managerial utility if not wealth. Another class of choices would involve charitable donations, discretionary protection afforded the environment, and other public service activities which may build corporate images more than corporate sales. And, of course, even this list far from exhausts the possible motivations for managerial behavior, which may conflict to some degree with shareholder wealth maximization.

nomically and legally sound criterion resulting in equity (literally and figuratively) for shareholders. Second, it is as realistic as any alternative goal while having the important virtue of allowing our theory to give logical, unambiguous predictions and providing a measure of the costs of alternative behavior. Thus, we shall proceed with the maximization of shareholders' present wealth as the fundamental purpose of corporate financial decision making.

From the standpoint of continuing to develop the theory of corporate finance, our job has now become clearer: We must discover the effects various corporate financial decisions can have on shareholder present wealth. Our method of analyzing these decisions will involve nothing more than the basic ideas that we have already developed about capital markets and corporate valuation in the first part of this book.

We can think of corporate financial decisions as fitting into two general categories: investment decisions and financing decisions. Investment decisions have to do with the acquisition, maintenance, and divestment of real operating assets of the corporation.‡ We shall deal with the theory of corporate investment decisions in Section V. Corporate financing decisions in our theory are themselves separable into two categories: the *capital structure decision,* which we will address in this section, and the *capital acquisition and disbursement decision.* The theory of capital acquisition and disbursement examines how shareholder present wealth is affected by various time patterns of disbursements of cash to and acquisitions of cash from all classes of capital suppliers. We will explore such decisions in Section IV.

‡See footnote 5 in Chapter 7 (p. 108) regarding the conceptual treatment of maintenance expenditures.

The Theory of Capital Structure

This section is concerned with the theory of capital structure. Here we wish to discover how shareholder wealth is affected by the corporation's decision as to the *mix or proportion of debt and equity claims outstanding against its future cash flows.* Corporate capital structure is simply the relative value of debt versus equity claims in the financing of a company.* Because corporations can alter the proportions of debt and equity in their capital structure, we are interested in the shareholder wealth effects, if any, of this financing decision. The three chapters in this section will give us an introduction to the basic concepts and relationships important to the capital structure decision (Chapter 8), illustrate the basic economics of how capital structure influences shareholder wealth (Chapter 9), and treat more realistic situations (Chapter 10 and Conclusion to Section III).

*We shall deal with only these two general types of capital claims, again leaving the extensions and elaborations of these basic ideas to texts concerned with more complex applications.

Capital Structure and Risk

INTRODUC-
TION TO
CAPITAL
STRUCTURE
In all of our examples so far, companies' capital structures were already decided. The financial decision as to the proportion of capital value claimed by equity, VE_T/VF_T, and that claimed by debt, VD_T/VF_T, was already contained in the cash-flow expectations of the firms. Further, these proportions were constant for each time period (you can, if you wish, check back to Section II to verify this). As a result, we are now able to value an existing capital structure, but we have not yet learned how to judge the effect of any particular capital structure or the effect of *changing* the capital structure of a corporation. That will be our task this section.

We shall develop the theory of capital structure and all other financial decisions under what economists call *ceteris paribus* conditions. This means that when we examine capital structure decisions we shall hold constant the effects of all other financial decisions that the corporation could make. Since investment and capital acquisition/disbursement decisions may also affect shareholder wealth, if we allowed those effects to appear along with capital structure effects, we might find it difficult to see which action is responsible for each part of any total effect. By isolating the capital structure decision, we can be sure that whatever changes show up in shareholder present wealth are due exclusively to the capital structure decision that has taken place.

You have probably gathered from the discussion so far that capital structure refers specifically to the value proportion of debt claims and equity claims on a corporation's total value:

$$\text{capital structure is given by } \frac{VD_T}{VF_T} \text{ and } \frac{VE_T}{VF_T}$$

But remember that

$$VF_T = VD_T + VE_T$$

and, therefore,

$$VE_T = VF_T - VD_T$$

We can substitute this way of looking at VE_T into equity's capital structure proportion:

$$\frac{VE_T}{VF_T} = \frac{VF_T - VD_T}{VF_T}$$

Expanding, we have

$$\frac{VE_T}{VF_T} = \frac{VF_T}{VF_T} - \frac{VD_T}{VF_T}$$

and reducing, we get

$$\frac{VE_T}{VF_T} = 1 - \frac{VD_T}{VF_T}$$

so that capital structure is also given by VD_T/VF_T and $1 - (VD_T/VF_T)$. In words, this tells us that the proportion of debt to total value is sufficient to describe capital structure since equity's proportion is merely $1 - (VD_T/VF_T)$. All we are really saying is that since the two claims must constitute 100% of the corporation's value, if debt constitutes some percentage, equity must constitute 100% minus debt's percentage.[1] Hence, in order to specify the capital structure of a corporation at time T, all we need to know is VD_T/VF_T. And equity's proportion will merely be the complement of that ratio. Since VD_T/VF_T is a somewhat awkward piece of notation, we shall simplify it a bit by letting the lowercase Greek letter theta (θ) stand for the ratio of VD to VF (the capital structure of the corporation). Thus, from now on

$$\theta_T = \frac{VD_T}{VF_T}$$

We shall characterize a firm's capital structure as being θ_T. Specifically, debt's proportion of VF_T is θ_T, equity's is $1 - \theta_T$, and θ_T will always have a value in the range of zero to 1.

Now we are ready to begin developing the theory of capital structure. Perhaps the first question that we should address is why we want to study capital structure at all. What is there about the capital structure decision that might possibly have an effect on shareholder wealth? Suppose we are considering a firm that has an existing capital structure (θ_0 and expectations for all other θ_T's are known, as they would be for any of our Section II companies). If we were to alter the capital structure of the firm at t_0, would this have any effect on the present wealth of the company's shareholders? For example, suppose that without altering any other financial decision (the *ceteris paribus* condition, you recall) we were to issue a debt claim at t_0 and at the same time

---

[1] Of course, it is also true that debt's percentage equals 100% minus equity's percentage. However, to avoid unnecessary complications or confusion, our convention is to specify capital structure using only the proportion of value claimed by debt.

give the dollar inflow from that debt issue to equity suppliers.[2] The θ_0 in this situation would probably increase, since we have increased the debt claim on future cash flows, and thus capital structure would have changed. But what about the effect, if any, on equity suppliers' present wealth?

Two things have happened to equity suppliers. First, they have received a t_0 cash payment (the dollar proceeds of the debt issue) that they would not have gotten if capital structure had not been altered. That would increase their present wealth. But something else has also happened. The sizes of the *higher-priority* claims (debt) on corporate cash flows in the future have increased, also because of the new debt issue. This means that the market value of equity's *residual* claim on future corporate cash flows must now be valued

[2]Our cash-flow diagram could be used to show this action as the cash flow from NDC to CDE:

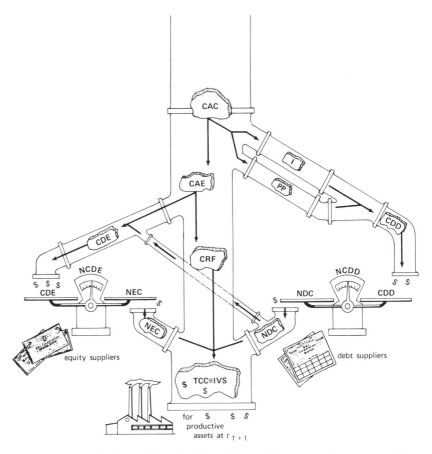

The reverse action, issuing equity and retiring debt, would appear as the same type of flow, going from NEC to CDE.

lower than it was before capital structure was changed.[3] That would decrease equity suppliers' present wealth.

So a change in capital structure of the sort we have just described could easily have *some* effect on shareholder present wealth. But because the effects include both an increase (t_0 cash payment) and a decrease (t_0 market value decrease), we are not sure whether the net effect of the capital structure change on shareholder wealth is positive, negative, or, perhaps, even zero.

If you think about this illustration for a moment, you can see that the real difficulty in discovering the effect of a capital structure change on shareholder wealth is in saying exactly what happens to the market price of equity at t_0 when the θ_0 change takes place. We know exactly the dollar amount of the t_0 cash payment to equity caused by the capital structure alteration: it is the proceeds of the debt issue. Whatever amount of debt capital we raised went directly to equityholders. What we do not know is how much the market price of equity decreased in reaction to the larger higher-priority claim on future cash flows.[4]

We do know, however, where to turn for the answer: the price setting authority itself, the capital market. The price change in equity due to the capital structure alteration is, of course, decided by the capital market. The effect on shareholder present wealth is dependent on how the capital market views the changes in future cash-flow expectations to equity suppliers caused by the change in θ. We know that the capital market is interested in only the size, risk, and timing of expected future cash flows. If we can discover the effects of a capital structure change on the size, risk, and timing of future cash-flow expectations, we can combine that information with what we already know about the pricing mechanism of an efficient capital market and be able to know exactly what the present wealth effects of capital structure changes are. The rest of this section will be devoted to doing just that.

The discussion that follows on the next several pages will probably seem tedious and even frustrating the first time you read it. Our approach will be to attack the question of capital structure wealth effects from the basis of valuation developed in the previous sections. This will take us down several paths, which appear initially to be of questionable value to the problem at hand and only vaguely related to each other. Before very long, however, the paths will merge into a quite coherent group of ideas about capital structure and wealth, and the groundwork that we have laid will prove its usefulness. So, please bear with us for the next few sections of the chapter; the eventual insights into capital structure will soon prove worth the effort.

---

[3]This must be true unless the residual claim has also become less risky. As we shall see shortly, that would be impossible.

[4]The same difficulty exists for a change in the opposite direction in θ. If we issued equity and retired debt, we would know the cash t_0 payment by equity suppliers, but would not know the exact increase in equity market price due to the lower amount of the higher-priority claim on future cash flows.

CAPITAL STRUCTURE AND RISK

We are interested in market-price reactions to capital structure changes. We know that market prices are a function of future cash-flow expectations and rates of return required by capital suppliers. As we shall see, discovering the effect on the size and timing of cash-flow expectations is not very difficult. If the overall corporate cash-flow expectations are known, cash flows to capital suppliers can be found quite easily. That merely involves splitting up the available cash consistent with debt's new priority claim expectation. Whatever is left is available to equity. Then the existing capital acquisition/disbursement policy is applied, and the new CDE and NCDE expectations result. We shall work through numerical examples of this process shortly.

But the real problem is how those new cash-flow expectations are *valued*. From our work in Section II you know that we need an important piece of additional information; we need the new required rates for equity suppliers. And from our Section I discussions you also know that the required rates will be a function of the riskiness of the new cash-flow expectations. Thus, our goal now becomes very specific: we must find the relationship between capital structure and required rates of return to capital suppliers. Once we have that information, finding shareholder present wealth effects will be a simple mechanical calculation. We shall apply new required rates to new cash-flow expectations in order to find market value, and we shall add that value to the cash distribution received or given as part of the capital structure change. The result will be the new t_0 shareholder wealth.

We are now ready to begin investigating the relationship between capital structure and required rates of return. Whatever the relationship is, it must operate through changes in the riskiness of future cash flows caused by the changes in θ. In order to isolate *equity* wealth effects, we are, of course, primarily interested in the relationship between ke and θ. But we shall find that it is also worth the effort to study the relationships between θ and other required rates, kd and kf, and their attendant capital costs, kd^* and kf^*. If we can manage to understand the entire spectrum of capital structure effects on capital-market rates, we will have advanced our theory significantly.

As a first step we can review what we already know about the risk characteristics of capital claims on a corporation's cash flow. Section II showed that when we split a risky overall corporate cash-flow expectation into two parts, a debt expectation with a higher-priority claim and an equity expectation with a residual claim, the risk of the overall stream was shared unequally by the two capital claims. The higher-priority debt claim's risk, portrayed by the level of kd, was always less than the residual claim's risk shown by ke. For a given capital structure, ke is always greater than kd. Equity is riskier than debt. If we were to plot this statement on a graph, it might appear as Figure 8.1, where required rates of return are plotted on the vertical axis and the level of θ on the horizontal axis. We have used the actual required rates and θ of our two-period firm from Chapter 6 to illustrate this.

But what happens when θ is altered? We know that ke must still be

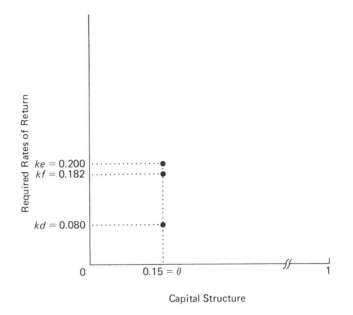

FIGURE 8.1   Capital Structure and required rates for our two-period firm

greater than kd, but can we say anything more than that? As a matter of fact, we *can* make a number of general statements about the behavior of required rates as θ changes.

***ke* AND θ**   First let us consider ke. As θ is increased above an existing level by substituting debt for equity in the capital structure, our cash-flow knowledge tells us that the higher-priority claims against corporate cash flows increase. Whatever risk is contained in the total cash available to service capital claims will therefore be even more disproportionately shared by equity since its claims are residual to the now-larger higher-priority claims of debt. Given a risky CAC expectation, the now higher CDD claim causes equity's residual cash-flow expectation to be more risky than it was before θ was raised. Generally then, *ke must increase as θ increases.* Holding all other financial decisions constant, the risk of the equity claim increases as capital structure shifts to higher debt levels. θ and ke are positively related.

***kd* AND θ**   How about kd? Is it affected by capital structure changes? Although the relationship might not be as intuitively straightforward as that for equity, kd also generally increases as θ increases. Think about the risk of a debt claim. When a corporation has very little debt in its capital structure, the debt claim probably constitutes only a small part of the expected cash available to service all capital claims at any time point. Since debt has the higher-priority claim on those cash flows, its risk is less than the risk of the total flow. Since at low levels of θ, debt needs only a small portion of whatever becomes available, its expectations are quite likely to be met even though the CAC flow is risky.

But as θ increases, the proportion of CAC claimed by debt also increases, and it becomes more likely that debt's actual cash return could differ from its expectation. Since the *actual* CAC realized could be less than that *expected*, it is possible that debt's actual cash flow (which has first claim on CAC) might also be less than expected. The larger the proportion of expected CAC claimed by debt, the more likely it is that even a *small* shortfall in actual CAC from expected CAC would cause debt's actual cash flow to be less than debt suppliers expect. Debt becomes more risky as θ increases because its priority claim constitutes a larger proportion of the risky overall cash flow. kd, then, *also increases as θ increases.*[5]

We can be even more specific about the relationship between kd and θ. Suppose that we have a corporation with no debt in its capital structure. We call such a firm unlevered. ("Leverage" is a term often used to mean the amount of debt in a company's capital structure; θ can be thought of as the "leverage ratio."[6]) This company, of course, has no kd because it has no debt outstanding. The unlevered corporation is such a convenient theoretical reference point that we reserve a special notation for its required rate of return, ku.

An unlevered firm has no debt, so it must be entirely financed by equity, and its $\theta = 0$ since VD $= 0$. *For an unlevered firm, $ku = ke = kf$.* The required return on equity must be the same as the overall or weighted-average required rate because equity is the whole of the firm's financing. The situation of an unlevered firm can be seen in Figure 8.2. Notice that when the firm is unlevered, $\theta = 0$ and $ku = ke = kf$ appears as a point on the vertical axis.

But what does all this have to tell us about the relationship between kd and θ? Suppose now that the unlevered firm issues a very tiny amount of debt and distributes the proceeds to equity. What is kd likely to be for this very tiny θ? From our discussions above, the risk of that debt claim will be very low. If the amount of debt issued is extremely tiny, kd will probably be very close to the risk-free required rate we used in introducing financial markets in Chapter 1. We call this rate i. It appears on the vertical axis of Figure 8.2 well below the point $ku = ke = kf$. (Since this latter rate is determined by operating risks of the corporation which is not risk-free, it must

---

[5]In the terminology of Appendix II.D, as θ increases the chances increase that debt's actual return will be less than its promised return; therefore, the risk of the debt claim increases as θ increases.

[6]In most English-speaking countries more recently associated with England than is the United States, the term "gearing" is used in lieu of "leverage" to identify precisely the same concept.

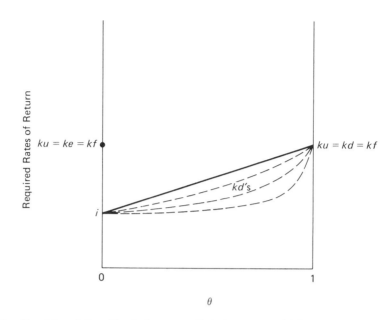

FIGURE 8.2   Possible relationships between capital structure and *kd*.

necessarily be larger than *i*.) And at miniscule levels of θ, *kd*, representing miniscule risk, must be close to *i*, the risk-free rate.

When θ is increased further, however, we know that *kd* will also increase. Suppose that we increase θ all the way to its upper limit. That would be $\theta = 1$, because the maximum $\theta = VD/VF$ must occur when $VD = VF$. With $\theta = 1$, the corporation would be totally financed by debt. What would *kd* be for a company like this? From Chapter 5 we know that debt now claims the entire cash flow of the company, since there is no equity claim. How risky is debt that claims a company's total cash flow? *It is exactly as risky as the equity claim was when the firm was unlevered.* When equity was the only claim, the risk of that claim required a rate of $ku = ke = kf$. Now that debt is the only claim, its risk indicates that *kd* must have increased all the way from *i* up to *ku* as θ went from 0 to 1.[7]

kd must increase from *i*, the risk-free rate, up to *ku*, the all-equity rate, as θ goes from 0 to 1. One such relationship is shown as the solid straight line from *i* at $\theta = 0$ to $ku = kd = kf$ at $\theta = 1$ in Figure 8.2. Since we only know the beginning and ending points for the line (*kd* = *i* when $\theta = 0$, and *kd* = *ku* when $\theta = 1$) and that *kd* must continually increase with θ, there

---

[7]If the reasons why *kd* = *ku* at $\theta = 1$ puzzle you, it might help to consider the argument that an all-debt firm is not really any different from an all-equity firm. Both are merely single capital-claim organizations. The debt in a $\theta = 1$ firm also has, in effect, a residual claim.

are many possible shapes to the relationship between kd and θ. A few others are shown as dashed lines in Figure 8.2. All are allowable.[8]

kf AND θ

We now know that the required return on equity and the required return on debt capital both increase as we increase the ratio of debt to the total value of the firm, assuming that we do not change any other financial decision the company has made. But how about the value-weighted average of ke and kd, kf? How does this overall required rate of return for the firm, kf, react to changes in θ?

Since kf depends on both ke and kd, and since they both increase with θ, doesn't that mean that kf also increases with θ? No, not necessarily. Remember that kf is a weighted average of ke and kd and lies somewhere between the two. As we increase θ, kd and ke each increase as we just discovered: kd moves upward from i toward ku; ke simply moves upward from ku. Figure 8.3 illustrates these general relationships. But as θ increases, some other things also change. VD goes up and VE goes down, thus increasing the weight applied to the lower required return of debt and decreasing the weight applied to the higher equity return in the calculation of kf. Mathematically, it is entirely possible that kf could increase, decrease, or even remain unchanged as θ increases. Figure 8.3 shows three such possibilities for kf, each of which necessarily begins at ku when $\theta = 0$ and ends at ku when $\theta = 1$, for the reasons we have discussed previously.

[8] There are no dashed lines wholly or partially above the straight line from i (at $\theta = 0$) to ku (at $\theta = 1$) in Figure 8.2. While the straight line depicts an allowable relationship between kd and θ, no allowable relationship can exist at any point above that line. Given that kd must equal ku at $\theta = 1$, any relationship that ventures above the straight line must eventually come back to meet the line. This would mean that at some level of θ the risk added by the next dollar of debt substituted for equity would be strictly less than the risk added by the immediately preceding dollar of debt. Realistically viewed, each additional dollar of debt *must* increase the overall risk of debt by at least as much as the preceding dollar did, so relationships that do not exhibit this characteristic over the entire range of $0 \leq \theta \leq 1$ are not allowed. This condition, of course, is also a requirement for any possible $kd \longleftrightarrow \theta$ relationship that lies wholly on or below the straight line from i (at $\theta = 0$) to ku (at $\theta = 1$).

For those of you familiar with differential calculus, the mathematical statement of the conditions that are necessary and sufficient to provide an allowable $kd \longleftrightarrow \theta$ relationship is as follows: f is an allowable function to describe this relationship if and only if for every $\theta' \in [0, 1]$:

$$\frac{df}{d\theta}(\theta') > 0$$

and

$$\frac{d^2 f}{d\theta^2}(\theta') \geq 0$$

In other words, the derivative of f at every point $\theta' \in [0, 1]$ must be greater than zero and the second derivative of f at every point $\theta' \in [0, 1]$ must be greater than or equal to zero.

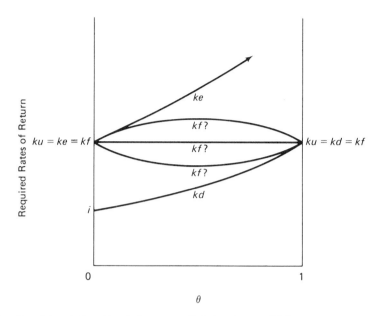

FIGURE 8.3   **Possible relationships between capital structure and** *kf*

From Section II we have the formula for calculating *kf* as a function of *kd* and *ke*:

$$kf = \frac{VD}{VF}kd + \frac{VE}{VF}ke$$

Using our θ notation, we get

$$kf = \theta kd + (1 - \theta)ke \qquad\qquad [8.1]^9$$

From just what we know so far, it would seem that *kf* could bear almost any relationship to θ. A glance at formula 8.1 shows that as θ increases, *kd*, which is lower than *kf*, gets more weight and *ke*, which is higher, gets less. Whether or not *kf* increases or decreases with θ thus depends on exactly how *kd* and *ke* react to capital structure changes.

Geometry and arithmetic have now taken us as far as they can in our pursuit of the relationship between *kf* and θ. There *is* a specific relationship between the two, but it is only accessible through the use of economics.

---

[9] This formula and the immediately preceding one are not time-subscripted. In our discussions of capital structure theory and decisions we shall assume that all θ_τ's for any corporation are the same across future time periods, and that if we choose to alter θ_0, we shall also choose to alter all other θ_τ's identically. The reason for this, as we shall see, is that there is nothing inherent in the mere passage of time that would indicate that capital structure should change. So, if there is a correct θ for a company at t_0, it will also be the correct θ at $t_1, t_2,$ and so on.

Analyzing graphs or performing algebraic manipulations in an economic vacuum will not do the job.

As we develop this relationship we shall also be answering our major question about the effect of the capital structure decision on shareholder wealth. Look back at formula 8.1. We already have a fairly good idea of how kd and θ relate to each other. Figure 8.2 shows several acceptable ways, any of which we can choose. If, then, we can find the relationship between kf and θ, we can also use formula 8.1 to find how ke is related to capital structure. As we saw earlier, it is a simple calculation from there to find shareholder wealth effects.

θ AND VF   This brings us to the final link in our chain of important capital structure relationships: that between θ and the total value of the firm, VF. From Section II we know that kf can be considered the overall required rate of return for the whole corporation. It is the rate appropriate for discounting the total net cash flows back to equal the total market value of the firm, VF, which, of course, equals VE plus VD. Our next major step forward in studying capital structure theory will be to specify the relationships among θ, kf, and VF.

How will adding VF to our investigation help us? Recall our original illustration of a capital structure change. We issue debt and give the resulting cash to equity suppliers. The value of the debt claims against the firm increases by the amount of cash we take in.[10] *If the value of the firm as a whole stays the same, then equity value must drop by exactly the amount of cash equity suppliers receive from the proceeds of the debt issue.* Thus, with VF remaining the same, *equity suppliers' present wealths would not have changed.* However, if VF *decreases*, VE must decrease by *more* than shareholders' cash receipts, and shareholders are thus worse off. And if VF *increases*, VE does not decrease as much as the cash amount that shareholders receive, and they are, therefore, better off. Algebraically:

1. Since $VF_0 = VE_0 + VD_0$, and if
2. Shareholder present wealth (PWE) before a θ change is VE_0, then
3. With an increase in θ, VD_0 increases by \$X (the cash taken in from debt suppliers), \$X flows to equity holders, and VE_0 decreases (ΔVE_0) by the net amount of \$X and the VF_0 change (ΔVF_0). Line 1 has now been altered as follows:
4. $(VF_0 + \Delta VF_0) = (VE_0 \underbrace{- \$X + \Delta VF_0}_{\Delta VE_0}) + (VD_0 \underbrace{+ \$X}_{\Delta VD_0})$.
5. Shareholder wealth after a θ change ($PWE_0 + \Delta PWE_0$) is the \$X received plus $VE_0 + \Delta VE_0$, or

$$PWE_0 + \Delta PWE_0 = \$X + (VE_0 + \Delta VE_0)$$
$$PWE_0 + \Delta PWE_0 = \$X + (VE_0 - \$X + \Delta VF_0)$$

[10]This point was developed in Chapter 7 in our discussion of the ongoing firm, and we shall re-demonstrate it later in this section.

and

$$PWE_0 + \Delta PWE_0 = VE_0 + \Delta VF_0$$

But originally

$$PWE_0 = VE_0$$

so

$$\Delta PWE_0 = \Delta VF_0$$

That is, *the change in shareholder wealth must equal the change in the value of the firm.*

Finally, we can conclude that as a result of a θ change:

6. If VF_0 increases (ΔVF_0 is larger than zero), then shareholder wealth will increase by that same amount; if VF_0 is unchanged (ΔVF_0 is equal to zero), then shareholder wealth will remain unchanged; and if VF_0 decreases (ΔVF_0 is smaller than zero), then shareholder wealth will decrease by that same amount.

Note that the conclusions in step 6 apply to any θ change, be it an increase or a decrease. Since the $X amounts canceled out in step 5, all that is left that really matters is the change in the value of the firm, all of which accrues, plus or minus, to the equity holders.

REVIEW We have discussed several ways of approaching capital structure theory. Although they probably appear quite distinct and discouragingly complex right now, we shall see shortly that all the approaches, shareholder wealth, required returns, and market valuations are closely related to each other and not nearly so complicated as this lengthy introduction might lead you to believe.

To review, we have seen one example of a *ceteris paribus* capital structure alteration consisting of substituting debt for equity financing. It produced:

1. Increased VD_0/VF_0, or θ_0.
2. Simultaneous changes in shareholder wealth equal to:
   a. A t_0 wealth increase equal to the amount of the debt flotation
   b. A t_0 wealth decrease equal to the necessary decrease in VE_0 because of the new higher-priority claim by debt suppliers on future cash flows.

Our introductory ideas about the size of the VE_0 decrease told us that a primary question to be answered is how the altered net cash-flow expectations to equity would be valued. Seeking that answer led us to consider the riskiness of ke and its relationship to θ, the capital structure. We saw that ke would generally increase above ku as θ increased above zero. Although that is valuable knowledge, it is not sufficient to specify exactly the ke or VE_0

changes. This realization, in turn, directed our attention to kd. kd is also positively related to θ, increasing from i when $\theta = 0$ to ku when $\theta = 1$. We then looked at kf and decided that it could be another way of approaching the capital structure effect on shareholder wealth. We saw that if both the $kf \leftrightarrow \theta$ and $kd \leftrightarrow \theta$ relationships are known, our familiar weighted-average formula can tell us the $ke \leftrightarrow \theta$ relationship.

Finally, we realized that information about how VF changes with θ alterations would also solve our problem, since the decrease in equity value would equal the known increase in debt value plus any change in VF. We can see that all of these approaches to capital structure must be interrelated theoretically since kf is the appropriate discount rate for obtaining VF; ke performs the same function relative to VE; and kf, ke, kd, and θ constitute all the component parts of our overall weighted-average required return formula.

If we can succeed in specifying any one of the relationships that we have identified, all the rest will be easy. We must now analyze the basic economics of a capital structure change to see how the capital market views this decision.

INTUITIONS ABOUT CAPITAL STRUCTURE THEORY

Probably the best way to begin thinking about the economics of capital structure theory is on an intuitive level. From what we already know about the capital market, we might be able to predict its reaction to a capital structure change. Since the changes in the total value of the firm seem to be the most straightforward candidates for answering the capital structure question, we can start by considering how the capital market might value this sum of capital claims when θ changes.

The capital market, of course, never actually computes VF. It is interested only in VE and VD as distinct claims on future cash flows. But there is no reason why capital-market participants could not hold both the equity and debt claims of a corporation at the same time. Suppose for the moment that they do; suppose a corporation has both equity and debt claims outstanding and that those claims are held by the same capital-market participants. For them, VF_0 is a very real amount. It is the value of all their holdings in the firm, all their combined claims on the future cash flows from the firm. How would those participants regard a change in the capital structure of the firm?

Suppose you are one of those participants (you hold all the debt and equity of a corporation) and the company announces that it plans to increase the proportion of debt in its capital structure without in any way altering its asset operations. As far as you are concerned, the θ change means that you pay the corporation some cash for a higher debt claim and then receive that same amount back as an equity cash distribution. So your t_0 cash position is unchanged. But how about your valuation of the firm now that its capital structure has been altered? Will it be higher, lower, or unchanged? If you are a capital-market participant of the variety we have been working with all along, your reaction will be consistent with our valuation formulas from Section II:

1. If the amounts of your cash-flow expectations are lower or their risks higher, or both, the total value that you assign to the firm will be lower. VD_0 increases, VF_0 decreases, and VE_0 decreases by *more* than the increase in VD_0.[11] The capital structure alteration has caused the future cash-flow expectation of the firm to change for the worse. Your present wealth has decreased.

2. If the amounts and risks of your total net cash-flow expectations are unchanged, you will value the firm in total exactly as you did before the capital structure alteration. VF_0 is constant and VE_0 decreases by *just* the amount that VD_0 increases. Part of your equity claim has been bought by part of your debt claim, but since the total of your cash-flow expectations and risks is unaffected, the total value you place on the claims remains unchanged, as does your present wealth.

3. If the amounts of your future cash-flow expectations are higher or their risks lower, or both, the total value that you place on the company will be higher. VF_0 increases, VD_0 increases, and VE_0 decreases by *less* than the amount of the VD_0 increase. Expectations have improved because of the capital structure alteration. Your present wealth has increased.

As you can see, the general point of these three statements is that the importance of capital structure, if any, depends on what happens to future cash-flow expectations of the whole company as θ is altered. If expectations change for the better, equityholder present wealth increases; if expectations worsen, equityholders lose present wealth. If total corporate future cash-flow expectations are unaffected by a change in capital structure, equityholder present wealth is also unaffected.

Remember, we are still assuming that the same participants hold all the equity and debt of a corporation. As θ increases, t_0 cash goes from debt to equity as payment for the larger higher-priority claim. VD_0 increases by that amount. VE_0 decreases because of the larger higher-priority claim. The decrease in VE_0 will be less than the t_0 cash payment received if *overall* corporate cash-flow expectations have improved due to the θ change. Equity, being the residual claimant, gets all the net benefits: an increase in shareholders' present wealth equal to the change in VF_0. If overall corporate expectations are unaffected by the θ change, VE_0 will fall by exactly the amount of the t_0 cash received. No benefits accrue from the capital structure alteration, and there is no change in shareholders' present wealth. If expectations worsen,

---

[11]$\Delta VE_0 = -(\Delta VD_0) + (\Delta VF_0)$; $-(\Delta VD_0)$ is equal to the cash you received, and since here ΔVF_0 is negative, you are worse off. Equity value has decreased more than debt increased.

VE_0 decreases by more than the t_0 cash received, and shareholders' present wealth again reaps the net change in VF_0, this time a decrease.[12]

If it is at all reasonable to think of the capital market as being made up of participants who own both the debt and the equity claims of corporations, we have come a large step closer to unraveling the question of capital structure. We still need to discover what effect, if any, capital structure alterations have on the future cash flows of the firm as a whole. Once we have decided that question, the calculation of total firm value, VF_0, merely involves applying the correct formula from Section II. And once the new VF_0 is known, the changes in VE_0 are simply arithmetic involving the relationship $VF_0 = VD_0 + VE_0$.

"Why," one might ask, "bother with VF_0 and total firm cash flows when what we are really interested in is VE_0 and equity cash-flow expectations? Would it not be more direct to question the equity flows themselves rather than deduce from total corporate valuations what the change in VE_0 is?"

Actually, there is a valid reason for our use of overall cash flows rather than equity alone. We saw earlier the difficulty in trying to work with equity expectations directly: the only thing we are now able to say about the change in riskiness of equity's claim is that it is positively related to θ. The larger higher-priority claim (more debt) definitely makes equity's cash-flow expectations more risky. But since we have not quantified a risk measure for equity, we cannot say more than this: ke will increase with a θ increase and decrease with a θ decrease. But how much the ke change will be, we do not know.

With total cash flows, however, we do not need to worry about how a capital structure alteration proportions the risk of overall flows between capital claims. All we need to know is whether the *sum* of the $NCDE_\tau$ and $NCDD_\tau$ expectations have changed in size, timing, or risk. As we shall soon see, this is a much easier question to answer.

THEORY OF CAPITAL STRUCTURE

We have talked long enough about the questions raised by capital structure. It is now time to begin answering them. The first thing we must do is make sure that our capital market behaves the way we described it in connection with our decision to concentrate our efforts on the $\theta \leftrightarrow VF_0$ relationship. You remember that this market must value the debt and equity of a corporation as if participants hold both simultaneously. This is not a terribly difficult task. As a matter of fact, all we need to do is to specify that *in the efficient capital market we have had since Section I, participants can borrow and lend money on the same terms as corporations.* Thus capital-market participants

---

[12]Again, we have been illustrating a capital structure change with an increase in θ. A decrease implies t_0 cash paid from equity to debt, a VD_0 decrease as debt is retired, and the question then becomes one of an increase in VE_0 greater than, equal to, or less than the dollars paid to debt. The answer, however, still depends in the same way on the nature of the changes, if any, in future corporate cash flows. The net change in shareholders' present wealth remains equal to the net change in VF_0.

in our theory face *individual kd* $\leftrightarrow \theta$ relationships that look just like those of a corporation. A capital-market participant can lever his personal portfolio of assets by borrowing money at t_0 in exactly the same way a corporation can. In addition, we shall continue to specify that our capital-market participants are not subject to personal income taxes.

Let us examine how the opportunity for individual participant borrowing and lending results in a capital market which behaves the way we require. Suppose that a company is thinking of increasing its θ by issuing debt and distributing the proceeds to equityholders. How will the market react to this action? How will the resulting capital claims be viewed (and valued) by market participants? Will the capital market attach a premium to the equity shares of the corporation because of the θ change? (Will VE_0 decrease by less than the cash distribution which equityholders receive from the proceeds of the debt issue?)

The answer to all these questions is that *participant (and therefore market) reaction to the θ change will depend on whether the corporate capital structure alteration gives something to participants which they could not have received without the corporate θ change.* Actual and potential equityholders now have the opportunity to alter their own *personal* θ's just as corporations do. They could, for example, have raised their personal θ's to the new corporate level merely by borrowing the same amount of money the corporation would have distributed as the proceeds of the debt issue. The θ would be personal rather than corporate, but the effective leverage and the cash position of the participant are the same. Similarly, the corporate θ change could be canceled in personal portfolios merely by using the cash inflow amount to buy the corporation's debt. Therefore, participants will attach no importance to a corporate θ change that can be duplicated (or canceled) in their personal portfolios unless something happens to corporate cash flows which is *not* duplicable in participants' own portfolios when their personal capital structures are altered.

The same argument holds for a corporate θ decrease. Equityholders could lower their own personal θ's by merely lending dollars appropriately in the capital market. The only reason for a wealth-changing reaction by the capital market to a corporate θ change would be if there is a unique effect of corporate capital structure changes on cash-flow expectations that is not attainable by individual participants through their own personal borrowing and lending.

So, because participants can borrow and lend on the same terms as corporations (corporate and individual $kd \leftrightarrow \theta$ relationships are identical), the market reacts to a corporate capital structure alteration just as if participants did hold both the debt and equity claims of a corporation: a wealth change will occur in response to a θ change only if something happens to overall corporate cash flows which cannot be produced by personal lending and borrowing.

The capital market is not in the habit of giving away something for nothing. If share prices are already based on the capabilities of participants to borrow and lend personally, and if corporate leveraging results in cash-flow expectations to equity suppliers no different than they could achieve by personal leveraging, then no corporate capital structure change can add anything of value to (or subtract anything of value from) the capital market. A debt issue or redemption that changes a firm's capital structure under these conditions would merely cause equity value to decrease by exactly as much as the cash that equity suppliers receive (the proceeds of the debt issue) or increase by exactly as much as the cash that equity suppliers pay (the amount of the debt redemption).

If, however, corporate debt does provide something in the way of cash-flow size, timing, or risk that capital-market participants cannot duplicate (even though they can borrow and lend like a corporation), then capital structure is an important consideration. If a corporate θ increase provides net benefits over and above what participants themselves could produce by altering their personal capital structures in the same way, we would expect to see equity prices adjust downward *less* than the amount of cash equity suppliers receive when debt is substituted for equity. Conversely, if such a corporate θ change is a net detriment, equity prices would decline *more* at t_0 than the amount of t_0 cash received. The reverse of these, of course, would apply to a decrease in the proportion of debt in a company's capital structure.

The only major question that we still need to answer is the effect of capital structure on overall corporate cash-flow expectations. Once we know that, all our remaining issues can easily be resolved by invoking our valuation relationships from Section II. How difficult will it be to settle this last question? Fortunately, our analysis of corporate financial cash flows in Chapter 5 will now produce a return on our investment. As we shall see, the effect of capital structure on overall corporate cash flows is especially easy to decipher in our financial cash flow (FCF) statement and diagram.

Chapter 9

Capital Structure
Theory—I

CAPITAL
STRUCTURE
THEORY
WITHOUT
INTEREST
DEDUCT-
IBILITY

We shall begin answering the question raised at the end of Chapter 8 by illustrating a condition in which overall corporate cash flows (and therefore shareholder wealth) are unaffected by corporate capital structure changes. To accomplish this we must alter one characteristic of corporations which has been part of our theory until now. This characteristic is *interest deductibility*. When we have completed this illustration, deductibility will be reinstated. For the moment, however, corporate interest payments will not be deductible for income tax purposes so that we can view θ changes which leave overall corporate cash flows unchanged. For this example, the absence of personal income taxes remains.

ONE-PERIOD
EXAMPLE
WITHOUT
DEDUCT-
IBILITY

As is our habit, we shall proceed cautiously, by first attacking a simple example. Suppose that in our capital market there is a corporation with the following characteristics:

1. It is a *one-period* firm, whose capital suppliers expect to claim a set of corporate cash flows at t_1, and none thereafter.

2. The firm is *unlevered*; it has no debt outstanding, having been 100% equity-financed. The capital market, in assessing the risk of the t_1 cash-flow expectations to the capital suppliers, has assigned a $ku = ke = kf$ of 20%.

3. The firm is subject to a corporate tax rate, τ, of 52%, but the tax laws have been amended so that interest payments, if any, are *not* deductible for tax purposes. This company, being unlevered, of course, has no interest payments.

4. The corporation's expected FCF statement for t_1 is as follows:

$RCPT	$10,000.00
$EXPT	5,102.00
GCFO	4,898.00
GTAX	2,546.96
NCFO	2,351.04
DTS	648.96
CAU	3,000.00
ITS	0.00
CAC	3,000.00
I	0.00
PP	0.00
CDD	0.00
NDC	0.00
NCDD	0.00
CAE	3,000.00
CRF	0.00
CDE	3,000.00
NEC	0.00
NCDE	3,000.00
TCC ≡ IVS	0.00

Notice that the interest tax subsidy (ITS) is zero. Since this company has no debt, it pays no interest or principal. Even if it did, however, there would be no ITS, since in this illustration interest is not deductible for tax purposes.

Calculating the value of this firm is simplicity itself. There is only one type of capital claim outstanding, equity. Its riskiness requires a 20% return. Therefore, the t_1 payment of $3000.00 has a t_0 value of

$$VE_0 = VU_0 = \frac{NCDE_1}{1+ke} = \frac{\$3000.00}{1.20} = \$2500.00$$

The value of the equity and of the entire corporation at t_0 is $2500. VU_0 indicates the value of the unlevered firm.

Now suppose that the corporation were to alter its capital structure at t_0 by issuing $900 of debt. The capital market looks at the riskiness of that debt claim and assigns a required return of 10%. kd is less than ku (20%), because the debt expectation at t_1 is both a priority claim and less than expected cash available. This means that debt suppliers will have an expectation of receiving $900 plus 10% of $900, or $90, at t_1. $NCDD_1$ now becomes $900 + $90, or $990.

But what happens to the $900 that the company takes in at t_0 as the proceeds of the debt issue? If the company were to keep it until t_1, we know from Section II that it would necessarily be altering its investment decision at t_0. In this chapter, however, we are holding investment decisions constant, so the $900 cash must be distributed to equity suppliers at t_0. In essence, the equity suppliers are selling for $900 at t_0 a $990 priority claim on their t_1 cash-flow expectation. This, of course, reduces the size and increases the risk of their t_1 cash flow. VE_0 will therefore drop below $2500. But how much below? From our previous discussions, you know that depends on what happens to overall corporate cash flows.

Let us look at those. With its new capital structure the firm's new FCF expectations for t_1 become

$RCPT	$10,000.00
$EXPT	5,102.00
GCFO	4,898.00
GTAX	2,546.96
NCFO	2,351.04
DTS	648.96
CAU	3,000.00
ITS	0.00
CAC	3,000.00
I	90.00
PP	900.00
CDD	990.00
NDC	0.00
NCDD	990.00
CAE	2,010.00
CRF	0.00
CDE	2,010.00
NEC	0.00
NCDE	2,010.00
TCC $\equiv$ IVS	0.00

Compare these expectations to those of the same firm at t_1 when it was unlevered. The operational flows, $RCPT, $EXPT, GCFO, GTAX, NCFO, DTS, and CAU, are the same. They must be unchanged if we have not altered the firm's investment or operating expectations. And these, in turn, remain unaltered since we assume that plant and equipment, labor, sales personnel, customers, suppliers, and so on, will all behave exactly as they would have, quite independent of the firm's capital structure.

ITS_1 remains zero since interest is not deductible. So *the overall cash flow for the corporation at t_1 is still $3000 and has the same risk as it had before capital structure was changed.* All we have done is split the $3000 overall flow into two parts: a priority claim of $990 to debt suppliers and a residual expectation of $2010 to equity. Nothing new has been added or subtracted from corporate cash flows due to the θ change. According to our previous discussion of the way the capital market works, the firm must therefore still be worth $2500 *in total* at t_0. Since debt is worth $900 ($= VD_0$), equity must now be worth $1600 ($= VE_0$).

By using the ability of capital-market participants to borrow just as corporations do, we can illustrate specifically why equity's market price must behave exactly the way we say it will. That is, VE_0 will fall from $2500 to $1600, its drop exactly matching the cash that equity suppliers receive at t_0 as the proceeds of the debt issue when capital structure is changed.

Suppose that the company we have been studying is still unlevered and that there are several other companies exactly like it in the capital market, all having a $VU_0 = \$2500$ and identical t_1 cash-flow expectations.[1] Now suppose that our company changes its capital structure the way we have described, but the resulting equity price after the change is something other than $1600. Let us say it is $1650. Now we shall show how the capital market recognizes that it has made a mistake, and corrects that mistake.

Assume that you are a capital-market participant thinking of buying some common stock. Specifically, you have $1650 cash at t_0 and are interested in the firms we have been talking about, both leveraged and unlevered. First you consider a leveraged firm, whose equity sells for $1650. This would give you t_1 cash-flow expectations of

$3000	CAC_1
− 90	I_1
−900	PP_1
$2010	$NCDE_1$

If you bought this leveraged equity for $1650, you would receive an expectation of $NCDE_1 = \$2010$ coming from an overall corporate cash flow of $3000 with a $990 priority claim.

Now consider the unlevered firms. They cost $2500. To buy one of them you could borrow $900 at t_0 for 10%. The market would let you do that if you gave it a priority (debt) claim of $990 on *your* t_1 expectations, just as the leveraged firm did. You will recall that as a participant in our capital market, you can lend and borrow on the same terms as corporations. If you bought an unlevered firm this way, your t_1 cash-flow expectations would be:

$3000	CAC_1
− 0	I_1
− 0	PP_1
$3000	$NCDE_1$
− 90	personal loan interest at t_1
−900	personal principal repayment at t_1
$2010	personal cash-flow expectation at t_1

This is identical to your t_1 expectations as an equityholder of the leveraged firm. But wait a moment. Let us review what you have done. You have $1650 at t_0; you borrowed $900 and bought the unlevered firm for $2500. This gave you a t_1 expectation personally identical to the leveraged equity. *But you have*

[1]This assumption is not a strict necessity, as we shall demonstrate shortly. The same price changes would take place in our capital market even without such firms. However, because we have not yet developed a quantified risk measure, their presence makes the illustration simpler.

$50 at t_0 left over. $1650 was yours to begin with, the $900 you borrowed gave you $2550, and you paid only $2500 for the unlevered firm. Had you bought the leveraged equity, your t_1 expectations would have been the same, but you would have no t_0 money left over, no $50 in your pocket.

Obviously you would always choose the unlevered firm over the leveraged firm. But so would all other capital-market participants. Nobody would pay $1650 for the leveraged equity when unlevered firms are selling for $2500 and personal borrowing is the same as corporate borrowing. With no bids, the leveraged equity price must fall. How much? By $50, to exactly $1600. At that price the leveraged equity costs the same as the unlevered equity with $900 of personal borrowing. That personal borrowing results in the same prior claim which exists on the cash flows of the leveraged firm.

If the leveraged company's equity sold for less than $1600, capital-market participants would bid its price back up to the $1600 cost of getting the same t_1 expectation through the unlevered equity and personal borrowing of $900. Thus, even if VE_0 of the levered firm starts out at a value different from $1600, it will very quickly return to be valued at exactly $1600 in our capital market, since the total value of the firm, levered or not, remains at $2500. Equity suppliers' present wealth thus has not been affected by the capital structure change. VE_0 before the change was $2500. When the debt claim was issued, equity suppliers got $900 at t_0, and the t_0 value of their claim dropped to $1600. So the sum of their t_0 cash inflow and the new VE_0 is $2500. They are exactly as well off as they were when the firm was unlevered. The capital structure alteration caused no change in the overall cash-flow expectations of the firm, and therefore equity suppliers are unaffected as to wealth. VF_0 is constant.

θ AND *ke* WITHOUT DEDUCT-IBILITY We now know that equity suppliers' present wealth is unaffected by a capital structure change for this firm. VE_0 drops by exactly the amount of cash that they receive from the debt flotation. We also know that the leveraged equity claim is now more risky. The capital market recognizes this by raising the return required by equity suppliers. Since we know the cash that equity expects to receive at t_1, and we know VE_0, we can deduce the new required rate of return to equity for our one-period firm:

$$VE_0 = \frac{NCDE_1}{1 + ke}$$

$$\$1600 = \frac{\$2010}{1 + ke}$$

$$1 + ke = \frac{2010}{1600}$$

$$= 1.25625$$

$$ke = 0.25625 \quad \text{or} \quad 25\tfrac{5}{8}\%$$

The $ke = ku = kf$ of the unlevered firm is 20%; the increased risk to equityholders due to the prior debt claim has caused an increase in ke for the levered firm to $25\frac{5}{8}\%$.

Now that we have found the required rate of return for the equity of the leveraged firm, we can attach a more intuitive interpretation to the equity price adjustment that was described in the previous section when the corporation altered its capital structure. Look at Figure 9.1. We have reproduced there the security market line, which shows the capital market equilibrium relationship between the risk of cash-flow expectations and their required rates of return. It shows that the riskiness of the $CAU_1 = NCDE_1 = \$3000$ cash-flow expectation requires a rate of $ku = ke = 0.20$ in the capital market, as we saw for the firm originally (unlevered). When the capital structure is altered, equity's expected cash flow becomes more risky, to the level of riskiness indicated by $R_{NCDE=\$2010}$ for the $\$2010$ $NCDE_1$ expectation. The efficient capital market assigns a required rate to that risk level such that ke now increases to 0.25625, as we have just calculated, above. *That is the rate of return that the capital market would require on any cash-flow expectation having the same risk as the $NCDE_1$ leveraged equity cash flow for this firm.* Regardless of where a cash flow originates, be it from a corporation, a personal investment, a gold speculation, or whatever, as long as its risk is the same as the $R_{NCDE=\$2010}$ level and it is priced in the capital market, it would require a return of 0.25625.

Notice what this means for the equity price that must prevail after the capital structure change. On the vertical axis of Figure 9.1 we show the rates

FIGURE 9.1   Leverage and equity rates in the capital market

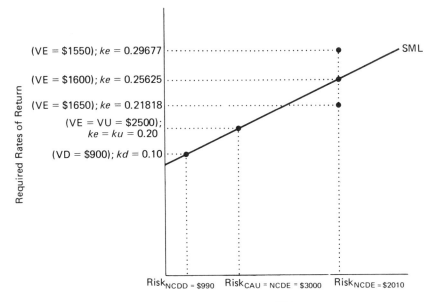

of return that would exist if the equity price for this firm fell to either $1550 or $1650, both of which differ from the equilibrium price of $1600. With a cash-flow expectation of $2010 at t_1, the three prices imply required rates of

$$1 + ke = \frac{\$2010}{\$1550} = 1.29677$$

$$ke = 0.29677$$

$$1 + ke = \frac{\$2010}{\$1650} = 1.21818$$

$$ke = 0.21818$$

$$1 + ke = \frac{\$2010}{\$1600} = 1.25625$$

$$ke = 0.25625$$

Thus, $1600 is the *only* price that can exist for that claim, given the riskiness of the cash flow and the equilibrium structure of required rates shown for the capital market in Figure 9.1. At any other price, the return being offered is a disequilibrium one (it would lie, as do the rates implied by the $1550 and $1650 prices, off the SML), and would adjust immediately to the appropriate capital-market rate. As we saw in Section I, the mechanism for adjusting required rates is the market price, so the price would immediately move to $1600, neither more nor less.

   Notice also that this equilibrium pricing process does not necessarily require the presence of other unlevered but otherwise identical firms. Although it was convenient to use such firms in the "personal versus corporate leverage" illustration in the previous section, *the influence of the general capital-market rate structure alone is enough to bring prices into line*. That structure, of course, is influenced by the other risks and returns available to participants, including other corporations of all types, real asset investments, and personal borrowing and lending.

θ AND *kf* WITHOUT DEDUCT-IBILITY   The overall required return for the levered firm can, of course, be calculated as the weighted average of the equity and debt rates:

$$kf = \frac{VD_0}{VF_0} kd + \frac{VE_0}{VF_0} ke$$

$$= \frac{900}{2500}(0.10) + \frac{1600}{2500}(0.25625)$$

$$= (0.36)(0.10) + (0.64)(0.25625)$$

$$= 0.20 \quad \text{or} \quad 20\%$$

The $ku = ke = kf$ of the unlevered firm was 20%, and the leveraged firm also has an overall required rate of 20%. In weighted-average terms, the required return on equity has increased just enough to offset exactly the lower required rate on debt. As a result, *kf is unaffected by capital structure*. This should not come as a surprise. The overall cash-flow expectations ($CAC_1 -$ IVS_1) are unchanged, and VF_0 is unchanged, so *kf* must also be unchanged. As another approach, if you can think of *kf* as being determined solely by the risk of the overall cash-flow expectation in the same way that *ke* and *kd* are determined by equity and debt cash-flow risks, you can see why *kf* is constant. The *riskiness* of the overall cash-flow has not changed but has merely been reapportioned between equity and debt.

With this information we can depict the required return and capital structure relationships that we were concerned about earlier in the chapter. These are shown in Figure 9.2. The θ for the unlevered firm is of course zero, and for the leveraged firm is \$900/\$2500, or 0.36. Note that *kf* is constant at 20%, *kd* increases from the risk-free rate *i* at $\theta = 0.00$ to 10% at $\theta = 0.36$, and *ke* increases from 20% at $\theta = 0.00$ to $25\frac{5}{8}\%$ at $\theta = 0.36$. *ke*, *kd*, and *kf* behave the way they do in relation to θ because capital structure changes for this firm do nothing but reapportion a constant risk and unchanging overall cash-flow expectation between debt and equity claims.

We can further illustrate this by allowing our leveraged firm to move to an even higher θ. Suppose that it wants to have a total of \$1875 of debt outstanding. The capital market requires an even higher *kd* for this because the debt claim now covers more of the risky operational cash flow. Assume that *kd* increases to 15%.[2] $NCDD_1$ becomes \$1875 $\times$ 1.15, or \$2156.25, and

FIGURE 9.2   Capital structure and required rates without deductibility

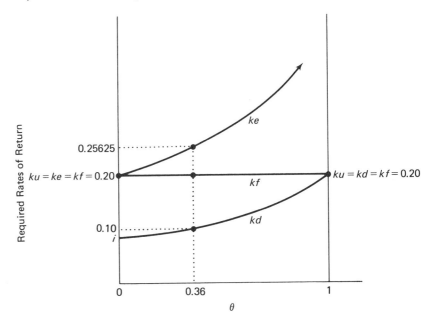

[2]The debt issuance, for simplicity, can be thought of as the firm paying off the \$900 debt by first unlevering itself and then issuing a new \$1875 debt claim, all at t_0. Issuing \$975 of new debt on top of the existing \$900 also works, if both issues have the same priority, that is, if *kd* is raised from 10% to 15% on the original \$900. The new debt suppliers expect \$975(1.15) = \$1121.25 at t_1 and the old now expect \$900(1.15) = \$1035 at t_1. \$1121.25 + \$1035.00 = \$2156.25, $NCDD_1$ for the higher θ.

$NCDE_1$ becomes $3000.00 - $2156.25 = 843.75. The *economics* of the situation are the same as for the $900 debt issue. VF_0 is constant at $2500. VE_0 changes to $625 since VD_0 is now $1875. The ke must increase just enough to offset the added risk to equityholders of the new prior debt claim on CAC:

$$VE_0 = \frac{NCDE_1}{1 + ke}$$

$$\$625.00 = \frac{\$843.75}{1 + ke}$$

$$1 + ke = \frac{843.75}{625.00} = 1.35$$

$$ke = 0.35 \quad \text{or} \quad 35\%$$

which, of course, is precisely the ke that will offset the new kd so as to hold kf constant:

$$kf = \frac{1875}{2500}(0.15) + \frac{625}{2500}(0.35)$$
$$= (0.75)(0.15) + (0.25)(0.35)$$
$$= 0.20 \quad \text{or} \quad 20\%$$

Figure 9.3 graphs the relationships between capital structure and required rates of return, and Figure 9.4 shows the θ and market-value relationships that we have discovered for this firm. The only aspects of these figures which we have not already commented on are some things that occur when $\theta = 1$. At that point in Figure 9.3, $kd = ku = kf = 20\%$ and ke is

FIGURE 9.3   **Capital structure and required rates without interest deductibility: a one-period example**

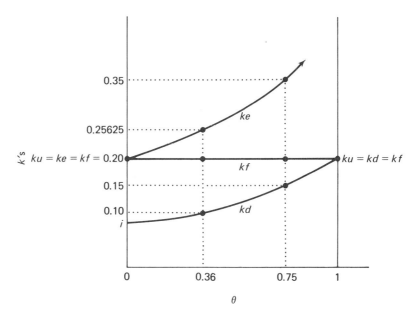

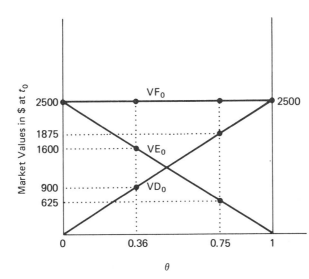

FIGURE 9.4   Capital structure and market values without interest deductibility: a
one-period example

undefined, since there is no equity. Similarly in Figure 9.4, equity value
steadily decreases toward zero as θ moves to 1 and, concurrently, debt value
steadily increases toward \$2500, the constant total corporate value.

REVIEW   Having come this far with our numerical example, we are ready to make
a few generalizations about the theory of capital structure. In this illustration
of a corporation whose interest payments were not deductible for tax purposes we have discovered that:

1. Equityholders' present wealth is unaffected by capital structure. Changing the proportionate claims of debt and equity causes equity market
   value to change by exactly the same amount as the cash received from
   or paid to the priority claim.
2. Total corporate value is unaffected by capital structure since overall
   cash flows are unaffected when interest is not deductible. Capital structure changes merely reapportion the same risky operating cash-flow
   expectations between debt and equity.
3. ke and kd increase as θ increases and decrease as θ decreases because
   their risks are positively related to the level of θ. But since the risk of
   the overall cash flows is constant with θ changes, kf must be constant.
   Therefore, ke and kd are related to θ such that their weighted average,

$$kf = \theta kd + (1 - \theta)ke$$

   is constant. As θ increases, kd and ke increase, but the higher θ weight
   on the lower kd, and the lower θ weight on the higher ke exactly offset
   each other and keep kf constant.

Statements of capital structure relationships such as those described in point 3 can sound very complicated. And it is easy to become so involved in deciphering their algebra and geometry that you lose sight of the really important lessons in the *economics* of capital structure. What we are saying in essence is that when interest is not deductible by a corporation for income tax purposes, capital structure does not matter. It has no effect on anyone's present wealth or on corporate value. If equityholders do not like their particular corporate θ, they can borrow or lend personally to bring their own θ into line, and neither lose nor gain present wealth. The market therefore attaches no wealth-changing importance to corporate capital structures.

Corporate capital structure changes under these conditions offer the capital market nothing new in terms of corporate cash-flow expectations. Nor do they allow capital-market participants to arrive at risk-return expectations that the participants could not have achieved by themselves.

The capital market, as we continue to discover, is a fair, yet rigorous judge of the values of claims offered for sale in it. If the same thing is being offered in a different package, the capital market may alter the prices of the parts but will continue to value the firm itself, as a whole, independently of the packaging of the parts. The firm's worth remains the same.

Naturally, these general statements also hold true for multiperiod corporations whose interest payments are not deductible. We have used the single-period example merely because the arithmetic is simpler. The economics of capital structure does not change with the number of periods a firm is expected to operate, as we shall see in Appendix III. A.

Chapter 10

Capital Structure Theory—II

CAPITAL STRUCTURE THEORY WITH INTEREST DEDUCT-IBILITY

Depending on one's level of intellectual curiosity, our study of capital structure thus far could be regarded as theoretically interesting, but somewhat of a flop otherwise. Capital structure certainly does not appear to be a very important financial decision. In the situations that we have examined up to this point, a firm could choose *any* capital structure, or change its existing capital structure as much as it wanted to, and the wealth of equity suppliers would stay the same. That is not very encouraging in a world where equity present-wealth maximization is the *raison d'etre* of corporate financial decision making. But do not despair. Capital structure *can* be an important financial decision, as we shall now discover.

In Chapter 9 we saw that corporate capital structure changes offered the capital market nothing that it could not do for itself. Consequently, capital structure did not matter. Overall cash-flow expectations were unaffected by θ changes. But the corporations we considered there had one characteristic that set them apart from all the others we have seen in the book. Interest was not deductible for tax purposes. That particular characteristic relegated capital structure to an interesting but financially unimportant artifact. Our purpose in introducing capital structure that way, however, was not gratuitous. The "without-deductibility" illustrations are convenient vehicles for a first pass at how the capital market reacts to θ changes under all circumstances. The basic economics of capital structure are as present in those illustrations as in any other. They correctly emphasize the importance of capital structure effects on future cash-flow expectations. Actually, all we must do to incorporate "with-deductibility" situations into our generalized capital structure theory is discover any *additional* effects that interest deductibility has on cash-flow expectations as capital structure is changed.

So the important question to ask now is: Does interest deductibility make corporate cash-flow expectations different from what they are without deductibility of interest? As you no doubt have already guessed, the answer is yes. Interest deductibility offers something to the capital market that is otherwise not there. That something, as we know from Chapter 5, is the interest tax subsidy.[1] Because its interest was not deductible, our corporation in the previous section had no ITS expectation regardless of how much interest it paid. For that reason, overall cash-flow expectations did not change when θ did. But if the chance for interest tax subsidies exists, overall cash flows can change with θ. Remember that the ITS, if present, is a legitimate part of overall cash flows. As interest payment expectations increase with θ, so will interest tax subsidies, and so, also, will resulting overall cash flows. A leveraged corporation can offer the capital market something an unlevered firm cannot: ITS cash flows.

What effect does a capital structure change with deductibility have on the present wealth of existing equity suppliers? The best way for us to approach that question is the same way we did in the without-deductibility situation: We shall examine the effect of deductibility on overall cash flows and total corporate value. The only difference here will be that corresponding to each capital structure will be a different ITS (or set of ITS_τ's in a multi-period corporation).

For every capital structure a firm could have, we already know the total value of its overall cash flows not including the ITS_τ's. It is simply the value of the firm when it is unlevered. The previous section dealt with valuing at various θ's the cash flows of corporations having no interest tax subsidies. We learned that the total value of such firms was constant at VU_0, the value of an unlevered firm. So the value of a leveraged firm when its interest payments are deductible must be

$$VF_0 = VU_0 + VITS_0$$

The value of a leveraged firm must be equal to the value of that firm when unlevered, plus the value of its future interest tax subsidy expectations.[2]

Think of the theoretical argument this way: We have set up our capital market so that it places a total value on the capital claims of a corporation as if participants held both the company's equity and its debt. Participants, in

---

[1]Interest deductibility is, of course, only one of a number of phenomena that can produce similar effects. Such effects may most generally be characterized as feedback from a payment (or effective payment) of cash to a capital supplier which impacts overall corporate cash flow (CAC). Other examples which are seriously proposed from time to time in the United States include dividend deductibility and the acceptance of corporate taxes as pro rata prepayment of (credit toward) equityholders' personal income taxes.

[2]Note that $VITS_\tau$ is the value of ITS flows occurring at time points $\geq \tau + 1$.

effect, value the whole firm on the basis of its overall cash-flow expectations. And we saw that corporate value is constant at VU_0 for all θ's when no interest tax subsidies are present in the cash-flow expectations. So when ITS's *are* present in cash-flow expectations, the overall value of the leveraged firm will differ from its unlevered value by the value of those interest tax subsidies.

Overall cash flows do not change with θ when interest is not deductible. Referring to our FCF statement, you can see that overall cash flows are constant at CAU_T for any capital structure. Without deductibility, CAC_T equals CAU_T for all θ's, so overall cash flows are unaffected by θ. But when interest payments become deductible, overall corporate cash-flow expectations at each time point (CAC_T) increase by ITS_T. For leveraged firms with interest deductibility, CAC_T is larger than CAU_T by the amount of ITS_T. And the difference, ITS_T, will increase as θ increases because we expect more interest to be paid at higher levels of debt in the capital structure.

We can therefore discover the effect of capital structure on overall corporate value by adding the present value of expected interest tax subsidies to the unlevered value of the firm. And, as we saw in the without-deductibility discussion, it is then a simple step to find the effect of capital structure on the present wealth of existing equity suppliers. But what exactly *is* the present value of the interest tax subsidies? How is this $VITS_0$ measured?

As we have seen so many times, value in a capital market is determined by the size, timing, and risk of future cash-flow expectations. And the same things determine the value of future interest tax subsidies. The size and timing of each ITS_T expectation is not difficult to figure. ITS_T is, of course, simply the interest expectation, I_T, times the tax rate, τ. In order to calculate $VITS_0$, all we need do is discount our ITS_T expectations back to the present at rates appropriate to the risks of the interest tax subsidies.

But what rates are those? Or, more specifically, how risky are future ITS_T expectations? Think back to our cash-flow diagrams in Section II. ITS_T flows to the corporation from the government. Short of a change in tax laws, interest tax subsidies will be paid when and if interest is paid. If I_T is not paid, neither will ITS_T be paid. *Interest tax subsidies must have the same risk as interest payments.* And we already know the discount rates which recognize the riskiness of interest, kd_P. So kd_P must also be the appropriate rates at which to discount ITS_T expectations in order to find $VITS_0$.[3]

[3]This implies three other conditions which we should point out to you. First, we are assuming that expected interest and principal payments are equally risky, and therefore can separately be discounted at kd. Corporate bond contracts could, for example, provide that actual payments to interest and principal be proportionate to their promised amounts. This is not a vital theoretical necessity. We could have one rate for interest and another for principal; in such a situation, $VITS_0$ would be determined using the rate for interest payments. But our debt value and kf formulas in Chapter 7 would be more complicated than necessary, so the assumption of equal risk for principal and interest is probably worthwhile. The second condition is that companies can sell accounting "tax losses" for their full value. We must allow this because a firm pays no taxes when it has no accounting income. In that situation the firm would have no ITS even though it did pay interest. In our capital market,

In other words, the value of a corporation's interest tax subsidy expectations is

$$\text{VITS}_0 = \sum_{\text{T}=1}^{T} \frac{\text{ITS}_\text{T}}{\prod_{\text{P}=1}^{\text{T}}(1 + kd_\text{P})} \qquad [10.1]$$

or, for constant *kd*,

$$\text{VITS}_0 = \sum_{\text{T}=1}^{T} \frac{\text{ITS}_\text{T}}{(1 + kd)^\text{T}} \qquad [10.1a]$$

VITS$_0$ *equals the future ITS*$_\text{T}$ *expectations discounted back to the present at the required rate of return to debt suppliers.*

We have already said that the value of a leveraged firm must equal the value of that firm when unlevered plus the value of its interest tax subsidy expectations. This must be true since the ITS$_\text{T}$'s are the only differences in the overall cash flows between the levered and unlevered firms. In formula terms,

$$\text{VF}_0 = \text{VU}_0 + \text{VITS}_0$$

$$\text{VF}_0 = \text{VU}_0 + \sum_{\text{T}=1}^{T} \frac{\text{ITS}_\text{T}}{\prod_{\text{P}=1}^{\text{T}}(1 + kd_\text{P})} \qquad [10.2]$$

or

$$\text{VF}_0 = \text{VU}_0 + \sum_{\text{T}=1}^{T} \frac{\text{ITS}_\text{T}}{(1 + kd)^\text{T}} \qquad [10.2a]$$

if *kd* is constant. This formula applies to all corporations regardless of whether interest is deductible. If it is not, there are no ITS$_\text{T}$ expectations, and the formula reduces to our finding in the previous section that $\text{VF}_0 = \text{VU}_0$.

Formula 10.2 (or its alternative, 10.2a) is a very important one. As a matter of fact, it tells us exactly what we must know to complete our development of capital structure theory. Rather than discuss this in the abstract, we shall apply the knowledge to another simple numerical example.

ONE-PERIOD EXAMPLE WITH INTEREST DEDUCTIBILITY

Again we shall begin with a one-period firm. Assume a corporate tax rate (τ) of 48% with interest deductibility:

1. The corporation is unlevered, and the capital market judges this all-equity firm's required return to capital suppliers to be $ku = ke = kf = 25\%$.
2. The firm and the capital market expect that at t_1, operations will

therefore, companies can sell VITS$_0$. (Historically, this has been one reason for mergers of companies. Further, in real capital markets, the existence of tax loss carry-back and/or carry-forward provisions can to some extent insure realization of VITS$_0$ in accounting loss situations.) Finally, the use of *kd* is conditioned on a risk-free government. That is, we are certain of a whole range of things, such as government allowance of the interest deduction, government maintenance of the legal provisions of deductibility, and government acceptance of tax losses once sold. In other words, nothing about the government increases the risk of the ITS$_\text{T}$ flows.

generate a CAU_1 of \$3630. The cash flow expectations at t_1 are

\$RCPT	\$15,000
\$EXPT	9,750
GCFO	5,250
GTAX	2,520
NCFO	2,730
DTS	900
CAU	3,630
ITS	0
CAC	3,630
I	0
PP	0
CDD	0
NDC	0
NCDD	0
CAE	3,630
CRF	0
CDE	3,630
NEC	0
NCDE	3,630
TCC $\equiv$ IVS	0

As before, calculating the value of this one-period unlevered firm consists simply of dividing the t_1 equity cash-flow expectation by $1 + ku$:

$$VU_0 = \frac{\$3630}{1.25} = \$2904$$

Now suppose that the company changes its capital structure. For example, say that an \$1800 debt issue is floated and that the capital market, looking at the resulting cash-flow expectations, requires a $12\frac{1}{2}\%$ return on that amount of debt capital for this particular company. The transaction at t_0 is accomplished by debt suppliers giving \$1800 to the firm in exchange for an expectation of $\$1800(1.125) = \$2025$ as $NCDD_1$. The \$2025 expectation is composed of $\$1800(0.125) = \$225$ of interest and \$1800 of principal repayment. The \$1800 which is received by the company at t_0 is immediately distributed to equity suppliers so as not to violate the firm's t_0 investment decision.

The \$225 of interest at t_1 is therefore expected to generate an interest tax subsidy of $\$225(0.48) = \$108$; $ITS_1 = \$108$. *That \$108 t_1 cash-flow expectation is not there when the firm is unlevered.* You can check back to verify this. The t_1 cash flows become

\$RCPT	\$15,000
\$EXPT	9,750
GCFO	5,250
GTAX	2,520
NCFO	2,730
DTS	900

CAU	3,630
ITS	108
CAC	3,738
I	225
PP	1,800
CDD	2,025
NDC	0
NCDD	2,025
CAE	1,713
CRF	0
CDE	1,713
NEC	0
NCDE	1,713
TCC $\equiv$ IVS	0

At this point, knowing the new cash-flow expectations, we can calculate the value of the now leveraged firm using formula 10.2a:

$$\begin{aligned}
VF_0 &= VU_0 + \sum_{\tau=1}^{T} \frac{ITS_\tau}{(1 + kd)^\tau} \\
&= VU_0 + \frac{ITS_1}{1 + kd} \\
&= \$2904 + \frac{\$108}{1.125} \\
&= \$2904 + \$96 \\
&= \$3000
\end{aligned}$$

By issuing \$1800 of debt and distributing the proceeds to equity the company has increased its market value from \$2904 to \$3000. That \$96 increase in value is the present value of the t_1 interest tax subsidy of \$108. As debt was substituted for equity, the ITS_1 cash flow appeared and the t_0 value of the firm increased by the present value of that amount; $VITS_0 = \$96$.

Again, our capital market values the capital claims of a corporation as if participants did hold both debt and equity. Since the overall amount of cash expected to go to all claims has increased by the amount of the interest tax subsidy, participants raise the value of the total claims by what the ITS_1 is worth at t_0.

How have the equityholders fared in this capital structure alteration? Well, we know they started off with a VU_0 of \$2904, and when debt was issued they received the \$1800 proceeds at t_0. But the new debt issue constitutes an expected priority claim of \$2025 on overall cash flows at t_1. This makes equity's t_1 expectation lower and more risky, so VE_0 must drop. But by how much? Since we already know that the value of the total corporation has increased to \$3000 and that the debt value is \$1800, VE_0 is equal to the difference, \$1200. So the capital structure change has caused the value of equity to fall from $VU_0 = \$2904$ to $VE_0 = \$1200$, a decrease of \$1704.

But remember that the equity suppliers received \$1800 in cash at t_0 from the new debt suppliers. *So the present wealth of equity suppliers has* *increased by $1800 − $1704 = $96*. We have seen that $96 before. It is the value of the interest tax subsidy. Equity prices, therefore, adjust downward by less than the t_0 cash that equity suppliers receive from the increase in θ (θ now equals $1800/$3000 = 0.6). The difference between the price decrease and the cash inflow is the value of the interest tax subsidy. Equity present wealth increases by that much. On the other hand, if, with deductibility, θ is lowered, the $VITS_0$ would decrease and equityholders would lose present wealth. You can see that this would be true by observing what would occur if we allowed the example firm to unlever itself again: Equity buys out debt for $1800 and present wealth decreases from $3000 to $2904, because the $96 $VITS_0$ disappears.

Why does equity's market price react in this way to increases and decreases in θ? The answer is simple: Since interest is deductible, corporate leverage gives capital-market participants something they could not get by themselves. That something is the interest tax subsidies.[4] Think of the economics of the equity valuation this way: When the company is unlevered, actual and potential shareholders value its equity at $2904. This is based on the size, timing, and risk of the company's operating cash-flow expectations, CAU_τ. When the company substitutes debt for equity in the way we have described, two things happen simultaneously:

1. A priority claim against future cash flows is created, causing the equity claim to be valued at less than it was when the firm was unlevered.
2. The deductibility of expected interest payments to debt suppliers causes overall cash flows to be incremented by an interest tax subsidy, the risk of which is the same as the interest payment.

Because overall cash flows now include the ITS_τ expectations, equity's value, as the residual claimant on those cash flows, does not behave as it did in the nondeductibility case; now it does not decrease by the whole amount of the value of the new debt claim. If it did, no one would be claiming the interest tax subsidy. Since equity gets the deductibility benefit, its market price decreases by only ($VD_0 − VITS_0$). Equity's cash inflow from the debt issue is equal to VD_0, so its present wealth has actually increased by $VITS_0$.[5]

We can again use an illustration of personal versus corporate leverage to show that the value of the equity of the firm must fall from $2904 to $1200 when it undertakes the capital structure change. We shall assume the same condition that we did in the without-deductibility illustration, that is, a number of identical unlevered firms and personal leveraging allowed. Assume also that capital-market participants still are not subject to personal income taxes.[6]

---

[4]This remains true even if personal interest is deductible for personal income tax purposes. We shall illustrate this in Appendix III.B.

[5]The wealth increase is $VITS_0$ when moving from an unlevered to a leveraged firm. When moving from one level of leverage to another the wealth change is, of course, the *difference* between the "before" and "after" $VITS_0$'s.

[6]Personal income taxes, again, merely make the calculation more complicated. Appendix

Now suppose that our corporation issues $1800 of debt at $12\frac{1}{2}\%$ and distributes the proceeds to equity, but somehow or other the market price of the equity of that firm falls only to $1250 rather than to $1200. You are a capital-market participant with $1250 of cash, thinking of buying some equity. What would you think of the shares of this now leveraged firm?

If you bought the leveraged equity for $1250, your t_0 cash-flow expectations would be

CAU	$3,630
ITS	108
CAC	3,738
I	225
PP	1,800
CDD	2,025
NDC	0
NCDD	2,025
CAE	1,713
CRF	0
CDE	1,713
NEC	0
NCDE	1,713

You would expect an overall corporate flow of $3738 with a $2025 prior claim netting you a $1713 NCDE at t_1.

But remember, shares of the unlevered but otherwise identical firms are also available. Suppose that you borrowed $1704 at t_0, put up $1200 of your own money, and bought all the equity of the unlevered firm for $2904. You could borrow the $1704 at $12\frac{1}{2}\%$ because you can issue a priority claim on your personal t_1 cash flows similar to that which the leveraged company did. If it could obtain a kd of $12\frac{1}{2}\%$, so can you.[7]

If you bought the unlevered firm's shares this way, your t_1 cash flows would be

$3630	CAU_1
— 0	ITS_1
3630	CAC_1
— 0	I_1
— 0	PP_1
3630	$NCDE_1$
−1704	personal loan repayment at t_1
— 213	personal loan interest payment at t_1 ($12\frac{1}{2}\%$ of $1704)
$1713	personal cash-flow expectation at t_1

III.B will show that the presence of personal taxes (with or without interest deductibility) does not change the economics of capital structure with deductibility.

[7]Notice that you can only borrow $1704 at $12\frac{1}{2}\%$, not $1800 like the corporation. Since you pay no taxes, there is no ITS in your personal t_1 expectation. The $96 difference is just that.

Personal borrowing to buy the unlevered firm results in the same $1713 t_1 cash-flow expectation as the unlevered firm's equity does.[8] But that cash-flow expectation costs only $1200, while the leveraged firm's cost $1250. Obviously, no one would bid $1250 for the leveraged equity, and its price would fall to the level that equated its cost to that of the "unlevered firm with personal leverage". As we have seen, that level is $1200.

Should the leveraged equity's price fall below $1200, participants would bid it back up when they compared it to the cost of obtaining the $1713 t_1 expectation through using personal borrowing to buy the unlevered firm.

In sum, the change in price of equity when a firm moves from an unlevered to a leveraged position is a decrease, but not so much as to offset totally the cash that equityholders receive from the proceeds of the debt issue.[9] The difference between the price decrease and the cash inflow is the present value of the interest tax subsidy. That is the value benefit of deductible leverage, and the increase in equityholder present wealth.

θ AND
REQUIRED
RATES WITH
INTEREST
DEDUCT-
IBILITY:
θ AND ke

Interest deductibility, as you doubtless already expect, also affects the relationship between capital structure and required rates of return on corporate capital claims. In the without-deductibility situation we saw that both the equity and debt required rates, ke and kd, increased with increases in θ because of the greater risk that each type of claim experienced. However, we also discovered that the increase in ke exactly offset the lower kd as debt was substituted for equity. This meant that the overall required rate, kf, was constant. The risk of the company's overall cash-flow expectations was constant. This is not the case when interest payments are deductible.

Rather than try to predict what the "with-deductibility" relationships will be, we can use those which exist in our example. The debt rate, kd, has obviously increased from the risk-free rate i when $\theta = 0$ to $12\frac{1}{2}\%$ when

---

[8]This $1713 is just as risky as the leveraged firm's $1713 $NCDE_1$, since the leveraged corporate CAC is higher than your CAU by the $108 ITS_1, and its debt payment of $2025 is higher than your $1917 debt payment by the same, identical risk, $108.

[9]There is one loose end we can tie up here. The cash taken in from debt suppliers can also be distributed to equity by buying back $1800 worth of shares at a price per share equal to

$$\frac{VE_0(\text{before } \Delta\theta) + \Delta VITS_0}{\text{no. of shares}_0(\text{before } \Delta\theta)} = \frac{\$3000}{\text{no. of shares}_0(\text{before } \Delta\theta)}$$

Suppose that there are 100 shares outstanding before the capital structure change. They will sell for $2904/100 = $29.04 each. The company issues $1800 of debt at $12\frac{1}{2}\%$ and buys back $1800 worth of shares at $3000/100 = $30 each, or $1800/$30 = 60 shares. Each shareholder then gets the correct present wealth increase:

$$\frac{\Delta VITS_0}{\text{no. of shares (before } \Delta\theta)} = \frac{\$96}{100} = \$0.96 \text{ per share}$$

Those who sell back their shares get the 96 cents in cash: $30.00 payment compared to the previous value of $29.04. Those who do not sell their shares back to the firm are holding 40 shares worth $1200 in aggregate, or $1200/40 = $30 per share, a 96-cent gain in market value.

$\theta = 0.6$. The equity rate, ke, began at $ku - ke = 25\%$; now, for this one-period firm,

$$VE_0 = \frac{NCDE_1}{1 + ke}$$

$$\$1200 = \frac{\$1713}{1 + ke}$$

$$1 + ke = \frac{1713}{1200} = 1.4275$$

$$ke = 0.4275 \quad \text{or} \quad 42\tfrac{3}{4}\%$$

The equity rate has increased to $42\tfrac{3}{4}\%$ from 25% as a result of the increased risk of the larger higher-priority debt claim.

The price-adjustment process for the equity of the leveraged firm can be described through the structure of equilibrium rates based on risk in the capital market, just as we did for the without-deductibility corporation in Chapter 9. Figure 10.1 shows the relationship for the equity claim of this with-deductibility firm. The unlevered equity requires a $ku = 0.25$. When capital structure is altered, the capital market judges the riskiness of the $NCDE_1$ cash flow to require a return of $0.4275 \,(= ke)$. The market would assign this rate to any cash-flow expectation having the same risk as this $NCDE_1$, regardless of the source of that cash flow. Note that the $1250 equity price and the $1150 equity price result in incorrect rates. The *only* VE_0 that can prevail in the capital market for the leveraged corporation is

FIGURE 10.1   **Leverage and equity rates in the capital market**

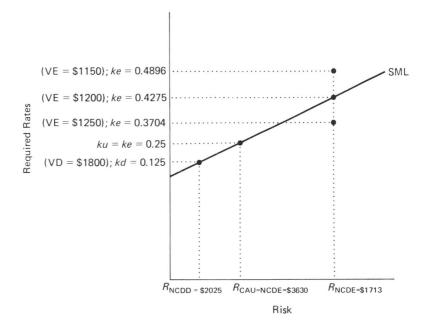

$1200. Any other price would imply a *ke* that is not in equilibrium with the structure of capital-market rates, and the price would adjust to $1200 to give the necessary $ke = 0.4275$.

θ AND *kf* WITH DEDUCT-IBILITY

The overall required rate, *kf*, calculated as a weighted average of *ke* and *kd*, has become

$$kf = \theta kd + (1 - \theta)ke$$
$$= (0.6)(0.125) + (0.4)(0.4275)$$
$$= 0.246 \quad \text{or} \quad 24.6\%$$

The overall required rate has *declined* from $ku = kf = 25\%$ at $\theta = 0$ to 24.6% at $\theta = 0.6$. This means that the overall cash flows of the firm are less risky than they were when the firm was unlevered. The reason is not difficult to understand. An ITS_1 has been added to the overall flow. As we have argued, ITS's risk is that of interest payments whose *kd* of $12\frac{1}{2}\%$ indicates a lower risk than does the unlevered flow's 25% *ku*. Since *kf* depends on the combination of the riskinesses of two cash flows, CAU_1 requiring 25% and ITS_1 requiring $12\frac{1}{2}\%$, *kf* must therefore lie between the two and be less than 25%. As it turns out, it is 24.6%.[10]

Figure 10.2 graphs these results. Visually, this does not appear to be very much different from the without-deductibility graph of Figure 9.3. The economic differences, however, are quite important. As we *begin* to increase θ (from $\theta = 0.0$ to $\theta = 0.6$), *ke* increases, but not enough to offset completely the lower *kd*, and, therefore, *kf* declines. The reason, as we have stressed, is because at low levels of θ the risk of the interest tax subsidy is quite low.

Notice in Figure 10.2 that we have drawn *kd* as continuing to increase with θ until, at $\theta = 1$, $kd = ku = kf = 25\%$. This is similar to the $kd \leftrightarrow \theta$ relationship in our without-deductibility example. It means that, even *with*

[10]Indeed, *kf* is also a weighted average of the returns required by the two component streams, where the weights are the relative values of each to their combination:

$$kf = \frac{VU_0}{VU_0 + VITS_0}ku + \frac{VITS_0}{VU_0 + VITS_0}kd$$
$$= \frac{\$2904}{\$3000}(25\%) + \frac{\$96}{\$3000}(12\frac{1}{2}\%)$$
$$= (0.968)(0.25) + (0.032)(0.125)$$
$$= 0.242 + 0.004$$
$$= 0.246 \quad \text{or} \quad 24.6\%$$

Since $VF_0 = VU_0 + VITS_0$, we can rewrite the preceding formula for *kf* as

$$kf = \frac{VU_0}{VF_0}ku + \frac{VITS_0}{VF_0}kd$$

or, equivalently,

$$kf = \frac{VU_0}{VF_0}ku + \left(1 - \frac{VU_0}{VF_0}\right)kd$$

If we let the lowercase Greek letter phi (ϕ) stand for the proportion of VF_0 attributable to VU_0, we get

$$kf = \phi ku + (1 - \phi)kd \qquad [10.3]$$

This formula applies to single-period firms and to perpetuity situations but needs some modification in most other cases, as we shall discover in Appendix III.C.

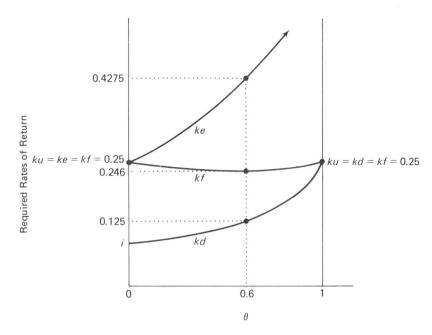

FIGURE 10.2   **Capital structure and required rates with interest deductibility:
a one-period example**

deductibility, when the corporation is totally financed by debt, debt's cash flows are just as risky as equity's are when the firm is totally financed by equity.

We had no difficulty seeing why $kd = ku$ when $\theta = 1$ in the without-deductibility situation. There, debt's cash-flow expectation is the corporation's CAU = CAC cash flow which has risk requiring a rate of ku. Since debt is claiming that whole cash flow, its required rate must be $kd = ku$. But what about the with-deductibility situation? Here at $\theta = 1$ debt again claims the entire corporate cash flow, as in the without-deductibility case, but here the entire cash expectation claimed by debt includes not only the CAU cash flow, but also the ITS cash flow. CAC = CAU + ITS. Since debt claims all this CAC, kd will be determined by CAC's risk.

And how risky is CAC in an all-debt firm with deductibility? We can find out by considering each of its parts, CAU and ITS. First, CAU's risk calls for a rate of ku, as we know. What about ITS? We know that the interest tax subsidy is a payment purely contingent on the amount and timing of the interest payment. But, since the payment of interest is directly depen-dent on the realization of CAU, just as ITS depends on the actual payment of interest, ITS is itself contingent on debt's receipt of CAU.[11] So *both*

---

[11]Remember our assumption that interest and principal are of equal risks carries the impli-cation that actual CAU will always be split between interest and principal in proportion to promised interest and principal payments.

parts (ITS and CAU) of the CAC claimed by debt have CAU's risk, which requires a *ku* rate of return. This is the reason why *kd* equals *ku* when $\theta = 1$ "with deductibility."

Figure 10.2 also shows that the overall required rate, *kf*, first decreases as θ moves up from zero, and later begins increasing, until at $\theta = 1$, $kf = ku = kd$. (The vertical dimension of the *kf* curve in Figure 10.2 has been slightly exaggerated to make it easier for you to see how *kf* changes with θ.) It is easy to see why $kf = kd$ at $\theta = 1$. An all-debt firm must have an overall required rate equal to the debt rate. And we have just finished showing that $kd = ku$ at $\theta = 1$. So *kf* must also end up where *kd* does at $\theta = 1$; that is, at *ku*. The overall cash-flow expectations at $\theta = 1$ are exactly as risky as they were when $\theta = 0$.

Why does *kf* first go down, and then back up again as θ moves from zero to 1? The important things to remember are that overall cash flows, CAC, are made up of operating flows, CAU, and interest tax subsidies, ITS; and that *kf* depends on the riskiness of overall flows, CAC. At all levels of leverage below $\theta = 1$, debt claims only a portion of the operating flow, and so interest payments and therefore ITS are less risky than CAU. That means that CAC is less risky than CAU, and thus *kf* is less than *ku*, as we demonstrated in footnote 10 (p. 202). As θ increases, debt claims larger proportions of operating flows and ITS becomes more risky. The *kf* continues to decline for a while as the increasingly risky (but still lower-risk) ITS begins to make up a larger proportion of CAC. Eventually, however, the increases in ITS's risk cause CAC to stop becoming less risky, and, instead, to begin becoming more risky. At that point, *kf* begins to increase with θ.[12] Finally, at $\theta = 1$, debt is claiming the entire overall cash flow; ITS is just as risky as CAU. The overall cash flow (CAC) must also, therefore, have the same risk as the operating cash flow (CAU), and $kf = ku = kd$.

θ AND CAPITAL COSTS WITH DEDUCTIBILITY

We have seen in some detail how deductibility of interest affects required rates of return to capital suppliers as we alter capital structure. Our theory would not be complete, however, if we did not also investigate the effect of capital structure on the firm's *capital costs*. You remember from Section II that our *kd** and *kf** rates can be thought of as the corporation's debt and overall capital costs, net of tax.

We did not discuss capital costs in the without-deductibility section because, there, *kd* and *kd** (and *kf* and *kf**) did not differ. Without deductibility of interest, you recall, required rates and capital costs are the same thing. With deductibility, however, they are not.

---

[12]An obvious question which probably occurs to you is: At what θ does *kf* reach its lowest value? We will deal with this question briefly in Appendix III.C. As it happens, the answering of this simple question is a very difficult task, and is, in general, well beyond what seems reasonable for a basic text such as this. Fortunately, as we shall see shortly (when we deal with the relationships between θ and market values), the question and its answer are of no real economic significance, being, rather, only academically interesting.

Since we know the relation between θ and required rates, and also the relationships (from Section II) between required rates and capital costs, we can develop the capital cost–capital structure relationships quite easily. For example, we know that, with deductibility,

$$kd_{\mathrm{P}}^* = kd_{\mathrm{P}}(1 - \tau) \qquad [7.2]$$

At $\theta = 0.6$, for example,

$$
\begin{aligned}
kd^* &= (0.125)(0.52) \\
&= 0.065 \quad \text{or} \quad 6.5\%
\end{aligned}
$$

So kd^* will always be $(1 - \tau)$ times kd as kd increases with θ.

Substituting θ for VD/VF in formula 7.6, we get

$$kf^* = \theta kd^* + (1 - \theta)ke \qquad [10.4]$$

Calculating for $\theta = 0.6$, we get

$$
\begin{aligned}
kf^* &= (0.6)(0.065) + (0.4)(0.4275) \\
&= 0.039 + 0.171 \\
&= 0.21 \quad \text{or} \quad 21\%
\end{aligned}
$$

The overall cost of capital, kf^*, continually decreases as debt is added to the capital structure, and reaches a minimum at $\theta = 1$ where kf^* equals kd^*. Notice in Figure 10.3 that as θ increases from 0 to 1, the kf^* for our corporation decreases from 0.25 at $\theta = 0$, through 0.21 at $\theta = 0.6$, all the way to 0.13 at $\theta = 1$. It is easy to see why kf^* must decrease all the way to 0.13 at $\theta = 1$. You have no doubt already discovered that 0.13 is also the value of kd^* at $\theta = 1$. $kd^* = kf^*$ when $\theta = 1$ is the simple statement that, for an all-debt firm, the overall cost of capital is equal to the cost of debt. No great surprise there.

The $kf^* \longleftrightarrow \theta$ relationship in Figure 10.3 is drawn as a smooth, always-decreasing curve. Actually, at this point we have not really demonstrated that to be necessarily true. We have, of course, calculated three values of the overall cost of capital for our company which are consistent with such a relationship, but a rigorous demonstration that kf^* "monotonically decreases" across θ is reserved for Appendix III.C.[13]

[13]Recalling from footnote 10 our definition of ϕ as VU_0/VF_0 (and $1 - \phi$ as $VITS_0/VF_0$), we can describe kf^* in the one-period firm as

$$
\begin{aligned}
kf^* &= \frac{VU_0}{VF_0}ku - \frac{VITS_0}{VF_0} \\
&= \phi ku - (1 - \phi) \\
&= \phi(1 + ku) - 1 \qquad [10.5]
\end{aligned}
$$

We shall fully develop formula 10.5 in Appendix III.C and use it there to show formally that kf^* continually decreases as θ increases, reaching its lowest value (equal to kd^*) at $\theta = 1$.

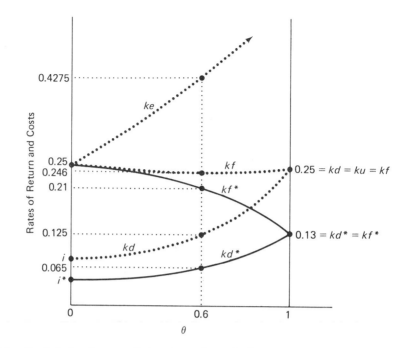

FIGURE 10.3 Capital structure, capital costs, and required rates without interest deductibility

It is possible, however, to offer an intuitive argument in support of the $kf^* \leftrightarrow \theta$ relationship in Figure 10.3. If we think of the overall cost of capital as a weighted average of ke and kd^*, the argument would say that the overall cost of capital declines because subsidized debt capital is being continuously substituted for unsubsidized equity capital as $\theta = VD_0/VF_0$ increases. Unlike the overall required rate, the overall capital cost never starts to increase as θ does. Even though ke and kd^* go up as θ does, they do not increase enough to offset the much cheaper subsidized debt cost.

From a purely theoretical point of view, the kd^* and kf^* capital costs add little to our knowledge of corporate finance. Given the capital structure relationships we had already developed, the capital cost formulations essentially "fall out" as mostly mechanical calculations. As we have argued in Section II, however, capital costs do have their uses in assisting management to view implications of financial decisions *from the perspective of the firm*. Further, as we shall see next, kf^* has more intuitive appeal than kf in relating θ to the overall value of the firm. And finally, for better or for worse, kf^* is widely accepted in theory and practice as a valid investment decision-making tool. But we shall discuss that in more depth in Section V.

θ AND MARKET VALUES WITH DEDUCTIBILITY

Now that we have completed our short excursion through capital costs, let us finish the main work of this chapter by examining what, ultimately, is all that matters: *value* as affected by capital structure. Figure 10.4 shows the relationships between capital structure and the market values of capital claims in this one-period example. The major difference between these relationships and those without deductibility shown in Figure 9.4 is that the value of the firm, VF_0, is no longer constant across capital structure changes. With interest deductibility, VF_0 gradually increases as θ increases.

As we have suggested, the reason for this is the ever higher interest tax subsidies as θ increases. Although it is difficult to see in this graph, the equity values decrease less than the debt values increase for any given upward alteration in θ. The difference is equal to the change in the overall value of the firm, which is, of course, the change in the value of the interest tax subsidy.

We can be much more precise, however, in convincing you that VF_0 must continually increase as the capital structure changes from $\theta = 0$ to $\theta = 1$. We need only combine two things we already know to be true. First, from the previous section on capital costs, remember that kf^*, because of the effect of interest deductibility, continually *decreases* across θ. Next, from

FIGURE 10.4   **Capital structure and market values with interest deductibility: a one-period example**

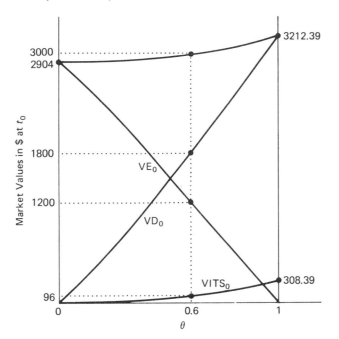

Section II, recall the overall valuation formula:

$$VF_0 = \sum_{T=1}^{T} \frac{CAU_T - IVS_T}{\prod_{P=1}^{T}(1 + kf_P^*)} \qquad [7.11]$$

Every numerator of this summation comprises CAU_T and IVS_T, both of which are absolutely unaffected by capital structure in our theory. Each ($CAU_T - IVS_T$) term will be exactly the same at $\theta = 0$ as at $\theta = 1$ or anywhere in between. But since every kf_P^* declines as θ increases, each denominator of the summation will be smaller at a higher θ. Thus, every term of the summation must increase as θ increases, and the total VF_0 must continually increase as we move from $\theta = 0$ to $\theta = 1$.

It is also worth noting here that the maximum VF_0 (and, therefore, shareholder present wealth) occurs at $\theta = 1$, the capital structure at which kf^* has its minimum value ($= kd^*$). Thus, *maximum VF_0 is associated with minimum overall cost of capital, kf^**, and *not* with minimum overall required rate of return, kf, which occurred somewhere between $\theta = 0$ and $\theta = 1$.

Since we also know that

$$VF_0 = VU_0 + VITS_0$$

and the VU_0 is constant with respect to θ, it follows that, like VF_0, $VITS_0$ *must continually increase as θ does* and by the same dollar amount as does VF_0. ($VITS_0$ as it is related to θ is also shown in Figure 10.4.) This is the basis, of course, for our frequent statement that it is the interest tax subsidy from government that makes the difference in value as capital structure changes with deductibility. In fact, the above equation shows emphatically that the reason why VF_0 increases with θ is simply because $VITS_0$ does.

As proportionately more of the capital structure of the firm becomes debt, VF_0 must continually increase, specifically reflecting the identical dollar increase in $VITS_0$. Looking to the calculation of $VITS_0$,

$$VITS_0 = \sum_{T=1}^{T} \frac{ITS_T}{\prod_{P=1}^{T}(1 + kd_P)} \qquad [10.1]$$

it is not intuitively obvious that $VITS_0$ must necessarily increase with θ. Of course, interest expectations will be higher for each higher θ (since both VD_0 and kd will have increased), and so, therefore, will be ITS_T. This means that even with θ very close to 1, a little more debt will generate a little more ITS_T. But, of course, kd is also increasing so that we have both larger numerators and larger denominators in formula 10.1. Fortunately, from our previous analysis we know that the value of the ITS_T's does increase with θ, notwithstanding the higher kd_P's, and so what we could not see directly in the formula for calculating $VITS_0$, we have accomplished through the total valuation approach using kf^*.

The specific value of the firm, VF_0, at $\theta = 1$ is approximately

$3212.39.[14] That figure is not terribly important, and the formulas for calculating it will be developed in Appendix III.C. The important thing to understand is that *shareholder wealth continues to increase as debt is substituted for equity.* And the reason it does is that government is providing ever higher interest tax subsidies as θ approaches 1, which, even as kd also increases, result in a continuously increasing value of those subsidies.

REVIEW   We have now completed the purely theoretical development of capital structure in the theory of corporate finance. Our findings are:

1. Capital structure affects shareholder wealth when interest payments to debt suppliers are deductible for corporate income tax purposes. Substituting debt for equity causes ever higher interest tax subsidies in a corporation's future cash-flow expectations. This, in turn, allows equity's market value to fall by less than the cash paid in by debt suppliers. For any given capital structure alteration the change in shareholder wealth will equal the change in the value of the interest tax subsidies.

2. Total corporate value with interest deductibility steadily increases as debt is substituted for equity, reaching a maximum at an all-debt capital structure. VF_0 increases because of the ever-higher interest tax subsidies. The market value of equity does not decrease as much as the market value of debt increases, so VF_0 goes up as θ does.

3. As in the without-deductibility situation, ke and kd increase as debt is substituted for equity, reflecting the increasing risk of each type of capital claim with increasing leverage. With deductibility, however, kf first declines, then increases, until at $\theta = 1$ it again equals ku. This is because overall cash flows include higher and higher proportions of lower-risk interest tax subsidies as θ increases. Thus, riskiness of overall cash flows is not constant with capital structure changes, and even declines over some range of θ increases.

4. Because interest payments are subsidized, the cost of debt capital, kd^*, is always less than kd and increases with θ at a lesser absolute rate than does kd. For the same reason, the overall cost of capital of a corporation, kf^*, continually declines as θ increases, moving from ku at $\theta = 0$ to $kd^* = ku(1 - \tau)$ at $\theta = 1$.

As a general statement it is fair to say that capital structure really does matter when interest is deductible. By comparing our statements above to

---

[14]In this example, a complete substitution of debt for equity calls for the firm to issue about $3212.39 of debt at t_0 and buy out all equity suppliers for that amount. This increases their present wealth by $3212.39 − $2904.00 = $308.39. Interest on the new debt is $3212.39(0.25) = $803.10; $NCDD_1 = $4015.49. At t_1, debt then expects to receive $(CAU_1 = $3630.00) + (ITS_1 = $385.49) = $4015.49.

If you think about this, you can see that the same thing would happen if the unlevered firm had suddenly told government that its shareholders were really debt suppliers receiving 25% interest. Government would then reduce the firm's tax bill by the $385.49 of ITS at t_1. We shall examine the likelihood of that happening in our discussion of imperfections in the conclusion to this section.

those we made in the review of the without-deductibility chapter, you can see that the differences are significant and due totally to the presence of interest tax subsidies in the future cash-flow expectations of leveraged corporations.

Conclusion to Section III

Capital structure has finally proved to be an important financial consideration. As soon as we let capital structure affect the future overall cash-flow expectations of corporations, CAC_T's, θ becomes a significant influence on capital claim values and equityholder present wealth. Capital structure is definitely something with which financial managers must reckon.

According to our theory, however, financial managers' analyses of optimal capital structure should not be very difficult. As a matter of fact, since shareholder wealth is maximized at $\theta = 1$, the best capital structure strategy for corporations is quite simple: become an all-debt firm. As we have seen, that maximizes the value of interest tax subsidy expectations and therefore of shareholder wealth. As anyone can plainly see, however, approaching a 100% debt level is not something that very many corporations do with their capital structure.[15]

Why not? Is something wrong with real-world financial managers? Or is our theory wrong? Why have not companies taken full advantage of government's largess? These questions have been and continue to be debated in financial academe. Although we have no intention whatsoever of reviewing the debate in detail, we *can* make a few observations. First, real-world financial managers, although perhaps not overly concerned with theoretical issues, are hardly likely to overlook benefits of the magnitude implied by capital structure theory. And, to some degree, they do seem to be taking advantage of interest deductibility.

IMPERFEC-TIONS   This tends to make us think that there must be something about real capital markets which limits the complete applicability of this theory. For the most part the academic debate has centered around certain of the assumptions as to the way our theoretical capital market works. For example, it is claimed that the theoretical model cannot be perfectly applicable to actual markets since individual capital-market participants cannot really borrow and lend on the same terms as can large corporations. (If corporate borrowing is somehow accomplished on better terms than individual borrowing, however, it would seem to reinforce our ultimate result.)

[15]We would note, however, that with a somewhat liberalized definition of capital, one can argue that many financial corporations, particularly deposit institutions, are in the θ range of 0.90 to 0.99.

On other fronts, some also claim that the presence of capital flotation and transaction costs in real markets injure the theoretical pricing process. Similarly, the notion that a company can always sell its tax losses (thereby guaranteeing that ITS's do not disappear when a company earns no accounting income) is sometimes singled out as unrealistic. Further, it is often claimed that primary capital markets are not really efficient at all. In reality, it is alleged, they are made up of commercial and investment bankers who depend on historical relationships and rules of thumb rather than on future cash-flow expectations for making lending decisions.

There are arguments and counterarguments, empirical studies and counterstudies on each of these issues, but little resolution has occurred so far. Someday, perhaps, there will be definitive answers. Until then, however, there *are* two real-world considerations, which are of clear significance in explaining why corporations do not use capital structure in exactly the way our theory would indicate. The first of these is both obvious and often understressed. We are, of course, speaking of the role of the tax collector (for example, the Internal Revenue Service in the United States) in enforcing government's taxation intentions.

As we developed the theory of capital structure with interest deductibility, we allowed our corporation to substitute debt for equity in any proportion. Interest deductibility was allowed over all θ's up to and including $\theta = 1$. This meant that total corporate value and shareholder wealth were maximized when debt was completely substituted for equity. Such an optimum (from the viewpoint of shareholders) is, of course, rarely approached.

The IRS, for example, would never allow a corporation to declare itself an all-debt-financed firm for tax purposes. As we suggested earlier in footnote 14 (p. 209), this would be equivalent to an unlevered firm claiming that (1) its equityholders were really debt suppliers, and (2) a good portion of the dividend payments were really interest and therefore deserving of deductibility. Government's interest tax subsidies may be generous, but they are not *that* generous.[16]

The fact remains, however, that government does allow deductibility up to some point. Beyond this point the firm could call some of its payments "interest" if it wished to, but they would not be deductible. This brings us to the question of an optimal capital structure. For each corporation there is some maximum θ above which the taxation authorities will provide no more interest tax subsidies and may well levy some type of penalty. That level of θ is the best capital structure for a corporation in the absence of any other

---

[16]The intent of government in legislating interest deductibility is ostensibly to foster capital formation and real investment within the nation's economy. To this point it is not at all obvious how deductibility could be expected to have such effects. Indeed, about the only major effect we have seen so far is that of increasing equityholder wealth over what it would have been without deductibility. By the time we complete Section V, however, our theory will be much more capable of judging the likelihood of government's aims being accomplished.

imperfections in the capital market. Since penalties could be imposed above that level, VF_0, VE_0, and therefore shareholder wealth might suffer if this optimum θ were exceeded.

With this in mind, our theoretical prescription for the capital structure decision still reads: Maximize the value of interest tax subsidies. The difference made by the imperfection is that the maximum is now somewhat less than $\theta = 1$, the exact level being determined by the taxation authorities, other legal arms of executive or legislative branches of government, and/or courts of law.

The second imperfection which unambiguously has important real-world influence on the capital structure decision arises from the legal power that debt suppliers have to disrupt the operations of a corporation. As we know, corporate debt claims are not risk-free. There is at least some chance, however small, that even the best corporate bonds may not deliver promised interest and/or principal payments. Such a situation is usually termed a "default." As we also know, default per se causes no particular problems within our theory. Whatever risks of default the capital market perceives are explicitly taken into account by the market with setting of the rate of return required by debt suppliers, kd. Since such risks increase as θ does, so does kd.

There is, however, another dimension to corporate debt default which is not explicitly included in capital structure theory but which is probably an important determinant of real corporations' capital structures. This is the real-world *cost* of corporate debt default. Whenever the promised cash flows or any other contractual debt provision is not met, creditors, as we mentioned above, usually have the legal right to disrupt the operations of a corporation. The disruptions may take the form of automatic restrictions on the corporation's capital-raising capabilities, its credit policy, and even its productive asset operations. In addition, the company may face lengthy court actions, or even loss of control to creditors. Such exigencies are not only unpleasant but are very costly to a corporation. (Consider, for example, the always-high cost of litigation.) Restrictions on how the firm may run its business also imply indirect costs likely to be borne by equityholders. Specifically, operational decisions such as those mentioned above are likely to be made in a manner suboptimal from the equityholders' viewpoint (that is, wealth-reducing). In addition, suppliers of capital, labor, and material, as well as customers, tend to avoid corporations in such situations, even those whose managements are confident that earlier expectations can be met. Hence, desirable investment opportunities may have to be foregone.

Obviously, for the sake of existing shareholders, the corporation would like to avoid these situations. The odds of successfully avoiding such contingencies are increased by having lower levels of debt in its capital structure. Whether or not these levels are above or below the θ allowed by taxation authorities' standards is very much dependent on the operational characteristics of the company, its debt suppliers' proclivities for causing a fuss, and, of course, the taxation procedures of government.

The implication of these two imperfections (interest tax subsidy limitations and default costs) is that corporations probably are faced with a complex capital structure decision which involves weighing the benefits of increased interest tax subsidies against the costs of taxation authority sanctions and the functional costs of defaulting on its debt claims, all of these, of course, in present value terms. Since both the costs and the benefits of debt increase in proportion to its presence in the capital structure of a corporation, there is probably an optimal level of θ for real firms.

Formally, we could respecify the corporate valuation formula with deductibility as

$$VF_0 = VU_0 + VITS_0 - VCD_0 \qquad [10.6]$$

where VCD_0 is the present value of the expectations of future default costs implied by a particular capital structure. The optimal capital structure for a corporation is the θ which maximizes VF_0. As θ increases from zero, $VITS_0$ increases to the maximum allowed by taxation authorities, then ceases to increase, and, eventually, probably decreases. VCD_0, however, also increases as θ increases, and since the present value of default costs is a negative value factor, there is probably some proportion of debt less than 100% in a company's capital structure which maximizes its VF_0.

Just because such optima exist, however, does not mean that they are easily discernable. The simple listing of factors we have seen above indicates that such optimal θ's can and doubtless do differ significantly among corporations, for a multitude of real-world reasons. Even the most expert financial practitioners cannot claim to reach exact capital structure optima. Such advice as is available appears in the references cited at the end of this section.

In situations where real decision-making prescriptions are difficult or impossible to specify fully, the theoretical bases of the situation become of primary importance. The corporate capital structure decision is one of these.

SUMMARY This section has extended our theory of corporate finance to include the corporate capital structure decision. By relying on the concepts of corporate valuation developed in Section II and our knowledge of the workings of efficient capital markets, we are now able to analyze the effect of capital structure on equityholders' present wealth, on capital claim values, and on required rates of return and capital costs. Although the arguments occasionally became somewhat intricate, we were always able to fall back on our theoretical conviction that value in the capital market is purely a function of the size, timing, and risk of future cash-flow expectations.

One of our more important conclusions is that when corporate interest payments are deductible, capital structure has definite and predictable effects on financial values and capital market rates. Our financial cash-flow analyses of Chapter 5 were most valuable in helping us to concentrate our attention on the specific cash flows that make capital structure important, the *interest tax subsidies*.

Even more important than these specific capital structure ideas, are two basic economic concepts which were illustrated by our theoretical development in this section. The first of these was the detailed study of the workings of the capital market. One basic economic idea was ratified again and again in our capital structure analyses: Regardless of capital claim alterations and imperfections of various sorts, the underlying capital-market mechanism will value future cash-flow expectations exclusively on the basis of their size, timing, and risk. The second, equally important concept is that any corporate financial decision has significance only to the extent that it offers cash-flow opportunities to the corporation's equity holders which they could not attain by themselves. These two concepts will continue to be of primary importance as we study the remainder of corporate financial theory in Sections IV and V.

Appendix III.A demonstrates that the capital structure ideas we have developed using single-period corporations apply equally well to multiperiod and perpetuity firms. Appendix III.B discusses capital structure theory when capital-market participants are subject to personal income taxes with and without personal interest deductibility. Appendix III.C offers the algebraic statements of capital structure theory for those readers who prefer that more rigorous, less verbally embellished approach. And finally, for those readers who appreciate a purely graphical viewpoint, Appendix III.D provides this approach to capital structure theory.

Appendix III.A: Capital Structure and Multiperiod Corporations

This appendix will briefly demonstrate that our theory of capital structure applies as well to multiperiod as to single-period corporations. We shall first examine a capital structure change for our two-period corporation from Chapter 6. The relevant financial cash flows, required rates, and market values for this company are shown in Table III.A.1 as they appeared initially. Now suppose that the company decides to alter its capital structure at t_0. It does this by issuing \$1991.40 of new debt at t_0, paying off the existing debt suppliers their \$450.00 market value, and distributing \$1541.40 to equity suppliers. The new debt issue carries principal repayment expectations of $PP_1 = \$1009.17$ and $PP_2 = \$982.23$, and interest expectations of $I_1 = \$239.19$ and $I_2 = \$117.87$. The capital market evaluates the riskiness of this issue to require $kd_1 = 12.011\%$ and $kd_2 = 12\%$.[17]

---

[17]The debt rates differ in the two periods because of (1) the assumptions made as to the determination of kd_P based on ku_P and θ, and (2) the fact that the implied ku_P's of this firm are not constant across time. Appendix III.C elaborates these relationships. This also means that the true kd_1 for the original θ is slightly above the 8% rate used in the numerical illustration ($kd_1 = 0.08000625$), but, rounded to the nearest cent, the results in the text of Section II are unaffected.

The company's financial cash-flow expectations after the capital structure alteration are shown in Table III.A.2. From Chapter 10, we can calculate the value of the firm by

$$VF_0 = VU_0 + \sum_{\tau=1}^{T} \frac{ITS_\tau}{(1 + kd)^\tau}$$ **[10.2a]**

TABLE III.A.1   Initial capital structure, two-period firm: financial cash flows, rates, and values

	t_1	t_2
CAU	$2027.28	$1763.64
ITS	18.72	9.36
CAC	2046.00	1773.00
I	36.00	18.00
PP	225.00	225.00
CDD	261.00	243.00
NDC	0.00	0.00
NCDD	261.00	243.00
CAE	1785.00	1530.00
CRF	0.00	0.00
CDE	1785.00	1530.00
NEC	0.00	0.00
NCDE	1785.00	1530.00
TCC $\equiv$ IVS	0.00	0.00

$$kd = 0.08$$
$$ke = 0.20$$
$$kf = 0.182$$
$$kd^* = 0.0384$$
$$kf^* = 0.17576$$
$$\tau = 0.52$$

$VF_0 = \$3000$	$VF_1 = \$1500$
$VD_0 = 450$	$VD_1 = 225$
$VE_0 = 2550$	$VE_1 = 1275$

TABLE III.A.2   New capital structure, two-period firm: financial cash flows

	t_1	t_2
CAU	$2027.28	$1763.64
ITS	124.38	61.29
CAC	2151.66	1824.93
I	239.19	117.87
PP	1009.17	982.23
CDD	1248.36	1100.10
NDC	0.00	0.00
NCDD	1248.36	1100.10
CAE	903.30	724.83
CRF	0.00	0.00
CDE	903.30	724.83
NEC	0.00	0.00
NCDE	903.30	724.83

All we need to know is VU_0. This can be calculated by using the values and cash flows for the company before the change:

$$VF_0 = VU_0 + VITS_0$$
$$VU_0 = VF_0 - VITS_0$$
$$= \$3000.00 - \frac{\$18.72}{1.08} - \frac{\$9.36}{(1.08)^2}$$
$$= \$2974.64$$

So the new value of the firm is

$$VF_0 = VU_0 + VITS_0$$
$$= \$2974.64 + \frac{\$124.38}{1.12011} + \frac{\$61.29}{(1.12011)(1.12)}$$
$$= \$3134.54$$

The value of the debt is given by

$$VD_0 = \sum_{T=1}^{T} \frac{NCDD_T}{(1 + kd)^T} \qquad \text{[7.1a]}$$
$$= \frac{\$1248.36}{1.12011} + \frac{\$1100.10}{(1.12011)(1.12)}$$

which is, of course,

$$VD_0 = \$1991.40$$

and the equity value is

$$VE_0 = VF_0 - VD_0$$
$$= \$3134.54 - \$1991.40$$
$$= \$1143.14$$

If our capital structure theory is correct, equity value should not have decreased by the full amount of the $1541.40 that equityholders received. VE_0 initially was $2550.00; now it is $1143.14. $2550.00 − $1143.14 = $1406.86. Equity value has not decreased by the full $1541.40, so equityholders' present wealth has increased by $1541.40 − $1406.86 = $134.54. Why $134.54? Calculating the value of the *new* interest tax subsidies, we get

$$VITS_0 \text{ (new)} = \frac{\$124.38}{1.12011} + \frac{\$61.29}{(1.12011)(1.12)}$$
$$= \$159.90$$

But the capital structure change also implies that the *initial* interest tax subsidies no longer exist. They were worth

$$VITS_0 \text{ (initial)} = \frac{\$18.72}{1.08} + \frac{\$9.36}{(1.08)^2}$$
$$= \$25.36$$

So the difference between the new and initial $VITS_0$'s is

$$\Delta VITS_0 = \$159.90 - \$25.36 = \$134.54$$

With the capital structure change, equity suppliers' present wealth has increased by the difference between the $VITS_0$ they gave up, and the $VITS_0$ they acquire under the new capital structure. This is exactly as our theory predicts.

We can, from Section II, also test the validity of our capital structure theory on the perpetuity corporation. The initial characteristics of this company appear in Table III.A.3.

Now suppose that the perpetuity decided to alter its capital structure at t_0. It does this by issuing \$11,063.11 of new debt, paying off initial debt suppliers their \$3850.00 market value, and distributing the difference, \$7213.11, to equity suppliers at t_0.[18] The new debt issue carries principal repayment expectations of \$400.00 per period, and interest expectations become \$1659.47 per period forever.[19] The capital market, because of the increased risk, raises the required rate of debt to $kd = 15\%$ (up from 7% initially). Table III.A.4 displays the altered financial cash-flow expectations for this perpetuity. (The cash flows, values, and rates which appear in the remainder of this appendix are the result of calculations carried to an accuracy of ten digits.)

TABLE III.A.3   Initial capital structure, perpetual corporation: financial cash flows, rates, and values

t_1 *through* t_∞	
CAU	\$2759.86
ITS	140.14
CAC	2900.00
I	269.50
PP	280.00
CDD	549.50
NDC	280.00
NCDD	269.50
CAE	2350.50
CRF	220.00
CDE	2130.50
NEC	200.00
NCDE	1930.50
TCC $\equiv$ IVS	700.00

$$ke = 0.27$$
$$kd = 0.07$$
$$kf = 0.20$$
$$kf^* = 0.18726$$
$$kd^* = 0.0336$$
$$\tau = 0.52$$
$$VF_0 = \$11,000$$
$$VD_0 = \ \ 3,850$$
$$VE_0 = \ \ 7,150$$

[18]The amount of new debt issued is designed to bring the level of θ to 0.75. The relationship used to calculate the \$11,063.11 appears in Appendix III.C to this section.

[19]As we shall explore further in Section IV, the PP amount is essentially arbitrary.

TABLE III.A.4   Altered capital structure, perpetual corporation: financial cash flows

	t_1 through t_∞
CAU	$2759.86
ITS	862.92
CAC	3622.78
I	1659.47
PP	400.00
CDD	2059.47
NDC	400.00
NCDD	1659.47
CAE	1563.31
CRF	200.00
CDE	1363.31
NEC	100.00
NCDE	1263.31
TCC $\equiv$ IVS	700.00

VU_0 can be calculated, as for the two-period firm, from the following initial capital structure information:

$$VU_0 = VF_0 - VITS_0$$
$$= \$11{,}000.00 - \frac{\$140.14}{0.07}$$
$$= \$8998$$

Hence, the new total firm value is

$$VF_0 = VU_0 + VITS_0$$
$$\simeq \$8998.00 + \frac{\$862.92}{0.15}$$
$$\simeq \$14{,}750.82$$

and since debt value for a perpetuity is

$$VD_0 = \frac{NCDD}{kd}$$
$$\simeq \frac{\$1659.47}{0.15}$$
$$= \$11{,}063.11$$

equity value becomes

$$VE_0 = VF_0 - VD_0$$
$$\simeq \$14{,}750.82 - \$11{,}063.11$$
$$\simeq \$3687.71$$

How have equityholders been affected? They received $7213.11 in cash at t_0, and their equity value has decreased by $3462.29 (= $7150.00 − $3687.71). So their present wealth increased by their cash receipt of $7213.11 less the value decrease, $3462.29, or $3750.82. Where did this wealth increase come from? It should be equal to the difference between the initial and new values of the interest tax subsidies:

$$\mathrm{VITS}_0 \text{ (initial)} = \frac{\$140.14}{0.07} = \$2002.00$$

$$\mathrm{VITS}_0 \text{ (new)} = \frac{\$862.92}{0.15} = \$5752.82$$

$$\mathrm{VITS}_0 \text{ (new)} - \mathrm{VITS}_0 \text{ (initial)} = \$3750.82$$

So when we alter its θ, the perpetuity also behaves consistently with our capital structure theory. We can also use this example to check the behavior of required rates and capital costs under a capital structure change.

The initial ke, kd, kf, kf^*, and kd^* appear in Table III.A.3. For the new capital structure, equity's required rate is:

$$ke = \frac{\mathrm{NCDE}}{\mathrm{VE}_0} \quad \text{for perpetuities}$$

$$\simeq \frac{\$1263.31}{\$3687.71}$$

$$\simeq 34.3\%$$

Debt's, as we know, is

$$kd = 15\%$$

And the overall required rate becomes

$$kf = \frac{\mathrm{CAC} - \mathrm{IVS}}{\mathrm{VF}_0} \quad \text{for perpetuities}$$

$$\simeq \frac{\$3622.78 - \$700.00}{\$14,750.82}$$

$$\simeq 19.8\%$$

Also, $kd^* = kd(1 - \tau)$. So $kd^* = 0.15(1 - 0.52) = 7.2\%$. And, finally,

$$kf^* = \frac{\mathrm{CAU} - \mathrm{IVS}}{\mathrm{VF}_0} \quad \text{for perpetuities}$$

$$\simeq \frac{\$2759.86 - \$700.00}{\$14,750.82}$$

$$\simeq 14.0\%$$

Figure III.A.1 graphs the behavior of required rates and capital costs as we, in this example, change $\theta = \mathrm{VD}/\mathrm{VF}$ from 0.35 to 0.75. Notice that the capital structure relationships are exactly as Chapter 10 would predict. The ke steadily increases from

$$ku = \frac{\mathrm{CAU} - \mathrm{IVS}}{\mathrm{VU}_0}$$

$$= \frac{\$2759.86 - \$700.00}{\$8998.00}$$

$$\simeq 22.9\%$$

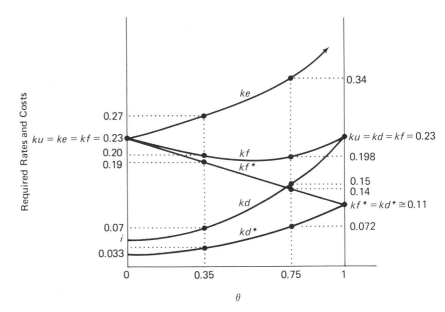

FIGURE III.A.1   Capital structure, required rates, and capital costs: perpetuity example

The kf declines from ku, reaches a minimum, and then increases back to ku.[20] The kd steadily increases from i to ku. The kd^* also increases but more slowly than kd. And kf^*, the overall cost of capital, steadily decreases from ku to $ku(1 - \tau)$, where it equals kd^*.

Finally, Figure III.A.2 graphs the relationship between capital structure and market values for this company. By comparing it with Figure 10.4 you can see that the theory of Chapter 10 is again verified.

FIGURE III.A.2   Capital structure and market values: perpetuity example

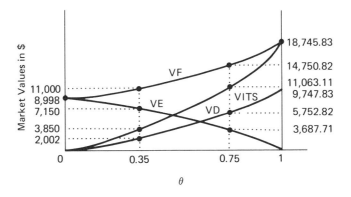

[20]Appendix III.C elaborates the particular turning points.

Appendix III.B: Personal Income Taxes and Interest Deductibility

In Chapter 10 we stated that corporate interest deductibility gives capital-market participants something they cannot get for themselves, namely, the value of corporate ITS's. That particular assertion is a crucial one to the shareholder wealth effects, market valuations, and required rate relationships in our capital structure theory.

In the absence of personal income taxes, corporate interest deductibility was the critical variable that caused capital structure to matter, in contrast to the without-deductibility situation, where the corporation could not do anything for capital-market participants which they could not do for themselves independent of corporate capital structure decisions.

But what about the existence of *personal* income taxes, either in addition to or in place of corporate income taxes? Does it matter whether or not personal interest payments are deductible? And if they are, does that not mean that personal interest tax subsidies will provide capital-market participants with the same benefits as those coming from corporate borrowing?

This appendix will address these questions, and, in particular, we will begin by showing that the answer to that last question is, in general, no. Except under very special circumstances, personal borrowing is not substitutable for corporate borrowing for ITS purposes, even when personal interest payments are deductible. Said another way, capital-market participants cannot, in general, reproduce wealth effects through personal leverage equal to those produced by corporate leverage.

To prove this, all we need show is that the equityholder ends up with a higher cash-flow expectation at no more risk when he allows the firm to leverage itself rather than carry a comparable amount of deductible debt in his own portfolio. A very simple example will suffice to show that this must be true. Suppose there are two corporate perpetuities, identical except for leverage. They each perpetually expect CAU of $500 per period and IVS of $50 per period. But one has debt outstanding that requires a perpetual $100 interest payment; the other has no debt. Assume that the corporate tax rate, τ_c, is 60% and the personal tax rate, τ_p, is 40%, and that interest payments of each type are deductible for the paying entity's income tax purposes.

The equityholders of the leveraged firm expect to have, after *all* taxes, personal cash (PC) as follows:

$$\begin{aligned} PC &= (\text{NCDE from the firm}) - \tau_p(\text{NCDE from the firm}) \\ &= (\text{CAU} + \text{ITS} - \text{I}_c - \text{IVS}) - \tau_p(\text{CAU} + \text{ITS} - \text{I}_c - \text{IVS}) \\ &= (\text{CAU} + \text{ITS} - \text{I}_c - \text{IVS})(1 - \tau_p) \end{aligned}$$

which, since ITS $= I_c \cdot \tau_c$, gives us, in this case,

$$PC = \$[500 + (100)(0.6) - 100 - 50](1 - 0.4)$$
$$= \$410(1 - 0.4) = \$246$$

By comparison, suppose that equityholders of the unlevered firm had duplicated the leveraged firm's debt by borrowing in their personal portfolios. This means that they expect to pay $100 of personal interest each period, and, assuming deductibility of personal interest, they also expect to receive the appropriate personal interest tax subsidy. Their expected PC position after all taxes is

$$PC = (NCDE) - \tau_p(NCDE) - (\text{personal interest})$$
$$+ (\text{personal interest tax subsidy})$$
$$= (CAU - IVS) - \tau_p(CAU - IVS) - I_p + I_p\tau_p$$
$$= (CAU - IVS)(1 - \tau_p) - [I_p(1 - \tau_p)]$$
$$= (CAU - IVS - I_p)(1 - \tau_p)$$

which evaluates to

$$PC = \$(500 - 50 - 100)(1 - 0.4)$$
$$= (\$350)(0.6) = \$210$$

The personally leveraged shareholders have not been able to duplicate the benefits of corporate leverage. The leveraged firm's shareholders expect $246 per period; the personally leveraged shareholders net only $210. So long as individuals and corporations can borrow on the same terms ($kd \leftrightarrow \theta$ relationships are the same for each; $I = I_c = I_p$), then regardless of the levels of τ_c and τ_p (even including $\tau_c = \tau_p$), the amount of personal cash resulting from corporate leverage will always be greater than that resulting from equal personal leverage. Notice that the leveraged firm shareholders get

$$\$(CAU + ITS - I - IVS)(1 - \tau_p)$$

whereas the personally leveraged shareholders get

$$\$(CAU - I - IVS)(1 - \tau_p)$$

The difference between the two is

$$(ITS)(1 - \tau_p)$$

What personal leveraging misses is the corporate interest tax subsidy, ITS, times $(1 - \tau_p)$. Regardless of the specific τ_c and τ_p rates, some dollar difference will always remain. For our example,

$$(ITS)(1 - \tau_p) = (I \cdot \tau_c)(1 - \tau_p)$$
$$= (\$100)(0.6)(1 - 0.4)$$
$$= \$36$$

The difference between $246 and $210 is $36.

There is no mystery involved in this. With corporate leverage the interest deduction is recognized earlier in the cash-flow stream, lowering the tax liability on both the corporate and personal cash flows. With personal leverage, interest lowers the tax liability on only the personal cash flows.

Given the existence of corporate income tax, there are many personal cash-flow situations that might obtain, depending on the presence or absence of corporate interest deductibility, personal income taxes, personal interest deductibility, and whether leverage is contracted at the corporate or personal level. Table III.B.1 arrays the seven substantive personal cash-flow situations that equityholders may experience as the conditions listed above vary. Table III.B.2 presents the formulations of the equityholder cash-flow expectations for each of the seven situations. (Perpetuities are assumed.)

Earlier, in Chapter 9, we discussed the irrelevancy of capital structure in the absence of corporate interest deductibility (and personal interest deductibility since there were no personal income taxes). Situations E and G in Table III.B.2 illustrate this same point: equityholders' total expectations are identical whether leverage is corporate or personal. Also, we just demonstrated in this appendix that situations A and B are not equivalent. When corporate

TABLE III.B.1   Equityholder cash-flow situations

Situs of leverage	*Personal income taxes*	*Corporate interest deductibility**	*Personal interest deductibility*,†*	*Situation identification*
Corporate	Yes	Yes	Irrelevant	A
Personal	Yes	Irrelevant	Yes	B
Personal	Yes	Irrelevant	No	C
Corporate	No	Yes	Irrelevant	D
Personal	No	Irrelevant	Irrelevant	E
Corporate	Yes	No	Irrelevant	F
Corporate	No	No	Irrelevant	G

*Corporate or personal interest deductibility is, of course, irrelevant if the situs of the leverage is, respectively, personal or corporate.
†Personal interest deductibility is also irrelevant in the absence of personal income taxes.

TABLE III.B.2   Equityholder cash-flow expectations after all taxes (perpetuities)

Situation identification*	*Corporate distribution* $(NCDE)$ $\overline{(CAU-I-IVS)+ITS}$	$-$ *Personal interest* $-$	*Personal income taxes*	$=$	*Total expectation*
A	$(CAU-I-IVS)+\tau_c\cdot I$	$-$ 0	$-\tau_p(CAU-I+\tau_c\cdot I-IVS)$	$=(CAU-I+\tau_c\cdot I-IVS)(1-\tau_p)$	
B	$(CAU-IVS)+0$	$-$ I	$-\tau_p(CAU-IVS-I)$	$=(CAU-I-IVS)(1-\tau_p)$	
C	$(CAU-IVS)+0$	$-$ I	$-\tau_p(CAU-IVS)$	$=(CAU-IVS)(1-\tau_p)-I$	
D	$(CAU-I-IVS)+\tau_c\cdot I$	$-$ 0	$-$ 0	$=CAU-I+\tau_c\cdot I-IVS$	
E	$(CAU-IVS)+0$	$-$ I	$-$ 0	$=CAU-I-IVS$	
F	$(CAU-I-IVS)+0$	$-$ 0	$-\tau_p(CAU-I-IVS)$	$=(CAU-I-IVS)(1-\tau_p)$	
G	$(CAU-I-IVS)+0$	$-$ 0	$-$ 0	$=CAU-I-IVS$	

*From Table III.B.1.

interest is deductible, not only does capital structure matter when there are *no* personal income taxes, it remains relevant when personal income taxes *are* introduced.

We can also see from situations C and F that even in the absence of corporate interest deductibility, capital structure does matter if there are personal income taxes also without deductibility. If the personal income tax law does allow personal interest deductibility, however, then we see from situations B and F that capital structure is once again irrelevant because equityholders' personal leverage can exactly reproduce the wealth effects of corporate leverage. Whether the corporation or the equityholder pays the interest, there is no impact on NTAX and identical impact on personal taxes.

Appendix III.C: Algebraic Capital Structure Relationships

In developing the algebraic expressions describing capital structure relationships, we shall focus on the with-deductibility situation because that model is the most complex. Hence, we shall build on the proposition that we defended in Chapter 10:

$$\text{VF}_0 = \text{VU}_0 + \sum_{\text{T}=1}^{T} \frac{\text{ITS}_{\text{T}}}{\prod_{\text{P}=1}^{\text{T}} (1 + kd_{\text{P}})} \qquad \textbf{[10.2]}$$

PERPE-TUITIES FIRST We shall begin, however, using the perpetuity model. This is done to keep the algebra as simple as possible. Thus, the following are perpetuity relationships unless stated otherwise. We shall also present single- and multiperiod formulas toward the end of this appendix.

For a perpetuity,

$$\text{VF} = \text{VU} + \frac{\text{ITS}}{kd}$$

or

$$\text{VF} = \text{VU} + \frac{\tau \text{I}}{kd}$$

Since $\text{I}/kd = \text{VD}$,

$$\text{VF} = \text{VU} + \tau \text{VD}$$

Dividing by VF,

$$1 = \frac{\text{VU}}{\text{VF}} + \tau\theta$$

and

$$\text{VF} = \frac{\text{VU}}{1 - \tau\theta} \qquad \textbf{[III.C.1]}$$

Note that when $\theta = 1$,

$$VF = \frac{VU}{1 - \tau}$$

Recalling that ϕ is defined as VU/VF, we get, from formula III.C.1,

$$\frac{VU}{VF} = 1 - \tau\theta$$

and

$$\phi = 1 - \tau\theta \qquad \text{[III.C.2]}$$

so

$$VF = \frac{VU}{\phi} \qquad \text{[III.C.1a]}$$

For a perpetuity, ϕ decreases linearly from 1 to $1 - \tau$ as θ moves from zero to 1, and consequently VF steadily increases (hyperbolically) over the same range. This is consistent with our theory developed in Chapter 10.

Now take the relationship

$$CAC = CAU + ITS$$

Dividing by VF,

$$\frac{CAC}{VF} = \frac{CAU}{VF} + \frac{ITS}{VF}$$

Since $ITS = \tau kd VD$ and, for perpetuities, $CAC/VF = kf$, we get

$$kf = \frac{CAU}{VF} + \tau kd \frac{VD}{VF}$$

or

$$kf = \frac{CAU}{VF} + \tau kd\theta$$

Using Formula III.C.1 to substitute for VF,

$$kf = \frac{CAU}{VU}(1 - \tau\theta) + \tau kd\theta$$

Since $CAU/VU = ku$,

$$kf = ku(1 - \tau\theta) + \tau\theta kd$$

This is simply formula 10.3,

$$kf = \phi ku + (1 - \phi)kd \qquad \text{[10.3]}$$

with the perpetuity value of ϕ, $1 - \tau\theta$, substituted. It can also be rewritten as

$$kf = ku - \tau(ku - kd)\theta \qquad \text{[III.C.3]}$$

and from

$$kf = \theta kd + (1 - \theta)ke \qquad \text{[8.1]}$$

we get

$$ke = \frac{ku(1 - \tau\theta) - \theta kd(1 - \tau)}{1 - \theta} \qquad \text{[III.C.4]}$$

or, equivalently,

$$ke = \frac{\phi ku + kd(1 - \phi - \theta)}{1 - \theta} \qquad \text{[III.C.4a]}$$

Formula III.C.4a is generally true for all corporations, not just perpetuities, since it is expressed in terms of ϕ, rather than in terms of the perpetuity value for ϕ ($= 1 - \tau\theta$) as is formula III.C.4.

If we were to choose any reasonable $kd \leftrightarrow \theta$ relationship of the general form

$$kd = i + (ku - i)\theta^n \qquad \text{[III.C.5]}$$

(where n is any real number greater than or equal to one) and plot all the preceding formulas for kf, ke, and kd for all levels of θ, the relationships would appear exactly as those for our with-deductibility graphs in Chapter 10. Formula III.C.4 can also be used to derive the following relationship for perpetuities:

$$kf^* = \phi ku = (1 - \tau\theta)ku \qquad \text{[III.C.6]}$$

Using the relationship

$$kf^* = \theta kd^* + (1 - \theta)ke \qquad \text{[10.4]}$$

we can rewrite in terms of ke to get

$$ke = \frac{kf^* - \theta kd^*}{1 - \theta} \qquad \text{[III.C.7]}$$

which is generally true for all corporations. Then we take the relationship

$$kd^* = kd(1 - \tau) \qquad \text{[7.2]}$$

substitute for kd^* in formula III.C.7, and compare the result with formula III.C.4 to see that formula III.C.6 must be true.

These capital cost $\leftrightarrow \theta$ relationships (formulas III.C.6, 10.4, and 7.2) are also algebraically identical to those shown graphically in the main body of Chapter 10.

For those readers who may be interested, the minimum level of kf as θ goes from 0 to 1 for a perpetuity (although the particular point has no economic significance) is

$$kf_{\min} \text{ at } \theta^* = \left(\frac{1}{n + 1}\right)^{1/n} = (n + 1)^{-1/n} \qquad \text{[III.C.8]}[21]$$

where n is the exponent of θ in the formula

$$kd = i + (ku - i)\theta^n \qquad \text{[III.C.5]}$$

You may have noticed that in our perpetuity capital structure example in Chapter 10, kf reached a minimum between the two θ's we were using, 0.35 and 0.75. We knew that kf's minimum was necessarily at $\theta \simeq 0.58$ because the $kd \leftrightarrow \theta$ relationship we used (not explicitly stated) approximated $n = 2$.

[21]The derivation of the perpetuity kf minimum is presented in C. W. Haley and L. D. Schall, *The Theory of Financial Decisions* (New York: McGraw-Hill Book Company, 1973), pp. 323–324.

MORE GENERAL RELATION- SHIPS

For single-period and multiperiod nonperpetuity corporations the relationships between capital structure, market values, required rates, and capital costs are, as we know, economically the same as those for constant perpetuities which appear above. Algebraically, however, the relationships are more intricate.[22]

We do, however, wish to explore some aspects of these relationships for single-period and multiperiod nonperpetuity corporations. To do this we need first to define some new concepts. ku_P^ψ shall be the single-period required rate of return on the equity of a corporation when the company is unlevered for period P but not for any other period. Similarly, VU_{T-1}^ψ is defined as the value of a company unlevered for the period P (with $P = T$), but not thereafter. If we unlever a firm for only period P, we give up its ITS_T, and

$$VU_{T-1}^\psi = VF_{T-1} - \frac{ITS_T}{1 + kd_P} \qquad \text{where } P = T \qquad \text{[III.C.10]}$$

In Section II we argued that one-period required rates on beginning value are equal to that period's cash-flow expectations plus any value change over the period divided by the value at the beginning of the period. So for a firm unlevered for only time period P (ending at time point T), the cash-flow expectation is $CAU_T - IVS_T$, the value change from time point $T - 1$ to T is $VF_T - VU_{T-1}^\psi$, and the initial value is therefore VU_{T-1}^ψ. Thus, with $P = T$,

$$ku_P^\psi = \frac{CAU_T - IVS_T + VF_T - VU_{T-1}^\psi}{VU_{T-1}^\psi} \qquad \text{[III.C.11]}$$

or

$$ku_P^\psi = \frac{CAU_T - IVS_T + VF_T}{VU_{T-1}^\psi} - 1 \qquad \text{[III.C.11a]}$$

If ke_P, kd_P, and kf_P for a firm are constant across time, then ku_P^ψ will also be constant across time. In general, however, it is extremely unlikely that such conditions will exist. Even if ku_P is constant across time (because the capital market views all $CAU_T - IVS_T$ flows to be of equal risk—that is, business risk is invariant) and even if management holds θ constant (these two conditions implying no change in kd_P over time), kf_P will, in general, vary from period to period. In finite multiperiod cases, kf_P is constant only for constant

---

[22]For example, the θ which generates the minimum kf in a one-period firm is given by the $\theta*$ which solves the following cubic equation:

$$(\theta*)^{3n}(n + 1)q^2 + (\theta*)^{2n}[2i(n + 1) + 1 - q + 2n]q$$
$$+ (\theta*)^n[(n + 1)(i^2 + i - q) - 2qi] - i(i + 1) = 0 \qquad \text{[III.C.9]}$$

where n is defined as before and $q = ku - i$. Although clearly more complex, the derivation of this formula follows the same logic and procedures as that for the perpetuity case. Although it was not previously specified, we used $n = 2$ and $i = 5.46875\%$ for our single-period example in Chapter 10. In that example, minimum kf occurs at $\theta \simeq 71.75\%$ with a corresponding kd of 15.511%.

perpetuities and two other very restrictively defined firms.[23] The reasons we are interested in ku_{P}^{ψ} even though it is not generally constant across time is that it is relatively easy to compute and from it we can quickly and directly arrive at kf_{P} and other parameters that vary from period to period in the nonperpetuity multiperiod world. The general relationships between ku and other rates as a function of and in relationship to capital structure are most complex and difficult, if not impossible, for the usual type of finite multi-period firm. Based on ku_{P}^{ψ}, however, one-period relationships can be isolated. Some of these are presented below.

The final new variable we need to define is ϕ_{P}^{ψ}:

$$\phi_{\text{P}}^{\psi} = \frac{\text{VU}_{\text{T}-1}^{\psi}}{\text{VF}_{\text{T}-1}} \qquad \text{[III.C.12]}$$

ϕ_{P}^{ψ} has the valuable characteristic of being invariant over time as long as θ is held constant. It is this invariance that will allow us to proceed with our analysis of multiperiod firms using relatively simple algebra. Also keep in mind that for a single-period firm and for the final period of a multiperiod firm, $ku^{\psi} = ku$, $\text{VU}^{\psi} = \text{VU}$, and $\phi^{\psi} = \phi$.

For single-period corporations and for single periods of multiperiod corporations having constant θ and kd, the following relationships hold:

$$kf_{\text{P}} = ku_{\text{P}}^{\psi} - \tau(ku_{\text{P}}^{\psi} - kd)\theta\frac{kd}{1 + kd} \qquad \text{[III.C.13]}$$

This formula is the general statement of

$$kf = ku - \tau(ku - kd)\theta\frac{kd}{1 + kd} \qquad \text{[III.C.13a]}$$

the single-period-firm counterpart of formula III.C.3,

$$kf = ku - \tau(ku - kd)\theta \qquad \text{[III.C.3]}$$

which we developed above for perpetuities. Similarly,

$$\phi^{\psi} = 1 - \theta\tau\frac{kd}{1 + kd} \qquad \text{[III.C.14]}$$

$$1 - \phi^{\psi} = \theta\tau\frac{kd}{1 + kd} \qquad \text{[III.C.14a]}$$

$$\text{VF} = \frac{\text{VU}^{\psi}}{\phi^{\psi}} \qquad \text{[III.C.15]}$$

$$kf_{\text{P}} = \phi^{\psi}ku_{\text{P}}^{\psi} + (1 - \phi^{\psi})kd \qquad \text{[III.C.16]}[24]$$

$$ke_{\text{P}} = \frac{\phi^{\psi}ku_{\text{P}}^{\psi} + kd(1 - \phi^{\psi} - \theta)}{1 - \theta} \qquad \text{[III.C.17]}$$

$$kf_{\text{P}}^{*} = \phi^{\psi}(1 + ku_{\text{P}}^{\psi}) - 1 \qquad \text{[III.C.18]}$$

[23]If kf is constant across time, the risk of the overall cash flow, CAC − IVS, must also be constant. This implies that if both components of CAC, CAU and ITS, have constant risk, they must constitute the same proportions of CAC over time for kf to be constant. The second possible case would involve a changing ku which would exactly offset the change in kf caused by the altering proportions of CAU and ITS in CAC.

[24]This is the modification we promised to formula 10.3 to allow its general application.

Formula III.C.18 is the general version of the single-period counterpart,

$$kf^* = \phi(1 + ku) - 1 \qquad \qquad \textbf{[10.5]}$$

Footnote 13 (p. 205) in the main body of Chapter 10 promised a derivation of this formula and a proof that kf^* continually decreases as θ increases from 0 to 1. We used this assertion about kf^* to show that VF, and hence VITS, both continually increase over the same range of θ.

First, we need to express ϕ in terms of θ. Starting with the facts that

$$\phi = \frac{\text{VU}}{\text{VF}}$$

$$\text{VF} = \text{VU} + \text{VITS}$$

and, for the one-period firm,

$$\text{VITS} = \frac{\text{ITS}}{1 + kd} = \frac{\theta kd\tau \text{VF}}{1 + kd}$$

we get

$$\text{VITS} = \frac{\theta kd\tau(\text{VU} + \text{VITS})}{1 + kd}$$

$$= \frac{\theta kd\tau \text{VU}}{1 + kd - \theta kd\tau}$$

and

$$\phi = \frac{\text{VU}}{\text{VU} + \dfrac{\theta kd\tau \text{VU}}{1 + kd - \theta kd\tau}}$$

The latter expression reduces to

$$\phi = 1 - \frac{\theta kd\tau}{1 + kd}$$

and

$$1 - \phi = \frac{\theta kd\tau}{1 + kd} \qquad \qquad \textbf{[III.C.19]}$$

Recalling that

$$kf^* = \theta kd^* + (1 - \theta)ke \qquad \qquad \textbf{[10.4]}$$

and

$$kd^* = kd(1 - \tau) \qquad \qquad \textbf{[7.2]}$$

we get

$$kf^* = \theta kd - \theta kd\tau + (1 - \theta)ke$$
$$= [\theta kd + (1 - \theta)ke] - \theta kd\tau$$
$$= kf - \theta kd\tau$$

Substituting for kf from formula 10.3,

$$kf^* = [\phi ku + (1 - \phi)kd] - \theta kd\tau$$
$$= \phi ku + [(1 - \phi)kd - \theta kd\tau]$$
$$= \phi ku + [(1 - \phi)kd - (1 - \phi)(1 + kd)]$$

the last step being derived from the use of formula III.C.19. Then

$$\begin{aligned}
kf^* &= \phi ku + (1 - \phi)(kd - 1 - kd) \\
&= \phi ku - (1 - \phi) \\
&= \phi ku - 1 + \phi \\
&= \phi(ku + 1) - 1 \qquad\qquad\qquad \textbf{[10.4]}
\end{aligned}$$

or, in terms of θ,

$$kf^* = \frac{\tau kd\theta}{1 + kd}(1 + ku) \qquad\qquad \textbf{[III.C.20]}$$

The first derivative of kf^* with respect to θ is given by

$$\frac{d}{d\theta} kf^* = \frac{-a}{(1 + kd)^2}(kd^2 + kd + bn)$$

where $a = \tau(1 + ku)$, $b = kd - i$, and n is from formula III.C.5. Since kd is always $\geq i$ in the range $0 \leq \theta \leq 1$, and $\tau > 0$, and ku and kd are > 0, this tells us that the slope of the kf^* curve must always be negative, as was depicted in Figure 10.1.

HOW MUCH DEBT? Another interesting question is that of how much debt must be issued by an unlevered firm in order to become levered to a particular level of θ. We leave as an exercise for the reader the demonstration that for all firms, VD is given by

$$VD_{T-1} = \frac{\theta VU_{T-1}}{\phi_P} \qquad \text{where P} = \text{T} \qquad \textbf{[III.C.21]}$$

It is, of course, also true that

$$VD_T = \frac{\theta VU_T^{\psi}}{\phi^{\psi}} \qquad\qquad\qquad \textbf{[III.C.21a]}$$

Appendix III.D: Graphical Capital Structure

In this appendix we shall present the theoretical results of Section III in graphical form. As we indicated in Section I, graphical displays being limited to two dimensions requires us to use only single-period corporations for this type of analysis. In addition, although the numerical illustrations are exact, we have occasionally taken liberties with the axis scales of the graphs so as to emphasize a relationship which is difficult to see with normal scaling.

Figure III.D.1 presents the graph of our single-period unlevered without-deductibility firm from Chapter 9. You recall that the firm's expected CAU_1 was $1500, which with a $ku = 20\%$ gave a t_0 market price = VU_0 = $1250. As in Chapter 1, the vertical axis of the graph is the t_1 cash flow, and the horizontal axis is the t_0 (present) value of the t_1 flow. The line joining CAU_1 and VU_0 represents the capital-market rate appropriate for discounting the risky CAU_1 expectation back to equal VU_0. That rate, of course,

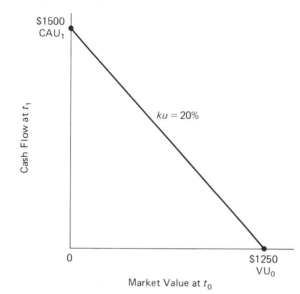

FIGURE III.D.1   Graphical one-period firm—unlevered

is ku. [The slope of that diagonal line is equal to $-(1 + ku)$ or -1.20.] Thus, by using our simple one-period graphical display from Chapter 1, we can depict the cash-flow expectation, required rate, and market value of an unlevered firm.

But how about capital structure relationships? Look at Figure III.D.2. You recall that this one-period company issued $450 of debt at t_0, with the expectation of a $495 t_1 payment to debt suppliers. On the vertical axis of Figure III.D.2, we have indicated that this action splits the unchanged CAU_1 of $1500 into a $495 $NCDD_1$ and a $1005 $NCDE_1$. The valuation of these two streams is indicated on the horizontal axis. The unchanged $VF_0 = VU_0 = 1250 is split into $VD_0 = 450 and $VE_0 = 800. Graphically, required rates are indicated by the negative of 1 plus the slope of the line joining each cash-flow expectation to its market value. Look at the shaded triangle in the upper left. That is the one-period debt supplier's situation. The vertical axis $= 495; the horizontal $= 450. So kd is

$$kd = -\left(1 + \frac{-495}{450}\right) = 0.10 \quad \text{or} \quad 10\%$$

The slope of the hypotenuse of that triangle indicates a $kd = 10\%$. Similarly, the lower-right shaded triangle is equity's situation:

$$ke = -\left(1 + \frac{-1005}{800}\right) = 0.25625 \quad \text{or} \quad 25\tfrac{5}{8}\%$$

These are the same rates that we calculated in Chapter 9.

More generally, notice that the slope of debt's hypotenuse is less steep than the $kf = ku$ overall rate of 20%, and equity's slope is steeper than the

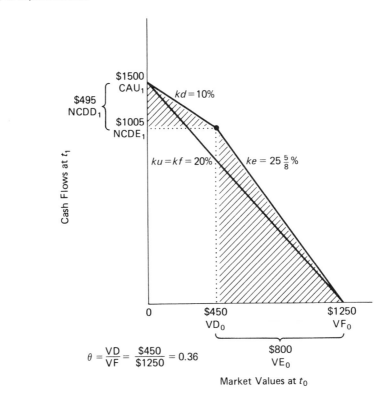

FIGURE III.D.2 Graphical one-period capital structure without deductibility (I)

overall line's slope. Our without-deductibility theory predicts this result. The kf is, of course, unchanged at 20% after the capital structure change. In graphical terms it is easy to see that all the firm has succeeded in doing is to split the 20% overall rate into two parts, a 10% debt rate weighted at $450/1250 = \theta$, and a $25\frac{5}{8}$% equity rate weighted at $800/1250 = 1 - \theta$. The overall rate and value of the firm are unaffected by capital structure because we are still working with the identical overall cash-flow expectation, CAU_1.

Further, Figure III.D.3 indicates that as long as CAU_1 is constant with respect to capital structure, these general relationships hold. Here we have again altered capital structure to $VD_0 = \$800$. kd increases to $14\frac{3}{8}$%, as indicated by the steeper kd line, and ke increases to 30%, as shown by the steeper ke line. kf, their weighted average, is constant. These relationships continue (ke and kd both increasing, kf constant) until $\theta = 1$ is reached, where, as you can imagine, the kd line becomes the same as the $ku = kf$ line $= 20$%. Value, of course, remains unchanged.

The with-deductibility case can also be shown graphically. Recall our one-period with-deductibility firm in Chapter 10. $CAU_1 = \$3630, ku = 25$%,

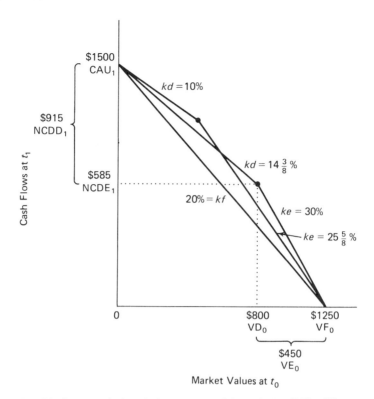

FIGURE III.D.3 Graphical one-period capital structure without deductibility (II)

and $VU_0 = \$2904$. When capital structure was changed by issuing $1800 of debt, CAU_1 was incremented by a less-risky $ITS_1 = \$108$. This resulted in a decrease in kf to 24.6%, and an increase in kd to 12.5% and ke to 42.75%. All of this is shown in the rather baroque Figure III.D.4.[25] Again, the vertical axis depicts t_1 cash flows, showing the increase of $108 due to the interest tax subsidy. The horizontal axis shows that market value of the firm increases from $VU_0 = \$2904$ to $VF_0 = \$3000$. Note that the overall required rate with leverage is the negative of 1 plus the slope of the line joining $CAC_1 = \$3738$ to $VF_0 = \$3000$, and that its slope is less steep than that of the unlevered line joining $CAU_1 = \$3630$ to $VU_0 = \$2904$. The shaded triangles are again the debt- and equityholders' one-period displays, and we leave the interpretations to you. They are geometrically done the same way as for the without-deductibility case.

The dotted lines in Figure III.D.4 indicate capital costs. kd^*, you recall, discounts $NCDD_1 - ITS_1$ to equal VD_0. The dotted line through the

[25]Alternatively, one may prefer to describe Figure III.D.4 as "rather rococo," feeling that, in the financial world, it is probably considered gauche to "go for baroque."

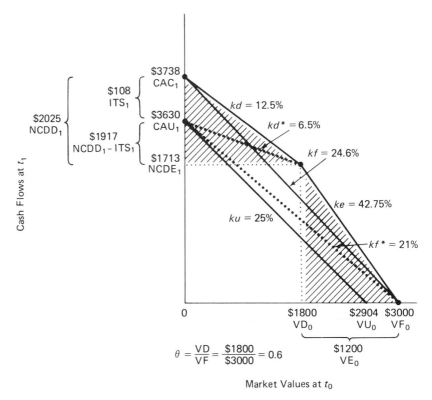

FIGURE III.D.4   **Graphical one-period capital structure with deductibility (I)**

shaded upper-left triangle is debt's cost, $kd^* = 6.5\%$. Note that its slope is less than the kd line's, as it should be. kf^* discounts $CAC_1 - ITS_1 = CAU_1$ to equal VF_0. kf^* is indicated by the dotted line joining $CAU_1 = \$3630$ to $VF_0 = \$3000$; $kf^* = 21\%$. Note that its slope is less steep than the overall leveraged rate of $24.6\% = kf$, as it should be.

Figure III.D.5 shows graphically what happens to this one-period with-deductibility corporation when it becomes an all-debt firm. (The \$1800 debt situation is also shown for reference.) Total firm (and therefore debt) value is approximately \$3212, its maximum.[26] $kd = kf$ has increased to equal ku at 25%. Interest is $\$803.10 \simeq [\$3212.38 \times (ku = kd = kf = 25\%)]$ and therefore $ITS_1 = \tau I \simeq \$385.49$ and $CAC_1 \simeq \$4015.48$. Note that $kd^* = kf^* = 13\%$ is indicated by the dotted line joining CAU_1 to VF_0. This is the minimum cost of capital for the corporation. And finally, look at the line $kf = kd = ku$ for the all-debt firm. Although farther from the origin than the $kf = ke = ku$ line for the unlevered firm, it retains the identical slope, 25%.

[26]This is easily calculated. We know that $kf^* = kd^* = ku(1 - \tau)$ at $\theta = 1$, and since $VF_0 = CAU_1/(1 + kf^*)$ for this firm, we get $VF_0 = \$3630.00/1.13 \simeq \$3212.38$.

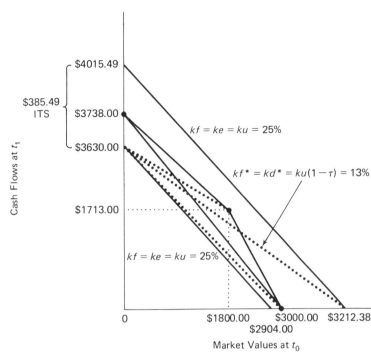

FIGURE III.D.5   Graphical one-period capital structure with deductibility (II)

Problems for Section III

1. The Levered Sisters Corporation is a one-period firm operating in a capital market where interest payments are not deductible for tax purposes, but otherwise like that of Section III. The debt suppliers of Levered Sisters expect a CDD_1 of $3300.00, which they value now (t_0) at $3000.00, and the equity-holders of Levered Sisters expect $4700.00 of CDE_1, which has a t_0 value of $3666.67. (No investment is planned.) Levered has investigated three capital structure alternatives:

   (a) Stay as is.
   (b) Issue new equity to pay off all debt suppliers now.
   (c) Issue debt to bring VD_0 in total to $6000, which they find would cause kd to be 18 % for the period.

Analyze the effects of these alternatives on Levered Sisters' required rates and capital costs, on market values, and on shareholder wealth.

2. The Unlevered Brothers Corporation is a one-period firm with an expected CAU_1 of $15,000. At t_0, Unlevered has no debt in its capital structure. The capital market has appraised the riskiness of Unlevered's equity as deserving a return for the period of 19 % $(ku = 0.19)$. Unlevered has dis-

covered that it can now issue $7000 of debt at a rate of 10% for the period ($kd = 0.10$). Since Unlevered plans no investment at t_0, the proceeds of the debt issue would be distributed to equityholders at t_0. Unlevered is subject to a corporate income tax rate of 40%, interest payments are deductible for tax purposes, and the capital market is as described in Section III.

(a) What would happen to the total value of Unlevered were it to undertake the capital structure alteration? Account quantitatively for the dollar change. Where did it come from?

(b) Calculate the effects of this proposed capital structure change on Unlevered's equity suppliers by illustrating their comparative wealth positions at t_0. How is shareholder wealth related to the total value of the firm?

(c) What would happen to Unlevered's kf as a result of the alteration? How would its cost of capital compare to the original, prealteration one?

(d) Suppose that Unlevered accomplished the proposed capital structure change and the price of its equity fell in the capital market to $VE_0 = \$6000.00$. Comment on this situation. Would you expect this price to be maintained at t_0? Show quantitatively why or why not.

(e) On a graph, plot the θ levels and associated rates you have found, and on another, the θ levels and market values. Are these relationships consistent with the theoretical ones in Chapter 10? Demonstrate this by completing the graphs theoretically for all θ levels.

3. Suppose that the Unlevered Brothers Corporation has undertaken the proposed capital structure change in Problem 2. Suppose now that Unlevered, in addition, can raise another $3000 of debt to total $10,000 at t_0. The required kd assigned by the capital market to this total amount of debt is 14%. Account quantitatively for the value and wealth changes which would take place, and repeat part (e) of Problem 2.

4. The Fezz Publishing Corporation produces and sells a book entitled *Fabricating Accounting Numbers in Earnest*. The company, not altogether surprisingly, is a one-period firm (not having sold very well, the book is being peddled to the Environmental Protection Fund paper drive) expecting operating cash flows (CAU_1) of $4024.68 at the next time point.

At the moment (t_0) Fezz has a debt issue outstanding from which debt suppliers are expecting interest and principal payments to total $1438.63 at t_1 of which $81.43 is interest. Fezz's debt value presently is $1357.20, and its equity suppliers are holding claims worth a total value of $2213.17. Fezz's interest payments are deductible for corporate income tax purposes, the tax rate being 52% of accounting income.

(a) Calculate Fezz's t_0 values, p_1 capital costs and required rates, and t_1 cash flow expectations.

(b) Suppose Fezz had no debt outstanding. What would be Fezz's value? Required rates? Capital costs? In an economic sense, why do these differ from Fezz leveraged?

(c) Fezz has discovered that it can alter its capital structure (from its original leveraged position) through an issue of debt at t_0 in the amount of \$2769.71. If Fezz were to split the proceeds of the issue by buying out the original debt holders at their t_0 market value and distributing the remaining cash to equity suppliers, the capital market would require a return of 10% on the new debt issue. Calculate Fezz's altered values, required rates, capital costs, and cash flows.

(d) Illustrate the effect, in *transactional* detail, of this capital structure change upon Fezz's equityholders' present wealth. Verify these calculations with the *economic* basis of the wealth change.

For parts (e), (f), and (g), assume *no* deductibility of personal interest payments for personal tax purposes.

(e) At Fezz's new capital structure, suppose you desired to create a similar *personal* capital structure in your own portfolio. Using the unlevered Fezz as a vehicle, and assuming you can borrow on the same terms as corporations, illustrate what your personal portfolio and cash-flow expectations would be, in comparison to Fezz's leveraged equity.

(f) The answer to part (e) is often used in the literature of finance to illustrate what the price of a leveraged firm's equity must be in market equilibrium. Is the existence of "identical but unlevered" corporations necessary to this line of argument? If not, offer an alternative.

(g) Since, in this example, corporate interest is deductible by corporations but personal interest is not deductible by individuals, would you be better off (1) as an equityholder of Fezz at the new capital structure, or (2) holding Fezz as unlevered with a comparable amount of personal borrowing? Explain.

(h) Suppose personal interest payments *were* deductible for personal income tax purposes, in addition to corporate interest deductibility for corporate tax purposes. Would you then be indifferent between altering your own versus corporate capital structure? Explain.

(i) Suppose Fezz became an all-debt ($\theta = 1$) firm. Calculate its value(s), capital costs, required rates, and cash flows.

(j) Graph the various rates, capital costs and values you have found in this problem, as they vary with Fezz's capital structure. Do they appear reasonable? What about kf?

(k) List what are considered to be the two major reasons why corporations in real capital markets do not adopt the theoretical wealth-maximizing capital structure strategy of part (i); explain each.

(l) Suppose in moving from its original capital structure to its \$2769.71 level of debt, Fezz chose to repurchase equity rather than declare a dividend. Assuming Fezz has 100 shares outstanding at t_0, calculate the price per share and number of shares of its tender offer so as to accomplish the identical effects of a dividend.

5. Suppose that the Perpetual Machine Corporation (Problem 5, Section II) were to float a debt issue equal in value to the sum of all capital claims against

it (that is, your VF_0 answer to the original problem) and use the proceeds of the issue to (1) pay off old debt suppliers and (2) distribute the remainder to equityholders. The capital market would require a 16% kd on the new debt issue.

(a) Calculate the equity, debt, and total values of the firm with its new capital structure, using the new FCF statement.

(b) Calculate the required rates and capital costs, and compare them to the original capital structure of Perpetual.

(c) Using the various VITS's, demonstrate the effect of this capital structure change on the equityholders of Perpetual.

(d) Suppose that Perpetual had become an all-debt firm. Calculate its values, rates, and FCF statements. Are they consistent with the theory of Section III?

(e) Comment on the likelihood of (d) occurring in real capital markets. Be specific in your argument.

References for Section III

The earliest recognition, albeit intuitive, of the basic economic ideas underpinning the relationship between corporate capital structure and value can be found in: John Burr Williams, *The Theory of Investment Value* (Cambridge, Mass.: Harvard University Press, 1938).

The specific economic mechanisms illustrating the market's appraisal of corporate capital structures first appeared in: Franco Modigliani and Merton H. Miller, "The Cost of Capital, Corporation Finance, and the Theory of Investment," *American Economic Review* (June 1958) and Franco Modigliani and Merton H. Miller, "Corporation Income Taxes and the Cost of Capital: A Correction," *American Economic Review* (June 1963).

Empirical studies of the theory and imperfections of capital structure are legion. A good start for reading would be: Merton H. Miller and Franco Modigliani, "Cost of Capital to the Electric Utility Industry," *American Economic Review* (June 1966).

One argument linking operational results to capital structure is found in: Alexander A. Robichek and Stewart C. Myers, *Optimal Financing Decisions* (Englewood Cliffs, N.J.: Prentice-Hall, Inc., 1965), pp. 40–42.

Research continues apace on these questions. Almost any issue of academic finance journals since 1960 will contain such references, many of which add to the understanding of how imperfections affect the outcomes predicted by the theory. For more complex theoretical and empirical extensions, see Charles W. Haley and Lawrence C. Schall, *The Theory of Financial Decisions* (New York: McGraw-Hill Book Company, 1973).

The Theory of Capital Acquisition and Disbursement

When introducing Part Two we said that corporate financing decisions are generally of two types: capital structure decisions, and capital acquisition and disbursement decisions. The theory of capital structure was developed in Section III. In this section we shall study the theory of capital acquisition and disbursement, usually called "dividend policy" in applied finance texts. Here we shall be concerned with the strategy a corporation uses to acquire cash from the capital market for corporate investment purposes, and distribute cash to the capital market for servicing capital claims. The reason we prefer "the theory of capital acquisition and disbursement" to "the theory of dividend decisions" is because the latter, as it is popularly used, does not cover the full range of alternative strategies that a corporation can pursue in acquiring and servicing capital sources. As we shall see, the dividend decision defined as choosing some proportion of the cash available to equity suppliers to be paid to them is only one part of a more general financing decision.

Chapter 11

Acquisition / Disbursement of Capital: Basics

MARKET CHARACTERISTICS As with our development of capital structure theory, we shall hold constant the effects of other financial decisions (investment and capital structure) as we study the theory of capital acquisition/disbursement. Our major concern, of course, continues to be the effect, if any, of this particular financial decision on the present wealth of existing equity suppliers.

Since, as always, the capital market will be the final judge of any financial decisions a corporation may make, it is worth the effort to remind ourselves of a few characteristics our theoretical capital market has which will be especially important to our work in this chapter. First, the capital market prices a capital claim on the basis of the size, timing, and risk of the future cash flows expected for that claim at the time it is valued. Second, neither corporations nor capital-market participants pay any transactions costs (like investment banking or stock brokerage fees). And third, capital-market participants are not subject to personal income taxes. As we progress through the chapter you will have no trouble seeing why we have given the capital market these characteristics. And after the purely theoretical ideas have been developed we shall, in the Conclusion to Section IV, discuss how the theory might be affected if these characteristics were changed.

CETERIS PARIBUS CONDITIONS As we study the theory of capital acquisition/disbursement we want to be able to isolate this financial decision from capital structure and investment decision effects. To do this we shall require the financing decisions we make in this section to have no impact on the investment and capital structure decisions that we assume have already been made.

By using our financial cash flow (FCF) format, we can be very explicit about which capital acquisition/disbursement actions are allowable and which are not, in terms of whether or not other decisions already made are left unaffected. Specifically, we shall see what boundaries are implied by what we know about the investment and capital structure decisions.

Let us look first at the investment decision. As we know, the decisions a corporation has made for its asset investments appear as IVS_T's in our FCF statements and diagrams. Those IVS_T cash-flow expectations must be unaffected by any financing decision considered in this section. If a single dollar of any IVS_T expectation is changed, then the investment decision has been altered and we cannot be sure that whatever wealth effects appear have been caused by a capital acquisition/disbursement decision and not by a change in investment expectations. In other words, we shall assume that our corporations have decided on a stream of IVS_T's, and those dollars *must* continue (as expectations) to be available at each time point regardless of our financing strategy.

We must also ensure that the financing alternatives we consider do not affect the companies' capital structure decisions. There are two ways to think about this constraint. First, Chapter 8 defined capital structure as θ_T, the ratio of VD_T to VF_T for a corporation. We learned that altering these ratios can, under common conditions, have an effect on shareholder wealth. So we must not allow any θ_T to be affected.

Our FCF statement presents another way of seeing how capital structure can be held unaffected. Again, Chapter 10 taught us that the shareholder wealth effects of capital structure are caused by interest-tax-subsidy cash-flow expectations. It is a logical consequence that if we require ITS_T's to be unaffected, then capital structure effects will also be unchanged, since a change in any θ_T would necessarily require a change in the corresponding kd_P's, I_T's, and ITS_T's. In essence, therefore, we can maintain the necessary *ceteris paribus* conditions by not allowing a capital acquisition/disbursement decision to affect any IVS_T (investment decision) or any ITS_T (capital structure decision).

Now that we have covered what we cannot do in this section, you might reasonably be wondering if we have not constrained ourselves to do nothing. Well, that is not quite true. Even when we hold investment and capital structure decisions constant, we still have a rather broad range of financing alternatives available, and our FCF diagrams can be quite helpful in allowing us to see what these alternatives are.

Look at Figure 11.1. The shaded portions are the FCF expectations which must be left unchanged by capital acquisition/disbursement decisions if we are to be able to understand the exclusive effects of those decisions on capital suppliers' present wealth. Your first impression may be that we have slipped many more conditions into Figure 11.1 than we suggested above. It

FIGURE 11.1 Capital acquisition and disbursement cash flows

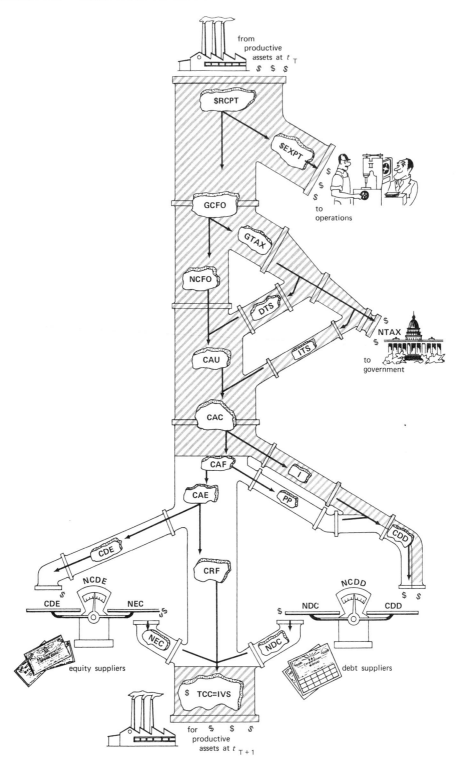

from
productive
assets at t_T
$ $ $

$RCPT

$EXPT

$
$
$
to
operations

GCFO

GTAX

NCFO

DTS

ITS

$
NTAX

$
to
government

CAU

CAC

CAF

I

CAE

PP

CDD

CDE

CRF

NCDE

NCDD

CDE   NEC

NDC   CDD

NEC

NDC

equity suppliers

debt suppliers

$ TCC≡IVS

for $ $ $
productive
assets at t_{T+1}

certainly has a lot more than just the IVS and ITS expectations marked as remaining unchanged. But, in fact, that is all we are doing. Let us run down the diagram to see why.

First, notice that all the operational cash-flow expectations ($RCPT, $EXPT, GCFO, GTAX, NCFO, DTS, and CAU) are shaded. This is because they are functions only of IVS_T expectations and operating conditions that are totally unaffected by financing decisions. As long as we maintain existing IVS_T expectations across time, the cash flows from $\$RCPT_T$ through CAU_T would be unaffected by financing decisions regardless of whether we wanted them to be or not.

Moving farther down, ITS_T is unaffected because capital structure remains unchanged, and therefore $CAU_T + ITS_T = CAC_T$ is also immune: *The overall cash-flow expectations of a firm are not affected by capital acquisition/disbursement decisions.* Note that I_T must also be maintained. This should not surprise you since $I_T = ITS_T/\tau$ and τ is, of course, assumed constant across time.

At this point in our FCF diagram (Figure 11.1) you will discover a new acronym: CAF. This stands for *cash available to the firm* and is equal to CAC_T minus I_T. Conceptually, CAF_T is the first cash over which the management of the firm has discretionary control for the purposes of capital acquisition/disbursement decisions. Specifically, management can allocate the CAF_T flow as it pleases among CDE_T, CRF_T, and PP_T (since, of course, $CAF_T = CDE_T + CRF_T + PP_T$). We shall illustrate shortly how management can opt to divide CAF_T in different situations.

Now skip down to the bottom of Figure 11.1. $TCC_T \equiv IVS_T$ is shaded because the investment decision must be unaffected by the capital acquisition and disbursement decision. $TCC_T \equiv IVS_T$ can be thought of as the ending level of cash which must be accumulated by management for asset acquisition after having exercised its discretionary control over capital acquisition/disbursement decisions.

At this point we can also note the impact of these decisions on the value of the firm, VF_0. Knowing that both CAC_T and IVS_T are given by a corporation's capital structure and investment decisions, and with reference to one of our valuation formulas from Section II:

$$VF_0 = \sum_{T=1}^{T} \frac{CAC_T - IVS_T}{\prod_{P=1}^{T} (1 + kf_P)} \qquad [7.9]$$

you can see that *the value of the firm as a whole is unaffected by the capital acquisition/disbursement decision.* Not only are the numerators of this summation unchanged, but so too are the denominators. Recalling Appendix II.C, we know that kf_P, the overall required rate of return for the corporation, is also unaffected because no cash flows that it values, or their risks, have been changed.

Finally, Figure 11.1 shows that $NCDD_\tau$ and $NCDE_\tau$ are also unaffected by this financing decision. Because $CAC_\tau - IVS_\tau = NCDE_\tau + NCDD_\tau$, we know that the sum of these net cash distributions to capital suppliers is unaffected. But why is each separately unaffected? The reason is that we are holding the capital structure decision intact. Remember that this *ceteris paribus* condition requires θ_τ to be unaffected by capital acquisition/disbursement. θ_τ, of course, equals VD_τ/VF_τ. We have just seen that VF_τ is unaffected, so for θ_τ to remain unaltered, VD_τ must also. But if any $NCDD_\tau$ is altered, one or more VD_τ's will also be changed. And we cannot allow that while holding the capital structure decision intact. So the $NCDD_\tau$'s must remain unaffected. If both the sum $(NCDD_\tau + NCDE_\tau)$ and $NCDD_\tau$ itself are unaffected, then $NCDE_\tau$ must be unaffected also. And finally, since nothing occurs to change the size, timing, or risk of the expected net cash distributions to capital suppliers, the kd_P's and ke_P's must also remain unaltered.

CAPITAL ACQUISITION/ DISBURSEMENT DECISION

We have now reached the point where we can specify the types of financing actions encompassed by the capital acquisition/disbursement decision. The unshaded cash flows in Figure 11.1 are those which can be affected by this decision. They are PP_τ, CAE_τ, CRF_τ, CDE_τ, NEC_τ, and NDC_τ. Any and all of these flows may be altered as long as the capital structure and investment decisions remain intact.

Conceptually, CAF_τ must be divided between PP_τ and CAE_τ, CAE_τ split into CRF_τ and CDE_τ, and appropriate amounts of NEC_τ and NDC_τ obtained to combine with CRF_τ to maintain $TCC_\tau \equiv IVS_\tau$.

DIVIDEND DECISION

Let's look more closely at the cash flows covered by this decision. First, we shall consider CAE_τ, CRF_τ, and CDE_τ. These three cash flows are the ones commonly thought of as constituting a corporation's *dividend decision*. Of the amount of cash available to equity suppliers (CAE_τ), it must be decided how much to retain (CRF_τ) and how much to distribute as dividends (CDE_τ). How is this a financing decision? Well, remember that a dividend decision (CDE_τ) also implies a retention decision (CRF_τ), since $CDE_\tau + CRF_\tau = CAE_\tau$. And our financial cash-flow diagram illustrates that CRF_τ is definitely part of TCC_τ, the source of IVS_τ.

We can get a better view of this dividend decision by concentrating on the lower part of our financial cash-flow diagram. In order to see the dividend decision clearly, we will hold PP_τ and NDC_τ, the other cash flows subject to the more general capital acquisition/disbursement decision, unaltered for the time being. This means that the amount of financing coming from debt suppliers at time τ, NDC_τ, is for the moment a given. But so is the total amount of outlay necessary for IVS_τ. Therefore, the total amount of investment cash coming from other than NDC_τ, namely $CRF_\tau + NEC_\tau$, must also be a given.

So the dividend decision is really a financing decision that asks: Given an amount of total investment capital to be provided by sources other than new debt suppliers, how much should come from cash retained by the firm (CRF_T) and how much should come from outside (NEC_T)? The dividend (CDE_T) is simply that portion of the cash available to equity (CAE_T) which is left after the amount to be retained (CRF_T) is decided by management.

Figure 11.2 illustrates what we have just described. It shows in situations A–C, the general types of dividend decisions a corporation can make from a given starting point defined by CAF_T, PP_T, NDC_T, and $TCC_T \equiv IVS_T$. Suppose that we have a company whose relevant time T cash flows are as follows:

	t_T
CAC	$1000
I	50
CAF	950
PP	100
CDD	150
NDC	120
NCDD	30
CAE	850
CRF	450
CDE	400
NEC	80
NCDE	320
CRF + NEC	530
TCC $\equiv$ IVS	650

These flows appear as situation A of Figure 11.2. At T the company is expected to have $1000 of overall cash available to pay interest of $50, leaving $950 of cash available to the firm to pay principal of $100 and dividends of $400, and to retain $450. The necessary $650 of investment at time T is supplied by the $450 of retained cash, $120 of new debt capital, and $80 of new equity capital. The existing dividend decision is to pay $CDE_T = \$400$ of the available $CAE_T = \$850$ to equity suppliers, and retain $CRF_T = \$450$ for time T investment purposes. Since, however, total non-NDC_T financing, $CRF_T + NEC_T$, must equal $530, $80 of NEC_T is raised from the capital market.

Situation B in Figure 11.2 illustrates this same company at time T but with a different dividend decision. Here the $850 of CAE_T is divided into a dividend of $320 and retained cash of $530. The necessary non-$NDC_T$ financing of $530 is entirely composed of retained cash, and no new equity capital is raised. Comparing situations A and B in Figure 11.2 we can see that situation B finances more internally and less externally than situation A. The situation B dividend decision has increased retained cash, CRF_T, by $80 while at the same time decreasing both dividends, CDE_T, and new equity contributions, NEC_τ, by the same amount, $80. Indeed, changes in CDE_τ must always be matched dollar-for-dollar by changes in NEC_τ in the same direction so as to maintain $NCDE_\tau$. Further, downward changes in CDE_τ and NEC_τ are, of course, constrained to the extent that neither flow can be negative.

For this company at time τ, $530 is the maximum amount of cash that it can retain without violating the investment decision. With the debt investment of $120 NDC_τ a given, and IVS_τ necessarily $650, $CRF_\tau + NEC_\tau$ must be exactly $530 for any acceptable dividend decision. Since NEC_τ cannot be less than zero, it follows that $530 is the effective maximum value for CRF_τ. A retained amount of greater than $530 would also force $NCDE_\tau$ to be less than $320, thus changing $VE_{\tau-1}$ and violating the capital structure decision. If the firm wishes to have internal financing, any amount of CRF_τ up to $530 is allowable, as long as new equity capital is raised in an amount so as to bring $CRF_\tau + NEC_\tau$ sources to the necessary level of $530 at time τ.

FIGURE 11.2 **Dividend decision (Situation A)**

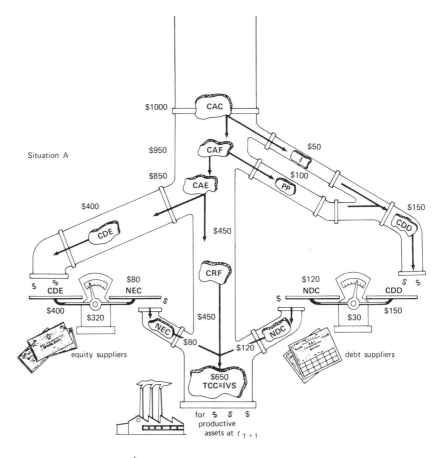

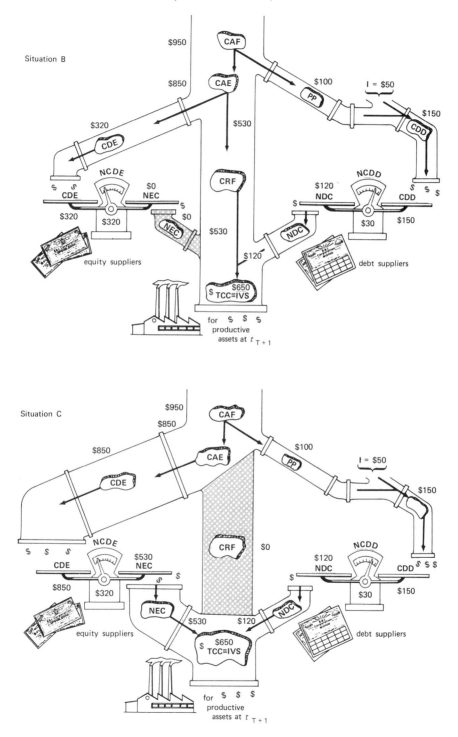

FIGURE 11.2   Dividend decision (Situations B and C)

Situation C in Figure 11.2 is again the same corporation at time T, but here it is minimizing its cash retention (and therefore maximizing its dividend to equityholders). The entire \$850 of CAE_T is paid as dividends, CDE_T. No cash is retained for investment purposes. The necessary addition of \$530 to the existing \$120 of new debt capital is raised entirely from a new equity capital flotation, $NEC_T = \$530$. Of course, had it wished, the firm could pay less than the \$850 dividend, as long as $NCDE_T = \$320$ remains intact and $CRF_T + NEC_T$ sum to \$530.

So the dividend decision essentially specifies how:

1. An available CAE_T is split between dividends (CDE_T) and retained cash (CRF_T).
2. Given the CRF_T, how much NEC_T is necessary to provide the needed supplement to NDC_T so as to maintain the required level of $TCC_T \equiv IVS_T$.

Remember, however, that to illustrate the dividend decision, we held constant PP_T and NDC_T. A glance at Figure 11.2 shows that if we had allowed those to vary also, CAE_T and the sum of CRF_T plus NEC_T themselves become decisions. That situation is the more general capital acquisition/disbursement decision, of which the dividend decision is only one part. We shall illustrate that shortly. But before we do, the dividend decision itself deserves a couple of comments.

First, you probably have noticed that none of the various dividend decisions had any effect on the net cash distributions to equity suppliers. From what you learned in Section II, this tells you immediately that the total market value of equity, VE_T, is unaffected by the dividend decision. That being the case, why should we bother to proceed further? If VE_T is unaffected, is not the dividend decision irrelevant? Not necessarily. Remember that though $NCDE_T$ was unchanged, the various decisions did result in different amounts of cash dividends paid and new equity capital raised at time T.

Recollect situation A in Figure 11.2 and think of the existing equityholders there. If the dividend decision were changed to that of situation B, the A equityholders would receive \$80 less cash at time T. But at the same time, \$80 less equity capital is raised. Now if the A equityholders were also supplying the new equity capital, they would be as well off in B as in A. In A they receive \$400 and give back \$80, netting \$320, and in B they receive \$320 and give back nothing, also netting \$320. But suppose that the A equityholders were not supplying the new equity capital. Suppose it was to be raised from other capital-market participants. What about the A equityholders in that situation?

Initially the A equityholders expect to receive \$400 at time T. But the new equity capital contributed in A by others means that the A equityholders also must share *future* cash flows past τ with the new capital contributors. The amount they must share, from what we know about capital-market participants, no doubt is related to the contribution that the new equity suppliers make at τ. Now consider the shift from A to B in Figure 11.2. True, the A equityholders receive less time τ cash. But because NEC_τ, the new equity capital supplied by others, is less than it was in A, A equityholders are giving up a smaller share of future cash flows past τ to the new equity suppliers. Are the A equityholders better or worse off in moving to B? The answer is, of course, that *if the present value of the decrease in new equity claims on cash flows past τ is greater than the $80 A equityholders give up in dividends when moving to B, they are better off. If it is less than $80, they are worse off.*

In plainer words, the move from dividend decision A to dividend decision B does two things to the A equityholders:

1. It costs them $80 in time τ cash dividends.
2. It decreases the claim by other new equity suppliers on cash flows further in the future than time τ.

The net effect on A equityholders of moving from A to B depends on the amount by which A equityholders' share of future (past τ) cash flows has been increased because less outside capital has been brought in. If the present value of what A equityholders gain is greater than $80, they are better off; if less, they are worse off; if equal to $80, their present wealth is unchanged.

Moving from A to C in Figure 11.2 is just the opposite. A equityholders get more time τ cash ($850 versus $400) but give up a larger share of future cash flows to outsiders. The net effect depends on the value of what they give up in moving from A to C, compared to the value of the additional CDE_τ they receive in situation C.

Presented this way, discovering value implications through the analysis of a dividend decision might seem rather ominous, approaching the complexity of capital structure theory. But do not despair. As we shall discover shortly, these valuation questions are easily answered from what we already know about efficient capital markets. Before we do that, however, we must extend the dividend decision to cover the more general capital acquisition/disbursement decision.

GENERAL DECISION

In addition to deciding how much cash to retain and how much to distribute as dividends to equity (and, therefore, how much new equity capital to raise), the general capital acquisition/disbursement decision also encompasses the PP_τ and NDC_τ cash flows. Depending on the provisions of the existing debt contract, a corporation may be able to alter principal repayment and new debt capital acquisition plans without violating its investment and capital structure decisions.[1] In a sense this decision is the debt counterpart of the dividend decision. Figure 11.3 illustrates how this works for the time τ cash flows introduced in Figure 11.2.

Situation A in Figure 11.3 presents the same set of time τ cash-flow expectations that were depicted as situation A in Figure 11.2. Now, however, the corporation may also decide to alter the $PP_\tau = \$100$ and $NDC_\tau = \$120$ cash-flow expectations, in addition to those involved in the dividend decision. Look at the time τ cash flows shown as situation F in Figure 11.3. Here the company has decided to decrease PP_τ to zero. This reduces the cash distribution to debt suppliers, CDD_τ, to the minimum necessary for preserving the capital structure decision, namely $\$50 = I_\tau$, which leaves ITS_τ unaffected. $NCDD_\tau$ equal to $\$30$ is also given, as we know, by the capital structure decision. Thus, the cash-flow relationship $CDD_\tau - NCDD_\tau = NDC_\tau$ tells us that new debt capital must be $\$50 - \$30 = \$20$. If the debt contract permits fully compensated principal payment delays, the corporation could choose a principal repayment anywhere from $\$100$ to zero.

In general the minimum principal payment allowable to a corporation is given by the cash-flow relationship

$$NCDD_\tau = I_\tau + PP_\tau - NDC_\tau$$

which implies that

$$PP_\tau = (NCDD_\tau - I_\tau) + NDC_\tau$$

We know that (1) NDC_τ cannot be less than zero, (2) PP_τ cannot be less than zero, and (3) $(NCDD_\tau - I_\tau)$ must remain unchanged. Because (3) is an absolute constraint, it should be clear from the formula above that any change in PP_τ must be matched dollar-for-dollar by a change in NDC_τ in the same direction. (Note that this is for debt what the CDE_τ and NEC_τ matching is for equity in the dividend decision.)

But are there limits other than non-negativity on PP_τ and NDC_τ? Looking again at the formula for PP_τ above, think about lowering PP_τ. As we lower PP_τ and therefore NDC_τ, if PP_τ reaches zero before NDC_τ does, zero is PP_τ's lower limit. If, however, NDC_τ reaches zero first, PP_τ's lower limit must be $(NCDD_\tau - I_\tau)$ so as to leave that amount unchanged and not violate any other financial decision. In other words, if NDC_τ were less than PP_τ, the principal repayment could only be reduced by the expected amount of NDC_τ without violating $NCDD_\tau$ and thereby the capital structure decision.[2]

---

[1]There are two basic provisions which must appear in the bond indenture or debt contract to allow management to do this. These are that the firm must have the options of (1) total or partial principal prepayment at market value of the debt, and (2) delayed payment of principal. If the latter option is exercised, the firm must pay accrued interest on the market value of the delayed amount at the rate of kd_P for each period of payment postponement. These two contractual provisions allow flexibility in refinancing debt while preserving debt suppliers' present wealth.

[2]You can convince yourself of this by substituting $NCDD_\tau = \$70$, $NDC_\tau = \$80$, and $IVS_\tau = \$610$ into situation A in Figure 11.3. The minimum principal repayment in situation F is then $\$20$ in order to preserve $NCDD_\tau = \$70$ with $NDC_\tau = 0$.

FIGURE 11.3   Capital acquisition/disbursement decision (Situations A and F)

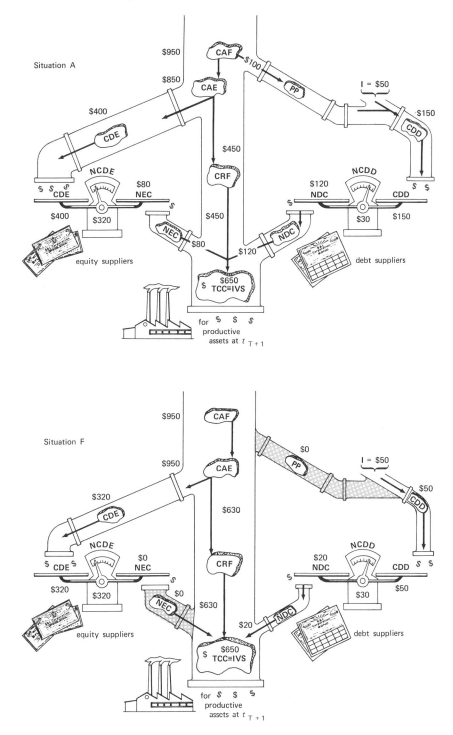

FIGURE 11.3   Capital acquisition/disbursement decision (Situations E and D)

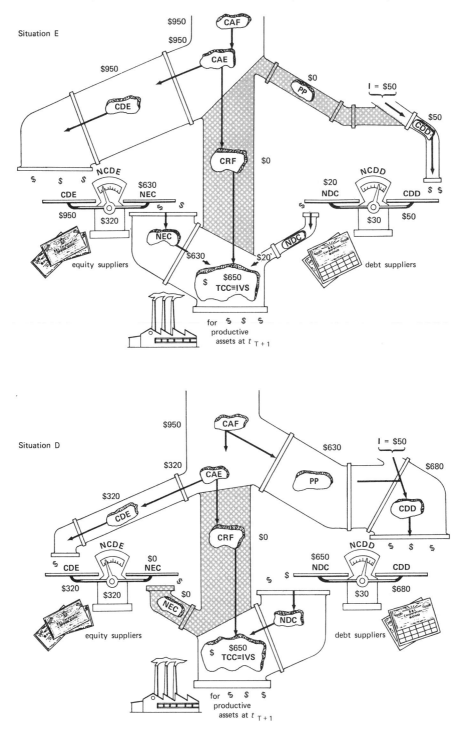

Reducing PP_τ by \$100 in situation F means that the cash available to equity suppliers is increased by that amount. In situation A, CAE_τ was \$850; in situation F, CAE_τ becomes \$950. Now we are back to the dividend decision. In F the corporation decides to retain \$630 of the \$950 CAE and pay a dividend of \$320. This is the maximum allowable retention because with \$20 of NDC_τ debt financing, the non-NDC_τ contribution must be \$630 to total $IVS_\tau = \$650$. With the maximum retention, no new equity capital is raised; $NEC_\tau = \$0$.

Compare situation F in Figure 11.3 to situation B in Figure 11.2. In essence, situation B maximized internal financing through the dividend decision alone, and resulted in a $CRF_\tau = \$530$. Situation F, however, *maximizes cash retention through the more general capital acquisition/ disbursement decision*, and $CRF_\tau = \$630$. The increase in CRF_τ from B to F is due to the reduction in principal repayment and new debt capital acquisition.

Situation E of Figure 11.3 also reduces the principal repayment at time τ by the maximum \$100, but instead of maximizing cash retention, maximizes dividend payout. Here the shareholders receive the largest amount of cash at time τ that is possible without violating the capital structure decision, which requires an interest payment expectation of \$50. With total cash available to all capital suppliers, CAC_τ of \$1000, equity suppliers receive everything but the interest payment as time τ dividends; 100% of CAF_τ constitutes the expected distribution to equityholders. In situation E, $CRF_\tau = \$0$, and therefore the necessary non-NDC financing of \$630 is raised entirely outside the firm as new equity financing; $NEC_\tau = \$630$. Situation E is the general capital acquisition/disbursement decision counterpart of situation C in Figure 11.2.

Finally, look at situation D in Figure 11.3. Here the principal repayment, PP_τ, is *maximized* rather than minimized as it was in E and F.[3] In order to maintain the investment and capital structure decisions, \$320 of dividends are paid, no cash retained, no new equity capital raised, and the entire financing is accomplished through a \$650 flotation of new debt capital.

Table 11.1 summarizes the algebra defining the limits of the allowable outcomes for the various flows which the capital acquisition/disbursement decision can alter without affecting the capital structure or investment decisions. The only statement in Table 11.1 that has not been mentioned or at least implied by our previous discussions is that the maximum allowable dividend, CDE_τ, is the smaller of CAE_τ, or $VE_{\tau-1}(1 + ke_P)$, where $P = \tau$. The first sounds logical enough; we cannot pay out more than is available. The second, however, is a bit more subtle. Actually, it is the equity counter-

[3]We must assume here that $VD_{\tau-1} \geq \$630$; otherwise, we would be giving debt suppliers more than they deserve.

TABLE 11.1   Allowable cash-flow ranges for the capital acquisition/disbursement decision

Flow	Minimum value	Maximum value
PP_T	max [zero, $(NCDD_T - I_T)$]	min [VD_{T-1}, CAF_T, $(CAF_T - NCDE_T)$*]
CAE_T	$CAF_T - $[max PP_T]	$CAF_T - $[min PP_T]
CRF_T	max [zero, $(CAF_T - $max $PP_T - $max $CDE_T)$]	min [CAE_T, $(CAE_T - NCDE_T)$]
CDE_T	max [zero, $NCDE_T$]	min [$VE_{T-1}(1 + ke_P)$†, CAE_T]
NEC_T	max [zero, $-NCDE_T$]	[max CDE_T] $- NCDE_T$
NDC_T	max [zero, $-(NCDD_T - I_T)$]	[max PP_T] $+ I_T - NCDD_T$

*The quantity $(CAF_T - NCDE_T)$ can be equivalently viewed as $(IVS_T - I_T + NCDD_T)$.
†Where $P = T$; note also that $VE_{T-1}(1 + ke_P) = VE_T + NCDE_T$

part of the debt constraint that PP_T cannot exceed VD_{T-1}. Since, for equity, CDE_T is both "principal" *and* "interest," a CDE_T greater than $VE_{T-1}(1 + ke_P)$, where $P = T$ would be granting equity suppliers more than their required returns *of* and *on* capital, something the capital market would not allow. Were CDE_T to be increased past this point, no new equity capital would be supplied at the going market price, for future cash flows would not compensate the new suppliers.

SCOPE OF THE DECISION

When we first began discussing the capital acquisition/disbursement decision, it seemed as if constraining ourselves not to violate existing investment and capital structure decisions would result in there being practically no financing latitude remaining. This was because we found it necessary to hold CAC_T, I_T, $NCDD_T$, $NCDE_T$, and IVS_T all inviolate. But a glance at Figure 11.3 shows our original impression to have been quite misleading. The range of financing alternatives we have discovered is quite broad and varied. Financing can be preponderantly by new *debt* capital (D), by new *equity* capital (E), or by *internal retention* (F). These options have no differential effects on overall corporate cash flows, interest, net cash distributions to debt or to equity, or investment at time T.

And, of course, the decisions that are shown in Figure 11.3 are extremes. They constitute the maximum allowable amount of the type financing they represent. The company could choose among an infinite number of other time T capital acquisition/disbursement decisions somewhat less extreme than the D, E, and F alternatives of Figure 11.3; for example, management might choose situation A. Now things are really beginning to sound ominous. How can we possibly reach any conclusion about shareholder wealth effects of the capital acquisition/disbursement decision when the alternatives are so many and so varied? Admittedly at this point the analysis yet to be done seems quite arduous. But that, too, is deceptive. We have an ace in the hole yet to be displayed: the capital market.

EFFECTS OF THE CAPITAL ACQUISITION/ DISBURSEMENT DECISION

Our earlier brief comments on the dividend decision indicated that the shareholder wealth effects of that decision depended upon:

1. In the case of *increasing* dividend and *increasing* new equity capital, whether the value of current equityholders' *reduced* claim on future cash flows was bigger or smaller than the cash dividend increase.
2. In the case of *decreasing* dividend and *decreasing* new equity capital, whether the value of current equityholders' *increased* claim on future cash flows was bigger or smaller than the cash dividend decrease.

Figure 11.3 indicates that these same conditions are true for the capital acquisition/disbursement decision. In changing from A to D or F, dividends and new equity capital acquisitions are reduced. In changing from A to E, dividends and new equity capital are increased. *In any possible financing decision the net effect on shareholder wealth will depend on the comparison of the cash dividend change to the change in value of the current shareholders' claim on future cash flows.* By allowing PP_T and NDC_T to vary, the more general financing decision recognizes that as long as the capital structure and investment decisions remain intact, current equityholders can trade-off current dividends against future expected CAF_T flows rather than against just those flows expected for equity.

But what will the change in value of current equityholders' claims be? Will it be greater, less than, or equal to the cash dividend change? The answer depends on the nature of the capital market and its participants. Consider the dividend decision, leaving aside for the moment questions of changing PP_T and NDC_T. We are now considering a change in time T cash dividends. As implied earlier, and as you can verify from Figures 11.2 and 11.3, any change in dividends (CDE_T) must be matched exactly by an equal change in new equity capital (NEC_T) so as to hold unchanged non-NDC time T contributions. Suppose that it is a dividend increase we are considering. What will be its effect on shareholder wealth?

Well, we know that equityholders will receive a higher time T cash dividend, which would tend to increase wealth. And we also know that their equity value at T will decrease because receiving a higher dividend means issuing new equity claims which share in future cash flows. What we really need to know is how much the time T equity value of existing shareholders decreases.

Think of the new equity suppliers. They are capital-market participants who require a return on their capital contributions such that the claim they receive is worth at least what it costs them. If it were not, they would provide no capital. Similarly, existing shareholders will certainly not be willing to give up part of their claim on future cash flows unless the increased dividend they receive fully compensates them for it. If it did not, they would either refuse the dividend and maintain their claim, or provide the increased new equity capital themselves with the increased dividend cash they receive. The translation of all this is: *For a dividend increase, the increase in value of new equity claims exactly equals the increase in cash dividend to existing shareholders.* If the increase in new equity value were greater than the cash dividend increase, existing shareholders would take action to provide the new capital themselves, thereby preserving their claim on future cash flows. If the increase in new VE were less than the dividend increase, no new capital would be forthcoming because new equity suppliers would be receiving an equity claim worth less than their cash contribution.

Now we know a little more than we did before. We know:

$$\text{\$ increase in existing equityholders' dividend} = \text{\$ increase in } VE_\tau \text{ due to new equity} \qquad [11.1]$$

But we also know that the total value of all equity claims, both new and existing, is unaffected by a dividend change because $NCDE_\tau$ is unaffected. Therefore, since

$$VE_\tau(\text{total}) = VE_\tau(\text{existing}) + VE_\tau(\text{new}) \qquad [11.2]$$

The value of existing shareholders' claims must decrease by exactly the amount that new equity's claim increases:

$$\text{\$ decrease in } VE_\tau(\text{existing}) = \text{\$ increase in } VE_\tau(\text{new}) \qquad [11.3]$$

in order for $VE_\tau(\text{total})$ to remain unaffected. But we just said that the increase in $VE_\tau(\text{new})$ is also equal to the amount of the dividend increase to existing shareholders. Look at formulas 11.1 and 11.3. Taken together they show that

$$\text{\$ increase in existing equityholders' dividend} = \text{\$ decrease in } VE_\tau(\text{existing}) \qquad [11.4]$$

In plain words, the increased dividend is exactly matched by a decrease in market value for existing equityholders.

The same net result occurs with a dividend decrease. There, existing shareholders exchange a decrease in current dividends for an increased claim on future cash flows due to the lower need for new equity capital. The increase in value of existing shares exactly equals the decrease in value of new shares (from what the new shares would have been worth with the original dividend decision). That increase is the same number of dollars as the cash dividend decrease. *The present wealth of existing equity suppliers is unaffected by the dividend decision*, be it an increase or a decrease.

But how about the more general capital acquisition/disbursement decision? Does that affect shareholder present wealth? The answer again is no, and the argument is quite similar to that for the dividend decision. Remember that debt suppliers also are capital market participants. Just like equity suppliers, they require full compensation for any change in their time τ cash receipts (PP_τ included) or their claims on future cash flows.

Any decrease in principal payments to existing debt suppliers is compensated by an increase in their claims on future cash flows and hence in their present debt values. But total VD_T is constant because new debt claims are less by the amount that existing claims have increased. Similarly, an increased principal payment is exactly matched by an increased NDC_T, and VD_T is left unchanged. Hence, existing debt suppliers are left unaffected by these acquisition/disbursement alterations. And existing equityholders are also unaffected by such debt payment and issuances because the net effect coming from the debt side of the cash-flow statement is unchanged. Any increase in equity dividends due to a lower principal repayment also necessitates a corresponding increase in new equity capital claims to hold investment dollars unchanged (because NDC_T has decreased by the same dollar amount as the PP_T decrease). Similarly, a decrease in dividends due to an increased principal repayment is exactly offset by the need for less new equity capital (and more new debt capital). Therefore, we find ourselves in identically the same conceptual situation that we encountered in the more limited case of the dividend decision, and we already know *that* decision does not affect shareholder wealth. *Consequently, the entire capital acquisition/disbursement decision is irrelevant to existing shareholders' present wealth levels as long as existing investment and capital structure decisions are held intact.*

Perhaps the best intuitive way to appreciate capital acquisition/disbursement irrelevancy is to think of existing equityholders also as potential new equity suppliers. Such capital-market participants are completely indifferent as to whether or not they receive a higher cash dividend and simultaneously contribute the same amount back to the firm as NEC_T. Their old shares decline in value by the same amount that their new shares increase in value. They would be just as happy not getting the dividend increase in the first place.

Is, then, the whole question not worth considering? Why spend all this time and trouble with a theoretical exercise that nets nothing? Be careful not to jump to the conclusion that we have learned nothing of (or about) value. There are at least two very important lessons to be learned from capital acquisition/disbursement theory. One is related to real-world financial decisions and the other is of theoretical interest.

As to the first lesson, begin by thinking of the various transactions that may well be required to take place when a financial decision of this sort is executed. Cash dividends may be changed. Principal payments to debt suppliers may be altered. Equity and debt issues may have to be floated in primary capital markets. And, in addition, price changes in equity and debt holdings are likely to occur. In our capital market, all these phenomena net to produce no effect. But how about in real capital markets? Are there differences between our market and those that actually exist that would cause us to alter our irrelevancy statement? You may be surprised to hear that the answer is almost certainly yes.

The basic economic tendencies that we have outlined here *do* apply fully to real capital markets. Our capital market is not a bogus one designed merely for entertainment in the classroom. But we *have* assumed away several features of real capital markets in order to concentrate on the pure economics of capital acquisition/disbursement. Some of those features must be considered as potential amending influences to capital acquisition/disbursement irrelevancy. Consider, for example, the fact that investment bankers charge corporations a fee for capital-raising services. Might this not impact the theory's pure results? How about taxes assessed on capital-market participants' income? In real markets, dividends are taxed differently from gains in equity values. What does this mean for equityholders' present wealth changes?

You can see that our discussion of capital acquisition/disbursement theory would not be complete unless we gave some consideration to such questions. We shall do just that later in the section. But remember that had we not gone to the trouble of developing the theory first, real-world questions like those above would have had no theoretical foundation on which we could build practical answers.

This brings us to the second lesson to be gleaned from capital acquisition/disbursement theory. This second point is, in a sense, a rerun of something we learned in developing capital structure theory: *There is no such thing as lagniappe in capital markets; you do not get something for nothing.* The capital acquisition/disbursement decisions we have studied were supplying nothing in the way of new net cash-flow expectations to the capital market, and therefore no wealth changes occurred. The basis for shareholder wealth remained the operations, investment, and capital structure expectations of the corporation. The only possible significance of the capital acquisition/disbursement decision will be from transaction, taxation, or other such considerations which we shall discuss shortly.

Before that, however, in keeping with our approach to the theory of corporate finance, we shall offer a complete numerical example of this section's financial decision so that you can review your understanding of the theory.

Chapter 12

Acquisition/Disbursement of Capital:
Illustration and Discussion

Suppose that we have a two-period corporation with the following t_1 and t_2 cash-flow expectations:

TABLE 12.1

Expected flow	t_1	t_2
$RCPT	$8,850.00	$10,395.00
$EXPT	3,982.50	4,677.75
GCFO	4,867.50	5,717.25
GTAX	2,531.10	2,972.97
NCFO	2,336.40	2,744.28
DTS	439.00	528.50
CAU	2,775.40	3,272.78
ITS	54.60	38.22
CAC	2,830.00	3,311.00
I	105.00	73.50
CAF	2,725.00	3,237.50
PP	850.00	1,050.00
CDD	955.00	1,123.50
NDC	400.00	0.00
NCDD	555.00	1,123.50
CAE	1,875.00	2,187.50
CRF	200.00	0.00
CDE	1,675.00	2,187.50
NEC	300.00	0.00
NCDE	1,375.00	2,187.50
CRF + NEC	500.00	0.00
TCC ≡ IVS	900.00	0.00

In judging the riskiness of the capital claims on this company, the capital market has decided that, for both time periods, $kd = 7\%$ and $ke = 25\%$. The corporate income tax rate, τ, is 52%.

At t_0 the values of the capital claims are

$$VD_0 = \sum_{\tau=1}^{T} \frac{NCDD_\tau}{(1 + kd)^\tau}$$
$$= \frac{\$555.00}{1.07} + \frac{\$1123.50}{(1.07)^2}$$
$$= \$1500.00$$

and

$$VE_0 = \sum_{\tau=1}^{T} \frac{NCDE_\tau}{(1 + ke)^\tau}$$
$$= \frac{\$1375.00}{1.25} + \frac{\$2187.50}{(1.25)^2}$$
$$= \$2500.00$$

Therefore, the value of the firm at t_0 is

$$VF_0 = VD_0 + VE_0$$
$$= \$1500.00 + \$2500.00$$
$$= \$4000.00$$

The financial cash flows for this corporation indicate an existing capital acquisition/disbursement decision for the t_1 expectations. The company is expected to repay some principal to debt suppliers, raise some new debt capital, retain some cash, pay some dividend, and raise some new equity capital at t_1. All in all, the existing decision for this firm is generally the same type as that for situation A in Figures 11.2 and 11.3.

TYPE A DECISIONS

The equityholders at t_0 have claims valued at $2500. The company also plans to issue new equity capital at t_1 which will share with t_0 equityholders in t_2 cash flows. Assuming the new equity capital, NEC_1, will be supplied by other capital-market participants, let us examine how the two sets of equity suppliers share the cash-flow expectations.

The new equity suppliers at time point t_1 (E_1 suppliers) are expected to contribute $300 of capital. Since their claim has the same priority as all other equity claims, they require the same $ke = 25\%$ per period. At t_2, therefore, the E_1 suppliers require a net cash flow of

$$RRE_2^{E_1} = VE_1^{E_1}(ke_1) = \$300(0.25) = \$75$$

$RRE_2^{E_1}$ means "the required cash return *on* capital to E_1 suppliers at time point t_2." $VE_1^{E_1}$ is the value of the E_1 suppliers' claim at t_1, which we know must equal their capital contribution in an efficient market. So the new equity suppliers require a $75 cash return *on* capital at t_2. And since t_2 is the terminal point, their $300 capital contribution must also be returned (RC), so

$$NCDE_2^{E_1} = RRE_2^{E_1} + RC_2^{E_1} = \$75 + \$300 = \$375$$

This t_2 total of \$375, of course, discounts back to t_1 at 25% to give $VE_1^{E_1} = \$300$.

So the NEC_1 suppliers have a claim on \$375 of the equity cash disbursement at t_2. What about the original equity suppliers? Let us see what they get. At t_2 \$2187.50 of $NCDE_2$ is distributed to both sets of equity suppliers, and since the new people get \$375:

$$NCDE_2^{E_0} = NCDE_2 - NCDE_2^{E_1} = \$2187.50 - \$375.00 = \$1812.50$$

The E_0 suppliers expect to receive a net cash flow of \$1812.50 at t_2. At t_1 these original equity suppliers expect to receive a dividend equal to $CDE_1 = \$1675$. Their *net* receipts at t_1 are also \$1675 since the \$300 of NEC_1 is supplied by outsiders:

$$NCDE_1^{E_0} = NCDE_1 - NCDE_1^{E_1} = \$1375 - (\$-300) = \$1675$$

If the E_0 suppliers expect $NCDE_2^{E_0} = \$1812.50$ and $NCDE_1^{E_0} = \$1675.00$, the t_0 value of their claim is

$$\begin{aligned} VE_0^{E_0} &= \frac{NCDE_1^{E_0}}{1 + ke} + \frac{NCDE_2^{E_0}}{(1 + ke)^2} \\ &= \frac{\$1675.00}{1.25} + \frac{\$1812.50}{(1.25)^2} \\ &= \$2500.00 \end{aligned}$$

which is the same as our original value.

The value of the original equityholders' claim at t_1 is expected to be

$$VE_1^{E_0} = \frac{NCDE_2^{E_0}}{1 + ke} = \frac{\$1812.50}{1.25} = \$1450.00$$

which, when added to the E_1 suppliers' t_1 value, is

$$VE_1 = VE_1^{E_0} + VE_1^{E_1} = \$1450 + \$300 = \$1750$$

That value is consistent with our Section II method of calculating equity values:

$$VE_1 = \frac{NCDE_1}{1 + ke} = \frac{\$2187.50}{1.25} = \$1750$$

Let us pause a moment to review what we have done. The purpose of the rather lengthy explanation above was to separate the cash flows and values of the E_0 suppliers from those of the E_1 suppliers. Table 12.2 reviews the

TABLE 12.2   **Type A decision**

NCDE's		$NCDE_1^{E_0} = \$\ 1675.00$ $+\ NCDE_1^{E_1} = \$-300.00$ $\overline{NCDE_1\ \ \ = \$\ 1375.00}$		$NCDE_2^{E_0} = \$1812.50$ $+\ NCDE_2^{E_1} = \$\ 375.00$ $\overline{NCDE_2\ \ \ = \$2187.50}$
VE's	$+$	$VE_0^{E_0} = \$\ 2500.00$ $VE_0^{E_1} = \$\ \ \ \ \ 0.00$ $\overline{VE_0\ \ \ = \$\ 2500.00}$	$+$	$VE_1^{E_0} = \$1450.00$ $VE_1^{E_1} = \$\ 300.00$ $\overline{VE_1\ \ \ = \$1750.00}$

results of our analysis. The t_2 equity cash flow is split into a $375.00 expectation for E_1 suppliers and a $1812.50 expectation for E_0 suppliers. We arrived at that split by calculating what amount of cash the E_1 suppliers require at t_2 for their capital return.[1] The t_1 equity cash flow $NCDE_1 = \$1375$ is split into two parts, $NCDE_1^{E_0}$ of $1675 to E_0 suppliers and $NCDE_0^{E_1}$ of $-\$300$ for E_1 suppliers.

The value of the claim held by E_0 suppliers at t_1 is expected to be $VE_1^{E_0} = \$1450$, which is the discounted value of their t_2 cash flow. At t_1, the value of the claims held by the E_1 suppliers is $300 = VE_1^{E_1}$. The two sum to $1750 = VE_1$ as determined per our Section II discussions. At t_0, the value of the t_0 equityholders' claim is the discounted value of their t_1 and t_2 cash-flow expectations, $NCDE_1^{E_0} = \$1675.00$ and $NCDE_2^{E_0} = \$1812.50$. At $ke = 25\%$, these discount to $VE_0^{E_0} = \$2500$. The E_1 suppliers naturally have no claim at t_0; $VE_0^{E_1} = \$0$ because they have not yet contributed anything. Consequently, $VE_0 = VE_0^{E_0} + VE_0^{E_1}$; $2500 = \$2500 + \$0$.

So for this firm, $VE_0 = VE_0^{E_0}$. The total value of equity at t_0 is the same as the value of the claim of the t_0 equityholders. Both values are $2500. But if you check back to our calculations, you will see that we arrived at those two equal dollar amounts by discounting different cash flows. Specifically,

$$VE_0 = \frac{NCDE_1}{1 + ke} + \frac{NCDE_2}{(1 + ke)^2} \qquad [12.1]$$

$$= \frac{\$1375.00}{1.25} + \frac{\$2187.50}{(1.25)^2} = \$2500.00$$

which is our Section II valuation formula for equity. By contrast,

$$VE_0^{E_0} = \frac{NCDE_1^{E_0}}{1 + ke} + \frac{NCDE_2^{E_0}}{(1 + ke)^2} \qquad [12.2]$$

$$= \frac{\$1675.00}{1.25} + \frac{\$1812.50}{(1.25)^2} = \$2500.00$$

By comparing these two valuation calculations we can see in detail the numerical implications of the capital acquisition/disbursement decision.

TYPE B DECISIONS   Suppose that instead of issuing $NEC_1 = \$300$, the company altered the decision by reducing NEC_1 to zero, and retaining $300 more at t_1, which would be accomplished by reducing dividends (CDE_1) by $300. This preserves the non-NDC contribution because NEC_1 is reduced by the same amount that CRF_1 is increased. The cash-flow expectations of the firm are now as given in Table 12.3. You may recognize these t_1 cash flows as corresponding generally to the type of decision shown as situation B in Figure 11.2. New equity capital and dividends have been decreased, and retentions increased, all by the same amount.

[1] The E_0 suppliers require $RRE_2^{E_0} = VE_1^{E_0}(ke) = \$1450.00(0.25) = \$362.50$ plus $RC_2^{E_0}$ of $1450.00. Therefore, $NCDE_2^{E_0} = \$1450.00 + \$362.50 = \$1812.50$. Appendix II.A shows another method of arriving at these cash flows.

TABLE 12.3

Expected flow	t_1	t_2
CAC	$2830.00	$3311.00
I	105.00	73.50
CAF	2725.00	3237.50
PP	850.00	1050.00
CDD	955.00	1123.50
NDC	400.00	0.00
NCDD	555.00	1123.50
CAE	1875.00	2187.50
CRF	500.00	0.00
CDE	1375.00	2187.50
NEC	0.00	0.00
NCDE	1375.00	2187.50
CRF + NEC	500.00	0.00
TCC $\equiv$ IVS	900.00	0.00

For this decision, the calculation of VE_0 remains exactly the same as it was originally in the Type A decision. While the calculation of $VE_0^{E_0}$ is, of course, given by the same formula (12.2) as before,

$$VE_0^{E_0} = \frac{NCDE_1^{E_0}}{1 + ke} + \frac{NCDE_2^{E_0}}{(1 + ke)^2} \qquad [12.2]$$

the cash flows that now appear have changed, and $VE_0^{E_0}$ is calculated as

$$VE_0^{E_0} = \frac{\$1375.00}{1.25} + \frac{\$2187.50}{(1.25)^2}$$

which is *identical* with respect to cash flows to the calculation of VE_0 following formula 12.1.

By decreasing dividends, increasing retention, and decreasing new equity contributions at t_1, the E_0 suppliers lose $300 of t_1 cash and gain ($2187.50 − $1812.50) = $375 of t_2 cash. At their required rate of $ke = 0.25$, the loss of $300 of t_1 cash cost them $300/1.25 = $240 of value at t_0, but the t_2 cash they gain is also worth $375/(1.25)^2 = $240 at t_0. The net effect of E_0 suppliers' wealth is $0. The Type B decision shifts some cash receipts forward in time but compensates at the appropriate required rate, ke.

TYPE C DECISIONS Suppose that instead of changing to a Type B decision, the company alters its capital acquisition/disbursement decision to one corresponding to situation C in Figure 11.2. You recall that this decision involves reducing retention, increasing dividends, and increasing new equity capital contributions. If this were done to the maximum, consistent with the investment and capital structure decisions, the relevant cash flows of the firm become those shown in Table 12.4.

Compared to the original t_1 cash-flow expectations, these show $200 less retained cash, $200 more dividends, and $200 more new equity capital.

TABLE 12.4

Expected flow	t_1	t_2
CAF	$2725.00	$3237.50
PP	850.00	1050.00
CDD	955.00	1123.50
NDC	400.00	0.00
NCDD	555.00	1123.50
CAE	1875.00	2187.50
CRF	0.00	0.00
CDE	1875.00	2187.50
NEC	500.00	0.00
NCDE	1375.00	2187.50
CRF + NEC	500.00	0.00
TCC $\equiv$ IVS	900.00	0.00

In terms of the cash-flow expectations to the two sets of equity suppliers, we know that $VE_1^{E_1} = \$500 = NEC_1$, and $ke_1 = 0.25$. Therefore, the cash return *of* and *on* capital required by the E_1 suppliers at t_2, $RRE_2^{E_1} + RC_2^{E_1}$, is $VE_1^{E_1}(ke) + VE_1^{E_1} = VE_1^{E_1}(1 + ke) = \$500(1.25) = \$625$ as $NCDE_2^{E_1}$. The t_1 equity suppliers expect to get \$625 of cash at t_2 in exchange for their \$500 at t_1.

Table 12.5 details the resulting cash flows and values for the two sets of equity suppliers and the firm as a whole under this decision. The important calculation, $VE_0^{E_0}$, is

$$VE_0^{E_0} = \frac{NCDE_1^{E_0}}{1 + ke} + \frac{NCDE_2^{E_0}}{(1 + ke)^2} \qquad \text{[12.2]}$$

$$= \frac{\$1875.00}{1.25} + \frac{\$1562.50}{(1.25)^2}$$

$$= \$2500.00$$

TABLE 12.5 Type C decision

NCDE's		$NCDE_1^{E_0} = \$\ 1875.00$ $+ \ NCDE_1^{E_1} = \$ -500.00$ $\overline{NCDE_1 \ \ \ = \$\ 1375.00}$			$NCDE_2^{E_0} = \$1562.50$ $+ \ NCDE_2^{E_1} = \$\ 625.00$ $\overline{NCDE_2 \ \ \ = \$2187.50}$
VE's	$+$	$VE_0^{E_0} = \$\ 2500.00$ $VE_0^{E_1} = \$\ \ \ \ \ 0.00$ $\overline{VE_0 \ \ = \$\ 2500.00}$		$+$	$VE_1^{E_0} = \$1250.00$ $VE_1^{E_1} = \$\ 500.00$ $\overline{VE_1 \ \ = \$1750.00}$

Once again, the original equity suppliers' present wealth is unaffected. As far as they are concerned, moving from a Type A decision to a Type C decision (higher dividends, lower retention, higher new equity flotation) gives them expectations of \$200 more cash at t_1 and \$250 less cash at t_2. ($NCDE_1^{E_0}$ for Type A = \$1675, for Type C = \$1875, a difference of \$200; and $NCDE_2^{E_0}$ for Type A = \$1812.50, for Type C = \$1562.50, a difference of

$250.00 at t_2.) The t_0 values of the differences are $200/1.25 = 160$, and $250/(1.25)^2 = 160$. What E_0 suppliers gain in wealth at t_0 ($160) from the t_1 increase in dividends they exactly lose at t_0 ($-$160) as a result of the $250 that must now be paid at t_2 to the E_1 suppliers.

As an exercise, you might find it worthwhile to perform these calculations for a decision to change from Type B to Type C. If done correctly, the present wealth of t_0 equityholders will be unaffected.

TYPE F DECISIONS
Type F decisions, as shown in Figure 11.3, involve increasing internal ("firm") financing (CRF_T) by decreasing dividends, decreasing principal payments, and decreasing both new equity and debt issuances. Were our company to do this at t_1 to the allowable maximum (Table 11.1), its relevant cash-flow expectations would be as listed in Table 12.6. The company is now expecting to finance the necessary $IVS_1 = 900$ totally by cash retention internal to the firm.

TABLE 12.6

Expected flow	t_1	t_2
CAF	$2725.00	$3237.50
PP	450.00	1050.00
CDD	555.00	1123.50
NDC	0.00	0.00
NCDD	555.00	1123.50
CAE	2275.00	2187.50
CRF	900.00	0.00
CDE	1375.00	2187.50
NEC	0.00	0.00
NCDE	1375.00	2187.50
CRF + NEC	900.00	0.00
TCC $\equiv$ IVS	900.00	0.00

Demonstrating that t_0 equityholders' present wealth is unaffected by the shift from Type A to Type F capital acquisition/disbursement policy is quite easy. If you compare these Type F cash flows to those for the Type B decision you can see that, as far as equityholders are concerned, the two are identical. At t_1 they expect $NCDE_1^{E_0}$ of $1375.00 and at t_2, $NCDE_2^{E_0}$ of $2187.50 in either situation. We have already shown that the value of those flows is the same as the $VE_0^{E_0}$ for Type A: $2500.00.

What, then, is the difference between Type B and Type F decisions? The difference is in debt financing. Debt suppliers at t_0 (D_0 suppliers) have agreed to forego part of their t_1 principal repayment in exchange for higher t_2 interest and principal payments. In situation F, the D_0 suppliers have, in effect, agreed to finance the $400 NDC_1 Type A debt contribution (provided in situation A by D_1 suppliers) by allowing the corporation to reduce their t_1 principal payment expectation by that amount.

The original debt suppliers have given up \$400 of t_1 cash. By doing that, they no longer must share t_2 cash with new debt (D_1) suppliers. In the Type A decision, D_0 suppliers expected to receive at t_1:

$$\text{NCDD}_1^{p_0} = \text{NCDD}_1 - \text{NCDD}_1^{p_1}$$
$$= \$555 - (\$-400)$$
$$= \$955$$

and at t_2

$$\text{NCDD}_2^{p_0} = \text{NCDD}_2 - \text{NCDD}_2^{p_1} = \text{NCDD}_2 - [\text{NDC}_1(1 + kd)]$$
$$= \$1123.50 - \$400(1.07)$$
$$= \$1123.50 - \$428.00$$
$$= \$695.50$$

which had a t_0 value of

$$\text{VD}_0^{p_0} = \frac{\$955}{1.07} + \frac{\$695.50}{(1.07)^2}$$
$$= \$1500$$

Under the Type F decision, the D_0 suppliers' expectations change to

$$\text{NCDD}_1^{p_0} = \text{NCDD}_1 - \text{NCDD}_1^{p_1}$$
$$= \$555 - \$0$$
$$= \$555$$

and

$$\text{NCDD}_2^{p_0} = \text{NCDD}_2 - \text{NCDD}_2^{p_1}$$
$$= \$1123.50 - \$0.00$$
$$= \$1123.50$$

which, of course, are the cash flows of our original debt value computation, where again $\text{VD}_0 = \$1500 = \text{VD}_0^{p_0}$. So debt suppliers' present wealths remain intact, and they should be willing to go along with any such Type F decisions. They give up, in this example, \$400 of t_1 cash for \$428 of t_2 cash, each of which has the same t_0 value of \$373.83. And equity suppliers' present wealth also is unchanged, so this decision, under our capital-market conditions, does not affect the wealth of either debt or equity suppliers.

TYPE E DECISIONS

Type E financing decisions involve increasing outside *equity* financing. Figure 11.3 shows that this is accomplished by reducing principal payments and new debt financing, reducing retained cash, increasing dividends, and increasing new equity capital contributions. Were our firm to move as far in this direction as possible per Table 11.1, its cash-flow expectations would be as shown in Table 12.7. Compared at t_1 to the A decision, principal payments and new debt capital are less by \$400, retained cash less by \$200, dividends more by \$600, and new equity capital more by \$600. The new expectation under E is that the $900 of IVS_1 needed will now be supplied totally by a new equity capital issue.

TABLE 12.7

Expected flow	t_1	t_2
CAF	$2725.00	$3237.50
PP	450.00	1050.00
CDD	555.00	1123.50
NDC	0.00	0.00
NCDD	555.00	1123.50
CAE	2275.00	2187.50
CRF	0.00	0.00
CDE	2275.00	2187.50
NEC	900.00	0.00
NCDE	1375.00	2187.50
CRF + NEC	900.00	0.00
TCC ≡ IVS	900.00	0.00

First, the original debt suppliers' cash-flow expectations have become identical to those of the Type F decision we just studied. Since that situation did not affect them, neither will this one. The original equity (E_0) suppliers are now expecting to receive a higher t_1 cash dividend, but because the new NEC_1 is also higher, they must share more of the t_2 cash with new equity (E_1) suppliers. Splitting these cash-flow expectations in our usual way,

$$\begin{aligned} NCDE_1^{E_0} &= NCDE_1 - NCDE_1^{E_1} \\ &= \$1375 - (\$-900) \\ &= \$1375 + \$900 \\ &= \$2275 \end{aligned}$$

and

$$\begin{aligned} NCDE_2^{E_0} &= NCDE_2 - NCDE_2^{E_1} = NCDE_2 - [NEC_1(1 + ke)] \\ &= \$2187.50 - \$900.00(1.25) \\ &= \$2187.50 - \$1125.00 \\ &= \$1062.50 \end{aligned}$$

The value of the original shareholders' claim under the Type E decision is then:

$$\begin{aligned} VE_0^{E_0} &= \frac{NCDE_1^{E_0}}{1 + ke} + \frac{NCDE_2^{E_0}}{(1 + ke)^2} \qquad \text{[12.2]} \\ &= \frac{\$2275.00}{1.25} + \frac{\$1062.50}{(1.25)^2} \\ &= \$2500.00 \end{aligned}$$

the same as always. Compared to their Type A cash flows, E_0 suppliers have gained an additional \$600 of t_1 cash at the expense of \$756 of t_2 cash. The t_0 values of these differences are each \$480, so they cancel each other and shareholder present wealth is unaffected.

Essentially, a Type E decision depicts the original debt suppliers leaving their capital in the firm longer, the original equity suppliers withdrawing sooner, and the new equity suppliers taking up the slack left by the withdrawal of the E_0 suppliers. As before, however, no one's present wealth is affected as long as the investment and capital structure decisions remain intact.

TYPE D DECISIONS
Finally, Type D decisions involve increased external (new) *debt* financing. This is accomplished by decreasing dividends and new equity capital, decreasing cash retention, increasing principal repayment, and increasing new debt capital flotation. The cash flows shown in Table 12.8 indicate that our firm is maximizing new debt financing at t_1. Here, dividends are less than situation A by \$300, and new equity capital is less by the same \$300. Notice that this means the original equityholders' cash-flow expectations are identical to the Type B and Type F decisions we have already studied. Since their present wealth was unaffected by those decisions, it is also unaffected here. CRF_1 is less by \$200, and the entire IVS_1 is supplied by \$900 of new debt capital.

TABLE 12.8

Expected flow	t_1	t_2
CAF	\$2725.00	\$3237.50
PP	1350.00	1050.00
CDD	1455.00	1123.50
NDC	900.00	0.00
NCDD	555.00	1123.50
CAE	1375.00	2187.50
CRF	0.00	0.00
CDE	1375.00	2187.50
NEC	0.00	0.00
NCDE	1375.00	2187.50
CRF + NEC	0.00	0.00
TCC $\equiv$ IVS	900.00	0.00

But how about the original debt suppliers? Will they go along with this decision? Our analysis of cash flows shows:

$$\text{NCDD}_1^{p_0} = \text{NCDD}_1 - \text{NCDD}_1^{p_1}$$
$$= \$555 - (\$-900)$$
$$= \$1455$$

and

$$\begin{aligned}
\text{NCDD}_2^{D_0} &= \text{NCDD}_2 - \text{NCDD}_2^{D_1} = \text{NCDD}_2 - (\text{NDC}_1)(1 + kd) \\
&= \$1123.50 - \$900.00(1.07) \\
&= \$1123.50 - \$963.00 \\
&= \$160.50
\end{aligned}$$

Thus, the t_0 value of the D_0 suppliers' claim is

$$\begin{aligned}
\text{VD}_0^{D_0} &= \frac{\text{NCDD}_1^{D_0}}{1 + kd} + \frac{\text{NCDD}_2^{D_0}}{(1 + kd)^2} \\
&= \frac{\$1455.00}{1.07} + \frac{\$160.50}{(1.07)^2} \\
&= \$1500.00
\end{aligned}$$

which is the same value as under the Type A and all other decisions. Original debt suppliers, in accepting an early principal repayment, have gained $500 at t_1 and lost $535 at t_2.[2] The t_0 values of each of these amounts are $467.29, so present wealth is unaffected.

The Type D decision, increasing external debt financing, essentially leaves equity financing in the firm longer, and substitutes larger amounts of new debt capital for original debt capital. Since the investment and capital structure decisions are not affected, in our capital market this financing decision alters no t_0 values nor anyone's present wealth.

SUMMARY   With this admittedly lengthy numerical example, we have examined each of the major financing alternatives available under what we call the capital acquisition/disbursement decision. Probably the most familiar strategies appeared in the Type F, Type D, and Type E decisions. Those entailed financing as much as possible *with retained cash* (F), *with new equity capital* (E), and *with new debt capital* (D). Table 12.9 summarizes for each decision type the discretionary flows to be maximized and minimized, along with the calculations for the amounts of each, given in terms of cash flows which must remain invariant for the pure capital acquisition/disbursement decision. Clearly, as we have seen, capital acquisition/disbursement is rich in alternatives, but when viewed in terms of wealth effects on existing equityholders, that richness pales in the pure theory. We have demonstrated that $\text{VE}_0^{E_0}$ remains unchanged regardless of whether an F, E, or D strategy is followed; indeed, we saw that current shareholder wealth did not vary even under a mixed strategy (A).

[2]By referring to our commentary about the Type F decision, you can see that $\text{NCDD}_2^{D_0}$ under Type A is $695.50, and here it is $160.50. $695.50 − $160.50 = $535.00 change in $\text{NCDD}_2^{D_0}$ from A to D.

TABLE 12.9 Implications of decision types F, E, and D for capital acquisition/disbursement cash flows

Decision type	Flows maximized	Flows minimized	If PP_T equals,	Then CAE_T equals,	CDE_T is given by,	And IVS_T comprises CRF_T +	NEC_T +	NDC_T	$= TCC_T$
F	CAE_T CRF_T	PP_T CDE_T NEC_T NDC_T	$\max \begin{cases} 0 \\ NCDD_T - I_T \end{cases}$	CAF_T $IVS_T + NCDE_T$	$\max \begin{cases} 0 \\ NCDE_T \end{cases}$ $\max \begin{cases} 0 \\ NCDE_T \end{cases}$	CAF_T $CAF_T - NCDE_T$ $IVS_T + NCDE_T$	$-NCDE_T$ 0 0	$I_T - NCDD_T$ $I_T - NCDD_T$ 0	
E	CAE_T CDE_T NEC_T	PP_T CRF_T NDC_T	$\text{mas} \begin{cases} 0 \\ NCDD_T - I_T \end{cases}$	CAF_T $IVS_T + NCDE_T$	$\min \begin{cases} VE_{T-1}(1+ke) \\ CAF_T \end{cases}$ $\min \begin{cases} VE_{T-1}(1+ke)* \\ (IVS_T + NCDE_T) \end{cases}$	$CAF_T - VE_T - NCDE_T$ 0 0	VE_T $CAF_T - NCDE_T$ VE_T IVS_T	$I_T - NCDD_T$ $I_T - NCDD_T$ 0	
D	PP_T NDC_T	CAE_T CDE_T CRF_T NEC_T	$\min \begin{cases} VD_{T-1}\dagger \\ CAF_T - NCDE_T \\ CAF_T \end{cases}$	$CAF_T - VD_{T-1}$ $NCDE_T$ 0	$\max \begin{cases} 0 \\ NCDE_T \\ NCDE_T \end{cases}$	$CAF_T - VD_{T-1}$ $CAF_T - VD_{T-1} - NCDE_T$ 0 0	$-NCDE_T$ 0 0 $-NCDE_T$	$VD_{T-1} + I_T - NCDD_T$ $VD_{T-1} + I_T - NCDD_T$ IVS_T $CAF_T + I_T - NCDD_T$	

*If the maximum value of CDE_T is constrained to equal $VE_{T-1}(1+ke)$, then the difference between CAF_T and CDE_T could flow to either PP_T or CRF_T. What is presented here assumes that the difference flows to CRF_T and that PP_T remains minimized as previously specified. As an exercise, you might write down the formulas for each flow which minimize CRF_T rather than PP_T, given this constraint on CDE_T.

†What follows to the right in the table assumes that CDE_T will be minimized, given the VD_{T-1} constraint on maximizing PP_T. An alternative you might explore is that of minimizing CRF_T instead of CDE_T in this situation.

Conclusion to Section IV

If you have found that the diagrammatic and numerical explanations offered for the financing decisions introduced in this section lack an intuitive economic appeal, consider the following idea (keep in mind that we are considering capital acquisition/disbursement decisions constrained not to affect capital structure or investment expectations). Our results pointing out the irrelevancy of such decisions turn out that way because *such decisions offer capital-market participants nothing they cannot provide for themselves.* We have seen, for example, that the effect of using more internal financing (F) is to lower new equity capital flotations and decrease dividends. Existing shareholders are compensated for their decreased dividends by their claim on future cash flows being higher because less new equity needs to be issued. *But the same thing could have been accomplished by the current shareholders themselves had they used their cash dividends to buy up the new equity issue.* Therefore, they are not likely to attach any premium or discount to a company that undertakes this financing policy.

Similarly, a company that decides to pay a higher dividend and raise more new equity capital provides its shareholders with higher cash flows in the near term, but compensatingly less in the future due to the new equity-holders' higher claims. If the existing shareholders prefer that strategy, they could accomplish the same thing on their own by selling some of their shares now, thus increasing their personal cash flow in the near term at the cost of future flows to the shares they sell.[3]

The net effects are the same whether the firm or the equityholders themselves choose the time pattern of cash flows to existing shareholders. The company can alter the time pattern of shareholders' cash receipts by choosing various retention, new equity-, and new debt-acquisition strategies. But the shareholders themselves could have duplicated any pattern the company chooses by selling shares to substitute personal "capital gain" cash flows for corporate dividends. And, furthermore, the individual equityholder can "undo" or negate any such decision the firm makes by taking opposite actions in his personal portfolio.

As we saw so emphatically in the theory of capital structure without deductibility, *when the capital market can arrive at the same cash-flow expecta-*

---

[3]Consider, for example, the Type C decision. Compared to A, our company issued $200 more NEC_1 and paid $200 more dividends at t_1. This gave the shareholders $200 of t_1 cash and cost them $250 of t_2 cash that went to new equityholders. If the company had kept its A decision, the t_0 shareholders could have sold $200 worth of their shares at t_1 after the t_1 dividend was paid, netting themselves $200 more at t_1, but then they would have lost out on $250 of t_2 dividends which would go to the people who bought the shares for $200 at t_1. In terms of the t_0 shareholders, this strategy gives them cash-flow expectations *identical* to the Type C decision, but in their own *personal* portfolio rather than through *corporate* cash-flow alterations.

tions independent of the corporation's actions, it will adjust values so that share-holder present wealth is unaffected by any such action the firm may take. Like capital structure without deductibility, capital acquisition/disbursement decisions can be duplicated by the capital market and therefore cause no wealth changes. Again, we return to the notion that only operating cash flows, interest tax subsidies, and investment expectations are the determinants of shareholder wealth in our capital market.

IMPERFEC-TIONS

Our market, however, is an abstraction from reality. We generally maintain that the simplifications which appear are worthwhile because they help us to clarify the basic economics that apply to even the most institutionally complex markets. This is true for the capital acquisition/disbursement decision we are studying in this section. The valuation tendencies we have outlined to this point are the same basic forces that you would see in the shares of a company traded on the New York Stock Exchange, were that company to alter its capital acquisition/disbursement expectations.

Nevertheless, real-world considerations that are not included in our capital market can affect real market values. The most obvious illustration of this so far is the presence of interest deductibility in the theory of capital structure. We could very easily have assumed that our corporations were not subject to income taxes. In that situation, interest deductibility would have appeared in the discussion of imperfections in Section III. We chose to include corporate income taxes and interest deductibility directly in the theoretical development because its effects have significant impact on real wealth, are economically interesting to study, and are subject to fairly straightforward analysis.

The real market considerations related to capital acquisition/disbursement theory are, however, not quite as clear-cut as interest deductibility. We can make statements about the likely effects of these imperfections, and this discussion is devoted to doing just that. Detailed numerical analysis of these effects, however, would prove to be either terribly intricate without much gain over our intuitive statements, or downright ambiguous. So our approach to discussing real-world considerations applied to capital acquisition/disbursement theory will be on an intuitive-descriptive level, recognizing that the alterations implied for our theory are not necessarily unimportant, merely difficult to quantify.

First, we must set the context in which to consider the imperfections that might affect the theory. As in the theoretical development itself, we shall assume that the company has already discovered an appropriate capital structure and investment plan. As you know, this specifies expectations for operational cash flows, interest payments and tax subsidies, net cash distributions to capital suppliers, and investment outlays for all future time points.[4] All

---

[4]Our numerical example demonstrated all of these for only a single time point. Appendix IV.A will show that the theory applies equally well to multiperiod situations.

we need do is specify how the IVS_T dollars are to be supplied at each time. To this point the theory tells us that how we specify that does not matter, as long as the other financial decisions are left intact.

That is the result for our idealized capital market. In real markets there are three major imperfections the effects of which we must consider:

1. *Corporate acquisition/disbursement costs.* These include:
    a. *Flotation costs* incurred by corporations when they issue new capital claims, either debt or equity securities.
    b. *Disbursement costs* associated with the transfer of monies to holders of capital claims.
2. *Personal taxes* levied on capital-market participants.
3. *Brokerage fees* charged participants when they buy or sell capital claims of corporations (securities).[5]

CORPORATE ACQUISITION/ DISBURSEMENT COSTS

When a corporation raises capital externally through a formal security issuance it must pay a fee for the investment banking services provided. We call these fees *flotation costs.*[6] Their effect is to make external capital issues more expensive than internal capital. For example, suppose that a corporation needs $1 million for investment purposes. If internally generated cash is used, there are no flotation costs incurred. But if external capital is raised, the corporation must issue claims totaling *more* than $1 million if it needs to *net* $1 million from the issue for investment purposes. The difference is, of course, the flotation cost.

You can see that this is not a good situation for current shareholders. By selling new shares, the company is, in effect, giving new shareholders a claim more than proportionate to the dollars received by the corporation for those new shares.[7] If the corporation must pay to "float" a new issue (equity or debt), current shareholders are worse off than if the company paid no such costs. Independent of other considerations, this makes internal financing (CRF_T) preferred to external (NEC_T and NDC_T).

The use of CRF_T, we know from our previous discussions, also implies lower dividends and principal payments. That means a reduction in the second kind of corporate cost associated with this financing decision: disbursement costs. The writing of thousands, possibly tens of thousands, of checks, the postage for mailing them, the bank fees for processing them, the audits of

---

[5]We include under the rubric "brokerage fees" all such transactions costs. Other examples in the United States would be odd-lot differentials, SEC fees, New York State transfer taxes, and so on.

[6]Other costs subsumed in this category would be expenditures for producing prospectuses, printing security certificates, the cost of management time, and so on.

[7]The new shareholders, however, *receive* a claim only proportionate to the dollars they pay in. The difference is what goes to the investment banker. Additionally, an even smaller number of dollars is actually applied to IVS_T once internal flotation costs are met (see footnote 6).

payments and dates of record for determining dividend ownership, the calling of bonds, trustee fees, and so on, and so on, do not improve current shareholders' present wealth. And these kinds of costs can also be significant in a firm of any size.

Thus, from the viewpoint of the corporation, there are clear cost-cutting incentives favoring CRF_τ financing from both the acquisition and disbursement dimensions. Indeed, the firm which both prepays principal and solicits NDC, or which both pays dividends and raises NEC, all at time τ, could be said to be reducing current equityholder wealth coming and going.

PERSONAL TAXES

Almost all real capital-market particpants subject to income taxes must pay taxes on their personal cash dividend receipts at each time point. If all such cash receipts are taxed at the same rate, such participants generally would prefer corporations to finance internally or by new debt issues (ignoring flotation costs). Think of the situation this way: If a company finances externally with new equity, the dividends received by current shareholders will be higher than if the company chooses another financing strategy. Those dividends are taxed immediately upon receipt by the participant. Even if she chooses not to consume all that cash now, she must pay tax on it.

If, however, dividends are lowered through internal or new debt financing, the current shareholders will receive their returns in the form of higher equity values than would have been the case if new equity had been issued. (You can check our numerical example to see that this is true right up until the terminal period.) *These value changes are not taxed.* Taxes on those gains are paid only when the ownership of the securities changes.[8] This means that if the participant consumes none of the return, he pays no tax. If he consumes some, he pays tax only on the amount he consumes. Of course, sooner or later the taxes will be paid. But if dividends are high because of new equity capital flotations, the tax is paid sooner than if returns are received through "capital gains." The further into the future you can push tax liabilities, the lower their present value, and the higher your personal present wealth.[9]

Further reinforcing this disadvantage of new equity financing is the fact that, in the United States, capital gains are taxed at rates lower than dividends. Thus, not only do the returns suffer from being taxed immediately rather than when equityholders decide to receive them, but they are also taxed

[8]This is not strictly true to the extent that some political jurisdictions impose *ad valorem* personal property taxes on holdings of securities. These taxes, where they exist, are sometimes called "intangibles taxes," but they apply to total value, not just to changes in value.

Taxes on gains may also be avoided in whole or in part by the transfer of ownership to certain specific econonic units such as charitable organizations or educational institutions (attention, alumni).

[9]Our examples in this chapter had no capital gains in the sense of increasing equity values across time because we were working with a firm that terminated quickly. To see a firm that does have capital gains, check back to our four-period corporation in Appendix II.B.

at higher rates if paid by the corporation as dividends rather than elected by the equityholders through personally acting to take capital gains.

On the other hand, there is one group of capital-market participants which might prefer dividends to capital gains. Consider persons who are subject to fairly low personal tax rates, and who consume all the dividend as paid. Remembering that, under present U.S. laws, the first $100 of dividends are tax-free,[10] and that, as the next section shows, consuming capital gains usually also involves brokerage fees to which dividends are not subject, such participants might well prefer to receive their returns from the corporation in the form of cash dividends.

BROKERAGE FEES

When capital-market participants buy or sell securities, they must pay a transaction cost called *brokerage*. The effect of such brokerage fees on financing theory is, at best, ambiguous. On the one hand, they add to the cost of receiving capital gains because brokerage fees must be paid when shares are sold. On the other hand, if dividends in excess of present consumption are paid, brokerage fees can be incurred when buying securities with the excess. From this point of view, brokerage fees are a friction in the cash flows but show no necessary bias one way or the other. The exception, again, is participants who consume all the dividend paid to them and who would therefore incur no reentry brokerage fees due to excess of dividend over consumption.

ADDITIONAL CONSIDERA- TIONS

As long as we are in the realm of real-market considerations, there are a few other potential effects on the capital acquisition/disbursement decision that should be mentioned. First, recognize that at some time points, corporations may be forced to go to external capital suppliers for necessary investment cash. Consider, for example, a situation where a very profitable investment opportunity exists for a corporation, but the investment outlay necessary is larger than the overall cash flow of the company for that period. Simple arithmetic indicates that external capital will be necessary.

There are two interesting comments we can make about this situation, one theoretical and one "practical." From the standpoint of our FCF statement, notice that this situation says simply that CAC_T is less than IVS_T. It therefore follows that $(CAC_T - IVS_T)$ is a negative amount. Since

$$CAC_T - IVS_T = NCDE_T + NCDD_T$$

it follows that the sum of the expected net cash distributions to capital suppliers at that time point is negative. This may sound startling at first, but in fact it is a quite common occurrence in real capital markets. It does not mean, for example, that dividends (CDE_T) are negative; they cannot be. It means simply that when $NCDE_T$ is negative, NEC_T must be larger than CDE_T; new equity capital flotations exceed the cash dividend paid at that

[10]$200 on a joint return.

time point. Similarly, should $NCDD_T$ be negative, it does not imply that interest has not been paid. Rather, it indicates that NDC_T exceeds CDD_T; new debt capital is larger than principal and interest paid against previous debt claims. Neither of these situations is at all uncommon in real capital markets, occurring almost certainly at any time point when new capital is raised. (This is due, in part, to the fixed nature of flotation costs, which, if at all independent of the amount of capital sought, are often spread over large blocks of new debt or equity. Thus, firms may raise new capital only once a year instead of monthly.) Negative $NCDD_T$ and/or $NCDE_T$ flows have no particular effect on the applicability of any theoretical formula or relationship that we have developed in the past few chapters. All it means is that in calculating VE_0 or VD_0, the $NCDE_T$ or $NCDD_T$ in question enters as a negative, rather than as a positive amount.

The second point is more practical. If corporations' productive asset investments tend to be larger than CAC_T when they occur, the company could conceivably choose to avoid external financing at those time points by retaining cash in previous periods, and holding it as liquid assets, say, marketable securities. The effect would be to raise each period's CRF_T and IVS_T, and lower dividends (CDE_T). Then, when the time for the large real-asset IVS_T rolled around, the liquid assets would be sold, and the cash used for real-asset investment (producing very large $\$RCPT_T$, CRF_T, and IVS_T that period).[11] Whether or not shareholders' present wealths are aided by this strategy is a function of at least all the following factors:

1. Issuance costs avoided.
2. Taxes on dividends avoided.
3. Returns from holding liquid assets rather than distributing dividends.
4. Capital gains taxes incurred.
5. Tax brackets of shareholders.
6. Consumption preferences of shareholders.

As you can see, such an analysis would be both complex and very much dependent on the characterstics of the particular firm and its shareholders.

REVIEW Reviewing our discussion of real-market influences on the capital acquisition/disbursement decision, we have made the following observations:

1. Flotation costs tend to make internal financing preferable to external new equity or debt financing.
2. Personal taxes favor internal or new debt financing over new equity,

[11]With reference to the parenthetical comments in the immediately preceding paragraph relating to flotation costs and economies of scale of capital claim issuance, note that this same liquid asset strategy can be employed in conjunction with the early issuance of capital claims for later real-asset investments.

both because of the possible delay of tax payments and because capital gains are often taxed at rates lower than dividends.[12] There is one group characterized by a low rate of personal income tax, $100 dividend tax exclusion, and current period dividend consumption who might prefer high dividends and new capital flotations, unless flotation costs were extremely high.

3. Brokerage fees cut two ways. They reduce capital gains and therefore favor dividends in one direction, but in the other, any dividends not consumed would incur reinvestment brokerage fees. Again, however, the dividend-preferring group above would have no such personal reinvestment needs and might prefer dividends rather than paying brokerage fees in order to convert capital gains on paper to real consumption.

As a general statement, then, for the great bulk of shareholders, firms that finance real investment internally whenever possible are probably more attractive (*ceteris paribus*) than those that do not. However, there is the "widows and orphans" group that might prefer the opposite strategy.

This brings us logically to the following observation: The chances are that whatever capital acquisition/disbursement policy a firm has adopted, it has attracted a clientele of shareholders which prefers that policy. Therefore, a corporation could conceivably reduce the present wealth of its existing equityholders by switching to a policy that was more generally acceptable, but unsuitable to its particular existing clientele. In any case, whatever policy is chosen should not be altered at the whim of management, because the transactions costs involved in clientele switching could be significant.

These generalizations, as you would expect, also have their exceptions. If too many corporations are serving a limited clientele, a switch from the common to the scarce policy could increase the value of the company's shares to potential shareholders from the "scarce policy" group, and existing shareholders from the "common policy" group could sell out to the potential shareholders who prefer the new policy. If the value increase exceeded the transaction costs the current shareholders would incur in switching to another common policy corporation, they would be better off.

Further, the investment and capital structure considerations we have held constant in this chapter can also change in real capital markets. A highly profitable new investment might be discovered that would warrant, because of its operational cash-flow effects in the future, a departure from existing capital acquisition/disbursement policy. Similarly, a change in corporate tax laws might call for revisions in financing strategy because of interest or other tax subsidy effects.

Finally, recall that our capital market is one where participants have easy access to the future cash-flow expectations of corporations traded in the

---

[12]Indeed, some countries assess *no* taxes on capital gains.

market. In effect, participants know the risky cash-flow expectations and are immediately aware of any changes in these expectations. Although real-world capital markets may approach this ideal, the information channels are not as perfect as in our market.[13] This implies that *corporate actions which have no value in our perfect market may contain "signaling value" or "informational content" in real capital markets where information flows are not perfect.* Dividend payments could possibly be one such signal. If corporations can use dividend cash flows to signal good and bad changes in future cash-flow expectations of management, some allowance for this might be worthwhile in capital acquisition/disbursement policy.

SUMMARY   In this section we have extended the theory of corporate finance to include capital acquisition/disbursement theory. We found that within our capital market, if we regard the corporation's investment and capital structure decisions as given, the capital acquisition/disbursement policy chosen has no effect on shareholder wealth. A company can choose to obtain the needed investment cash at each time point through new equity or new debt issues, or through retaining cash that would otherwise have been paid out to capital suppliers, all with no effect on the value of total equity (or debt) claims.

When new equity capital is issued at time τ, the current shareholders receive their required returns at the same time in the form of dividends. When the firm retains cash or issues new debt, current shareholders receive their returns as higher dividends further in the future than τ, or, if they choose, by selling some shares in the capital market in the current period. Shareholder wealth is the same under all capital acquisition/disbursement strategies, as long as investment and capital structure expectations remain intact.

The economic reason why this financing decision is irrelevant is the same as that for capital structure changes without interest deductibility: Nothing is provided to the capital market that particpants could not have done on their own. We saw that any cash-flow alteration caused by a change in capital acquisition/disbursement strategy could have been reproduced or canceled out by current shareholders' reinvesting dividends in new equity issues, or selling shares. When such is the case, the capital market adjusts values so that no wealth changes result from the corporate financing decision.

The introduction of real capital-market imperfections forced us to reconsider our theoretical findings. When corporate acquisition/disbursement costs, personal taxes, and brokerage fees exist, the "best" capital acquisition/disbursement policy for a corporation, if subject to definitive analysis at all, is a most complex question. We were able to make some general comments, but even those were subject to possibly significant exceptions.

[13]Remember that we are not saying that the expectations held by participants in our market are "correct" in the sense of being eventually borne out by actual cash flows. All we are saying is that, correct or incorrect, such expectations exist, and are agreed upon by (all) our participants.

To console ourselves for having devoted so much effort to developing this aspect of corporate financial theory, consider that without the theoretical statements, we would have had no basis for considering real-world complications. And this is equally true for the whole of corporate financial theory. We, as ever, have no pretensions toward offering detailed prescriptions to financial managers. But we *do* feel that the operational expertise of those managers (and managers to be) is greatly aided by understanding the basic economic tendencies they face when making financial decisions. If, in this section, we have taken a step in that direction, our effort has been worthwhile.

Appendix IV.A: Multiperiod Capital Acquisition/Disbursement Policy

This appendix will demonstrate that the theoretical statements of Section IV apply equally well to multiperiod financial situations as to the two-period firm we used to develop our capital acquisition/disbursement conclusions. Recall our five-period corporation from Chapter 7. Table IV. A.1 presents the relevant information about this firm. The results of Section IV indicate that we should be able to change the existing capital acquisition/disbursement decision(s) of this company and not affect the wealth of t_0

TABLE IV.A.1 Five-period corporation

	t_1	t_2	t_3	t_4	t_5
CAC	\$1341.06	\$1362.71	\$1281.94	\$1365.87	\$1262.24
I	78.96	72.51	61.43	47.35	25.80
CAF	1262.10	1290.20	1220.51	1318.52	1236.44
PP	107.44	284.80	234.64	484.04	430.07
CDD	186.40	357.31	296.07	531.39	455.87
NDC	0.00	100.00	0.00	125.00	0.00
NCDD	186.40	257.31	296.07	406.39	455.87
CAE	1154.66	1005.40	985.87	834.48	806.37
CRF	323.32	175.00	250.00	0.00	0.00
CDE	831.34	830.40	735.87	834.48	806.37
NEC	176.68	100.00	0.00	0.00	0.00
NCDE	654.66	730.40	735.87	834.48	806.37
CRF + NEC	500.00	275.00	250.00	0.00	0.00
TCC ≡ IVS	500.00	375.00	250.00	125.00	0.00

$ke = 0.25$ per period
$kd = 0.06$ per period

	t_0	t_1	t_2	t_3	t_4
VE_T	\$1973.98	\$1812.82	\$1535.62	\$1183.66	\$ 645.10
VD_T	\$1315.99	\$1208.55	\$1023.75	\$ 789.11	\$ 430.07
VF_T	\$3289.97	\$3021.37	\$2559.37	\$1972.77	\$1075.17

shareholders. Table IV.A.2 presents the cash flows for a Type F decision (low dividends and new equity, low principal repayment and new debt, high cash retention by the firm). Table IV.A.3 shows a Type E decision (high dividends and new equity, low principal payments and new debt, low cash retention by the firm). Then Table IV.A.4 gives the results of a Type D decision (low dividends and new equity, low retention, high principal repayment and new debt).

TABLE IV.A.2   Type F decisions

	t_1	t_2	t_3	t_4	t_5
CAF	$1262.10	$1290.20	$1220.51	$1318.52	$1236.44
PP	107.44	184.80	234.64	359.04	430.07
CDD	186.40	257.31	296.07	406.39	455.87
NDC	0.00	0.00	0.00	0.00	0.00
NCDD	186.40	257.31	296.07	406.39	455.87
CAE	1154.66	1105.40	985.87	959.48	806.37
CRF	500.00	375.00	250.00	125.00	0.00
CDE	654.66	730.40	735.87	834.48	806.37
NEC	0.00	0.00	0.00	0.00	0.00
NCDE	654.66	730.40	735.87	834.48	806.37
CRF + NEC	500.00	375.00	250.00	125.00	0.00
TCC ≡ IVS	500.00	375.00	250.00	125.00	0.00

TABLE IV.A.3   Type E decisions

	t_1	t_2	t_3	t_4	t_5
CAF	$1262.10	$1290.20	$1220.51	$1318.52	$1236.44
PP	107.44	184.80	234.64	359.04	430.07
CDD	186.40	257.31	296.07	406.39	455.87
NDC	0.00	0.00	0.00	0.00	0.00
NCDD	186.40	257.31	296.07	406.39	455.87
CAE	1154.66	1105.40	985.87	959.48	806.37
CRF	0.00	0.00	0.00	0.00	0.00
CDE	1154.66	1105.40	985.87	959.48	806.37
NEC	500.00	375.00	250.00	125.00	0.00
NCDE	654.66	730.40	735.87	834.48	806.37
CRF + NEC	500.00	375.00	250.00	125.00	0.00
TCC ≡ IVS	500.00	375.00	250.00	125.00	0.00

The first thing that we must do is sort out the equity claims and cash flows for the existing decision. Fortunately, Appendix II.A has already done this for us, and we merely reproduce those results from Tables II.A.2 and II.A.3 there as Table IV.A.5 here. (Some 1-cent discrepancies in the VE figures are due to rounding errors.) If your memory as to the sources of these cash flows and values is shaky, refer to Appendix II.A for an explanation. Note that the present decision calls for new equity issues at t_1 and t_2, and that the present shareholders' $VE_0^{E_0} = \$1973.99$.

TABLE IV.A.4   Type D decisions

	t_1	t_2	t_3	t_4	t_5
CAF	$1262.10	$1290.20	$1220.51	$1318.52	$1236.44
PP	607.44	559.80	484.64	484.04	430.07
CDD	686.40	632.31	546.07	531.39	455.87
NDC	500.00	375.00	250.00	125.00	0.00
NCDD	186.40	257.31	296.07	406.39	455.87
CAE	654.66	730.40	735.87	834.48	806.37
CRF	0.00	0.00	0.00	0.00	0.00
CDE	654.66	730.40	735.87	834.48	806.37
NEC	0.00	0.00	0.00	0.00	0.00
NCDE	654.66	730.40	735.87	834.48	806.37
CRF + NEC	0.00	0.00	0.00	0.00	0.00
TCC $\equiv$ IVS	500.00	375.00	250.00	125.00	0.00

TABLE IV.A.5 $NCDE_T^{E_i}$ and $VE_T^{E_i}$ for initial decision

	t_1	t_2	t_3	t_4	t_5
$NCDE_T^{E_0}$	$ 831.34	$ 749.47	$ 620.90	$ 704.11	$ 680.39
$NCDE_T^{E_1}$	(176.68)	80.93	67.05	76.03	73.47
$NCDE_T^{E_2}$	0.00	(100.00)	47.92	54.34	52.51
$NCDE_T^{E_3}$	0.00	0.00	0.00	0.00	0.00
$NCDE_T^{E_4}$	0.00	0.00	0.00	0.00	0.00
$NCDE_T$	$ 654.66	$ 730.40	$ 735.87	$ 834.48	$ 806.37

	t_0	t_1	t_2	t_3	t_4
$VE_T^{E_0}$	$1973.99	$1636.14	$1295.71	$ 998.74	$ 544.31
$VE_T^{E_1}$	0.00	176.68	139.92	107.84	58.78
$VE_T^{E_2}$	0.00	0.00	100.00	77.08	42.01
$VE_T^{E_3}$	0.00	0.00	0.00	0.00	0.00
$VE_T^{E_4}$	0.00	0.00	0.00	0.00	0.00
VE_T	$1973.99	$1812.82	$1535.63	$1183.66	$ 645.10

The Type F decision shown in Table IV.A.2 can be dispensed with rather easily. All IVS_T needs are supplied by retained cash ($CRF_T = IVS_T$), and new equity capital falls to zero at each time point. $NCDE_T^{E_0}$ is therefore equal to $NCDE_T$, and $VE_0^{E_0} = VE_0$, so current shareholder wealth is unaffected. Principal repayments and new debt capital decline at t_2 and t_4, releasing cash to CAE_2 and CAE_4, but this is retained within the firm and does not affect equity cash distributions.

In terms of specific cash flows, moving from the initial to a Type F decision means that E_0 suppliers' net cash flows shift from being the top $NCDE_T^{E_0}$ row of Table IV.A.5 to being the $NCDE_T$ row of that table, as shown in Table IV.A.6. When internal financing is substituted for external, net cash receipts close to t_0 decline, and further from t_0 rise. In effect, share-

TABLE IV.A.6

	t_1	t_2	t_3	t_4	t_5
Initial $NCDE_T^{E_0}$	$831.34	$749.47	$620.90	$704.11	$680.39
$-$Type F $NCDE_T^{E_0}$	654.66	730.40	735.87	834.48	806.37
Difference$_T$	$176.68	$ 19.07	$$-114.97$	$$-130.37$	$$-125.98$

$$\text{Value of} \atop \text{difference} = \frac{\$176.68}{1.25} + \frac{\$ 19.07}{(1.25)^2} + \frac{\$-114.97}{(1.25)^3} + \frac{\$-130.37}{(1.25)^4} + \frac{\$-125.98}{(1.25)^5}$$

$$= \$0.00$$

$$VE_0^{E_0} \text{ (initial)} = VE_0^{E_0} \text{ (Type F)}$$

holders are foregoing current (or near-term) dividends for future dividends. In value and wealth terms, however, there is no change.

Similarly, the Type D decision portrayed in Table IV.A.4 causes no particular problems in analysis. Here all IVS_T needs come from new debt issues, NDC_T. Principal repayments are higher and therefore CAE_T's lower, but the net cash receipts of current equity suppliers are the same as in the Type F decision discussed above. $VE_0^{E_0}$ must therefore remain at $1973.99.

Table IV.A.7 shows for the Type E decision from Table IV.A.3, the $NCDE_T^{E_1}$ flows, their values, and their comparison with flows under the initial capital acquisition/disbursement decision in our five-period corporation. The cash-flow allocations to the various categories of equity suppliers are calculated using the procedure introduced in Appendix II.A when we first considered distinct categories of equity claims. In Table IV.A.7, the $VE_T^{E_1}$ entries in the middle of the table are simply the results of discounting at $ke = 25\%$ the $NCDE^{E_1}$ flows at each time point greater than T. (Some 1-cent discrepancies in the VE figures are due to rounding errors.) Note, finally, that at the bottom of Table IV.A.7 when we contrast the $NCDE_T^{E_0}$'s of the initial mixed decision to those of the Type E decision (high dividends and new equity flotations), near-term net cash flows increase to existing shareholders. But because IVS_T is coming from new equity suppliers, future net cash flows to equity are shared with them, and are therefore lower for existing equityholders. In value and wealth terms, of course, there is no effect.

Finally, Table IV.A.8 shows the cash-flow expectations of our constant-perpetuity corporation for the three extreme capital acquisition/disbursement strategies. As an exercise, we suggest that you review the cash flows presented to make certain you understand the changes occurring with each decision, and then calculate $VE_0^{E_0}$ under each option. If you perform the calculations correctly, there are no changes in present wealth of t_0 shareholders under any decision.[14]

[14]*Hint:* Under the initial and Type E decisions, where NEC_T is issued every period, the t_0 equityholders' share of future equity cash flows must *decline* every period, even though overall corporate cash flows are constant across time.

TABLE IV.A.7 $\text{NCDE}_T^{E_i}$ and $\text{VE}_T^{E_i}$ for Type E decisions

	t_1	t_2	t_3	t_4	t_5
$\text{NCDE}_T^{E_0}$	\$1154.66	\$ 800.52	\$ 539.61	\$ 414.24	\$280.68
$\text{NCDE}_T^{E_1}$	(500.00)	304.88	205.51	157.77	106.90
$\text{NCDE}_T^{E_2}$	0.00	(375.00)	240.75	184.82	125.23
$\text{NCDE}_T^{E_3}$	0.00	0.00	(250.00)	202.65	137.31
$\text{NCDE}_T^{E_4}$	0.00	0.00	0.00	(125.00)	156.25
NCDE_T	\$ 654.66	\$ 730.40	\$ 735.87	\$ 834.48	\$806.37

	t_0	t_1	t_2	t_3	t_4
$\text{VE}_T^{E_0}$	\$1973.99	\$1312.82	\$ 840.51	\$ 511.03	\$224.55
$\text{VE}_T^{E_1}$	0.00	500.00	320.12	194.63	85.52
$\text{VE}_T^{E_2}$	0.00	0.00	375.00	228.00	100.18
$\text{VE}_T^{E_3}$	0.00	0.00	0.00	250.00	109.85
$\text{VE}_T^{E_4}$	0.00	0.00	0.00	0.00	150.00
VE_T	\$1973.99	\$1812.82	\$1535.63	\$1183.66	\$645.10

	t_0	t_1	t_2	t_3	t_4
$\text{NCDE}_T^{E_0}$ (initial mixed)	\$ 831.34	\$749.47	\$620.90	\$704.11	\$680.39
$-\text{NCDE}_T^{E_0}$ (Type E)	1154.66	800.52	539.61	414.24	280.68
Difference$_T$	\$$-323.32$	\$$-51.05$	\$ 81.29	\$289.87	\$399.71

$$\text{Value of differences} = \frac{\$-323.32}{1.25} + \frac{\$-51.05}{(1.25)^2} + \frac{\$81.29}{(1.25)^3} + \frac{\$289.87}{(1.25)^4} + \frac{\$399.71}{(1.25)^5}$$
$$= \$0.00$$

TABLE IV.A.8   Impact of different capital acquisition/disbursement decisions on constant-perpetuity cash flows

Cash flow	Initial	Decisions Type F	Type E	Type D
CAC	\$2900.00	\$2900.00	\$2900.00	\$2900.00
I	269.50	269.50	269.50	269.50
CAF	2630.50	2630.50	2630.50	2630.50
PP	280.00	0.00	0.00	700.00
CDD	549.50	269.50	269.50	969.50
NDC	280.00	0.00	0.00	700.00
NCDD	269.50	269.50	269.50	269.50
CAE	2350.50	2630.50	2630.50	1930.50
CRF	220.00	700.00	0.00	0.00
CDE	2130.50	1930.50	2630.50	1930.50
NEC	200.00	0.00	700.00	0.00
NCDE	1930.50	1930.50	1930.50	1930.50
CRF + NEC	420.00	700.00	700.00	0.00
TCC $\equiv$ IVS	700,00	700.00	700.00	700.00

$ke = 27\%$ per period
$kd = 7\%$ per period

Problems for Section IV

1. Quadper Industries is a four-period corporation with the following cash-flow expectations:

	t_1	t_2	t_3	t_4
CAC	$14295.10	$7370.53	$10530.39	$7126.45
I	642.17	476.03	352.28	179.17
CAF	13652.93	6894.50	10178.11	6947.28
PP	3969.01	2912.51	4165.17	2986.12
CDD	4611.18	3388.54	4517.45	3165.29
NDC	1200.00	850.00	1280.00	0.00
NCDD	3411.18	2538.54	3237.45	3165.29
CAE	9683.92	3981.99	6012.94	3961.16
CRF	3480.00	155.00	912.00	0.00
CDE	6203.92	3826.99	5100.94	3961.16
NEC	1320.00	195.00	818.00	0.00
NCDE	4883.92	3631.99	4282.94	3961.16
CRF + NEC	4800.00	350.00	1730.00	0.00
TCC ≡ IVS	6000.00	1200.00	3010.00	0.00

The market dictates a 6% return on debt and a 13% return on equity.

(a) Construct financial cash-flow statements for Quadper illustrating strategies of Types D, E, and F.

(b) Using the cash flows that equityholders expect to receive, demonstrate quantitatively the effects on shareholder wealth of each of these alternative policies. Assume that any new capital issuances will be made to participants other than those holding the shares at t_0.

(c) Suppose now that this corporation is real, that is, it is being valued in real rather than theoretical capital markets. Is there a particular capital acquisition/disbursement strategy that you would recommend? If so, defend that strategy, using whatever arguments you think relevant to real capital markets. If you can discover no unambiguously preferred strategy, say in detail why you cannot.

2. Hallelujah Perpetual, a corporation engaged in the manufacture of harps and harpstrings, is currently faced with its annual dividend decision. The corporation anticipates an unbroken string of annual revenues equal to $18,949.42, annual expenditures equal to $11,892.71, annual interest payments of $809.46, and annual investments of $2,700.00. Current practice is to go to the capital markets each period to raise $740.00 of new debt capital and $1,014.00 of new equity capital, the required rates of return for which are 11% and 16%, respectively. Ms. Daphne Divine, president of the company, is considering the possibility of switching to a different dividend distri-

bution policy but is unsure of the consequences. Hallelujah is faced with an annual corporate tithe of 52%, and, needless to say, operates in an ideal market.

(a) Prepare financial cash-flow statements for the current situation, as well as for situations of Types B, C, D, E, and F.

(b) Demonstrate for Ms. Divine the effects of each dividend policy on the present wealth of current equityholders. Are your results consistent with our theory?

3. Failsafe, Inc. sells finance examination answers to students at a well-known university. Because of legal threats, and because good students would never consider using the services of Failsafe, the company is expected to be in business for only three more time periods.

Failsafe's operating cash flow expectations are:

CAU_1	CAU_2	CAU_3
$6236.29	$4414.85	$5629.44

and the company plans investment outlays of $3400 at t_1 and $3100 at t_2, all of which is to be supplied through cash retentions. Failsafe has a debt issue outstanding upon which the capital market is requiring a 7% return per period, the interest and principal expectations for which are:

	t_1	t_2	t_3
I	$181.50	$137.69	$126.43
PP	$625.81	$160.94	$1806.08

The company's debt suppliers allow advanced or delayed principal payments, as long as their wealth is undisturbed.

Failsafe's equity suppliers require a 25% return per period, and Failsafe is subject to a corporate tax rate of 52% (interest is deductible).

(a) Detail Failsafe's financial cash flow expectations under its present capital acquisition/disbursement strategy. What would you think of this strategy were Failsafe a "real" corporation subject to usual capital market conditions (its capital suppliers would also be subject to realistic conditions)? Why?

(b) Failsafe is considering an alteration from its current capital acquisition/disbursement strategy to one which emphasizes as much cash dividend payout as possible, without altering its investment or capital structure decisions. Please show Failsafe's cash flow expectations under this strategy. Also, please indicate which cash flows are constrained from moving as far in the new direction as they would if unconstrained, and state the nature of the constraint.

(c) Under what realistic conditions would such a strategy as the emphasis of high cash dividends be desirable?

(d) Failsafe also would like to consider maximizing principal payments. Show the cash flows for such a strategy and detail which ones are constrained.

(e) Failsafe has also heard that stability in the cash dividend is a desirable characteristic. Show the company how it can achieve this stability (i.e. show the cash flows). ("Stability" in this sense would mean the same CDE in dollar terms at each time point). Give one good realistic reason why stability in cash dividends might be desirable, other than a consumption-based one.

(f) Failsafe has heard of something called the "clientele" effect, and wants to know how such a phenomenon might affect its capital acquisition/disbursement strategy. Please give Failsafe a sophisticated answer.

4. This section has isolated five strategies in the capital acquisition/disbursement decision, which we have labeled B, C, D, E, and F. Although the pure theory argues that the decision is irrelevant, arguments are also made that certain imperfections in real capital markets could cause the choice among such strategies to be important. No complete theory exists which fully incorporates these imperfections into the capital acquisition/disbursement decision. One first step toward such integration, however, could be a detailed specification of particular imperfections' effects on particular strategies. Construct this specification by detailing a two-dimensional matrix having the imperfections as rows, and strategies as columns, with the intersections describing the effect of a particular imperfection on a particular strategy.

References for Section IV

The rigorous economic proof of the neutrality of dividends vis-à-vis corporate value appears in: Merton H. Miller and Franco Modigliani, "Dividend Policy, Growth, and the Valuation of Shares", *Journal of Business* (October 1961), pp. 411–433; "Dividend Policy and Market Valuation: A Reply," *Journal of Business* (January 1963), pp. 116–119. An earlier and more intuitive approach is found in: James T.S. Porterfield, "Dividends, Dilution, and Delusion," *Harvard Business Review* (November-December 1959), pp. 156–161, and in a somewhat more refined version in his book *Investment Decisions and Capital Costs* (Englewood Cliffs, N.J.: Prentice-Hall, Inc., 1965), Chap. 6. The same subject is addressed at an intermediate level in: Alexander A. Robichek and Stewart C. Myers, *Optimal Financing Decisions* (Englewood Cliffs, N.J.: Prentice-Hall, Inc., 1965), Chap. 4.

For additional treatment of the theoretical irrelevancy of dividends including tests of the applicability of the theory to real markets and tax environments, see: John Linter, "Dividends, Earnings, Leverage, Stock Prices and the Supply of Capital to Corporations," *Review of Economics and Statistics* (August 1962), pp. 243–269; "Optimal Dividends and Corporate Growth Under Uncertainty," *Quarterly Journal of Economics* (February 1964), pp. 49–95; Eugene F. Fama and Harvey Babiak, "Dividend Policy: An Empirical

Analysis," *Journal of the American Statistical Association* (December 1968), pp. 1132–1161; Donald E. Farrar and Lee L. Selwyn, "Taxes, Corporate Financial Policy and Return to Investors," *National Tax Journal*, vol. 20 (1967), pp. 444–454; and Stewart C. Myers, "Taxes, Corporate Financial Policy and the Return to Investors: Comment," *National Tax Journal*, vol. 20 (1967), pp. 455–462.

The Theory of Asset Acquisition and Divestment

The introduction to Part Two said that there are three types of financial decisions made by corporations: (1) *the capital structure decision*, (2) *the capital acquisition/disbursement decision*, both of which are *financing* decisions, and (3) *the asset acquisition and divestment decision*, which is an *investment* decision.*

Sections III and IV extended our theory of corporate finance to include the two financing decisions. This section will do the same for the asset acquisition and divestment decision, or, as it is more commonly (if less accurately) termed, the "capital budgeting" decision. The theory of asset acquisition and divestment is concerned with the effects of corporate investment in assets. We shall use the term "investment decisions" to mean the same thing as "asset acquisition and divestment decisions" or "capital budgeting decisions."

But what really is the meaning of this financial decision? Until now our exposure to the investment decision has been limited to the knowledge that if any IVS_τ cash-flow expectation were altered, the investment decision would be changed. That, however, is not much information about the decision itself or its effects on the corporation and its capital suppliers. Our first task, therefore, must be to examine exactly what the corporate investment decision entails.

*As we have noted before (for example, pp. 108 and 162), the investment decision includes maintenance of real operating assets, even though such expenditures are usually "expensed" rather than "capitalized" (see footnote 5 of Chapter 7). It is also worth noting that the investment decision applies equally to financial as well as real assets.

CORPORATE INVESTMENT

In financial theory, corporate investments are most correctly thought of as "little corporations" in and of themselves which are to be attached to the existing corporation. Consider, for example, a corporation going into a new product line. This investment may have expectations of future cash receipts, expenditures, taxes, depreciation expenses, interest expenses, investment outlays, and so forth. If we were to detail all the financial cash flows associated with this investment, we would have a series of FCF statements relating just to the investment. And this FCF statement series would include each time point in the future through which the investment is expected to operate. But that is the same type of information we have been using in our study of corporations themselves. So a corporate investment is very much like a corporation, in that it carries expectations of future cash flows similar to those in our corporate statements.†

This way of thinking about corporate investment is very helpful to us in describing the investment decision. A corporation faced with this decision has an existing set of cash-flow expectations and risks for each future time point. If it chooses to reject the proposed investment, existing future cash flows are, naturally, unaffected. If it accepts the investment, however, its future cash-flow expectations must change to recognize that the investment cash-flow expectations and attendant risks have now been attached to those of the existing corporation.

In other words, a company considering an investment (or divestment) proposal must choose between two sets of future cash-flow expectations and risks: *Set I* is that for the existing corporation at each future time point *without* the proposal's acceptance; and *Set II* is what would result for the corporation at each future time point *with* the proposal's acceptance.‡ If the corporation rejects the proposal, its cash flows and risks will remain as specified in *Set I*. If it accepts the proposal, its future cash flows and risks will become those specified in *Set II*.

Notice that the decision is between *Set I* and *Set II* even if the proposal is to get rid of existing assets rather than to acquire new assets. The corporation still is faced with the choice between an existing *Set I* of future cash-flow expectations (that is, "do not get rid of the asset"), and a new *Set II* that includes the acceptance of the proposal (that is, "get rid of the asset").

Notice also that the choice of *Set II* includes the cash-flow expectations *and risks* of the proposed decision. This means that the "with-proposal-

---

†This analogy may appear to be inappropriate to "cost saving" investments, which in themselves generate no receipts. However, "negative expenditure" expectations are economically equivalent to "positive receipt" expectations.

‡The similarity between this terminology ("with" and "without") and that for a financial market participant's investment decision in Section I is both obvious and intentional, as we shall demonstrate.

acceptance'' corporation can differ from the ''without-proposal-acceptance'' corporation not only in the expected cash-flow dollars that appear in future FCF statements, but also in the risks associated with those cash flows. As you know, risk affects required rates of return in our capital market. So the with-proposal-acceptance corporation can have both different expected cash flows and different required rates of return in the future compared to what they would be if the proposal were rejected. If the acceptance of the proposal changes the risk of future cash-flow expectations, required rates of return will also change. If the proposed decision does not change the risk of future cash flows, the corporation with acceptance would have the same required rates as it would without acceptance.

INVESTMENT DECISION When faced with an investment (or divestment) decision, a corporation must decide between two sets of future cash flows and risks. But how does it make that decision? On what is the judgment based? The answer is the same as for all other financial decisions that we have studied: *The corporation chooses the set of future cash flows and risks which maximizes the present wealth of currently existing equityholders.* The remainder of this section is devoted to examining the investment decision from that point of view.

As we shall see, much of the groundwork for the investment decision has been provided by the theory in previous sections. What we already know about valuation, capital structure, and capital acquisition/disbursement will carry us a good distance in this analysis. Actually, as Section I promised, we are faced with only one rather formidable task: We must come to very specific grips with a risk measure for future cash-flow expectations. Until now (that is, prior to confronting the investment decision) we have been able to avoid the necessity of actually *measuring* risk because other financial decisions involved only allocating a given amount of overall corporate risk among capital claims.§ We were able to make those allocations by relying on our knowledge of claim priorities and the economic relationships between the claims of a corporation in the capital market.

But an investment decision may have risks quite different from those of the corporation considering it. In order to analyze that situation adequately we must develop a way of measuring the risks of investment proposal cash flows, and in the process, the risks of the cash-flow expectations associated with an existing firm. That task will constitute the largest part of our theoretical effort. Once it is done, the investment decision itself involves little more than applying ideas we have seen repeatedly in earlier sections.

As was also the case with our previous analyses, we shall examine the

§The with-deductibility capital structure analysis did involve corporate risk alterations, but those too were associated with the given risks of debt claims.

investment decision while holding constant the effects of other financial decisions. Within our theory this simply means that we intend to hold capital structure constant. Were it to be changed by an investment decision, equityholder present wealth would, as you know, also be affected by the capital structure alteration. And we would find it a tedious job to separate the capital structure and investment decision effects.

We need not, however, hold the capital acquisition/disbursement decision constant since, in our theory, capital acquisition/disbursement does not affect shareholder wealth. We can, if we wish, hold this decision constant also. But even if we do not, any wealth effects must necessarily arise from the investment decision alone, because the capital acquisition/disbursement decision has none to offer.

In sum, we shall hold capital structure constant while studying the theory of asset acquisition and divestment; the capital acquisition/disbursement decision may either be constant or changed because it does not matter.¶

We can now proceed to investigate the theory of corporate investment decision making.

¶In real-world terms, of course, if you have found an optimal capital acquisition/disbursement strategy, you would naturally tend to maintain it when making investments.

Chapter 13

The Corporate Investment
Decision: Risk Unaltered

The introduction to Section V has given us a number of basic observations about the corporate investment decision. Keeping these in mind, we are ready to incorporate this decision into our theory. As noted in the Section V introduction, we shall hold constant the effects of other financial decisions during the development of investment theory. Further, as is our usual procedure, we shall begin with the simplest of corporate investment decisions and gradually progress to the more complex.

Our first step will hold one other thing constant: risk. In this chapter our corporation will be faced with investment proposals which, if accepted, would leave the riskiness of corporate cash flows unchanged. Two questions immediately arise. First, why would we want to hold risk constant, and, second, what kind of investment could possibly leave the risk of cash-flow expectations unchanged?

The answer to the first question is easy. If risk is unaffected, so will be the required rates of return on corporate capital claims. This means that the with-proposal-acceptance corporate cash flows can be discounted at the same rates that apply to the existing firm. Here we do not need to have a specific risk measure because we know what required rates to use. This makes our job a lot easier than it would be if we were to consider an investment that altered the riskiness of cash flows. There we would need a mechanism for measuring the risk alteration and for specifying appropriate required rates to use for valuation purposes. We shall construct that mechanism shortly. But the theoretical development, we think, is more clear if cash-flow effects are handled first, and risk treated subsequently.

The answer to the second question is more difficult. Until we have a risk measure specified, it is impossible to be very clear about what it means to "hold risk constant." For the moment, however, you can regard this investment decision as something like a corporation merely expanding or contracting its current operations, that is, continuing to do what its existing expectations predict but on a larger (or smaller) scale.[1] Once we have specified a risk measure, we can return to this point with more clarity. But for now, the obvious importance of the simplification is that risk is, for the moment, "neutralized," and the same set of required rates apply to the firm with and without the acceptance of the investment (or divestment) proposal.

NUMERICAL EXAMPLE

The best vehicle for illustrating the effects of a "risk-constant" corporate investment decision is a simple numerical example. For this purpose, we recall our two-period corporation from Section II. To refresh your memory we have reproduced its full description in Table 13.1, to include its t_1 and t_2 cash-flow expectations, its required rates and costs, its θ and τ, and its values.

TABLE 13.1   Two-period corporation without proposal acceptance

	t_1	t_2	
$RCPT	$6250.00	$7500.00	$\theta = 0.15$
$EXPT	3976.50	4800.75	$\tau = 0.52$
GCFO	2273.50	2699.25	
GTAX	1182.22	1403.61	$ke = 0.20$
NCFO	1091.28	1295.64	$kd = 0.08$
DTS	936.00	468.00	$kf = 0.182$
CAU	2027.28	1763.64	$kd^* = 0.0384$
ITS	18.72	9.36	$kf^* = 0.17576$
CAC	2046.00	1773.00	
I	36.00	18.00	
CAF	2010.00	1755.00	$VF_0 = \$3000.00$
PP	225.00	225.00	$VD_0 = 450.00$
CDD	261.00	243.00	$VE_0 = 2550.00$
NDC	0.00	0.00	
NCDD	261.00	243.00	
CAE	1785.00	1530.00	$VF_1 = \$1500.00$
CRF	0.00	0.00	$VD_1 = 225.00$
CDE	1785.00	1530.00	$VE_1 = 1275.00$
NEC	0.00	0.00	
NCDE	1785.00	1530.00	
TCC $\equiv$ IVS	0.00	0.00	

In the context of Table 13.1, suppose that "now" is time point t_1 rather than t_0. All the t_2 cash-flow expectations and p_2 required rates of return are

[1]To be completely accurate, one would also have to assume that scale did not affect risk, which makes this a rather circular illustration; nevertheless, you can probably gather the intent of what we are saying.

as they were when we first saw this firm, except that now our time vantage point is t_1 instead of t_0. The t_1 cash flows previously expected when we were at t_0 are now actual amounts at t_1. For example, the company's equityholders would right now (t_1) be receiving a net cash flow of \$1785 ($NCDE_1$) and their stock would be worth \$1275 (VE_1), giving them a t_1 present wealth of \$3060, the sum of $NCDE_1$ and VE_1. They would also be expecting to receive a net cash distribution of \$1530 ($NCDE_2$) one period from now, and their required rate of return for p_2 is 20% ($ke = 0.20$). In other words, the company is completing its p_1 operations and is about to begin its last period's (p_2) operations. Note that the company, as matters now stand, has no investments planned; IVS_1 and IVS_2 are both equal to zero.[2]

Suppose that the company suddenly discovers the following investment opportunity. A \$1274.25 investment outlay at t_1 is expected to generate \$5000.00 more \$RCPT and \$2400.00 more \$EXPT for the corporation at t_2. The investment will not change the riskiness of any corporate cash flow (i.e., operating risks and capital structure of the corporation will remain unchanged). The entire \$1274.25 outlay is depreciable for income tax purposes at t_2, since the corporation ceases to exist at that time point. In terms of financial cash flows, this investment information is shown in Table 13.2. GCFO, GTAX, and NCFO recognize that $\tau = 52\%$; and the \$662.61 DTS is simply τ (\$1274.25). So the investment requires a \$1274.25 cash outlay at t_1 and adds \$1910.61 to CAU_2 while leaving risk unaffected.

TABLE 13.2 Investment proposal cash flows

	t_1	t_2
\$RCPT	\$ 0.00	\$5000.00
\$EXPT	0.00	2400.00
GCFO	0.00	2600.00
GTAX	0.00	1352.00
NCFO	0.00	1248.00
DTS	0.00	662.61
CAU	0.00	1910.61
IVS	1274.25	0.00

It may surprise you to hear that the company now has enough information to make the investment decision. How can that be? What about the ITS_T, CAC_T, CDD_T, I_T, PP_T, CAE_T, CDE_T, NDC_T, NEC_T, $NCDD_T$, and $NCDE_T$ flows associated with the investment? We have omitted a lot of familiar lines from our FCF statement for this investment. Do all these omissions matter at this point, and can we make the investment decision anyway?

---

[2]Somewhere in the past (t_0 or before) there were investment outlays; otherwise, the company would have no assets now. Those IVS's, of course, do not appear in the t_1 and t_2 FCF statements.

The answer is that they do not, and we can. We are trying to illustrate an investment decision, not fill out an FCF form. Before we leave this example we shall fill in the omitted lines. Right now, however, using just the information we have, let us see what the with-acceptance corporate cash flows would look like. To find these, all we need do is add the investment cash flows to those of the existing corporation. Or, add Table 13.1 to Table 13.2 to get Table 13.3.

TABLE 13.3   Total corporate FCF with acceptance = (corporate FCF without acceptance + investment proposal)

	t_1 (actual flows)	t_2 (expected flows)
$RCPT	$6,250.00 = ($6,250.00 + $ 0.00)	$12,500.00 = ($7,500.00 + $5,000.00)
$EXPT	3,976.50 = (3,976.50 + 0.00)	7,200.75 = (4,800.75 + 2,400.00)
GCFO	2,273.50 = (2,273.50 + 0.00)	5,299.25 = (2,699.25 + 2,600.00)
GTAX	1,182.22 = (1,182.22 + 0.00)	2,755.61 = (1,403.61 + 1,352.00)
NCFO	1,091.28 = (1,091.28 + 0.00)	2,543.64 = (1,295.64 + 1,248.00)
DTS	936.00 = (936.00 + 0.00)	1,130.61 = (468.00 + 662.61)
CAU	2,027.28 = (2,027.28 + 0.00)	3,674.25 = (1,763.64 + 1,910.61)
IVS	1,274.25 = (0.00 + 1,274.25)	0.00 = (0.00 + 0.00)

The cash flows in Table 13.3 are those for the company if it accepts the investment proposal. If we can discover what the resultant $NCDE_1$ and VE_1 figures are, we can compare their sum ("equity's present wealth with the proposal's acceptance") to the $3060 of "equity's present wealth without the proposal's acceptance" we derived from Table 13.1. If the equity present wealth *with* exceeds the *without*, the proposal will be accepted; if not, it will be rejected.

Before we proceed further we must introduce a bit of notation so that we can be sure which cash flows, discount rates, and values we are talking about during this section. As you can gather, there are three "corporations" involved in an investment decision: (1) the *without* corporation (the proposal not included), (2) the *with* corporation (the proposal included), and (3) the *investment* (the proposal) itself. The cash flows of the *without* corporation, its required rates, and values will be identified with a *wo* superscript; for example, CAU_2^{wo}, ke_3^{wo}, and VD_1^{wo} would be the CAU_2 cash flow, the ke_3 rate, and the VD_1 value for the corporation *without* the proposal's acceptance. Similarly, the *with* corporation's flows, rates, and values shall have w superscripts; for example, CAU_2^w, ke_3^w, and VD_1^w. And, finally, the proposal's flows, rates, and values are noted with *ivs* superscripts (for example, CAU_2^{ivs}, ke_3^{ivs}, and VD_1^{ivs}) when the proposal is an investment (acquisition of assets), and with *divs* superscripts (for example, CAU_2^{divs}, ke_3^{divs}, and VD_1^{divs}) when the proposal is to divest the firm of assets.[3]

[3]An example of the divestment of assets is presented in Appendix V.A.

VALUATION WITH ACCEPTANCE

As a first step in addressing the specific investment decision that we posed in Table 13.3, we need to find the t_1 market values of the with-acceptance cash flows. But how can we do that with only the information so far available? Recall from Section II that

$$VF_0 = \sum_{\tau=1}^{T} \frac{CAU_\tau - IVS_\tau}{\prod_{P=1}^{\tau} (1 + kf_P^*)} \qquad [7.11]$$

This valuation requires us to know CAU_τ and IVS_τ at each time point and kf_P^* for each time period. Table 13.3 indicates that CAU_2^w and IVS_2^w for the with-acceptance corporation are known. But what about kf_2^{*w}? *Remember that this investment will not change the risk of any cash flows. And, in addition, capital structure, θ, is not to change.* This means that kf_2^{*w} (with acceptance) is exactly the same as kf_2^{*wo} (without acceptance). Table 13.1 recalls that $kf^* = kf_2^{*wo} = 0.17576$. Therefore, we do have enough information to use formula 7.11:

$$
\begin{aligned}
VF_1^w &= \frac{CAU_2^w - IVS_2^w}{1 + kf_2^{*w}} \\
&= \frac{\$3674.25 - \$0.00}{1.17576} \\
&= \$3125.00
\end{aligned}
$$

VF_1^w, the value of the firm if it accepts the investment (*with*), is \$3125 at t_1.

"Well," you say, "that is really quite impressive. From just the information given, we can calculate that the value of the firm will increase from \$1500 = VF_1^{wo} (*without*, per Table 13.1) to \$3125 = VF_1^w (*with*, per our use of formula 7.11) if the firm accepts the proposed investment. The investment, if undertaken, would add \$1625 to the value of the firm. That's nice."

"But," you point out, "the value of the firm is *not* the value we are interested in. We were told only a moment ago that VE_1^w (*with*) will be the important market value in finding equity's present wealth *with acceptance*. How can we find out what *it* is?"

The answer of how to find VE_1^w is almost embarrassingly easy, now that we know VF_1^w. Recall that the company will have the same capital structure with acceptance as without. In Table 13.1 we reported the capital structure to be $\theta = 0.15$ without. You can verify this figure by recalling the basic definition of capital structure from Section III and inserting the appropriate numbers:

$$\theta^{wo} = \frac{VD_1^{wo}}{VF_1^{wo}} = \frac{\$225}{\$1500} = 0.1\dot{5}$$

$$1 - \theta^{wo} = \frac{VE_1^{wo}}{VF_1^{wo}} = \frac{\$1275}{\$1500} = 0.85$$

and, as is obvious,

$$VE_1^{wo} = VF_1^{wo}(1 - \theta^{wo})$$

But since we are holding capital structure constant as we consider the investment decision, we know also that

$$\theta^w = \frac{\text{VD}_1^w}{\text{VF}_1^w} = 0.15$$

that

$$1 - \theta^w = \frac{\text{VE}_1^w}{\text{VF}_1^w} = 0.85$$

and that, in general,

$$\text{VE}_1^w = \text{VF}_1^w(1 - \theta^w) \qquad [13.1]$$

So specifically for our firm,

$$\begin{aligned}
\text{VE}_1^w &= \text{VF}_1^w(0.85) \\
&= \$3125.00(0.85) \\
&= \$2656.25
\end{aligned}$$

Since the *value proportion* of equity will be the same with or without acceptance, to find VE_1^w under constant capital structure, all we need to know is $\theta^{wo=w}$, and VF_1^w. If the investment is accepted, the *with* value of equity will be $2656.25 at t_1.

WITH-ACCEPTANCE CASH FLOWS—II

Part of our problem has now been solved. We know that the *equity-value* portion of shareholder present wealth *with acceptance* is $2656.25 at t_1. But what about the *cash* portion of that wealth? Without-acceptance shareholders receive $1785 of NCDE at t_1. That is added to their VE_1^{wo} of $1275 to net a *without* present wealth of $3060. What happens to this NCDE cash flow at t_1 with acceptance? We must discover this in order to arrive at the with-acceptance equityholder present wealth.

In Table 13.3a we present an addition to the t_1 FCF statement for our firm *with*, which we began in Table 13.3. After the firm pays the $36 of t_1 interest, it will have $2010 in cash ($\text{CAF}_1^w$) before any principal payments, distributions to equityholders, new debt or equity flotations, and the $1274.25 IVS_1^w outlay. Is this enough information for us to work with so as to be able to discover the t_1 net cash receipts of equityholders with acceptance? Yes, it is.

We know from Section II that the $1274.25 of IVS_1^w must equal the sum of $\text{CRF}_1^w + \text{NEC}_1^w + \text{NDC}_1^w$. And we know from Section IV that the "mix" by which that $1274.25 IVS_1^w is supplied does not matter so long as we

TABLE 13.3a   Additional t_1 cash flows with acceptance

CAU_1^w	$2027.28
ITS_1^w	18.72
CAC_1^w	2046.00
I_1^w	36.00
CAF_1^w	2010.00
$\text{TCC}_1^w \equiv \text{IVS}_1^w$	1274.25

hold capital structure constant. Let us proceed, then, to make an allowable capital acquisition/disbursement decision at t_1, and see what happens.

First, note from Table 13.1 that at t_1, the *without* debt value, VD_1^{wo}, is $225, and that the debt suppliers are also expecting a PP_1^{wo} of another $225. Instead of that, let us buy out the D_0 suppliers altogether at t_1. That would require a total PP_1^w "with" of $450 = ($VD_1^{wo}$ of $225 + PP_1^{wo} of $225):

$$PP_1^w = \$450$$

This would mean, for the moment, that no debt claim is outstanding. But if capital structure, θ, is to be held constant, we also know that

$$VD_1^w = \theta(VF_1^w) \qquad \textbf{[13.2]}$$

must be true. Specifically, for our firm,

$$VD_1^w = (0.15)(\$3125.00)$$
$$= \$468.75$$

Therefore, our corporation *must* issue a new debt claim at t_1 to D_1 suppliers in the amount of $468.75. Thus,

$$NDC_1^w = \$468.75$$
$$CDD_1^w = I_1^w + PP_1^w$$
$$= \$36.00 + \$450.00$$
$$= \$486.00$$

and

$$NCDD_1^w = CDD_1^w - NDC_1^w$$
$$= \$486.00 - \$468.75$$
$$= \$17.25$$

Continuing through the FCF_1^w statement:

$$CAE_1^w = CAC_1^w - CDD_1^w = CAF_1^w - PP_1^w$$
$$= \$2046.00 - \$486.00 = \$2010.00 - \$450.00$$
$$= \$1560.00$$

Now we are faced with a dividend decision. Fortunately, we know that as long as we do not violate any other financial decision, this one does not matter. Specifically, since $NDC_1^w = \$468.75$, $CRF_1^w + NEC_1^w$ must equal $IVS_1^w - NDC_1^w$:

$$CRF_1^w + NEC_1^w = IVS_1^w - NDC_1^w$$
$$= \$1274.25 - \$468.75$$
$$= \$805.50$$

So whatever dividend decision we make, the sum of retained cash and new equity capital at t_1 must be $805.50.

To keep things as simple as possible, suppose that we just retain exactly $805.50 of the $1560.00 CAE_1^w and raise no new equity capital. Thus,

$$CRF_1^w = \$805.50$$
$$CDE_1^w = CAE_1^w - CRF_1^w$$
$$= \$1560.00 - \$805.50$$
$$= \$754.50$$

and since $NEC_1^w = \$0.00$, the $\$1274.25$ IVS_1^w is supplied by a TCC_1^w comprising $\$468.75$ of NDC_1^w and $\$805.50$ of CRF_1^w. Finally, then,

$$NCDE_1^w = CDE_1^w - NEC_1^w$$
$$= \$754.50 - \$0.00$$
$$= \$754.50$$

Let us examine what we have done. By collecting all these t_1 with-acceptance cash flows we have just calculated, we can produce a *complete* FCF_1^w statement as shown in Table 13.3b.

But even more important than the FCF statement, we have found the net cash receipts of the with-acceptance equityholders at t_1. They receive a cash dividend of $\$754.50 = CDE_1$ and supply no new cash ($NEC_1 = \$0.00$). So their net cash receipt at t_1 is $\$754.50 = NCDE_1$.

TABLE 13.3b   Complete FCF_1^w statement

$RCPT	$6250.00
$EXPT	3976.50
GCFO	2273.50
GTAX	1182.22
NCFO	1091.28
DTS	936.00
CAU	2027.28
ITS	18.72
CAC	2046.00
I	36.00
CAF	2010.00
PP	450.00
CDD	486.00
NDC	468.75
NCDD	17.25
CAE	1560.00
CRF	805.50
CDE	754.50
NEC	0.00
NCDE	754.50
TCC $\equiv$ IVS	1274.25

INVESTMENT DECISION AND EQUITY WEALTH

This information finally allows us to calculate equityholders' present wealth at t_1 *with acceptance* (PWE_1^w). This present wealth is given by the sum of the market value of their equity claim at t_1 plus their net cash receipts at the same time point, or

$$PWE_1^w = VE_1^w + NCDE_1^w$$
$$= \$2656.25 + \$754.50$$
$$= \$3410.75$$

The present wealth of equityholders at t_1 with acceptance is $\$3410.75$.

You will recall that we showed earlier that

$$PWE_1^{wo} = VE_1^{wo} + NCDE_1^{wo} = \$3060.00$$

So the adoption of the proposed investment will change equityholder present wealth at t_1 as follows:

$$\begin{aligned} \Delta PWE_1 &= PWE_1^w - PWE_1^{wo} \\ &= \$3410.75 - \$3060.00 \\ &= \$350.75 \end{aligned}$$

Thus, the change from *without* to *with* at t_1 leaves equity suppliers \$350.75 better off. If the proposed investment is accepted, they experience an increase in their market-value claim given by

$$\begin{aligned} \Delta VE_1 &= VE_1^w - VE_1^{wo} \\ &= \$2656.25 - \$1275.00 \\ &= \$1381.25 \end{aligned}$$

and simultaneously they sustain a decrease in their net cash receipts of

$$\begin{aligned} \Delta NCDE_1 &= NCDE_1^w - NCDE_1^{wo} \\ &= \$754.50 - \$1785.00 \\ &= \$-1030.50 \end{aligned}$$

The net wealth effect at t_1, ΔPWE_1, if the investment proposal is adopted, is also given by

$$\begin{aligned} \Delta PWE_1 &= \Delta VE_1 + \Delta NCDE_1 \\ &= \$1381.25 + (\$-1030.50) \\ &= \$350.75 \end{aligned}$$

as before.

To convince yourself that this \$350.75 is unaffected by the capital acquisition/disbursement decision which we designed arbitrarily, you might try any other PP_1^w less than \$450.00, as long as you come up with outstanding debt claims of $VD_1^w = \$468.75$.[4]

VALUING INVESTMENT CASH FLOWS DIRECTLY— THE NET PRESENT VALUE

As much fun as it may be to work through the equity wealth effects of the investment using corporate cash flows, you might be wondering if analyzing the investment decision will always require this much effort. Depending on your emotional attachment to our FCF statement, you will be either delighted or disappointed to hear that the answer is no. There is a much more direct way to arrive at equity wealth effects of investment decisions within our theory. We can, in fact, value the investment cash flows *directly*, as if the investment, as we said earlier, were a "little corporation" by itself.

---

[4]For example, if PP_1^w were \$225.00 (VD_1^{wo} being \$225.00), NDC_1^w would have to be \$243.75 to yield a VD_1^w of \$468.75. Then CDD_1^w would be \$261 and CAE_1^w would be \$1785. The amount of TCC_1^w from CRF_1^w and NEC_1^w combined must equal $IVS_1^w - NDC_1^w$, or \$1030.50. If this amount came totally from CRF_1^w, then CDE_1^w is given by \$1785.00 − \$1030.50 = \$754.50, and with NEC_1^w at zero, $NCDE_1^w$ remains at \$754.50. Hence equityholder wealth is the same as in the example we developed that has $PP_1^w = \$450.00$. Try one for yourself with $PP_1^w = \$0.00$.

Formula 7.11 will serve this purpose nicely. Table 13.2 shows that we have the necessary CAU_2^{ivs} and IVS_2^{ivs} cash flows for the investment to use in the numerator of formula 7.11. The only other thing we need is the appropriate discount rate as the denominator. But what rate is appropriate?

Remember we said that the risk of the overall corporate cash flows would not change even though adoption of the investment proposal results in the combination of the investment's cash flows with the corporation's without-acceptance cash flows. We shall see later in the section that *this means the investment cash flows have the same risk as the "without" corporate cash flows*. If we also assume that the investment will have the same capital structure as the existing firm, $kf_2^{*ivs} = kf_2^{*wo} = 0.17576$ is the appropriate rate to use for discounting the investment's $\text{CAU}_T^{ivs} - \text{IVS}_T^{ivs}$ cash flows in formula 7.11. Doing just that for our example:

$$\text{VF}_1^{ivs} = \frac{\text{CAU}_2^{ivs} - \text{IVS}_2^{ivs}}{1 + kf_2^{*ivs}}$$

$$= \frac{\$1910.61 - \$0.00}{1.17576}$$

$$= \$1625.00$$

VF_1^{ivs}, the value of the investment at t_1 as a "little corporation" is \$1625. If the investment were selling in the capital market as a separate corporation, its VF_1 would equal \$1625. Notice that $\text{VF}_1^{ivs} = \$1625$ is exactly the amount by which the value of the firm increases when it accepts the investment:

$$\Delta\text{VF}_1 = \text{VF}_1^w - \text{VF}_1^{wo}$$

$$= \$3125 - \$1500$$

$$= \$1625 = \text{VF}_1^{ivs}$$

The corporation's total value increases by the "market value" of the investment when it is accepted.

Notice also, however, that we have not yet accounted for the \$1274.25 IVS_1^{ivs} outlay. The corporation did not acquire the investment at zero cost. The t_1 value of the IVS_1^{ivs} outlay is, of course, the \$1274.25. And the t_1 value of the investment's t_2 cash flow is, as noted earlier, $\text{VF}_1^{ivs} = \$1625$. So the net t_1 value of the investment to the corporation is

$$\text{net value at } t_1 = \text{VF}_1^{ivs} - \text{IVS}_1^{ivs}$$

$$= \$1625.00 - \$1274.25$$

$$= \$350.75$$

The corporation, in essence, is paying \$350.75 less for the investment at t_1 than it would be forced to were the investment valued by the capital market. Since t_1 is the "present" time in this example, \$1625.00 is the "present value" of the investment's cash inflows, \$1274.25 is the present value of the investment's cash outflows, and \$350.75, their difference, is the investment's "net present value (NPV_1^{ivs})."[5]

[5]Good applied corporate finance texts, those solidly based in the theory of value, calculate an investment's NPV in exactly this way.

$$\text{NPV}_1^{ivs} = \$350.75$$

But wait a moment. We have already seen the $350.75 figure somewhere. In fact, we saw that $350.75 is the amount by which equityholder present wealth increases when the corporation accepts the investment; *the entire net present value of an investment goes to equityholders.* Why? It is simply because equityholders are the residual capital claimants of the firm. *Net present value is the amount by which investment cash flows exceed required cash returns to all capital claimants, discounted back to now. It is an "excess" of value left over after all capital claims are satisfied, and thus it reverts to the residual claimants, the equityholders.*

Investment net present value is directly calculated by

$$\text{NPV}_A^{ivs} = \Delta\text{PWE}_A = \text{PV}_A(\text{future investment cash flows}) - (\text{value of } t_A \text{ flows})$$

$$\text{NPV}_A^{ivs} = \left[\sum_{T=A+1}^{T} \frac{\text{CAU}_T^{ivs} - \text{IVS}_T^{ivs}}{\prod_{P=A+1}^{T}(1 + kf_P^{*ivs})} \right] + \text{CAU}_A^{ivs} - \text{IVS}_A^{ivs} \quad \textbf{[13.3]}$$

$$\text{NPV}_A^{ivs} = \text{VF}_A^{ivs} + \text{CAU}_A^{ivs} - \text{IVS}_A^{ivs} \quad \textbf{[13.3a]}$$

or, for constant cost of capital across time,

$$\text{NPV}_A^{ivs} = \sum_{T=A}^{T} \frac{\text{CAU}_T^{ivs} - \text{IVS}_T^{ivs}}{(1 + kf^{*ivs})^{T-A}} \quad \textbf{[13.3b]}$$

where CAU_T^{ivs} and IVS_T^{ivs} are the financial cash flows associated with the investment, and kf_P^{*ivs} is the weighted-average cost(s) of capital for the investment.[6] Formula 13.3 gives the change in present wealth of the currently existing equity suppliers when the investment is accepted. The formula may look a bit awesome, but it is nothing more than the calculations that we have just performed.[7]

If NPV_A^{ivs} is greater than zero, equityholder present wealth (at t_A) will increase by that amount, so the investment proposal will be accepted. If

[6]Here kf_P^{*ivs} is also equal to the weighted-average cost of capital for the corporation (both kf_P^{*w} and kf_P^{*wo}) because this particular example is of a risk-constant investment (that is, an investment proposal which, if accepted, will not alter the risk of the corporation, or equivalently—as we shall show later—which has risk equal to that of the *without* corporation.) kf_P^{*ivs}, as the overall capital cost of an investment, must, as any other kf_P^*, reflect the returns required by all capital market participants *claiming* future cash flows from the investment, *not* merely the returns required by those who *supplied* the cash to make the investment outlay (in general, claimants of investment flows are not limited to the same participants who supply IVS^{ivs}). We shall illustrate this idea soon.

[7]Formula 13.3 is essentially the same as formula 7.11 with the addition of the current cash flows CAU_A^{ivs} and IVS_A^{ivs}, which are not included in our Section II *ex dividend* valuation formulas. Notice that CAU_A^{ivs} is included in the formula. This allows for investment outlays which can be immediately "expensed" for income tax purposes; and further, there is a possibility of a cash *inflow* now (t_A) if the investment decision under consideration involves the divestment of assets. You will recall that, in our model, flows arising from the liquidation of assets are included in $RCPT (and, hence, in CAU). In the case of divestment, we would expect similar "reversed" flow effects on CAU and IVS in future periods as a result of a liquidation at t_A. Note also that the inclusion of $\text{IVS}_{T(>A)}^{ivs}$ in formula 13.3 implies the possibility of future cash outlays (past t_A). This is not at all unusual for actual investments, especially those in real assets which require periodic non-expensable renewal.

NPV is less than zero, equity present wealth will decline by that amount upon acceptance, so the investment will be rejected.

So you can see that a risk-constant investment is not a terribly difficult problem, either analytically or theoretically. The appropriate investment cash flows ($CAU_T^{ivs} - IVS_T^{ivs}$) are discounted back to the present at the investment's weighted-average cost(s) of capital, kf_P^{*ivs}. Any present outlay or inflow is included, and the result, NPV_A^{ivs}, is the equityholder wealth effect. It is the present value of the amount by which present and future cash returns from the investment exceed required cash returns from capital suppliers. Although working through the corporate cash flows *with acceptance* may well be a bit tedious, we should at least be encouraged that our theory of the first four sections served us well.

The general procedures that we have outlined, and formulas 13.3, 13.3a, and 13.3b, apply equally well to any investment proposal that does not alter the risk of the currently existing corporation. This includes both the acquiring and divesting of assets, both single- and multiple-period investments, and both new assets and the renewal of existing assets, as long as risk remains unchanged.[8]

WITH ACCEPTANCE CASH FLOWS REVISITED

We can now tie up a few loose ends. Recall that we have calculated all the t_1 cash flows and values for the with-acceptance corporation, but we have not yet specified fully the t_2 cash-flow expectations for that firm. To be honest, until the investment analysis was performed, we really did not know what these were. But now they present no problem.

We know already that VD_1^w is $468.75. I_2^w must be equal to debt suppliers' required rate of return applied to VD_1^w, so

$$I_2^w = VD_1^w(kd_1^w)$$
$$= \$468.75(0.08)$$
$$= \$37.50$$

and, therefore,

$$ITS_2^w = I_2^w(\tau)$$
$$= \$37.50(0.52)$$
$$= \$19.50$$

and

$$CAC_2^w = CAU_2^w + ITS_2^w$$
$$= \$3674.25 + \$19.50$$
$$= \$3693.75$$

[8]In fact, formulas 13.3, 13.3a, and 13.3b apply to *any* investment, risk constant or not, provided that each kf^{*ivs} is properly ascertained, as we shall explore later in the section. To exhaust the possibilities completely, the analysis also works correctly with "bad" investments, those which would, if accepted, decrease shareholder present wealth. If you care to see what such an investment looks like, try substituting a t_1 outlay of $1975.75 for the $1274.25 we used in this example.

Then

$$CAF_2^w = CAC_2^w - I_2^w$$
$$= \$3693.75 - \$37.50$$
$$= \$3656.25$$

Now we are again faced with a capital acquisition/disbursement decision. Were the firm to continue operations past t_2, we could choose any one which does not violate the other financial decisions. But the firm will stop operating at t_2, so the debt suppliers must be paid off then. In other words, PP_2^w must equal VD_1^w. Thus,

$$PP_2^w = \$468.75$$

Next

$$CDD_2^w = I_2^w + PP_2^w$$
$$= \$37.50 + \$468.75$$
$$= \$506.25$$

Since t_2 is the final time point at which our firm will exist,

$$NDC_2^w = \$0.00$$

so,

$$NCDD_2^w = CDD_2^w - NDC_2^w$$
$$= \$506.25 - \$0.00$$
$$= \$506.25$$

Moving to the equity cash flows,

$$CAE_2^w = CAC_2^w - CDD_2^w = CAF_2^w - PP_2^w$$
$$= \$3693.75 - \$506.25 = \$3656.25 - \$468.75$$
$$= \$3187.50$$

and, since the firm ends at t_2,

$$CRF_2^w = \$0.00$$

and

$$NEC_2^w = \$0.00$$

Thus,

$$CDE_2^w = CAE_2^w - CRF_2^w$$
$$= \$3187.50 - \$0.00$$
$$= \$3187.50$$

and

$$NCDE_2^w = CDE_2^w - NEC_2^w$$
$$= \$3187.50 - \$0.00$$
$$= \$3187.50$$

Finally, of course, TCC_2^w and IVS_2^w are both \$0.00.

Table 13.4 presents the complete synopsis of our corporation with acceptance. We have collected together there all the corporate cash flows expected at t_2 along with those realized and proposed for t_1 (the latter combining p_1 results, the investment decision, and our arbitrary capital acquisition/disbursement decision). Also presented are the firm's required rates and costs and its θ and τ, all of which have remained unchanged with the adoption of the proposed investment. Finally, the various t_1 values of capital claims and of the total firm are listed.

TABLE 13.4   **Two-period corporation with acceptance**

	t_1	t_2	
$RCPT	$6250.00	$12500.00	$\theta = 0.15$
$EXPT	3976.50	7200.75	$\tau = 0.52$
GCFO	2273.50	5299.25	
GTAX	1182.22	2755.61	
NCFO	1091.28	2543.64	
DTS	936.00	1130.61	$ke^w = 0.20$
CAU	2027.28	3674.25	$kd^w = 0.08$
ITS	18.72	19.50	$kf^w = 0.182$
CAC	2046.00	3693.75	$kd^{*w} = 0.0384$
I	36.00	37.50	$kf^{*w} = 0.17576$
CAF	2010.00	3656.25	
PP	450.00	468.75	
CDD	486.00	506.25	
NDC	468.75	0.00	
NCDD	17.25	506.25	$VF_1^w = \$3125.00$
CAE	1560.00	3187.50	$VD_1^w = 468.75$
CRF	805.50	0.00	$VE_1^w = 2656.25$
CDE	754.50	3187.50	
NEC	0.00	0.00	
NCDE	754.50	3187.50	
TCC $\equiv$ IVS	1274.25	0.00	

You might wish to check our calculations of these values by applying the various valuation formulas from Section II (for total corporate value, debt value, and equity value) to the t_2 cash flows shown in Table 13.4. This is also a nice opportunity for you to review footnote 4 (p. 301).

INVESTMENT DECISIONS AND CAPITAL MARKET ANTICIPATIONS

One sentence of caution: It is inappropriate to calculate t_0 values of these t_1 and t_2 flows. t_0 is "past"; that time point has already flown by. The investment decision was made at t_1, and was unanticipated at t_0, so values calculated for that time point using the Table 13.4 cash flows would be nonsense numbers. We realize that now you will probably calculate the t_0 values just to see what nonsense numbers look like, but your time would be better spent instead doing the exercises that we suggested in the last paragraph.

Since our advice is rarely so avuncular, we should perhaps explain this argument in a bit more detail. The problem, as we said, is that the investment decision made at t_1 was unanticipated at t_0. The values that apply to t_0 would *not* therefore include any investment cash flows. The cash flows in

Table 13.4 *do* include those of the investment. So they are inappropriate for t_0 value calculations.

But what if the t_1 investment *had* been anticipated at t_0? Would the Table 13.4 flows then be usable? Again, the answer is no. In that situation t_0 values *would* be affected by the anticipated investment. Specifically, VE_0^w would differ from VE_0^{wo}. And in order to hold capital structure constant, VD_0^w would, by necessity, be altered in the same general way that we changed VD_1^w in our example. But if, say, more debt is issued at t_0, I_1^w and ITS_1^w would differ from I_1^{wo} and ITS_1^{wo}, as they do not in our example. This implies that all the t_1 cash flows located below CAU_1^w on the cash-flow statement could differ from the ones in Table 13.4 if the investment to be made at t_1 were anticipated at t_0.

This is not to say such values and cash flows (and equity present wealth) could not be discovered. As a matter of fact, in Appendix V.B we shall do just that. There, we assume that the t_1 investment we used in this example *was* anticipated at t_0, and we show the cash flow, value, and wealth effects which apply in the situation where anticipation occurs.

It probably seems that we are spending a great deal of time on this apparently rather esoteric argument. In real-world terms, however, the point is not unimportant. *Capital markets often (for better or worse) anticipate corporate investment decisions yet to be made. Equity price changes of this sort, and the capital structure alterations they imply, are things financial managers should understand.* If they do not, equityholder present wealth may not be maximized.

INVESTMENT DECISIONS AND CAPITAL STRUCTURE

While the subject of capital structure is afoot, we might say a word about its relationship to the investment decision in general. In this section we are holding capital structure constant so as to be able to discern easily the exclusive wealth effects of investment or divestment decisions. To make such a decision, however, does not *require* that capital structure be held constant. Section III shows generally how required rates are affected by capital structure changes, so if you want to allow θ to change with an asset acquisition or divestment decision, feel free to do so.[9] Remember, however, that the with-acceptance cash flows must be discounted at the rates appropriate to the *new* capital structure. (As a good financial manager, you would already have found the optimal θ, and therefore would not wish to change it, unless, as noted in footnote 9, the very adoption of the proposed investment interacts with an imperfection so as to change the "optimum" θ.) When our risk measure is

---

[9]Depending upon which of the imperfections discussed under that heading at the end of Section III actually effect an upper bound on θ in the real world, it may be easier to push that limit as an investment decision concomitant than as an independent financial decision. It is also true that some investments may result in a lowering of the corporation's optimal θ. Both possibilities are especially true of "risk-altering" investments with which we deal later in this section.

developed later in this section, interrelationships between investment and capital structure decisions will be easier to understand *in toto*.

INVESTMENT CASH FLOWS REVISITED

Finally, now that the full financial cash-flow statement for the with-acceptance corporation has been completed, we can also finish the FCF display for the investment itself. Again, this will allow us to see the investment as if it were a separate corporation. We already have some of these cash flows. They appear in Table 13.2. To complete them now, we only need recall that the with-acceptance corporate cash flows (Table 13.4) are merely the without-acceptance corporate cash flows plus the investment cash flows. This implies that we can find the investment cash flows by subtracting the entries in Table 13.1 from their counterparts in Table 13.4. Table 13.5 shows the result of doing this. In addition to the cash flows, the usual parameter, rate, cost, and value information is reported, along with NPV_1^{ivs}, ΔPWE_1, and ΔPWD_1, were the investment decision to be accepted. Also shown is an alternative FCF_1^{ivs} statement which we shall explain below.

Remember, the cash flows that appear in Table 13.5 (other than the

TABLE 13.5 **Risk-constant investment**

		t_1		t_2	
		Original example	*Alternative*		
$RCPT	$	0.00	$ 0.00	$5000.00	
$EXPT		0.00	0.00	2400.00	$\theta = 0.15$
GCFO		0.00	0.00	2600.00	$\tau = 0.52$
GTAX		0.00	0.00	1352.00	
NCFO		0.00	0.00	1248.00	
DTS		0.00	0.00	662.61	
CAU		0.00	0.00	1910.61	
ITS		0.00	0.00	10.14	$ke^{ivs} = 0.20$
CAC		0.00	0.00	1920.75	$kd^{ivs} = 0.08$
I		0.00	0.00	19.50	$kf^{ivs} = 0.182$
CAF		0.00	0.00	1901.25	$kd*^{ivs} = 0.0384$
PP		225.00	0.00	243.75	$kf*^{ivs} = 0.17576$
CDD		225.00	0.00	263.25	
NDC		468.75	243.75	0.00	
NCDD		−243.75	−243.75	263.25	
CAE		−225.00	0.00	1657.50	
CRF		805.50	0.00	0.00	
CDE		−1030.50	0.00	1657.50	$VF_1^{ivs} = \$1625.00$
NEC		0.00	1030.50	0.00	$VD_1^{ivs} = 243.75$
NCDE		−1030.50	−1030.50	1657.50	$VE_1^{ivs} = 1381.25$
TCC $\equiv$ IVS		1274.25	1274.25	0.00	

$$NPV_1^{ivs} = VF_1^{ivs} + CAU_1^{ivs} - IVS_1^{ivs}$$
$$= \$1625.00 + \$0.00 - \$1274.25$$
$$= \$350.75$$

$\Delta PWE_1 = VE_1^{ivs} + NCDE_1^{ivs}$ ⠀⠀⠀ $\Delta PWD_1 = VD_1^{ivs} + NCDD_1^{ivs}$
$\quad = \$1381.25 + (\$-1030.50)$ ⠀⠀⠀ $\quad = \$243.75 + (\$-243.75)$
$\quad = \$350.75$ ⠀⠀⠀⠀⠀⠀⠀⠀⠀⠀⠀⠀ $\quad = \$0.00$

t_1 alternative) are the net of the *without* and *with* corporate cash flows. These cash flows are therefore those associated only with the investment itself. The t_1 cash flows, however, seem a bit strange. Notice that, for example, $225 of PP_1^{ivs} is paid even though CAC_1^{ivs} is zero. Where does the $225 come from? Think of it as being supplied by the new debtholders at t_1. The result is that the new debt suppliers claim not only the *investment's* debt cash flows, but also the *without* investment *corporation's* debt cash flows. This is because they have "bought out" the existing debt suppliers. If this idea bothers you, look at the alternative t_1 cash flows in Table 13.5. These assume a different capital acquisition/disbursement decision which, of course, affects no values, but makes the t_1 investment cash flows seem more reasonable (that is, does away with the negative CAE_1^{ivs} and CDE_1^{ivs} flows). Generally, it shows the entire $1274.25 IVS_1^{ivs} being raised from new debt and new equity sources. The $NCDE_1^{ivs}$ and $NCDD_1^{ivs}$ are unaffected, so investment values do not change.

You might wish to redo Table 13.4 with these t_1 alternatives. Be sure to calculate values there also, to verify that our assertions are correct. If you are really ambitious, you might want to separate out the "new" and "existing" equityholder returns. As you no doubt can guess, new equity suppliers at t_1 will share in the investment's net present value if the capital market has not anticipated the investment when the new shares are issued. If the investment has been anticipated by that time, new shareholders will earn only their required rates of return, and the entire $350.75 wealth increase will go to the old shareholders at t_1.

Table 13.5 also indicates the $VF_1^{ivs} = 1625.00 and $NPV_1^{ivs} = 350.75 which we calculated earlier. In addition, you also see $VE_1^{ivs} = 1381.25 and $VD_1^{ivs} = 243.75. These are the equity and debt values, respectively, of the investment. NPV_A^{ivs} is given by formulas 13.3, 13.3a, and 13.3b. For VF_A^{ivs}, we have

$$VF_A^{ivs} = \sum_{T=A+1}^{T} \frac{CAU_T^{ivs} - IVS_T^{ivs}}{\prod_{P=A+1}^{T} (1 + kf_P^{*ivs})} \qquad \textbf{[13.4]}$$

or, with constant cost of capital across time,

$$VF_A^{ivs} = \sum_{T=A+1}^{T} \frac{CAU_T^{ivs} - IVS_T^{ivs}}{(1 + kf^{*ivs})^{T-A}} \qquad \textbf{[13.4a]}$$

Then the investment's debt and equity values can be calculated in either of two ways. First, in relationship to capital structure,

$$VE_A^{ivs} = VF_A^{ivs}(1 - \theta^{ivs})$$
$$VD_A^{ivs} = VF_A^{ivs}(\theta^{ivs})$$

Second, by direct valuation, we have

$$VE_A^{ivs} = \sum_{T-A+1}^{T} \frac{NCDE_T^{ivs}}{\prod_{P=A+1}^{T} (1 + ke_P^{ivs})} \qquad \textbf{[13.5]}$$

or, for a constant required return on the investment's equity across time,

$$VE_A^{ivs} = \sum_{T=A+1}^{T} \frac{NCDE_T^{ivs}}{(1 + ke^{ivs})^{T-A}}$$ [13.5a]

Similarly,

$$VD_A^{ivs} = \sum_{T=A+1}^{T} \frac{NCDD_T^{ivs}}{\prod_{P=A+1}^{T} (1 + kd_P^{ivs})}$$ [13.6]

or, for kd constant across time,

$$VD_A^{ivs} = \sum_{T=A+1}^{T} \frac{NCDD_T^{ivs}}{(1 + kd^{ivs})^{T-A}}$$ [13.6a]

Note that the equity and debt *investment* values added to the equity and debt *without-acceptance* values yield the equity and debt *with-acceptance* values:

$$\begin{aligned} VE_1^w &= VE_1^{wo} + VE_1^{ivs} \\ &= \$1275.00 + \$1381.25 \\ &= \$2656.25 \end{aligned}$$

$$\begin{aligned} VD_1^w &= VD_1^{wo} + VD_1^{ivs} \\ &= \$225.00 + \$243.75 \\ &= \$468.75 \end{aligned}$$

and, of course,

$$\begin{aligned} VF_1^w &= VF_1^{wo} + VF_1^{ivs} \\ &= \$1500.00 + \$1625.00 \\ &= \$3125.00 \end{aligned}$$

This reinforces our view of the investment as a little corporation being attached to the without-acceptance corporation to result in the with-acceptance corporation.

Wealth effects also appear in Table 13.5. Essentially the wealth changes for capital suppliers of an investment are the difference between the present values received (VE_1^{ivs} and VD_1^{ivs}) and the present values paid ($NCDE_1^{ivs}$ and $NCDD_1^{ivs}$). As before, equity's wealth change equals the investment NPV. Debt experiences no wealth change; it merely receives its required return.

MEANING OF "FINANCING" Notice that the investment has the same capital structure ($\theta = 0.15$) as the corporation:

$$\theta^{ivs} = \frac{VD_1^{ivs}}{VF_1^{ivs}} = \frac{\$243.75}{\$1625.00} = 0.15$$

Be careful to remember that θ^{ivs}, like any other θ, is a ratio of *values*, not of cash flows. Thus, for example, θ^{ivs} is *not* equal to the quotient given by net debt capital supplied for the investment ($NDC_1^{ivs} - PP_1^{ivs} = \$243.75$) divided by total dollars invested ($IVS_1^{ivs} = \$1274.25$). That is,

$$\frac{\$243.75}{\$1274.25} \neq \theta^{ivs}$$

Conversely, it is obvious that applying θ^{ivs} to IVS^{ivs} will not tell us the actual amount of debt financing required. Rather, the amount of debt capital needed for an investment to attain a desired θ^{ivs} is given by

$$\text{Debt financing required} = VF_1^{ivs}(\text{desired } \theta^{ivs})$$
$$= \$1625.00(0.15)$$
$$= \$243.75 = VD_1^{ivs} = NDC_1^{ivs} - PP_1^{ivs}$$

A desired value proportion rather than a cash-outlay proportion is necessary because it is value proportions, as you recall from Section III, that determine the relationship between financing and rates of return required by capital suppliers.

A parenthetical remark about financing mix and required rates is also appropriate here. Beginning finance students are often puzzled by the following situation. An investment's cash outlays are to be supplied totally by a debt issue. Why is the cost of that debt capital *not* the appropriate discount rate to apply to the investment's future cash flows for decision-making purposes? The answer involves a more careful look at exactly what we mean by "financing." Think of the situation this way: An existing corporation is issuing a debt claim, the entire proceeds of which are used to supply the total cash outlay for an investment. Obviously some debt value has been created (VD^{ivs}) *but in addition, equity value* (VE^{ivs}) *has also been created.* This must be true, as we have seen, if the investment has positive NPV (and it would not have been accepted had it not). *Both claims, debt and equity, must expect to receive their required rates, the weighted average after tax cost of which is kf^{*ivs}.*

In essence, the determinant of return required on investment is not who supplies the actual cash for the necessary outlays, but the cash-flow expectations of those who claim the investment's future proceeds. Just as for entire corporations, the operating cash-flow risks and the value proportions (θ's) of the resulting capital claims determine an investment's required rates. Thus the appropriate discount rate to apply to the investment's overall cash flows must recognize *all* claims' requirements. kf^{*ivs}, the weighted-average rate for the investment, does this. The debt rate alone, of course, does not.

SUMMARY We have come just about as far as we can in developing the theory of asset acquisition and divestment with risk-constant corporate investments. And it has been a considerable distance we have come. Viewing corporate investments as separate corporations which are attached to an existing set of corporate financial cash-flow expectations is a valuable insight. As a matter of fact, it is the only basic theoretical point we have made. All the rest of our analysis has been derived from that single idea and what we have learned in previous chapters.

From a computational viewpoint we have seen that net present value analysis is the easiest and most direct method of making the risk-constant investment decision. *Investment NPV, if calculated correctly, is the addition to (if positive) or the decrement from (if negative) shareholder present wealth upon acceptance of the proposal.* This wealth change, in an efficient capital market, takes place as soon as the market realizes that the corporation has accepted the investment, even though the actual investment cash flows may be expected to take place well into the future.

Alternative methods of arriving at the wealth effects of corporate investments involve working with corporate cash flows themselves so as to value the with-acceptance and without-acceptance corporate capital claims and calculate present value of net cash receipt differences. Although this technique is more cumbersome than NPV analysis, its theoretical underpinnings (from Sections I–IV) are more obvious.

Indeed, it would be possible for us to rewrite all the valuation formulas in Section II for with-investment corporations. Rather than reproduce all dozen or so formulas, we show a representative few in Table 13.6. You can see that the changes from the original valuations involve nothing more than adding the investment cash flows to the existing corporate cash flows. The capital costs and required rates will be the same as the existing without-investment rates if the investment is risk-constant and the existing capital

TABLE 13.6   **Sampler of with-investment-decision corporate valuation formulas for risk-constant investments***

$$VF_0^w = \sum_{T=1}^{T} \frac{(CAU_T^{wo} + CAU_T^{ivs}) - (IVS_T^{wo} + IVS_T^{ivs})}{\prod_{P=1}^{T} (1 + kf_P^{*wo})} \qquad [13.7]†$$

$$VE_0^w = \sum_{T=1}^{T} \frac{NCDE_T^{wo} + NCDE_T^{ivs}}{\prod_{P=1}^{T} (1 + ke_P^{wo})} \qquad [13.8]$$

$$VD_0^w = \sum_{T=1}^{T} \frac{NCDD_T^{wo} + NCDD_T^{ivs}}{\prod_{P=1}^{T} (1 + kd_P^{wo})} \qquad [13.9]$$

*These formulas can be made perfectly general, that is, applicable to investments which would, if accepted, change the risk of the existing corporation. This is done by substituting w for the wo superscript in the discount rates which appear in each formula's denominator. For investments which would not alter existing corporate risk, the two rates are identical. For investments which *would* result in alteration of either operating-cash-flow risk or capital structure, w rates derived as weighted averages of wo and ivs rates must be used. We shall explore this process in Chapter 16.

†Including the cash-flow IVS_T^{wo} in formula 13.7 recognizes that a without-acceptance corporation may have existing expectations for investments other than the one under consideration. IVS_T^{ivs} are, of course, the future outlays that may be necessary for the investment proposal being considered.

structure is maintained. If capital structure is changed, or if the investment's risk differs from the existing corporation, new discount rates will be necessary. Section III shows us why different rates would be required by a different capital structure. The remainder of this section will show in some detail why differing investment risks also require different discount rates for the formulas shown, and will also demonstrate what those new rates should be.

Chapter 14

The Risk-Altering Corporate Investment Decision: Market Participants and Risk

**INVEST-
MENTS THAT
CHANGE
CORPORATE
RISK:
INTRODUC-
TION**

The remainder of this section, Chapters 14–16, will develop the theory of asset acquisition and divestment for decisions that would alter the risk of the existing corporation (risk-altering proposals). This is the last major topic covered in our treatment of the theory of corporate finance. There are two reasons why we have waited until now to begin treating risk as an explicit, measurable characteristic of financial cash flows:

1. As we said in Section I, even a basic intuitive appreciation of the ideas involved in appropriate corporate risk measures requires a fairly lengthy, rather complicated discussion. And the major part of corporate financial theory can be developed independent of, yet in a manner consistent with, these risk measures. That is what we have done to this point. The amount of effort necessary to arrive at risk measures early in our theoretical development would have, we feel, been both distracting and unnecessary to the ideas presented in Sections II through IV and the first part of this section.

2. The theory of risk measurement that we are about to discuss is less "mature" than the other components of corporate financial theory we have already seen. All theories, of course, are accepted only provisionally, until something better comes along. The theories of corporate valuation, capital structure, capital acquisition/disbursement, and risk-constant asset acquisition and divestment have been around long enough in their present forms to be considered well established. The theoretical basis for risk measurement, however, is much less unanimously accepted in a single form than these other theories. In other words, it is still being developed and debated by financial theoreticians.

For this reason we feel that relegating this theory of risk to the latter part of our treatment gives the correct impression that the preceding financial theory is not necessarily based on this specific risk model.

Neither of these reasons is intended to imply that the risk theory we are about to explore is either "weak" or unimportant. On the contrary, the concepts are probably some of the most important and economically substantive ever to appear in financial theory.

Our purpose in offering this lengthy apology is to prepare you for a presentation that may at first seem very complex, at times tedious, and until it is nearly complete, of dubious relevancy to corporate finance. We ask you to grit your teeth and bear with us. The theoretical insights you gain as you explore this financial frontier will be well worth your effort.

REQUIRE-MENTS OF THE RISK MEASURE

Our first task is to be more specific about exactly what our risk measure should be able to do. The introductory discussion about uncertainty (risk) in Chapter 4 is helpful here. To review a few of its more important points:

1. Uncertainty or risk is a characteristic appearing to a greater or lesser degree in all future cash-flow expectations.
2. Capital-market participants are "risk-averse"; that is, they require compensation for bearing risk. The higher the risk, the more compensation necessary. In our theory the risk compensation charged by capital-market participants appears as higher required rates of return on risky capital claims.
3. Similar to the way in which the financial market reaches an equilibrium market interest rate as "the price of time," the capital market, in equilibrium, also reaches a consensus as to how much compensation in the form of required return will be paid for each amount of risk bearing. You can think of this as the "price of risk." Just as all financial-market participants pay and receive the "price of time" for allocating their financial resources across time, capital-market participants in addition pay and receive the "price of risk" for decreasing and increasing the risk they bear.

These ideas, as in Chapter 4, can be collected graphically. To this purpose, we reproduce Figure 4.1 as Figure 14.1. In this graph, the SML curve (the security-market line) shows the equilibrium relationship between risk and required rates of return in the capital market. The SML intersects the vertical axis at i, the risk-free rate of return or financial-market interest rate. When risk is zero on the horizontal axis, the required return is equal to i, the risk-free rate. There is no compensation for risk, since no risk is present. As we increase risk by moving along the horizontal axis, the SML indicates that the required rate of return increases as the risk does.[1] For example, in

---

[1]The "market price of risk" in a graphical sense will be the slope of the SML. That would show the increases in required return due to increases in risk.

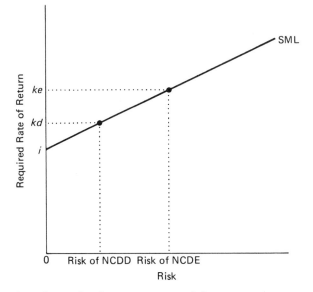

FIGURE 14.1   Security-market line or structure of share returns

Figure 14.1, *ke* and *kd* are shown related to their respective risky cash flows.

The security-market-line relationship, if we can discover how to use it, would give us the remaining information we need in order to solve the "risk-altering" corporate investment or divestment decision. The preceding chapter showed that the investment decision necessitates discounting the expected investment cash flows at rates appropriate to the riskinesses of those cash flows. If we can use the SML relationship to identify the appropriate discount rates for investment proposals, the investment analysis itself can be performed in exactly the same manner as the risk-constant decisions already described. The only difference will be that the rates used will not be those of the existing corporation.[2]

What more information is necessary, then, in order to use the SML relationship between risk and required rates of return in the capital market? A glance at Figure 14.1 will tell. We know that the SML intersects the vertical axis at the risk-free rate, *i*, and since participants are risk-averse, it slopes upward. But how much? How quickly do required rates increase as risk does? What *is* the "market price of risk"? That is one piece of information we must discover. *We must find the actual determinants of risk compensation in the capital market at equilibrium, or, in other words, we must be able to describe the slope of the SML.*

_____

[2]As we shall see, the resulting rates for the with-acceptance corporation are weighted averages of the rates for the without-acceptance corporation and the risk-altering proposal being considered.

In addition, of course, we must discover exactly what is being measured along the horizontal axis of Figure 14.1. We know that it indicates the risk of cash-flow expectations, but what are the units of measurement? Without those units, we would not know what location along the horizontal axis was appropriate for the cash flows being considered and therefore could not use the SML to find the appropriate rates for discounting those cash flows. In other words, *we need a specific measure of the risk of cash-flow expectations, one consistent with the determinants of the security-market line as the statement of capital-market participants' equilibrium compensation for risk bearing.*

Discovering those two pieces of information has claimed a great deal of financial theoreticians' time in recent years (and continues to do so). At the moment one set of answers appears to be the most widely accepted, so we shall devote our efforts to that one. It generally goes by the name "*capital asset pricing model,*" or CAPM. Our review of this capital-market risk–return theory is intended to be adequate enough for you to appreciate the risk measure and SML relationships that it implies but not exhaustive in the sense that rigorous derivations will be supplied for all its ideas.[3] Since entire texts have been devoted to complete treatments of this subject, we shall attempt to offer just enough proof so that our arguments are acceptable on an intuitive level.

CAPITAL-MARKET PARTICI-PANTS AND RISK

It is capital-market participants who, acting in accord with their risk aversions, set the market relationship between risk and required rates of return on capital claims. Our first step, therefore, will be to determine exactly what these participants regard as risk. To do this requires us to be more specific about our descriptions of future cash-flow expectations, the risk of which capital-market participants require compensation for bearing.

Until now we have talked about future cash-flow expectations using a single number. For example, $CF_1 = \$510$ indicates that the expected cash flow at t_1 is $510. That way of describing future cash flows was adequate and quite correct as we used it earlier. Now, however, we must expand the description. This will allow us to see what capital-market participants regard as "risk."

PROBABILITY DISTRIBU-TIONS

Cash flows to occur in the future are uncertain. No one really knows exactly what actual number of dollars will appear at future time points. But that is not to say there is no information available about future cash flows. Capital-market participants in our theory can agree about the likelihoods of various cash flows occurring. For example, the $510 is only one of several possible CF_1's that could actually result at t_1. And capital-market participants can

---

[3]The complete, economically and quantitatively rigorous development appears in several references indicated at the end of this section. Although offering this coverage in the body of the section is tempting, we have chosen to forego it in the interests of brevity and with a note of compassion for our less quantitatively inclined reader.

set odds or *probabilities* of occurrence for each of the possibilities. We say that participants agree on the *probability distribution* of future cash flows for the claims they value.

The idea of a probability distribution is not at all difficult to grasp. Suppose that participants, in studying their beliefs about the cash flow above, had decided there were five possible CF_1's that could occur and that the probabilities associated with each possible outcome were as given in Table 14.1.[4] By graphing this probability distribution we can get an even better view of what it is saying. Figure 14.2 shows this distribution, with the possible outcomes along the horizontal axis and their respective probabilities indicated vertically. When we speak of capital-market participants' t_1 cash-flow expectations, what we really mean is that their belief as to what is going to happen at t_1 is some kind of probability distribution of possible outcomes such as that shown in Figure 14.2.

TABLE 14.1

CF_1	Probability		
$258.00	11%	or	0.11
396.00	20%	or	0.20
510.00	37%	or	0.37
631.00	22%	or	0.22
749.00	10%	or	0.10
	100%	or	1.00

FIGURE 14.2   Probability distribution of CF_1

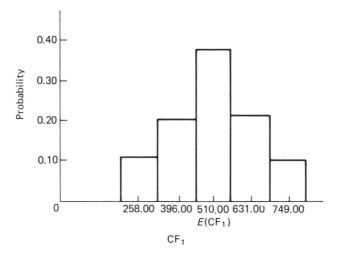

[4]If all possible outcomes are included, the probabilities must, of course, sum to 1.00, or 100%.

THE MEAN Why, then, did we represent those beliefs by saying, for example, that $CF_1 = \$510$? We did so because $510 is one widely used way of partially describing the probability distribution of CF_1. It is called the *expectation* or *mean* of the distribution. The expectation of a probability distribution tells us about the location of the distribution along the horizontal axis. Look back to the distribution itself and multiply each possible outcome by its probability. Then add up the products:

$$
\begin{aligned}
\$258.00 \times 0.11 &= \$28.38 \\
396.00 \times 0.20 &= 79.20 \\
510.00 \times 0.37 &= 188.70 \\
631.00 \times 0.22 &= 138.82 \\
749.00 \times 0.10 &= 74.90 \\
\hline
1.00 \quad &\$510.00 = E(CF_1)
\end{aligned}
$$

The expectation or mean of a probability distribution is the sum of the products of each possible outcome times its respective probability. It is the first and most important descriptive statistic or way of describing probability distributions of uncertain future cash flows.[5] *The future-cash-flow dollar amounts used in all our examples until now have been mean expectations of the probability distributions for the uncertain future cash flows indicated.* For example, our two-period firm without investment had a CAU_2^{wo} of $1763.64. We are now able to interpret that $1763.64 as the expectation of the probability distribution for the CAU_2^{wo} cash flow.

"Hold on a moment," you say. "In the financial cash-flow statement there was a lot of adding and subtracting of the dollars that appeared in them. And now you are telling us that those dollars represented entire probability distributions. So what we were really doing was adding and subtracting probability distributions, not just dollar amounts. Was that appropriate?" Fortunately, it was. Expectations of probability distributions are *additive*. That is, if you have one distribution whose mean is $3 and another whose mean is $2 and you add them together, the mean of the new distribution formed will be $5. So our additions and subtractions of probability distribution means in the financial cash-flow statement were allowable. For example, adding CAU_2 to ITS_2 gives us the expectation of the probability distribution for CAC_2.

[5]You have probably noticed that the mean of the CF_1 distribution, $510, was also one of the possible outcomes. Actually, the most correct way of thinking of a probability distribution is to consider the probabilities operating on intervals along the horizontal axis rather than on individual outcomes. Thus, the 0.37 probability of a $510 outcome is best thought of as a 0.37 probability of an outcome in the interval that includes $510 and other outcomes close to it. We use the $510 as a label to represent that whole interval, and you can also think of the $510 as the average (mean) of all possible outcomes in the interval it represents. The mean of the distribution, then, is the mean of all the interval means and may or may not be equal to any one of them. Note that we constructed Figure 14.2 using this interval scheme and chose our intervals so that the distribution's mean does equal the mean of one of the intervals.

Convenient as the mean is, however, it nevertheless is not a very complete description of a probability distribution for meeting the needs of capital-market participants. They certainly want to know what the expectations of distributions are, but they also need more information than that.

STANDARD DEVIATION Suppose that a capital-market participant is faced with the choice between acquiring either of two asset holdings, A and B. The acquisition of one or the other of A or B will entitle the participant to the actual t_1 cash-flow outcome associated with the assets acquired. The t_0 estimates of possible t_1 realizations are, of course, probability distributions of expected t_1 cash flows such as those shown in Figure 14.3. Distribution A (from holding A) is the CF_1 distribution we introduced a few pages ago. Distribution B represents the other holding's cash flow at t_1. Further, let us suppose that the underlying assets giving rise to distributions A and B each cost the same now (at t_0), and whichever one the participant chooses now will constitute her or his entire holding of risky assets during p_1.

Which alternative, A or B, will our participant choose? Look at Figure 14.3. To acquire either of the two distributions costs the same at t_0, and both distributions have the same mean or expected net cash flow at t_1 [$E(A) = E(B)$]. Yet, the distributions are not identical; even though they promise equal expectations, the two distributions differ substantially.

FIGURE 14.3   Two probability distributions with equal means and unequal standard deviations

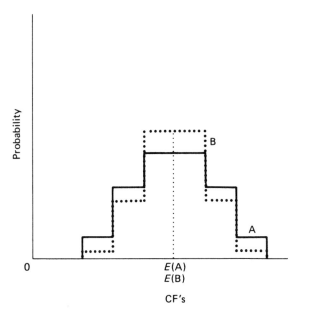

How do we describe this difference, which is visually apparent as you look at Figure 14.3? We say that distribution A is much more dispersed than distribution B. Our meaning is that more of the possible outcomes in B are closer to $E(B)$ than the outcomes of A are to $E(A)$. As measured by the distance between the highest and lowest possible outcomes, the actual width of the less dispersed distribution B may be smaller, larger, or, as in Figure 14.3, the same as that of the more dispersed distribution A. B, however, has a much stronger tendency to predict outcomes closer to its mean than does A, width notwithstanding. One descriptive statistic that is sensitive to this dispersion or lack thereof in probability distributions is called the *standard deviation* of a distribution. The higher the standard deviation, the more spread out the distribution is; the lower the standard deviation, the narrower is the distribution. A in Figure 14.3 has a higher standard deviation than B.

Examination of these two distributions shows it more likely that the actual cash flow from B will be near its expectation, $E(B)$, than the actual cash flow resulting from A will be near $E(A)$. Although the actual flows could be anywhere in the distributions, the odds are that B's will be closer to $E(B)$ than A's will be to $E(A)$. A's outcomes and probabilities are spread farther away from its mean (for example, they have a higher standard deviation) than B's.

To illustrate what a numerical standard deviation looks like, we can calculate the standard deviation of the CF_1 or A probability distribution. A useful process for calculating the standard deviation of a probability distribution is as follows:[6]

1. Find each possible outcome's deviation or difference from the expectation of the distribution (that is, the deviation of any outcome is numerically equal to the subtraction of the mean from that outcome).
2. Square each deviation.
3. Multiply each squared deviation by the probability of the occurrence of the outcome that generated it.
4. Add up the results (products) of these multiplications (this sum has a name also; it is called the *variance*).
5. Take the square root of that sum and you have the standard deviation.

For distribution A, then, the standard deviation is calculated as shown in Table 14.2. Thus, the standard deviation of distribution A is $136.08. This also tells us that the standard deviation of distribution B is necessarily less than $136.08. With this information, let us now return to our capital-market participant's problem of choosing between A and B.

[6]There are other techniques for calculating the standard deviation, but this one has a better intuitive basis for our discussion.

TABLE 14.2   Calculation of standard deviation

Step 1: *outcome − mean = deviation*	*Step 2:* *(deviation)²*	*Step 3:* *(deviation)² weighted* *by its probability*
$258.00 − $510.00 = $−252.00	$63,504.00	$63,504.00 × 0.11 = $ 6,985.44
396.00 − 510.00 = −114.00	12,996.00	12,996.00 × 0.20 = 2,599.20
510.00 − 510.00 = 0.00	0.00	0.00 × 0.37 = 0.00
631.00 − 510.00 = 121.00	14,641.00	14,641.00 × 0.22 = 3,221.02
749.00 − 510.00 = 239.00	57,121.00	57,121.00 × 0.10 = 5,712.10
Step 4: Sum the weighted squared deviations = variance		$18,517.76
Step 5: Take the square root of that sum		$ 136.08

STANDARD DEVIATION AS A RISK MEASURE FOR CAPITAL-MARKET PARTICIPANTS

Section I showed that market participants under certainty are utility maximizers; they choose the consumption patterns (and, therefore, particular collections of financial assets) that make them happiest. As you might expect, they behave the same way when uncertainty is present in capital markets. The only difference is that now they cannot maximize utility per se. Because future cash flows can only be described by probability distributions, the utility that participants will gain from consuming those cash flows must therefore also be described by probability distributions. Given that situation, capital-market participants do the best they can and maximize *expected* utility. They choose assets so that the uncertain future cash flows they get give them the highest expectation of utility or satisfaction.

"That sounds reasonable," you say, "but what does it mean specifically about choosing between uncertain cash-flow distributions such as A and B in Figure 14.3?" If the following conditions hold, it is possible to show that distribution B (with the lower standard deviation) results in higher expected utility and therefore will always be preferred to distribution A (with the higher standard deviation):[7]

1. Capital-market participants have reasonable utility relationships between consumption and satisfaction.
2. A and B cost the same.
3. A and B will constitute the only uncertain cash flows owned by the participants.

A's higher variability among possible cash-flow outcomes (which variability is reflected in the calculation of standard deviation) makes it less desirable than B to capital-market participants. If you will recall one of the basic characteristics of capital-market participants we identified in Table 4.2, it is that they are *risk-averse*. Inasmuch as the variability or uncertainty in future

---

[7]Conditions 2 and 3 for this conclusion appear to be rather restrictive, but we shall make them more general shortly. The proof of the assertion appears in several references cited at the end of the section.

cash flows associated with participants' total asset holdings is the fundamental manifestation of risk, and to the extent that this uncertainty is reflected in the magnitude of the standard deviation number, we can accept the standard deviation as a viable measure of the riskiness of these uncertain cash-flow outcomes. Given the risk-averse nature of our participants and if other things are held constant, they will prefer less standard deviation to more. They are standard-deviation-averse, if you like. Hence, with standard deviation as a measure of the riskiness to capital-market participants of Distributions A and B, participants will always prefer the total holding B with its equal cash-flow expectation but lower standard deviation.

RATES OF RETURN

So far we have suggested that standard deviation can be a useful measure of the risk of capital-market participants' total asset holdings or "portfolios" of assets, given certain conditions. It is now time to clean up our example somewhat so as to improve its usefulness. You will remember we assumed that the cost to the participant of acquiring the rights to the actual outcome from distribution A was the same as that for distribution B. This, of course, is not a very general situation. How can we deal with choices not costing the same? In Section I we made the point that capital-market participants are "perfectly competitive"; each is so small relative to the entire capital market that no action he or she takes has any measurable effect on market prices. This also implies that participants can buy as little or as much as they please of opportunities such as A and B. Their personal resources are tiny relative to the total value of A, B, and any other asset or set of assets. *In this situation, comparisons of one-period asset holdings based on expected rates of return are just as correct as those based on NPV's.* For example, A has an expected net cash flow at t_1 of $510.00, and so does B. Further, they both cost the same, say, $425.00 at t_1. As one-period investments, their expected internal rates of return are, therefore,

$$\text{IRR}_{A(B)} = \frac{\text{expected net cash flow}_{A(B)}}{\text{cost}_{A(B)}} - 1 \qquad \textbf{[14.1]}$$

$$= \frac{\$510.00}{\$425.00} - 1$$

$$= 0.20 \quad \text{or} \quad 20\%$$

A and B each have expected returns of 20% for the period; this comparison accomplishes the same thing as comparing their expected net cash flows when they cost the same.

When one-period holdings do not cost the same, expected rates of return are still appropriate for comparing participants' net cash-flow probability distribution expectations. Formula 14.1 shows expected return to be a basic measure of the "dollars of return per dollar of cost." Since participants can put as many or as few "dollars of cost" into an opportunity as they desire, the expected rate of return provides a kind of expected earnings rate adjusted for the dollar cost of buying the probability distribution of net cash flows. *The higher the expected return, other things held constant, the higher is the net cash-flow expectation for any given amount of cash outlay, and, therefore, the happier is the participant.*[8]

If participants are comparing net cash-flow probability distribution expectations on the basis of expected return, how do they compare the riskiness or standard deviations of the distributions? This presents no problem. The standard deviation of the future cash-flow distribution is directly related to the standard deviation of its rate-of-return distribution:

$$\frac{\text{standard deviation of rate of return}}{1 + \text{expected return}} = \frac{\text{standard deviation of cash flow}}{\text{expected cash flow}}$$

[14.2]

Specifically for distribution A,

$$\frac{\text{standard deviation of rate of return}}{1 + 0.20} = \frac{\$136.08}{\$510.00}$$
$$\text{standard deviation of rate of return} \simeq (1.20)(0.2668)$$
$$\simeq 32\%\,[9]$$

Distribution B has a lower cash-flow standard deviation and the same cost and expected rate of return, and so would also have a lower rate-of-return standard deviation, or risk. This means simply that the standard deviation of the rate-of-return distribution is just as good a risk measure for capital-market participants as is the standard deviation of the cash-flow distribution. As a matter of fact, the rate-of-return distribution is a somewhat better

[8]We did not advocate the use of the expected rate of return as a tool for corporations in making their investment decisions. One reason why the rate-of-return tool is inappropriate for corporations is that their real-asset investments probably do have dollar limits relative to the productive employment of the real asset. This distinction between investment opportunities of capital-market participants and those of corporations is typified by comparing (1) your purchasing a portfolio of securities traded on the New York Stock Exchange (into which you could place as little or as much of your resources as you chose without impacting your rate of return), with (2) American Telephone and Telegraph buying a particular kind of switching equipment for the Bell System. Whereas your rate of return would be unaffected by the amount of your cash outlay, AT&T could easily buy too much or too little equipment, thereby altering its rate of return as a result of the changing marginal productivity of additional switching units.

[9]The standard deviation of the distribution of rate-of-return outcomes may, of course, be calculated directly from the return probability distribution in exactly the same way we did the standard deviation calculation for the distribution of net cash-flow outcomes. Each rate-of-return outcome is simply the net cash-flow outcome, divided by the outlay, with one subtracted from the quotient. The expected IRR can be calculated using formula 14.1 or directly as the probability weighted average of 1 plus each respective rate-of-return outcome, with 1 subtracted from the sum. Rate-of-return deviations are simply each return outcome less the mean return and the calculation of standard deviation proceeds directly, using those deviations for steps 2–5 of the calculation method discussed earlier. We should stress that *the relationship* (formula 14.2) *between cash-flow and return expectations owes its simplicity to the single-period nature of this example.* Multiple-period complexities are discussed in both the conclusion and Appendix V.D.

candidate because it allows comparisons of alternative holdings *without questioning how much cash they require.* This is because capital-market participants can put as little or as much cash into a holding as they desire. *The higher the standard deviation of the rate of return, other things held constant, the less happy is the participant.*

PARTICI-
PANT
RISK–
RETURN
PREFER-
ENCES

To summarize our study so far of capital-market participants under uncertainty, we know the following things about the way they gain satisfaction from their total holdings of capital claims:

Situation 1: *The higher their expected return, other things constant, the happier they are.* This means simply that if two alternative sets of total holdings promise the same risk (that is, standard deviation of return), the one with the higher expected return will be preferred.

Situation 2: *The lower the risk or standard deviation of return, other things constant, the happier they are.* If two alternative sets of total holdings have the same expected return, the one with the lower standard deviation of return will be preferred.

Situation 3: Situations 1 and 2 imply that a total holding of assets promising higher expected return and lower standard deviation of return is preferred to one promising lower expected return and higher risk.[10]

[10]The literature of theoretical finance mentions other descriptive statistics of probability distributions which could be important to participants, but as yet they have not been widely accepted. Consider, for example, the following two distributions:

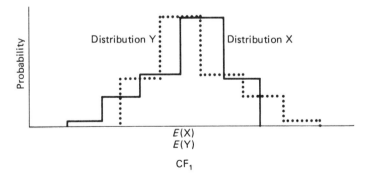

CF_1

Not only do distributions X and Y have the same expected cash flow (and expected rate of return based on equal cost), but they also have equal standard deviations, since each distribution is the mirror image of the other. Yet X and Y are clearly different distributions, and there is every reason to believe that most capital-market participants would prefer one to the other; that is, they would not be indifferent between the two. The tools that finance literature mentions for dealing with such situations are best left for more advanced treatments of the subject.

Those three statements carry us a long way toward specifying how a capital-market participant behaves when future cash flows are uncertain, but they do not cover all the possible choice situations:

Situation 4: Suppose that a participant is faced with two alternative total portfolios of assets, *one having only the higher return, while the other has the lower risk*. Which will the participant choose? We know that both higher return and lower risk are liked by participants. But in this case, those desirable attributes are present in different competing holdings.

Unless our theory can predict participant actions in cases such as situation 4, it is not very useful. Fortunately, the theory is capable of doing this.

We mentioned earlier that by examining a participant's utility relationship between satisfaction and consumption we could discover that distribution B with the lower standard deviation (risk) would be preferred to distribution A with the higher standard deviation (risk) when the expected returns of the two were equal. We can do the same thing to see how a specific participant will choose between *any* two distributions as long as we know his utility relationship and the risk–return attributes of the distributions he is considering. This includes choices such as situations 1, 2, and 3, and also choices such as situation 4. This process will indicate the satisfaction obtained by the participant through any combination of risk–return which is present in his holdings.

We can portray a participant's risk–return holding preferences by a system of *indifference curves between risk and return* such as the one shown in Figure 14.4.[11] Expected rate of return is measured on the vertical axis and noted as $E(r)$, and risk or standard deviation of return appears on the horizontal axis, noted as $\sigma(r)$. The participant's satisfaction increases as he moves to higher-numbered indifference curves. Note that distribution B lies on a higher indifference curve than does A. That comparison is a choice such as situation 2. B also lies on a higher indifference curve and is therefore preferred to C, which has the same risk, but a lower expected return than B. That comparison corresponds to situation 1. Similarly, a comparison between B and D is like situation 3. Finally, look at distribution E in Figure 14.4. It promises a higher return, but also higher risk, than B. This comparison is like situation 4; here the participant prefers B to E. Even though E has a higher expected return than B, E's higher risk causes this participant to choose B instead.

Indifference maps are very useful things for showing how a market participant will behave when returns are uncertain. But they do have one limiting characteristic we should stress. As we saw in Section I, *a particular*

[11]These are also developed extensively in references cited at the end of this section.

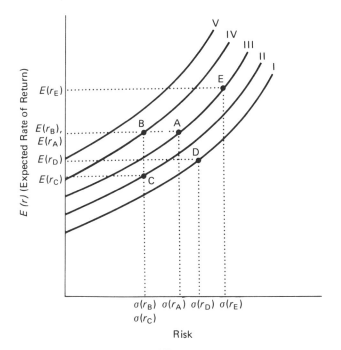

FIGURE 14.4   Participant's risk-return indifference map

set of indifference curves (and hence a particular utility function) *expresses the preferences of only a single individual participant.* All capital-market participants do not have exactly the same risk–return preferences.

"Now wait a minute," you say, "are you telling us we have gone to all this trouble to find out about just *one* participant? How does this help us to discover the way the market *as a whole* prices risk and return? Is that not the purpose of this whole discussion?" Yes, that is our purpose, and it is true that in order to specify fully participants' preferences we would need each individual utility function (or indifference map). But we also know that all participants are generally risk-averse. This means that we can always predict the actions of all participants in situations such as 1, 2, and 3. All participants will choose (1) less risk if return is the same, (2) more return if risk is the same, and (3) more return and less risk to less return and more risk. But in order to predict behavior in situation 4, we would need the indifference map for each individual.

Figure 14.5 can help to clarify this point. Here we have reproduced Figure 14.4 and superimposed another participant's risk–return indifference curves (as dashed lines). The new participant is also risk-averse but has differently shaped indifference curves. The important thing to notice about the new participant is that she, like the original participant, will choose B

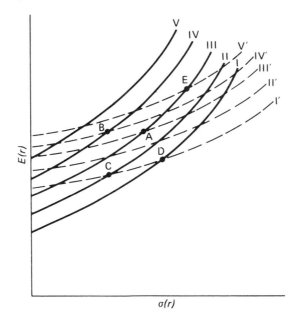

FIGURE 14.5   Two individual indifference maps for risk and return

over A, C, and D. Any participant would do that. She also happens to prefer E to B, since, compared with the original participant, she is somewhat less risk-averse than he.[12]

As we shall see, knowing that participants are generally risk-averse tells us enough about their risk–return preferences for us to discover how the capital market as a whole requires compensation for risk. The job of specifying each participants' particular risk aversions would be a monumental theoretical and realistically impossible task. Fortunately for us, it is also unnecessary.

SUMMARY   We now have a good idea of how capital-market participants behave in uncertain markets. Stated simply, each chooses the holding of assets (or portfolio) with the combination of expected return, $E(r)$, and standard deviation of return, $\sigma(r)$, that maximizes his or her expected utility. *Greater expected return tends to increase satisfaction; greater standard deviation of return (risk) tends to decrease satisfaction.* For our capital-market participants, an acceptable risk measure is the standard deviation of the return they expect from their total asset holdings, or portfolio.

[12]Indifference curves showing risk aversion must be positively sloped at all points along the curve. This general characteristic is enough to guarantee participant unanimity in comparisons described by situations 1, 2, and 3.

Chapter 15

The Risk-Altering Corporate Investment Decision: Diversification, a Risk Measure, and Capital-Market Required Rates

RISK MEASURES AND INDIVIDUAL ASSETS

In Chapter 14 we argued that the portfolio standard deviation is an acceptable measure of risk for participants in our capital market. Since $\sigma(r)$ is an acceptable risk measure, need we do anything more than discover the market's consensus as to the rates of return required for each level of $\sigma(r)$? Would that not satisfy our needs for a measure of the risk of corporate cash flows and the market SML relationship? Unfortunately, it would not, and as the remaining number of pages in this book implies, we are not yet done.

We have said that $\sigma(r)$, the standard deviation of expected return, is an appropriate risk measure for a capital-market participant. More specifically, it is a useful way to measure the riskiness of a participant's *entire holding*, or *portfolio*, of assets. That is not the object of our search, however. *We are trying to discover the appropriate risk measure for a corporate capital claim*, which claim probably constitutes only one small part of a participant's portfolio. Participants, therefore, are interested in individual capital claims only as actual or potential components of a portfolio of assets which can include many other capital claims. *Hence, an appropriate risk measure for a single claim must tell how it affects the riskiness of the portfolio in which it is held.* What remains for us to do is decide on such an "individual-asset-held-in-a-portfolio" risk measure, and the market's consensus about that risk measure's relationship to required rates of return.

Since we need an individual asset risk measure, why can we not use the standard deviation of the rate of return on that asset? If that asset is included in a portfolio with other assets, won't the portfolio's $\sigma(r)$ just be the average of the $\sigma(r)$'s of all the assets held in it? If this were true, would $\sigma(r)$ not be an appropriate individual-asset-held-in-a-portfolio risk measure? If it *were* true, $\sigma(r)$ *would* be the correct individual asset risk measure. *However, the $\sigma(r)$ of a portfolio is generally not just an average of the $\sigma(r)$'s of its constituent assets.*

PORTFOLIO RISK AND RETURN

To demonstrate this, assume that a participant is combining into a portfolio the two capital claims whose probability distributions of returns, expected returns, and standard deviations of return are shown in Table 15.1. The portfolio he forms from these claims will have *four*, not two potential outcomes, as shown in Table 15.2. These possibilities and their likelihoods can

TABLE 15.1

	Possible rate-of-return outcome r	Probability of return $P(r)$	Expected return $E(r)$	Standard deviation of expectation* $\sigma(r)$
Capital claim 1:	10%	0.45		
	20%	0.55		
		1.00	15.50%	4.97%
Capital claim 2:	7%	0.65		
	12%	0.35		
		1.00	8.75%	2.38%

*Calculated in accordance with footnote 9 of Chapter 14.

TABLE 15.2

Outcome	r_1	*and*	r_2
a	10%	*and*	7%
b	10%	*and*	12%
c	20%	*and*	7%
d	20%	*and*	12%

be shown by something called a *joint probability distribution*. One possible distribution for this situation is shown in Table 15.3.

A joint probability distribution is not difficult to decipher. The probabilities of the various "joint" outcomes appear inside the box, at the intersection of the appropriate rows and columns for the individual capital claim outcomes of which they are composed. For example, the probability that claim 1 will return 10% when claim 2 returns 7% is 0.35; or that claim 1 will return 20% when claim 2 returns 12% is 0.25; and so forth. The joint probabilities associated with such outcomes must of course sum to 1.0 if all potential outcomes are included. Note that the *individual* capital claim outcome probabilities appear on the right and lower margins of the box and are the

TABLE 15.3

| | | Claim 2 r_2 | | |
		7%	12%	$P(r_1)$
Claim 1 r_1	10%	**a** 0.35	**b** 0.10	0.45
	20%	**c** 0.30	**d** 0.25	0.55
	$P(r_2)$	0.65	0.35	1.00

sum of the rows or columns in which they appear. For example, the probability that claim 1 will return 20% is 0.55, the sum of 0.30 (with claim 2 returning 7%) and 0.25 (with claim 2 returning 12%).

Suppose that the composition of the portfolio which our participant is forming using claims 1 and 2 will be as follows: One half of the portfolio value will be placed in claim 1 and one half will be devoted to claim 2. By referring to the joint probability distribution we can discover the four possible outcomes for the portfolio and the probabilities for each. If portfolio outcome **a** occurred ($r_1 = 10\%$ and $r_2 = 7\%$), then, with a 0.35 probability, the portfolio return, r_p, would be

$$r_p = \text{(proportion of claim 1)}(r_1) + \text{(proportion of claim 2)}(r_2)$$
$$= (0.5)(10\%) + (0.5)(7\%) = 8.5\%$$

Doing the same thing for the other joint outcomes, we can obtain the *portfolio's* probability distribution, and can calculate its mean and standard deviation:[1]

TABLE 15.4

Outcome	r_p	$P(r_p)$	$E(r_p)$	$\sigma(r_p)$
a	8.5%	0.35		
b	13.5%	0.30		
c	11.0%	0.10		
d	16.0%	0.25		
		1.00	12.125%	3.008%

The portfolio formed with equal parts of claim 1 and claim 2 has an expected return of 12.125% and a standard deviation of return or risk of about 3%.

[1]The portfolio's return and standard deviation are calculated by using its probability distribution in the same manner as that for individual claims.

We could have found the portfolio's expected return by merely averaging the expected returns (proportionately) of its two securities:

$$
\begin{aligned}
E(r_p) &= (\text{proportion of claim 1}) \cdot E(r_1) \\
&\quad + (\text{proportion of claim 2}) \cdot E(r_2) \\
&= (0.5)(15.50\%) + (0.5)(8.75\%) \\
&= 12.125\%
\end{aligned}
$$

If, however, we had done the same for the two assets' standard deviations, we would have obtained

$$(0.5) \cdot \sigma(r_1) + (0.5) \cdot \sigma(r_2) = (0.5)(4.97\%) + (0.5)(2.38\%)$$

which evaluates to about 3.68%.

$$3.68\% \neq \sigma(r_p)$$

indeed,

$$\sigma(r_p) < 3.68\%$$

The proportionate averaging of individual capital claim standard deviations gives a result that is unequal to the portfolio standard deviation. The portfolio standard deviation is less than the weighted-average standard deviation of the securities making up the portfolio.

Figure 15.1 shows graphically what has happened. Again, expected return is measured on the vertical axis and risk, $\sigma(r)$, is measured on the horizontal axis. The risk–return locations of claim 1 and claim 2 are plotted on the graph, as is the risk–return location of the portfolio formed by holding

FIGURE 15.1   Portfolio risk and return

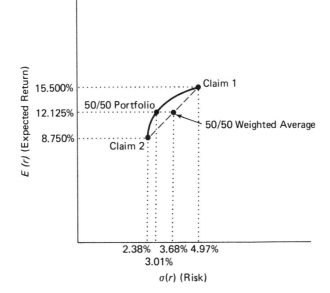

those two claims in equal proportions. The dashed line joining claim 1 to claim 2 shows the risk and return combinations we would find by merely averaging the $E(r)$'s and $\sigma(r)$'s of the two claims. (The equally-weighted average is, naturally, at the midpoint of the line.) The solid line joining claim 1 and claim 2, however, shows the risks and returns available to the participant by combining the two claims into various *portfolios*. The equal-proportion portfolio for which we calculated expected return and risk is indicated on the solid line. All portfolios formed from the two claims would plot somewhere along that line; the more of claim 1 in the portfolio, the closer to claim 1's risk–return location the portfolio location would be; the more of claim 2, the closer to claim 2's plot the portfolio plot would be. It is the solid line, not the dashed line, which indicates participants' risk–return expectations when combining these claims into portfolios.

Why does portfolio standard deviation behave the way it does? Why is portfolio risk generally less than the weighted-average standard deviations of individual capital claims making up the portfolio? The reason is that *the possible outcomes from the individual capital claims are related to each other in such a way that when the two claims are combined, their risks, to some extent, cancel each other out.* This is the essence of "diversification," the reason why participants hold combinations of claims or portfolios rather than individual capital claims. Visualize the participant indifference curves from Figure 14.5 superimposed on Figure 15.1. You can see that the odds are that the participants would be better off holding a portfolio rather than an individual claim. We shall return to this idea shortly.

First, to be more specific about the "relatedness" of capital claim outcomes and its effect on portfolio risks, we can calculate the risk of this two-claim portfolio directly by the formula

$$\sigma(r_p) = [X_1^2\sigma^2(r_1) + X_2^2\sigma^2(r_2) + 2X_1X_2\rho(r_1, r_2)\sigma(r_1)\sigma(r_2)]^{1/2} \quad \textbf{[15.1]}$$

where the X's are the proportions of the claims in the portfolio (for example, $X_1 = 0.5$, $X_2 = 0.5$) and where $\rho(r_1, r_2)$ is the *correlation coefficient* between the possible rate of return outcomes of the two claims indicated.[2]

The correlation coefficient is the only part of this formula that is new. For our purposes you can think of $\rho(r_1, r_2)$ as a measure of the relatedness of the returns from claim 1 and claim 2. $\rho(r_1, r_2)$ can have any value between -1 and $+1$. When $\rho(r_1, r_2)$ is somewhere between 0 and $+1$, the returns are "positively related"; that is, when claim 1's return is high, 2's tends also to be high; when 1's is low, 2's tends also to be low. $\rho(r_1, r_2) = +1$ is "per-

---

[2]Formula 15.1 has a more general form which can be used for any number of capital claims in a portfolio, say n claims:

$$\sigma(r_p) = \left[\sum_{i=1}^{n}\sum_{j=1}^{n} X_iX_j\rho(r_i, r_j)\sigma(r_i)\sigma(r_j)\right]^{1/2} \quad \text{or} \quad \left[\sum_{i=1}^{n}\sum_{j=1}^{n} X_iX_j\sigma(r_i, r_j)\right]^{1/2}$$

$\sigma(r_i, r_j)$ is defined as $\rho(r_i, r_j)\sigma(r_i)\sigma(r_j)$ and is called the *covariance*. Both formula 15.1 and this general formula are derived in references given at the end of the section.

fect positive correlation," the strongest possible positive relatedness between 1 and 2. When $\rho(r_1, r_2)$ is between 0 and -1, the returns are "negatively related"; that is, when 1 is high, 2 is low, and vice versa. $\rho(r_1, r_2) = -1$ is "perfect negative correlation," the strongest possible negative relatedness between the returns of 1 and 2.

A glance at formula 15.1 shows that the higher $\rho(r_1, r_2)$ is, the higher is portfolio risk; the lower $\rho(r_1, r_2)$ is, the lower is portfolio risk. Stated another way, the more negatively related (one high when the other is low), the more risk is canceled; the more positively related (one high when the other is high), the less risk is canceled. The particular $\rho(r_1, r_2)$ in our example is 0.2423, indicating a positive, but not "perfect" positive relatedness of returns from 1 and 2.[3]

Substituting our example's numbers into formula 15.1, we get

$$\sigma(r_p) = [(0.5)^2(0.0497)^2 + (0.5)^2(0.0238)^2$$
$$+ (2)(0.5)(0.5)(0.2423)(0.0497)(0.0238)]^{1/2}$$
$$\simeq 0.03008 = 3.008\%$$

which is the same portfolio standard deviation we found earlier. If the correlation coefficient had been higher, portfolio risk would have been higher; if $\rho(r_1, r_2)$ had been less than 0.2423, $\sigma(r_p)$ would have been less than 3.008%.

Figure 15.2 shows this idea graphically. The "portfolio lines" for various amounts of relatedness between the returns for claims 1 and 2 indicate that, the lower $\rho(r_1, r_2)$ is, the lower are the attainable portfolio risks, and therefore the greater are the gains to participants who diversify their holdings. Note that if returns are perfectly positively correlated, $\rho(r_1, r_2) = +1$, there are no real diversification benefits; portfolio risk is the weighted average of the $\sigma(r)$'s from the individual claims. Fortunately, this is a rare occurrence. Note also, however, that if $\rho(r_1, r_2) = -1$ (perfect negative correlation) participants can hold a portfolio that has no risk at all. Unfortunately, this is also a very rare occurrence. Most realistic capital claim ρ's are somewhere between 0 and $+1$, which indicates that some benefits will arise from diversifying.

---

[3]The mechanics of calculating the correlation coefficient obviously must involve the joint probability distribution of returns for claims 1 and 2. The product of each joint deviation is multiplied by its associated joint probability, those products are added together, and that sum is divided by the product of the two standard deviations of the return distributions. For our 2 $\times$ 2 joint distribution (see Tables 15.1, 15.2, and 15.3 for numerical values):

$$\rho(r_1, r_2) = \frac{\begin{aligned}&(r_{1_a} - E(r_1))(r_{2_a} - E(r_2))P(r_{1_a}, r_{2_a}) \\ &+ (r_{1_b} - E(r_1))(r_{2_b} - E(r_2))P(r_{1_b}, r_{2_b}) \\ &+ (r_{1_c} - E(r_1))(r_{2_c} - E(r_2))P(r_{1_c}, r_{2_c}) \\ &+ (r_{1_d} - E(r_1))(r_{2_d} - E(r_2))P(r_{1_d}, r_{2_d}) \\ &= (0.10 - 0.155)(0.07 - 0.0875)(0.35) \\ &+ (0.10 - 0.155)(0.12 - 0.0875)(0.10) \\ &+ (0.20 - 0.155)(0.07 - 0.0875)(0.30) \\ &+ (0.20 - 0.155)(0.12 - 0.0875)(0.25) \\ &= 0.24232\end{aligned}}{\begin{aligned}&\sigma(r_1)\sigma(r_2) \\ \\ &(0.049749)(0.023848)\end{aligned}}$$

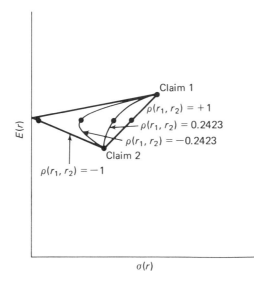

FIGURE 15.2   **Correlation and the gains from diversification**

RISKY-ASSET FRONTIER

We now have assembled sufficient tools to continue our quest for individual capital claim risk measures and the SML–market-risk relationship. Specifically, we know that capital-market participants maximize expected utility which depends on the expected return $[E(r)$, a positive utility factor] and risk $[\sigma(r)$, a negative utility factor] of the portfolios they hold. Furthermore, we know that the risks of portfolios are not likely to be mere averages of the individual claim standard deviations; portfolio risk also depends on the relatedness of the returns from the individual claims held in the portfolios.

We shall turn our attention now to the capital market as a whole. Our example of diversification to this point contains only two capital claims, 1 and 2. The capital market, however, has multitudes of risky capital claims, all of which are candidates to be held in participants' portfolios. If we were to describe the available risks and returns from holding portfolios of capital claims where (1) so many claims are available, and (2) any portfolio could contain any number of capital claims in any one of innumerable proportions, the "feasible set" of risk–return opportunities available to capital-market participants would appear as in Figure 15.3.

Here, individual claims are noted as c's and portfolios as p's. Notice that almost the entire upper-left (dashed-line) border of the feasible set of market risk–return opportunities comprises portfolios rather than individual claims. This should not be too surprising to you, given (1) the likelihood of diversification benefits such as we illustrated in our portfolio of two claims, and (2) the shape of the portfolio line in Figure 15.2. The amalgamation of all such portfolio lines generated by all possible combinations of two or more

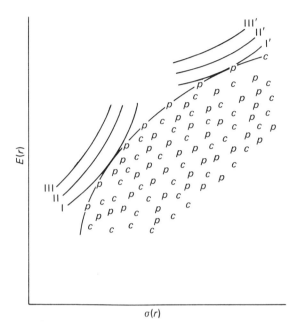

FIGURE 15.3 Feasible set of risk-return opportunities

claims in varying proportions is what generates the dashed-line border. Although it is not completely impossible for an individual claim to fall on this border, the conditions necessary to allow this to occur are so restrictive that we simply never actually see such an individual claim, except, possibly, for the highest-risk—highest-return point on the border. The rest of the border always represents *combinations* of claims (portfolios).

Figure 15.3 also shows how capital-market participants would choose their holdings from the set of capital claims and portfolios. As we know, participants are utility maximizers, which means they will attempt to reach as high an indifference curve as possible when deciding which capital claim or claims to hold. Figure 15.3 also shows representative sets of indifference curves; one set (I, II, III) is for a relatively more risk-averse participant, while the other set (I', II', III') represents a relatively less risk-averse participant. As indicated in the figure, the process of selecting a holding of capital claims which will place either participant on a higher indifference curve will naturally move the participants to the upper-left boundary (dashed line) of the set of all feasible holdings. Indeed, the highest indifference curve which any participant can reach is that curve which is just tangent to the feasible set of opportunities. That tangency is necessarily with the dashed-line boundary of the feasible set.

Since that boundary essentially comprises only portfolios and not individual capital claims, both individuals (whose indifference curves are depicted in Figure 15.3) will choose to hold *portfolios* of capital claims. Neither will choose to hold an individual capital claim. Given the risk-aversion characteristic of our participants, their utility-maximizing behavior will, in general, be that of portfolio holding.

Furthermore, in the situation represented by Figure 15.3, the portfolios that form the upper-left (dashed-line) border of the set of risk–return opportunities will be the only risky portfolios held by any market participants.

We call these portfolios the "efficient set" or, more descriptively, the "efficient frontier," because they are better than all other opportunities, both individual capital claims and all other inefficient portfolios that lie inside the efficient frontier.

To summarize, our capital market now can be described as comprising return-preferring, risk-averse (actually, standard-deviation-averse) participants who hold securities. They choose their security holdings on the basis of the rates of return and standard deviations of return expected, not for the individual securities, but for the *portfolios* which they can form from those securities. Because participants prefer higher portfolio returns to lower, and prefer lower portfolio standard deviations to higher, they are only interested in those portfolios which, for a given risk, $\sigma(r_p)$, offer the highest expected return, $E(r_p)$, and for a given $E(r_p)$, offer the lowest $\sigma(r_p)$. Being good portfolio analysts, our participants recognize that such portfolios would be those which are located along the upper-left border of the set of all feasible portfolios as depicted in Figure 15.3. This border is the efficient set or frontier of portfolios. All participants would, if their choices consisted of securities such as those described in Figure 15.3, choose a portfolio somewhere along the efficient frontier, depending upon their individual proclivities for expected return versus risk-bearing.

CAPITAL-MARKET EQUILIBRIUM

The set of risky capital claims and the portfolios they form, however, are not the only opportunities which our participants have. *We shall assume that participants can, if they wish, also use the financial market.* You recall from Section I that this means participants can borrow and lend at the risk-free rate of return, i.

When a risky portfolio can be combined with riskless borrowing or lending, a whole new group of possible portfolios becomes available. Figure 15.4 shows this situation. Portfolio a in Figure 15.4 is a risky portfolio comprising, say, a number of risky capital claims. If a participant held portfolio a alone, his expected return would be $E(r_a)$ and risk $\sigma(r_a)$. If, however, he combines portfolio a with lending at the risk-free rate, i, he can reach any risk-return position on the straight line joining portfolio a to i. The more lending, the closer to i will be his risk–return location; the less lending the closer to portfolio a he will be. When a is combined with borrowing at the risk-free rate, he can attain the risk–return combinations on the straight line

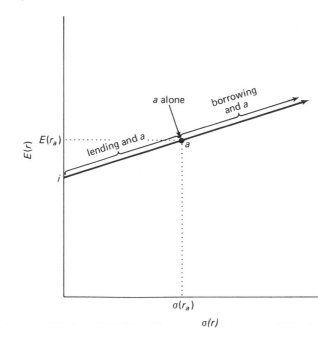

FIGURE 15.4   **Borrowing and lending**

above a. The less borrowing, the closer to a is the risk–return location of the new portfolio; the more borrowing the further from a (heading upward) is the new combination's risk–return location along the line.[4]

With all capital-market participants able to borrow and lend at i, their opportunities are shown in Figure 15.5. They can attain any risk–return combination on or below the line marked CML, where the CML (the capital-market line) is the straight line beginning at i, the risk-free rate, and extending indefinitely to the right, just tangent to the risky capital claim portfolio efficient frontier. In a mechanical sense, you can think of the CML as a line, hinged at i, which swings up and down until it just barely touches the efficient frontier of the feasible set of risk–return opportunities. The risky portfolio on the efficient frontier that lies on (is touched by) the CML is designated as m in Figure 15.5. The CML in relationship to portfolio m, then, is simply a particular case of the phenomenon shown in Figure 15.4, which is produced by combining any risky portfolio or asset (a) with borrowing and lending at i. Thus, the CML is the bounding of a new set of opportunities which includes

---

[4]Portfolios combining risky assets (or risky-asset portfolios) with borrowing/lending lie on a straight line because $\sigma(i) = 0$ and therefore $\rho(r_a, i) = 0$. Under these conditions, formula 15.1 gives a linear or straight-line relationship between the risk of such a portfolio and the proportion of it formed by the risky asset (or the risky-asset portfolio). Since rates of return are also linearly related to proportions, risk and return are linearly related to each other.

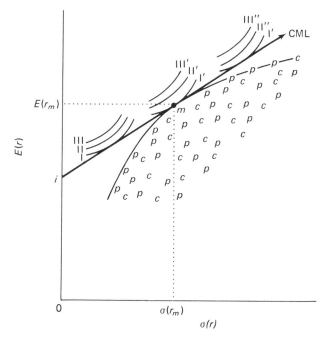

FIGURE 15.5 **Capital-market line**

all the original feasible set of purely risky individual claims and portfolios, plus all other risk–return combinations on or below the CML, attainable by borrowing or lending at i.[5]

Figure 15.5 also indicates that since participants are utility maximizers, they will all choose a portfolio somewhere on the CML regardless of their individual risk aversions. (Three representative indifference maps and their tangencies to the CML are shown in Figure 15.5.) Thus, we now have a new efficient set of risk–return portfolios, which is the CML itself. Specifically, it consists of four general strategies:

1. Only lending at i.
2. Lending at i and holding the risky capital claim portfolio m. This would place a participant somewhere between i and m on the CML, depending on the proportion of cash lent versus that placed in m.
3. Holding only the risky portfolio m.
4. Holding m and borrowing at the rate i, which places a participant on the CML above m, the particular location depending on the amount of money he borrows to invest in m along with his own cash.

[5]This new opportunity set cannot go above the CML because that would mean combining i with portfolios outside the risky efficient frontier. And it must reach all the way up to the CML since any point on the CML itself is attainable by holding m and either borrowing or lending.

The CML, in other words, has now become the efficient frontier of portfolios from which all capital-market participants will choose their utility-maximizing risk–return combinations.

Notice that the only risky capital claim portfolio held by participants is m. All holdings along the CML which are not purely *m* are some combination of *m* and either borrowing or lending at *i* (except, of course, for the pure strategy of only lending). No other risky asset portfolio will be held, in any proportion, by any participant. Since all capital claims must be owned by *someone*, *m* must therefore contain *all* risky capital claims. Because *m* is such an all-encompassing portfolio, we have a special name for it: "the market portfolio." [*m*'s expected return, $E(r_m)$, and risk, $\sigma(r_m)$, are indicated in Figure 15.5.]

Let's pause for a moment to collect our thoughts and see what we have accomplished. Remember that our goal is to discover an appropriate risk measure for individual capital claims, and to specify the "market price" of that risk. This would allow us to calculate required rates of return for the individual capital claims of corporations and for cash-flow expectations of corporate investments. The latter is the information we need to complete the theory of corporate asset acquisition and divestment for risk-altering investments.

Now consider the capital-market line in Figure 15.5. The risks and returns along the CML are generally available to all capital-market participants. We shall generally refer to any combination of the market portfolio *m* with borrowing or lending at *i* as an *efficient portfolio* and designate it with the letter *p*. *For any given portfolio risk along the horizontal axis, participants can expect to be compensated with the associated rate of return along the vertical axis, as indicated by the CML relationship.* The rates of return shown on the vertical axis are therefore legitate opportunity costs or *required rates of return* for the associated amounts of risk on the horizontal axis.

The CML relationship between risk and required rates of return can be stated in simple geometric terms as: The required return, k, on efficient portfolio p is equal to the risk-free rate, i, plus the product of the slope of the CML and the risk of the efficient portfolio. Algebraically,

$$kp = i + \frac{E(r_m) - i}{\sigma(r_m)} \sigma(kp) \qquad \textbf{[15.2]}$$

where $[E(r_m) - i]/\sigma(r_m)$ is the slope of the CML, $E(r_m)$ is the expected return on the market portfolio *m*, and $\sigma(r_m)$ is its standard deviation. Formula 15.2 tells us that, given any amount of efficient portfolio risk, $\sigma(kp)$, we can find the return which the capital market requires on that portfolio by multiplying its $\sigma(kp)$ by $[E(r_m) - i]/\sigma(r_m)$ and adding the result to the risk-free rate, i. The slope of the CML determines the "risk-premium" portion of the required return on an efficient portfolio; the CML slope therefore must be the "price of risk" for efficient portfolios when their risk is measured by standard deviation. Efficient portfolios, you recall, are those which lie on the CML.

This explanation of the capital-market line makes it sound very similar to what we are seeking. As a matter of fact, if corporate cash flows were efficient portfolios, we could use the CML relationship in formula 15.2 to discover their required returns based on their standard deviations. But corporate cash flows are not efficient portfolios. At best we can consider them as representing the cash returns to *individual* capital claims. Formula 15.2, however, applies only to efficient portfolios which lie on the CML. Individual corporate capital claims are neither efficient nor portfolios, so formula 15.2 would be inappropriate for finding their required rates.

But do not lose heart. We are very close to our goal. As we shall quickly see, the CML relationship is the key to the relationship between the risks of individual claims and their required rates of return.

CAPITAL-MARKET LINE AND INDIVIDUAL CAPITAL CLAIMS

As we said, the capital-market-line relationship between risk and required rates of return applies only to efficient portfolios. We also saw earlier that these efficient portfolios are composed of m, the market portfolio, in combination with borrowing or lending at the risk-free rate, i. Remember that the market portfolio is a portfolio of *all* the individual capital claims existing in the capital market. The market portfolio, m, is also an efficient portfolio. It lies on the CML. And it is composed of individual capital claims. *It stands to reason, therefore, that in order for m to exist in the way that we have defined it, the returns offered by the individual capital claims within the market portfolio must have adjusted relative to each other so as to reflect the respective risk that each contributes to m.* If this were not true, either m would not lie on the CML (which it does) or an individual claim would be excluded from the market portfolio (which cannot happen since all claims must be owned, and m is the only risky-claim portfolio held by anyone).

So the CML relationship in Figure 15.5 and formula 15.2 implies that individual capital claims are promising rates of return high enough to compensate for the risk which those individual claims contribute to the market portfolio. The risk of that portfolio is measured by $\sigma(r_m)$, the standard deviation of its expected return. We know, however, that individual claims' standard deviations do not just get averaged together to form portfolio standard deviations. We saw earlier that, depending on the relatedness of individual claims, some amount of their $\sigma(r)$ is *diversified away* when they are combined into portfolios. This, of course, holds true for their inclusion in the market portfolio as well. *The portion of individual capital claim $\sigma(r)$ which is not diversified away when it is included in m is the contribution to m's riskiness, $\sigma(r_m)$, and is therefore the riskiness of the claim itself and the basis for its required rate of return.*

In other words, the standard deviation of return on an individual capital claim is, essentially, made up of two parts:

1. A part that affects the riskiness of the market portfolio m (and all other efficient portfolios) in which it is held.
2. A part that is diversified away when it is held in m.

The only part of an individual claim's standard deviation which requires compensation is part (1), the risk that is *not* diversified away by capital-market participants holding it in an efficient portfolio. Remember, participants require compensation for risk-bearing. But they only require compensation for the riskiness of their *total* holdings. Since those holdings are always efficient portfolios, *each individual claim will have a required return based on that claim being held in the efficient market portfolio of claims, namely m.* The particular required return for each claim will be some function of the risk it adds to efficient portfolios, and which cannot therefore be diversified away. It is only this risk contribution to efficient portfolios which is borne by capital-market participants holding those portfolios, and it is this risk component alone that is the basis for their required rates of return on individual claims.

SECURITY-MARKET LINE

How do we discover the risk contribution of individual claims when they are held in efficient portfolios? The most logical procedure would be to find the expected rate of return that an individual claim would have to offer in order for it to be held in an efficient portfolio, specifically in m, the market portfolio. The condition that must be satisfied for an individual claim to be held in an efficient portfolio is

$$kc = i + \frac{E(r_m) - i}{\sigma(r_m)} \rho(kc, r_m)\sigma(kc) \qquad [15.3]^6$$

Formula 15.3 is a very important one. In fact, it is the basis for answering the questions which have been the purpose of this rather long discussion about risk in the capital market. Let us look at formula 15.3 in some detail. Again, it states the condition for an individual capital claim, c, to be held in m or any other efficient portfolio. kc is the required return for claim c. It is the rate of return necessary for c to be included in m. If the claim in question happened to be a debt issue of some corporation, we could change the c's in formula 15.3 to d's and thus have the relationship determining kd for that firm. Similarly, ke's and other familiar required rates can be ascertained by using this relationship.

Examining the right-hand side of formula 15.3, we see that the risk-free rate, i, makes up part of kc. You will recall that i represents the price of time. From Section I we know that in the absence of risk, kc would equal i.

---

[6] The derivation of formula 15.3 appears in several references cited at the end of this section.

This means that everything else on the right-hand side would have to equal to zero in the absence of risk. This further implies that everything in the second term of the sum on the right-hand side of formula 15.3 must be the risk-compensation part of kc. Therefore,

$$\left(\frac{E(r_m) - i}{\sigma(r_m)}\right)\rho(kc, r_m)\sigma(kc)$$

is the risk-compensation or "risk-premium" component of claim c's required rate of return. Like any figure representing total compensation, this risk-premium rate is the product of a price (of risk) times a quantity (of risk). The price component is the expression in parentheses, which we have seen before. It is the "market price of risk for efficient portfolios" we discovered in connection with our study of the CML, and, geometrically, it is the slope of the CML. Only a moment ago we said that the risk compensation necessary for an individual capital claim depends not only on the unit price but also on the quantity or amount of risk it adds to efficient portfolios. Since the expression in parentheses is the price of the risk, $\rho(kc, r_m)\sigma(kc)$ (the part outside the parentheses) must be the *quantity* of risk that claim c adds to efficient portfolios: $\rho(kc, r_m)\sigma(kc)$ *is the amount of claim c's standard deviation that is not diversified away when it is included in an efficient portfolio. It is therefore the risk for which compensation must be paid.* Notice that the proportion of $\sigma(kc)$ which is not diversified away is $\rho(kc, r_m)$, the correlation coefficient or relatedness between the returns from c and the returns on the market portfolio. From our earlier discussions about the gains from diversification being dependent on ρ, the correlation coefficient, the importance of $\rho(kc, r_m)$ in determining the risk compensation for claim c should have some intuitive appeal. If $\rho(kc, r_m) = 1$, all of c's $\sigma(kc)$ is "risk" and must be compensated for; none of its $\sigma(kc)$ is diversified away. If $\rho(kc, r_m) = 0$, as far as the capital market and its participants are concerned, c is riskless even though $\sigma(kc)$ may be large. Claim c would effectively be riskless because its inclusion in an efficient portfolio would have the same effect as lending at the risk-free rate. All of its $\sigma(kc)$ would be diversified away. If $\rho(kc, r_m) = 0$, then kc must equal i.[7]

If we were to graph formula 15.3 it would appear as shown in Figure 15.6. *A glance at that figure shows that formula 15.3 is indeed what we have been seeking all along: the security-market line.* Figure 15.6 tells us that, given the $\rho(kc, r_m)\sigma(kc)$ for any capital claim, formula 15.3 will produce the required return for that claim. When $\rho(kc, r_m) = 0$, $kc = i$. As the amount of risk, $\rho(kc, r_m)\sigma(kc)$, increases, so does the required return, kc. The location of the market portfolio is plotted on the security-market line (SML) in Figure 15.6

[7]If $\rho(kc, r_m)$ is negative $[-1 \leq \rho(kc, r_m) < 0]$, claim c actually has a negative risk effect on portfolio m. Clearly, it would require a return less than i, the risk-free rate. Not only *its* $\sigma(kc)$, but also part of $\sigma(r_m)$ is diversified away. Actually, if $\rho(kc, r_m)$ were negative enough, kc as a required return could itself actually be negative. Regrettably, as we mentioned earlier, real ρ's less than zero are very rare, and most $\rho(kc, r_m)$'s are between 0.3 and 0.9.

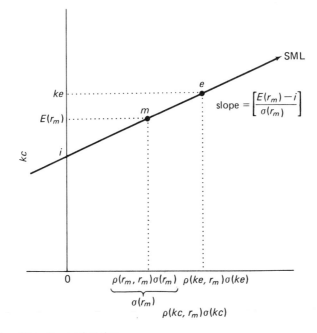

FIGURE 15.6   Security-market line

for reference. Note that its risk is $\rho(r_m, r_m)\sigma(r_m)$, but since $\rho(r_m, r_m) \equiv 1$, the market portfolio risk is simply $\sigma(r_m)$. We would expect this because none of $\sigma(r_m)$ can be diversified away. The m is already fully diversified because it contains all individual capital claims. If we knew the $\rho(ke, r_m)\sigma(ke)$ of an equity claim e, Figure 15.6 shows how its ke would be determined graphically.

As a summary of our discussion of formula 15.3, we present it again below with each of its economically important parts clearly identified:

$$kc = \underbrace{i}_{\text{price of time}} + \underbrace{\overbrace{\frac{E(r_m) - i}{\sigma(r_m)}}^{\substack{\text{market price} \\ \text{of risk}}} \overbrace{\rho(kc, r_m)\sigma(kc)}^{\substack{\text{amount of} \\ \text{undiversifiable} \\ \text{risk in } c}}}_{\text{risk premium}} \qquad [15.3]$$

required return on claim c

When the risk of an individual capital claim is measured by $\rho(kc, r_m)\sigma(kc)$, the required return on that claim is the amount of risk times the price of risk plus the risk-free return. That kc is the opportunity cost which capital-market participants incur when holding c in an efficient portfolio. All claims with equal $\rho(kc, r_m)\sigma(kc)$'s will have the same required return. $\rho(kc, r_m)\sigma(kc)$ is therefore an appropriate risk measure for individual capital claims. It is equal to the correlation of the return from that claim with the return on the market as a whole, times the standard deviation of that claim's rate of return.

$p(kc, r_m)\sigma(kc)$ is the amount of $\sigma(kc)$ that is not diversified away when c is included in participants' efficient portfolios and therefore is the portion of $\sigma(kc)$ that must be compensated for as risk.

CASH FLOWS AND RISK

There is one final step we must take to complete our development of risk. Examining the SML formula and graph to this point, you can see that the risk measure used is based on *rates of return* for individual capital claims. $p(kc, r_m)\sigma(kc)$ expresses a relationship between claim c's rate of return and the return on m, the market portfolio. What we really need, however, is an SML relationship stated in terms of the *cash flows* expected from a proposed investment. You recall that earlier in this section we referred to proposed investments (divestments) as little corporations. The final step we are about to take is simply to switch our viewpoint back from the rate-of-return perspective of formula 15.3, to the little corporation's cash-flow expectations. This step will complete the information that we must have in order to be able to address the risk-altering asset acquisition/divestment decision. In essence, we must now take Figure 15.6 and change the horizontal axis from a risk measure based on rates of return to a risk measure based on cash flows.

Fortunately, we already have the algebraic relationship between these two risk measures which we developed as formula 14.2 (p. 324). We have now developed sufficient notation so that we can restate formula 14.2 here without the necessity of writing out all the terms in words:

$$\frac{\sigma(kc)}{1 + kc} = \frac{\sigma(\text{CF})}{\text{CF}} \qquad [14.2]$$

where CF is the mean of the cash-flow probability distribution, and $\sigma(\text{CF})$, its standard deviation. Rearranging terms, we get

$$\sigma(kc) = \frac{\sigma(\text{CF}) \cdot (1 + kc)}{\text{CF}} \qquad [15.4]$$

and substituting this for $\sigma(kc)$ in the SML formula 15.3,

$$kc = i + \frac{E(r_m) - i}{\sigma(r_m)} p(kc, r_m) \frac{\sigma(\text{CF})(1 + kc)}{\text{CF}}$$

Since kc appears on both sides of this equation, we need to do some algebraic manipulation to put it in usable form. Doing that, we obtain

$$kc = \frac{1 + i}{1 - \dfrac{E(r_m) - i}{\sigma(r_m)} \dfrac{p(kc, r_m)\sigma(\text{CF})}{\text{CF}}} - 1 \qquad [15.5]$$

This is fine, except that our measure of relatedness is still based on the rate of return kc relative to the returns on the market portfolio. In general, proposed asset acquisitions or divestments are not couched in terms of probability distributions of rates of return. Common industry analysis forecasts *cash flows* and their variability. We can, of course, calculate a p which is cash-flow-based, $p(\text{CF}, r_m)$. Fortunately, this measure of relatedness,

$p(CF, r_m)$, is exactly numerically equal to $p(kc, r_m)$.[8] Thus, we can restate formula 15.5 using the cash-flow-based p as

$$kc = \frac{1 + i}{1 - \frac{E(r_m) - i}{\sigma(r_m)} \, p(CF, r_m)\sigma(CF)}{CF} - 1 \qquad \textbf{[15.6]}$$

This rather nasty-looking formula is the SML relationship for cash flows. Before you become discouraged at its complexity, however, consider that there is nothing unfamiliar about any of the parts of formula 15.6. Let us look at each in turn. kc is, of course, the required rate of return which the expected cash flow, CF, must achieve. If CF = NCDE, then $kc = ke$; if CF = CAU, $kc = ku$; and so on. The i represents, as we know, the risk-free rate of return. $[E(r_m) - i]/\sigma(r_m)$ is also well known to us. It is the famous (or infamous) market price of risk. The only substantive part remaining is

$$\frac{p(CF, r_m)\sigma(CF)}{CF}$$

which must be, of course, *the measure of the amount of risk in the expected cash flow CF which cannot be diversified away.* It is composed of $p(CF, r_m)$, $\sigma(CF)$, and CF.

The term $p(CF, r_m)$ represents the correlation coefficient between the cash flow CF and the rate of return on the market portfolio. As we said earlier, the correlation coefficient is a measure of relatedness. It shows whether the two things being examined tend to be positively related ($p > 0$) or negatively related ($p < 0$), and how strong a relationship exists (strongest positive is $p = 1$; strongest negative is $p = -1$; weakest is $p = 0$). If the investment's cash flows are positively related to r_m (as most probably are) and of "medium" strength, $p(CF, r_m)$ would probably be somewhere around 0.5. The specific numerical $p(CF, r_m)$ calculation, as we have seen earlier, would require the joint probability distribution of outcomes for CF and r_m.

The term $\sigma(CF)$ is simply the standard deviation of the cash-flow expectation. We studied these earlier in this section. And the CF that appears below $\sigma(CF)$ in formula 15.6 is the expectation or mean of the probability distribution of the possible cash-flow outcomes. The CF in formula 15.6 is the cash-flow number that we have been using throughout earlier chapters. Actually, the ratio $\sigma(CF)/CF$ is a common statistical measure called the "coefficient of variation," which is denoted by CV(CF). You can see that it gives the *standard deviation per dollar of expectation* of the cash flow.

[8]This is because the conversion of a one-period distribution of expected cash flows into a distribution of expected rates of return is accomplished by dividing each possible cash-flow outcome by a constant (the cash outlay) and subtracting another constant, 1, from each resulting quotient. It can be demonstrated mathematically that the distribution resulting from such a conversion will have the same correlation coefficient with any other distribution as did the original distribution.

Substituting this CV(CF) back in formula 15.6,

$$kc = \frac{1 + i}{1 - \dfrac{E(r_m) - i}{\sigma(r_m)} \rho(CF, r_m)CV(CF)} - 1 \qquad [15.7]$$

This is the final formula for required rates of return based on cash-flow expectations. As you would expect, it includes:

1. i, the price of time.
2. $[E(r_m) - i]/\sigma(r_m)$, the price of risk.
3. $\rho(CF, r_m)CV(CF)$, a measure of undiversifiable risk.

With (1) $\rho(CF, r_m)$ showing the relatedness between possible cash-flow outcomes and r_m, possible rates of return on the market portfolio, and (2) CV(CF) showing the standard deviation per dollar of cash flow, $\rho(CF, r_m)CV(CF)$ shows the cash-flow risk that is not diversified away when the investment (the little corporation) is held in efficient portfolios.

When we graph this new SML relationship for cash-flow expectations, it becomes more understandable. Formula 15.7, graphically displayed, appears in Figure 15.7. Note that the SML relationship is similar to the one we saw earlier except that the horizontal axis is now the cash-flow risk measure

FIGURE 15.7 **Security-market line for cash flows**

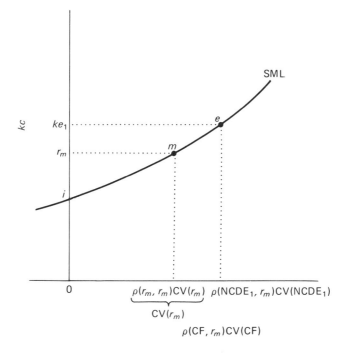

$\rho(\text{CF}, r_m)\text{CV(CF)}$.[9] When $\rho(\text{CF}, r_m)\text{CV(CF)}$ equals zero, kc equals i, the risk-free rate. As $\rho(\text{CF}, r_m)\text{CV(CF)}$ increases, so does kc. Notice that kc, the required return which a cash flow must achieve, increases with both the CV(CF) (per dollar standard deviation of the cash flow) and $\rho(\text{CF}, r_m)$, the degree of relatedness between the cash flow and "the market." The two multiplied together, $[\rho(\text{CF}, r_m)\text{CV(CF)}]$, constitute a measure of the amount of "risk" in the cash flow requiring compensation in the market.

We have also illustrated in Figure 15.7 the market determination of a required equity return, ke, based on the risk of the relevant NCDE flow.

SUMMARY After substantial effort, we have finally reached our goal: an individual cash-flow risk measure, and the market relationship which tells us the rate of return which that cash-flow risk requires. The risk measure is $\rho(\text{CF}, r_m)\text{CV(CF)}$; the SML relationship is given by formula 15.7 and depicted in Figure 15.7. In order to reach this point it was necessary for us to investigate in detail how capital-market participants behave in uncertain capital markets. We discovered them to be risk-averting portfolio analysts, or holders of efficiently diversified portfolios of capital claims. Of particular interest was that their satisfaction levels depended on the expected returns and risk (measured here by the standard deviation of returns) of the portfolios they held.

The preceding information was sufficient for us to arrive at the contribution of individual capital claims, and, in turn, cash-flow expectations, to the risk of efficient portfolios. The risk measure and market risk–return relationship we have discovered by these means will aid us greatly in completing the theory of corporate asset acquisition and divestment.

---

[9]The SML for cash flows does not plot precisely as a straight line, although it is very close to approximating linearity within reasonable ranges of $\rho(\text{CF}, r_m)\text{CV(CF)}$ values.

Chapter 16

The Corporate Investment Decision: A Risk-Altering Example

RISK-ALTERING INVESTMENT DECISIONS

Earlier in this section (Chapter 13) we studied the corporate investment decision under the condition that the acquiring (or divesting) of the asset would not change the risk (and hence required returns of) corporate cash flows. It is now time to abandon that condition and consider the more general situation where corporate investment can change the riskiness of the overall corporation and its required returns.

We asserted earlier that an investment which does not alter the risk of the existing corporation necessarily has the same risk as the existing corporation. An obvious corollary is that a risk-altering corporate investment must have risk which differs from that of the existing corporation. These assertions will be defended as we study the risk-altering corporate investment decision.

The procedural aspects of the risk-altering investment decision are very similar to the risk-constant decision that we saw in Chapter 13. First, the relevant corporate cash flows are calculated. With our knowledge of probability distributions we now know that the cash-flow numbers appearing in financial cash-flow statements are expectations of probability distributions for the respective flows and that it is quite appropriate to add and subtract the expectations as is done in the statement. Next, discount rates for the resulting expectations must be found. In the risk-constant situation this presented no particular problem. The rates for the existing (without-acceptance) corporation were appropriate. In the risk-altering situation, however, because of the differing risks, rates for the without-acceptance and with-acceptance corporation and for the proposal's cash flows are not all the same. The appropriate rates for discounting cash flows must be found by reference to the market risk–return relationship that we have just finished developing. Finally, using these market-derived discount rates, the values of the investment (VF^{ivs} and NPV^{ivs}), of the with-acceptance corporation, and of shareholder wealth changes are calculated in exactly the same way for risk-altering investments as we did for the risk-constant decision.

NUMERICAL EXAMPLE   Consider the risk-constant investment decision developed in Chapter 13. Table 16.1 shows the cash flows, discount rates, and values that we found. Suppose that exactly the same without-acceptance corporation, at exactly the same time (now $= t_1$) is faced with a different investment opportunity: If adopted by the corporation, a $1274.25 investment outlay at t_1 will give the following expectations of cash-flow probability distributions at t_2:

$$\$RCPT_2^{ivs} = \$5000.00$$
$$\$EXPT_2^{ivs} = 2400.00$$
$$GCFO_2^{ivs} = 2600.00$$
$$GTAX_2^{ivs} = 1352.00$$
$$NCFO_2^{ivs} = 1248.00$$
$$DTS_2^{ivs} = 662.61$$
$$CAU_2^{ivs} = 1910.61$$

The probability distribution of possible CAU_2^{ivs} outcomes indicates that the expected cash flow is $1910.61. Assume that it also provides us with a standard deviation of, say,

$$\sigma(CAU_2^{ivs}) = \$1301.38$$

Similarly, a careful forecast of the overall market (the market portfolio) suggests that

$$E(r_m) = 0.09$$
$$\sigma(r_m) = 0.10$$

From examining the joint probability distribution of the proposal's CAU_2^{ivs} cash-flow outcomes and possible overall market returns, it seems that

$$\rho(CAU_2^{ivs}, r_m) = 0.50$$

We shall maintain our previous assumption that the risk-free rate i for period p_2 will be 7.764%.[1]

This investment opportunity should appear familiar. In fact, the expectations of cash-flow probability distributions are exactly the same as the risk-constant opportunity we analyzed earlier in the section. The difference is, obviously, that this opportunity is not specified as being a risk-constant investment. The information which is given about the opportunity, however, is enough for us to use the capital market risk–return relationship to discover its risk and required rates. From the investment analysis procedure we have

---

[1] This assumption was used in Section III and in Appendix III.A even though it was never made explicit. Appendix V.C shows how i is determined and used.

TABLE 16.1 Risk-constant investment

A. Cash Flows	t_1 Without acceptance	t_1 Investment proposal	t_1 With acceptance	t_2 Without acceptance	t_2 Investment proposal	t_2 With acceptance
$RCPT	$6,250.00	$ 0.00	$6,250.00	$7,500.00	$5,000.00	$12,500.00
$EXPT	3,976.50	0.00	3,976.50	4,800.75	2,400.00	7,200.75
GCFO	2,273.50	0.00	2,273.50	2,699.25	2,600.00	5,299.25
GTAX	1,182.22	0.00	1,182.22	1,403.61	1,352.00	2,755.61
NCFO	1,091.28	0.00	1,091.28	1,295.64	1,248.00	2,543.64
DTS	936.00	0.00	936.00	468.00	662.61	1,130.61
CAU	2,027.28	0.00	2,027.28	1,763.64	1,910.61	3,674.25
ITS	18.72	0.00	18.72	9.36	10.14	19.50
CAC	2,046.00	0.00	2,046.00	1,773.00	1,920.75	3,693.75
I	36.00	0.00	36.00	18.00	19.50	37.50
CAF	2,010.00	0.00	2,010.00	1,755.00	1,901.25	3,656.25
PP	225.00	225.00	450.00	225.00	243.75	468.75
CDD	261.00	225.00	486.00	243.00	263.25	506.25
NDC	0.00	468.75	468.75	0.00	0.00	0.00
NCDD	261.00	−243.75	17.25	243.00	263.25	506.25
CAE	1,785.00	−225.00	1,560.00	1,530.00	1,657.50	3,187.50
CRF	0.00	805.50	805.50	0.00	0.00	0.00
CDE	1,785.00	−1,030.50	754.50	1,530.00	1,657.50	3,187.50
NEC	0.00	0.00	0.00	0.00	0.00	0.00
NCDE	1,785.00	−1,030.50	754.50	1,530.00	1,657.50	3,187.50
TCC ≡ IVS	0.00	1,274.25	1,274.25	0.00	0.00	0.00

B. k's with $\theta = 0.15$ and $\tau = 0.52$

	wo	ivs	w
ke_2	0.20000	0.20000	0.20000
kd_2	0.08000	0.08000	0.08000
kd_2^*	0.03840	0.03840	0.03840
kf_2	0.18200	0.18200	0.18200
kf_2^*	0.17576	0.17576	0.17576

C. Values ($V_T^{wo} + V_T^{ivs} = V_T^w$)

$$VE_1^{wo} = \$1275.00 \qquad VE_1^{ivs} = \$1381.25$$
$$VD_1^{wo} = 225.00 \qquad VD_1^{ivs} = 243.75$$
$$VF_1^{wo} = 1500.00 \qquad VF_1^{ivs} = 1625.00$$
$$VE_1^w = \$2656.25$$
$$VD_1^w = 468.75$$
$$VF_1^w = 3125.00$$

D. $NPV_1^{ivs} = VF_1^{ivs} + (CAU_1^{ivs} - IVS_1^{ivs}) = \$1625.00 + (\$0.00 - \$1274.25) = \$350.75$
$\Delta PWE_1 = VE_1^{ivs} + NCDE_1^{ivs} = \$1381.25 + (\$-1030.50) = \$350.75$

reviewed, you can see that once appropriate discount rates are discovered, the values and wealth changes in which we are interested are mere mechanical (or electronic) calculations.

INVESTMENT REQUIRED RATES

First, of course, we must find the appropriate discount rate. Recall formula 15.7, the SML relationship for cash flows:

$$kc = \frac{1+i}{1 - \dfrac{E(r_m) - i}{\sigma(r_m)}\rho(CF, r_m)CV(CF)} - 1 \qquad \textbf{[15.7]}$$

The first step in finding appropriate risk-adjusted discount rates for the investment cash flows is to substitute what we know about this opportunity into formula 15.7. The proposal's cash flow in which we are primarily interested at this stage is, of course, CAU_2^{ivs}, which is the most crucial flow for the NPV calculation.[2] The only part of formula 15.7 for which we do not already have a numerical value is CV(CF), the coefficient of variation of the cash flow (the standard deviation per dollar of expectation). We do, however, have all the information necessary to arrive at $CV(CAU_2^{ivs})$. We know that

$$CV(CF) = \frac{\sigma(CF)}{CF}$$

so

$$CV(CAU_2^{ivs}) = \frac{\sigma(CAU_2^{ivs})}{CAU_2^{ivs}}$$
$$= \frac{\$1301.38}{\$1910.61}$$
$$\simeq 0.681$$

Completing the substitutions in formula 15.7,

$$ku_2^{ivs} = \frac{1 + 0.07764}{1 - \dfrac{0.09000 - 0.07764}{0.10000}(0.5)(0.681)} - 1$$

$$= 0.125 \quad \text{or} \quad 12.5\%$$

The CAU_2^{ivs} cash flow has a required rate of return, ku_2^{ivs}, of $12\frac{1}{2}\%$.

"Is that all there is to it?" you ask. "Is $12\frac{1}{2}\%$ the correct discount rate to apply to the CAU_2^{ivs} cash flow in order to value the investment at t_1?" Slow down; it is not quite that simple. We are not yet finished considering the appropriate discount rates for this investment. Think about what the SML formulas show. They give the rate of return appropriate for an *individual* cash flow or capital claim. If this investment were to be traded in the capital market as a single type of capital claim, $12\frac{1}{2}\%$ would be its appropriate required return. But cash flows are not always represented in the capital market by a single type of capital claim.

Very often a cash flow is divided among more than one type of capital claim. *In other words, a cash flow such as* CAU_2^{ivs} *could have both equity and debt claims outstanding against it.* Since the $12\frac{1}{2}\%$ required rate is calculated as if there is only one type of claim against the CAU_2^{ivs} cash flow, that rate corresponds to the required rate of return on a corporation which has only one type of claim outstanding. Such a firm, as we saw in Section III, is an *unlevered* or all-equity firm. The $12\frac{1}{2}\%$ required rate which formula 15.7 indicates as the appropriate required rate for this investment assumes that it is an all-equity investment; $12\frac{1}{2}\%$ is the ku rate for the CAU_2^{ivs} cash flow.

Is the ku rate appropriate for this (or, for that matter, any) investment? The answer, as you no doubt have come to expect, is that it depends. Specifically, it depends on how the investment is *financed*. Figure 16.1 can help our understanding of this point. It essentially reproduces the general relation-

---

[2]More generally, the $(CAU_T^{ivs} - IVS_T^{ivs})$ cash flow is of interest in NPV calculations, and would be used here, except that $IVS_2^{ivs} = \$0.00$.

ships between various required rates, capital costs, and capital structure.[3] The $\theta \leftrightarrow k$ relationships shown in Figure 16.1 obey the general rules that Section III indicated as applicable to corporations whose interest payments are deductible for tax purposes, as are those of the corporation considering this investment.

In essence, the SML formula has given us the ku rate for this investment. In Figure 16.1 this is the rate for $\theta = 0$. This is the $ku_2^{ivs} = 0.125$ on the left-hand vertical axis; it would be the appropriate discount rate if the investment were to be entirely financed by equity (that is, generates only equity values). The procedure for finding the value of the investment in that situation would simply be to discount the CAU_2^{ivs} cash flow at $12\frac{1}{2}\%$. There is nothing particularly incorrect about doing that as long as we recognize that the resulting with-acceptance corporation would have a capital structure composed of the without-acceptance corporation's financing ($\theta = 0.15$) and the unlevered investment's financing ($\theta = 0$). The with-acceptance corporation's θ would thus be *less* than 0.15.

Let us assume, however, that the without-acceptance corporation knew what it was doing when it set its θ equal to 0.15, perhaps for such reasons as were mentioned in the conclusion to Section III. Unless someone

FIGURE 16.1   Investment required rates, costs of capital, and capital structure

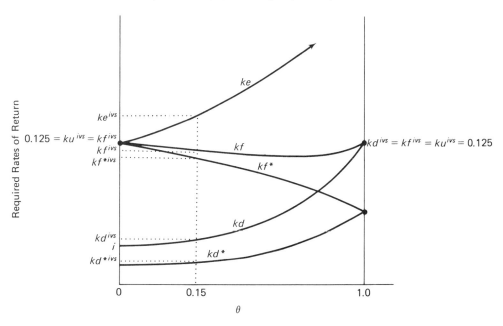

[3]The other financing decision (capital acquisition/disbursement), you recall, does not affect any of the required rates or capital costs.

tells us something to the contrary, we shall therefore assume that the with-acceptance corporation should also end up with a $\theta = 0.15$. Simple arithmetic tells us that $VD^{ivs}/VF^{ivs} = \theta^{ivs}$ must also equal 0.15. *The investment must be financed exactly the same way as the without-acceptance corporation if the with-acceptance corporation is to maintain the same capital structure it had previously.*[4] Therefore, the required rates and capital costs for this investment will be those indicated in Figure 16.1 for $\theta = 0.15$.

"Well, that sounds reasonable enough," you say. "And we already have a set of such rates for $\theta = 0.15$ from the without-acceptance corporation." Be careful here; don't leap too quickly. The rates for the without-acceptance corporation are indeed based on a $\theta = 0.15$, but they are also based on a *different ku* from that of the investment.[5] Since the *ku* of the investment is lower than the without-acceptance corporation, the investment's rates will show the same general behavior relative to θ, but will be lower, because the investment, even though financed in exactly the same mix of debt and equity, is, in a basic operational sense, less risky.

Finding the rates appropriate for an investment, therefore, requires both a knowledge of its basic riskiness (to get its ku^{ivs}) and its financing (to get its kf^{*ivs} and other rates).[6] We have its *ku*. All that remains is to find how that rate is affected by a $\theta = 0.15$, and we will have the rates appropriate for valuing the investment.

Figure 16.1 shows generally what the investment's required rates and capital costs are when its $\theta = 0.15$ and its $ku^{ivs} = 0.125$. The actual calculations of these rates involve using the capital structure relationships from Section III, and to save space here, we have placed these calculations in Appendix V.C. Specifically the rates are

$$ku^{ivs} = 0.12500$$
$$kf^{ivs} = 0.12474$$
$$kf^{*ivs} = 0.11860$$
$$kd^{ivs} = 0.07870$$
$$kd^{*ivs} = 0.03778$$
$$ke^{ivs} = 0.13286$$

If you wish, you can record these on Figure 16.1 to verify that their levels are reasonable.

---

[4]The easiest way to see this would be for you to return to Table 16.1 and find the θ^{ivs} for the risk-constant investment. It should and does equal 0.15, since we held that financing constant.

[5]The *ku* for the *without* corporation in period p_2 is 0.18259, as we saw in Section III. This indicates a higher operational risk than does the investment's *ku* at 0.125.

[6]This is true when interest is deductible for tax purposes. When it is not, $ku^{ivs} = kf^{ivs} = kf^{*ivs}$ for all θ's, as we saw in Section III. In that situation the SML rate is all we need for valuing an investment.

INVESTMENT NET PRESENT VALUE

We now have all the information necessary to complete this risk-altering corporate investment decision. The procedure from now on is identical to the risk-constant decision we studied earlier in this section. First, and most important, we shall see whether or not the investment is desirable. As we know, the best way to do this is to calculate the net present value of the investment. This will be the change in existing shareholder wealth if the investment is accepted:

$$\text{NPV}_1^{ivs} = \frac{\text{CAU}_2^{ivs} - \text{IVS}_2^{ivs}}{1 + kf_2^{*ivs}} + \text{CAU}_1^{ivs} - \text{IVS}_1^{ivs}$$

$$= \frac{\$1910.61 - \$0.00}{1.11860} + \$0.00 - \$1274.25$$

$$= \$433.79$$

The NPV of the investment is \$433.79. Existing shareholder wealth will increase by that amount if the investment is accepted, so it will be. Notice that the NPV of this investment is \$83.04 more than the risk-constant version we saw earlier (\$433.79 − \$350.75 = \$83.04). Since the investments are identical in every way but risk, the lower risk of this investment gives shareholders \$83.04 more present wealth than its risk-constant counterpart.

OTHER INVESTMENT VALUES

Calculating the little corporation values of the investment:

$$\text{VF}_1^{ivs} = \frac{\text{CAU}_2^{ivs} - \text{IVS}_2^{ivs}}{1 + kf_2^{*ivs}}$$

$$= \frac{\$1910.61}{1.11860}$$

$$= \$1708.04$$

And with $\theta = 0.15$ for the investment,

$$\text{VD}_1^{ivs} = \text{VF}_1^{ivs}(\theta^{ivs})$$

$$= \$1708.04(0.15)$$

$$= \$256.21$$

and, therefore,

$$\text{VE}_1^{ivs} = \text{VF}_1^{ivs} - \text{VD}_1^{ivs}$$

$$= \$1708.04 - \$256.21$$

$$= \$1451.83$$

WITH-ACCEPTANCE CORPORATE VALUES

Using these investment values we can easily find the corporate with-acceptance values:

$$\text{VF}_1^{w} = \text{VF}_1^{wo} + \text{VF}_1^{ivs}$$

$$= \$1500.00 + \$1708.04$$

$$= \$3208.04$$

$$\text{VD}_1^{w} = \text{VD}_1^{wo} + \text{VD}_1^{ivs}$$

$$= \$225.00 + \$256.21$$

$$= \$481.21$$

$$VE_1^w = VE_1^{wo} + VE_1^{ivs}$$
$$= \$1275.00 + \$1451.83$$
$$= \$2726.83$$

Note that the capital structure of the with-acceptance corporation is

$$\frac{VD_1^w}{VF_1^w} = \frac{\$481.21}{\$3208.04} = 0.15 = \theta^w$$

The corporate capital structure has been held constant with acceptance.

INVESTMENT AND WITH-ACCEPTANCE CORPORATE CASH FLOWS The cash-flow expectations for the risk-altering investment and with-acceptance corporation are calculated just as for the risk-constant example. Looking first at the t_2 cash flows for the investment, if VD_1^{ivs} is $256.21 and kd_2^{ivs} is 7.870%:

$$I_2^{ivs} = VD_1^{ivs}(kd_2^{ivs})$$
$$= \$256.21(0.07870)$$
$$= \$20.16$$

If $\tau = 0.52$,

$$ITS_2^{ivs} = I_2^{ivs}(\tau)$$
$$= \$20.16(0.52)$$
$$= \$10.49$$

And since t_2 is the terminal point,

$$PP_2^{ivs} = VD_1^{ivs}$$
$$= \$256.21$$

The remaining t_2 cash flows for the investment are mere arithmetic. Given the $CAU_2^{ivs} = \$1910.61$:

	t_2
$CAU_2^{ivs} =$	$1910.61
$ITS_2^{ivs} =$	10.49
$CAC_2^{ivs} =$	1921.10
$I_2^{ivs} =$	20.16
$CAF_2^{ivs} =$	1900.94
$PP_2^{ivs} =$	256.21
$CDD_2^{ivs} =$	276.37
$NDC_2^{ivs} =$	0.00
$NCDD_2^{ivs} =$	276.37
$CAE_2^{ivs} =$	1644.73
$CRF_2^{ivs} =$	0.00
$CDE_2^{ivs} =$	1644.73
$NEC_2^{ivs} =$	0.00
$NCDE_2^{ivs} =$	1644.73
$TCC_2^{ivs} \equiv IVS_2^{ivs} =$	0.00

The t_1 cash flows will be influenced, as we saw earlier in Chapter 13, by the way the investment outlay is supplied. Let us suppose that the company decides to repay all its outstanding debt at t_1, which you recall has a value of $VD_1^{ivs} = \$225.00$, and float a new debt issue at t_1 of that amount plus the investment debt capital necessary. Thus, $PP_1^{ivs} = \$225.00$, and $NDC_1^{ivs} = PP_1^{ivs} + VD_1^{ivs} = \$225.00 + \$256.21 = \$481.21$. As before, we shall also assume that the remaining cash necessary to come up with $IVS_1^{ivs} = \$1274.25$ is made up from retention of corporate cash at t_1. Therefore, $CRF_1^{ivs} = \$1274.25 - \$481.21 = \$793.04$, and no new equity cash is necessary.

The resulting investment cash flows at t_1 are:

$$t_1$$

$CAU_1^{ivs} = \$$	0.00
$ITS_1^{ivs} =$	0.00
$CAC_1^{ivs} =$	0.00
$I_1^{ivs} =$	0.00
$CAF_1^{ivs} =$	0.00
$PP_1^{ivs} =$	225.00
$CDD_1^{ivs} =$	225.00
$NDC_1^{ivs} =$	481.21
$NCDD_1^{ivs} =$	−256.21
$CAE_1^{ivs} =$	−225.00
$CRF_1^{ivs} =$	793.04
$CDE_1^{ivs} =$	−1018.04
$NEC_1^{ivs} =$	0.00
$NCDE_1^{ivs} =$	−1018.04
$TCC_1^{ivs} \equiv IVS_1^{ivs} =$	1274.25

Gathering these results together, we can present the cash flows, values, and required rates for the without- and with-acceptance corporations and for the risk-altering investment itself. We do that in Table 16.2. The values and cash flows of the with-acceptance corporation are merely the summed values and cash flows of the without-acceptance corporation and the investment itself.

The only part of Table 16.2 which is at all new in concept is section B, the required rates and capital costs. In the counterpart Table 16.1 for the risk-constant investment, the k's for the "with," "without," and investment were all the same; that is, $ke^{wo} = ke^{ivs} = ke^w$, $kf^{wo} = kf^{ivs} = kf^w$, and so forth. In this situation, however, since we are studying a risk-altering investment, the investment required rates differ from the without-acceptance corporate rates. A major part of this section has been devoted to explaining why and how the risk of the investment causes its required rates to be different from those of the firm considering it. The rates applicable to the invest-

TABLE 16.2 Risk-altering investment

A. Cash Flows	t_1 Without acceptance	t_1 Investment proposal	t_1 With acceptance	t_2 Without acceptance	t_2 Investment proposal	t_2 With acceptance
$RCPT	$6250.00	$ 0.00	$6250.00	$7500.00	$5000.00	$1250.00
$EXPT	3976.50	0.00	3976.50	4800.75	2400.00	7200.75
GCFO	2273.50	0.00	2273.50	2699.25	2600.00	5299.25
GTAX	1182.22	0.00	1182.22	1403.61	1352.00	2755.61
NCFO	1091.28	0.00	1091.28	1295.64	1248.00	2543.64
DTS	936.00	0.00	936.00	468.00	662.61	1130.61
CAU	2027.28	0.00	2027.28	1763.64	1910.61	3674.25
ITS	18.72	0.00	18.72	9.36	10.49	19.85
CAC	2046.00	0.00	2046.00	1773.00	1921.10	3694.10
I	36.00	0.00	36.00	18.00	20.16	38.16
CAF	2010.00	0.00	2010.00	1755.00	1900.94	3655.94
PP	225.00	225.00	450.00	225.00	256.21	481.21
CDD	261.00	225.00	486.00	243.00	276.37	519.37
NDC	0.00	481.21	481.21	0.00	0.00	0.00
NCDD	261.00	−256.21	4.79	243.00	276.37	519.37
CAE	1785.00	−225.00	1560.00	1530.00	1644.73	3174.73
CRF	0.00	793.04	793.04	0.00	0.00	0.00
CDE	1785.00	−1018.04	766.96	1530.00	1644.73	3174.73
NEC	0.00	0.00	0.00	0.00	0.00	0.00
NCDE	1785.00	−1018.04	766.96	1530.00	1644.73	3174.73
TCC $\equiv$ IVS	0.00	1274.25	1274.25	0.00	0.00	0.00

B. k's with $\theta = 0.15$ and $\tau = 0.52$

	wo	ivs	w
ke_2	0.20000	0.13286	0.16425
kd_2	0.08000	0.07870	0.07931
kd_2^*	0.03840	0.03778	0.03807
kf_2	0.18200	0.12474	0.15151
kf_2^*	0.17576	0.11860	0.14533

$$k_T^w = k_T^{wo} \frac{V_{T-1}^{wo}}{V_{T-1}^w} + k_T^{ivs} \frac{V_{T-1}^{ivs}}{V_{T-1}^w}$$

C. Values $(V_T^{wo} + V_T^{ivs} = V_T^w)$

$VE_1^{wo} = \$1275.00 \qquad VE_1^{ivs} = \$1451.83$
$VD_1^{wo} = \quad 225.00 \qquad VD_1^{ivs} = \quad 256.21$
$VF_1^{wo} = 1500.00 \qquad VF_1^{ivs} = 1708.04$
$VE_1^w = \$2726.83$
$VD_1^w = \quad 481.21$
$VF_1^w = \quad 3208.04$

D. $NPV_1^{ivs} = VF_1^{ivs} + (CAU_1^{ivs} - IVS_1^{ivs}) = \$1708.04 + \$0.00 - \$1274.25 = \$433.79$
$\Delta PWE_1 = VE_1^{ivs} + NCDE_1^{ivs} = \$1451.83 + (\$-1018.04) = \$433.79$

ment itself were finally developed only a few pages ago. We should therefore feel fairly comfortable with the first two columns of required rates in section B of Table 16.2.

WITH-ACCEPTANCE REQUIRED RATES AND CAPITAL COSTS But what about the third column, the one headed "with"? That implies the rates recorded below it are appropriate for the corporate cash-flow expectations with acceptance. Where did we get these rates? Actually, they are quite easy to find. As noted in the table, *the required rates and capital costs for the with-acceptance corporation are merely value-weighted averages of the rates for the investment and the without-acceptance corporation.* Thus,

$$ke_T^w = ke_T^{wo} \frac{VE_{T-1}^{wo}}{VE_{T-1}^w} + ke_T^{ivs} \frac{VE_{T-1}^{ivs}}{VE_{T-1}^w} \qquad [16.1]$$

so

$$ke_2^w = (0.20)\frac{\$1275.00}{\$2726.83} + (0.13286)\frac{\$1451.83}{\$2726.83}$$

and

$$ke_2^w = 0.16425$$

The other required rates and capital costs are calculated similarly for the with-acceptance corporation, their general formulas being

$$kd_{\scriptscriptstyle T}^w = kd_{\scriptscriptstyle T}^{wo}\frac{\mathrm{VD}_{\scriptscriptstyle T-1}^{wo}}{\mathrm{VD}_{\scriptscriptstyle T-1}^w} + kd_{\scriptscriptstyle T}^{ivs}\frac{\mathrm{VD}_{\scriptscriptstyle T-1}^{ivs}}{\mathrm{VD}_{\scriptscriptstyle T-1}^w} \qquad [16.2]$$

with kd^{*w} calculated using kd^{*wo}, kd^{*ivs}, and the same value weights; and

$$kf_{\scriptscriptstyle T}^w = kf_{\scriptscriptstyle T}^{wo}\frac{\mathrm{VF}_{\scriptscriptstyle T-1}^{wo}}{\mathrm{VF}_{\scriptscriptstyle T-1}^w} + kf_{\scriptscriptstyle T}^{ivs}\frac{\mathrm{VF}_{\scriptscriptstyle T-1}^{ivs}}{\mathrm{VF}_{\scriptscriptstyle T-1}^w} \qquad [16.3]$$

with kf^{*w} calculated using kf^{*wo}, kf^{*ivs}, and the same value weights. (Of course, as long as $\theta^{ivs} = \theta^{wo}$, the value weights in each of formulas 16.1, 16.2, and 16.3 will be identical—about 0.4676 and 0.5324, respectively, in this example). You may wish to verify the accuracy of these *with* rates in Table 16.2 by discounting the *with* cash flows and comparing the results to the *with* values listed. For example, from Section II we know that

$$\mathrm{VF}_1^w = \frac{\mathrm{CAC}_2^w - \mathrm{IVS}_2^w}{1 + kf_2^w}$$

Therefore,

$$\mathrm{VF}_1^w = \frac{\$3694.10 - \$0.00}{1.15151}$$

$$= \$3208.04$$

which is the same value we calculated by adding VF_1^{wo} to VF_1^{ivs}, ($1500.00 + $1708.04 = $3208.04). Before this section is finished we shall return to this point about with-acceptance required rates and discuss the *economic reason* why they are mere weighted averages of the "without" and investment/divestment proposal rates.

This completes the analysis of this particular investment example. The finding is that, if accepted, it will increase the wealth of the without-acceptance corporate equityholders by $433.79. It therefore is a good investment. As we saw in Section I, however, not all investments are good in the sense that present wealth increases upon their acceptance. A bad investment would have resulted in a decrease in shareholder wealth. One of the important lessons from the risk-altering example is that equity present wealth effects of corporate investments depend not only on the expected cash flows from the investment but also the risk associated with those cash flows. For example this particular investment increased equity wealth more than the risk-constant investment we examined, and the only difference between the two investments was their risks. Similarly, by making the assumption of a much higher

$\rho(\text{CAU}_2^{ivs}, r_m)$ CV(CAU_2^{ivs}) risk with the same cash-flow expectations, the investment can be rendered less good than the risk-constant version or even totally undesirable (a negative effect on shareholder wealth). The SML relationship would, in the latter case, indicate required rates which result in a negative net present value for the investment.

Conclusion to Section V

REVIEW OF RISK-ALTERING INVESTMENT DECISION PROCEDURES

The numerical example we have studied in Chapter 16 constitutes a bona fide risk-altering corporate investment decision with typical effects on market values and shareholder wealth resulting from acceptance. To review briefly our analytical procedure:

1. The investment proposal's cash-flow probability distributions were given in the form of expectations (means) of the distributions and standard deviations of the distributions. (Specifically, CAU_2^{ivs} and $\sigma(\text{CAU}_2^{ivs})$ are the necessary data.) In addition, expectations about returns from holding the market portfolio and the investment's relatedness to those returns were given. [Specifically, $E(r_m)$, $\sigma(r_m)$, and $\rho(\text{CAU}_2^{ivs}, r_m)$ were given, although all of the information, including CAU_2^{ivs} and $\sigma(\text{CAU}_2^{ivs})$, could have been calculated from a joint probability distribution of the r_m and CAU_2^{ivs} outcomes.]

2. Using formula 15.7, the SML relationship for individual cash flows, we calculated the required return on the CAU_2^{ivs} cash flow, which assumes it to be traded as an individual issue in the capital market. With that ku_2^{ivs}, we used the capital structure relationships from Section III and the knowledge of how the investment was to be financed to determine the appropriate required rates and capital costs for the investment: ke^{ivs}, kd^{ivs}, kf^{ivs}, kd^{*ivs}, and kf^{*ivs}.

3. Knowledge of the market rates appropriate for the investment and its financing allowed us to calculate the net present value (equity wealth effect) and the investment's or little corporation's market values. These values, added to the without-acceptance corporate values, yielded the with-acceptance values for the corporation were it to adopt the investment.

4. Making reasonable assumptions as to the capital acquisition/disbursement decision the corporation would make to be able to get the cash to invest, we were able to construct financial cash-flow statements for the investment and the with-acceptance corporation.

5. We discovered that the required rates of return and capital costs for the with-acceptance corporation are value-weighted averages of the "without" and investment rates and costs. We also found that all required rates and capital costs—investment, *without*, and *with*—when applied to the appropriate financial cash flows, gave values identical to

our previous calculations, and were entirely consistent with the theoretical valuation relationships developed in earlier shapters.

In sum, we have fully illustrated a corporate investment decision and its effects when the proposed investment has a risk which differs from that of the firm considering it.

Important as the analytical procedure is, perhaps even more important are the *economic* ideas involved in the risk-altering corporate investment decision. As we saw in the risk-constant example, a corporate investment decision involves a judgment as to whether or not a new set of future (and current) cash flows should be added to those of the existing corporation. A positive effect on shareholder wealth indicates yes, a negative effect, no. The risk-altering investment theory has disclosed elements of that decision, however, which were not obvious when the risk-constant example was studied. These are related to the risk measure employed, its economic basis in the capital market, and the risk-averting activities of capital-market participants.

Capital-market participants are the people who supply investment cash to corporations either through direct purchases of capital claims or through foregone corporate capital disbursements which permit the firm to retain needed corporate cash. Those participants are risk-averse. They require higher rates of return on their holdings (and hence the cash they contribute to corporations) for any higher risk they bear. Capital-market participants, however, do not hold only single corporate capital claims. Because they are risk-averse, they diversify their personal holdings so as to take advantage of the portfolio effect of risk reduction when claims' returns are less than perfectly correlated. Since all participants do this, the only risk of an individual claim for which compensation is required is the effect of including that claim in an efficiently diversified portfolio. The structure of rates of return in the capital market is based on participants holding efficient portfolios of individual capital claims. The return required on each claim is determined by the amount of individual claim risk which is not diversified away when the claim is held in efficiently diversified portfolios. The amount of compensation for each level of such "undiversifiable" risk is given by our SML formulas.

By interpreting the SML relationship for corporate cash flows, we can arrive at required rates of return for proposed corporate investments. *Basically, the rates that we develop in this way tell us the returns which the capital market would require if the investment existed as a little corporation whose capital claims were traded in the market, and which, of course, were also held in efficiently diversified portfolios by capital-market participants.* Such rates are appropriate for discounting the cash flows of the proposed investment, to see if it should be added to the existing corporation.[7]

---

[7]This does *not* imply that only investments which can exist independent of the corporation should be analyzed this way. Even those whose cash flows depend uniquely on the existing firm must pass this market test.

The risk measure and risk-adjusted required rates of return that we use are therefore correctly based both in capital-market participants' risk aversions and in portfolio-holding proclivities. The decision by a corporation to accept or reject an investment (or divestment) really requires an answer to the question of whether or not capital-market participants would be willing to hold that investment in (or exclude that divestment from) their efficient portfolios. Our risk measure and SML-related required rates of return answer that question and allow actual calculations of value and wealth changes which would result from the acceptance decision.

CORPORATE DIVERSIFICATION

There is one important observation that we should make about participants' risk aversions "feeding through" to corporate investment decisions. Consider the following: We know that by combining risky capital claims into efficient portfolios, market participants can decrease risk, and are made happier thereby. Should not the corporation also seek to combine its risky real investments into efficiently diversified portfolios of productive assets in the same way that participants do for capital claims? Why does our theory not mention such a possibility?

At first glance this seems an eminently reasonable query. If diversification to reduce risk is good, should not corporations do it, too? The answer, however, may surprise you. It is no. Think of the situation this way. As we have seen time after time, the capital market is only willing to value capital claims for what the claims *can* and the market *cannot* do by itself. For example, we know that capital structure alterations "without deductibility" have no effect on shareholder wealth, for such activities can be reproduced by participants within their own portfolios through personal borrowing and lending. Similarly, we saw that the capital acquisition/disbursement decision of the corporation is irrelevant for the same reason. Therefore, since capital-market participants can, in the same sense, choose the amount and type of diversification they desire by altering the composition of their personal portfolios, there is no value in a corporation doing it for them. Capital-market participants would be unwilling to pay a premium for the capital claims of a corporation merely because the company combined a set of activities under a single claim, when the participants, if they so desired, could have made that combination in their own portfolios.[8]

The argument that corporate diversification is irrelevant must be interpreted carefully. For example, we are not saying that corporate investment has no benefits for shareholders. We have just completed numerical examples which show that benefits are indeed possible. The wealth effects of corporate

---

[8]Perhaps the most intuitively pleasing illustration of this is the "conglomerate merger" merely for the purpose of portfolio-type risk reduction. Mergers of this type, which are purported to have occurred with great frequency in the 1960s, were often argued in terms of "stabilizing earnings per share." Such a merger could as easily be performed in participants' share portfolios, so would carry no benefits.

investment, however, are related to the returns and *nondiversifiable* risk of the investment. That is what the capital market examines when setting claim values. The corporation may, if it chooses, "diversify away" all or part of its diversifiable risk by adopting investments, each having the necessary relatedness to the existing corporation. But the capital market has already diversified away such corporate risk in the personal portfolios of its participants, so it pays no particular attention to the corporate activity of pure diversification.[9]

ELABORA-TIONS OF INVESTMENT THEORY

Our analysis of the corporate investment decision to this point is complete in its theoretical and conceptual coverage of the economic factors important to this decision. Some characteristics of the examples we have used, however, are not fully representative of the range of actual investment decisions that corporate financial managers face on a day-to-day basis. Although, again, our purpose is not to provide a detailed "cookbook" for corporate financial management, we would be doing a less-than-adequate job if we did not discuss the applicability of this theory to actual investment decisions.

We shall take two approaches to this discussion. First, we shall describe in the subsections that follow some of the applicabilities and limits of this theory of investment decision making. Second, we shall present some quantitative illustrations of the elaborations to the basic investment theory in appendixes to this section. Appendix V.A illustrates a divestment decision, Appendix V.B discusses the present impact of future asset acquisition/divestment decisions, Appendix V.C is the calculation of capital-structure-determined required rates for investment cash flows (mentioned earlier), Appendix V.D addresses the question of multiperiod required rates in the CAPM, and Appendix V.E illustrates the use of the FCF statement in estimating cash flows for real-world investments.

MULTI-PERIOD INVEST-MENTS

The most obvious artificiality of our investment theory to this point has been its single-period nature. The investment examples considered and the capital market risk–return relationships we developed have all used only "now" and "later" time points, with no continuation past "later." This is not, of course, a very common pattern of corporate investment cash flows; most extend for more than one period into the future. Our reasons for using this single-period development, however, should also be obvious: Single-period examples are the simplest, by far the most easily understood, and sacrifice nothing in the way of economically important concepts. All of the most important ideas of corporate investment theory appear in single-period illustrations. Complete

[9]This implies that the relatedness of the investment cash flows to the without-acceptance corporate cash flows is unimportant. Be careful to remember that the relatedness we are speaking of is a purely statistical or stochastic relatedness. If the investment's cash flows were *economically* related to the without-acceptance corporation's cash flows, such effects would appear in the investment cash-flow estimates directly.

honesty, however, also requires us to report that the development of corporate financial theory as it depends upon the SML relationships in this section has simply not progressed in a rigorous fashion beyond the single-period model of the capital market. In the sense of having a complete, fully applicable theoretical structure for multiperiod corporate investment decisions we are at somewhat of a loss. Nevertheless, there are important applications of the single-period ideas to multiple-period investment situations which we can feel fairly comfortable in discussing, and we shall now do just that.

The general procedure for making corporate investment decisions applies to multiperiod situations as well as to single-period. The expectations of investment cash-flow distributions are formulated for each future time point and these are discounted back to the present with the appropriate rates. A positive NPV indicates acceptance, a negative NPV, rejection. As Appendix V.B will show, the formulation of financial cash-flow statements for multiple future periods is no different from their single-period formulation. You can, however, begin to see the complexities of such decisions by considering a single investment opportunity that has cash-flow expectations for several future time points, when there are *different* riskinesses associated with the cash-flow expectations at each different time point. Conceivably then, each cash flow may deserve its own unique discount rate. Discounting the flows in such a situation would be a rather complicated, but nonetheless possible task. The real difficulty is in discovering exactly what those rates should be.

As we said before, the theory of capital-market risk–return relationships has been rigorously developed only for single-period situations. But the basic economics underlying the theory would apply to any number of time periods across which an investment is expected to have economic impact. In certain situations, we can proceed, based on this conviction, to find multiperiod rates. For example, if an investment under consideration has multiple future cash flows but is essentially a "scale" type of investment (risk-constant), the rates that apply to the existing enterprise apply as well to the investment. Furthermore, if the investment's required rates are not known, but future cash flows are each expected to bear about the same risk (that is, standard deviation per dollar of expected cash flow, and relatedness of expected cash flow to overall economic activity), their required rates must be comparable to what is being offered in the capital market by other claims of comparable risk. This latter example, if you consider it carefully, is not an unreasonable description of many real-world corporate investments. Given that some productive activity is to generate all the future cash flows, they probably all have much the same $\rho(CF, r_m)CV(CF)$. There is little reason to expect that the characteristics of the distribution of possible cash-flow outcomes for any one period would differ greatly from any other period's expected cash-flow deviation per dollar and relatedness to the market. If that is true, our SML relationship in formula

15.7 may well be appropriate for finding the single rate applicable to the multiple future cash flows of the investment.[10]

In more complex multiperiod investments, where future cash flows bear differing CV(CF)'s or $\rho(\text{CF}, r_m)$'s, theoretically acceptable rates are more difficult to describe. But the basic determinants of such rates must be generally those described in this chapter, and reasonable approximations of such rates can probably be found by finding what the market is allowing for cash flows with similar characteristics, either in a single claim or as separate claims.

RENEWAL DECISION

There is one final observation of practical importance that we should make about the multiperiod corporate investment decision. In Section II we pointed out that future periods' cash-flow estimates are valid only as of a single time point (now). It is entirely possible that when the next time point is actually reached, the estimates for future cash flows may be altered. *This implies that as time actually passes, even the existing corporation* (which we call the without-acceptance company in this section) *must make a decision at each time point whether or not to continue operating, and if so, whether existing investment plans should be altered.* Such a decision encompasses the renewal of existing productive assets (an "economic depreciation" investment decision) "as planned," and any necessary changes in those plans, including the option of divesting part or all (liquidation) of the productive assets of the corporation.

This observation may seem so obvious as to be trivial, but it is important to recognize that even when a corporation is not considering any new investments, the decision even to continue operating as planned for at least one more period requires, in theory at least, a multiperiod investment decision of the type we have described. From just the simple decisions that we have seen in this section, it should be apparent that allowing such renewal investment to be made by default can have very significant effects on shareholder present wealth.

MULTIPLE INVESTMENT OPPORTUNITIES

Thus far, our corporations have made their investment decisions while confronted with only a single investment opportunity. In fact, however, companies may find themselves considering *several* investments at each time point. How are such decisions made in a manner consistent with our theory? The answer depends on the economic relationships among the investment opportunities.

Recall that in Section I we distinguished between *economic* and *statistical* or *stochastic* relationships. Economic relatedness between investments means simply that the acceptance or rejection of one opportunity has some

---

[10] A constant required rate for all future periods would, of course, require not only $\rho(\text{CF}, r_m)\text{CV(CF)}$ constancy, but also the influences of i, $E(r_m)$, and $\sigma(r_m)$ to be constant.

effect on the cash-flow distribution of another opportunity. The most severe form of economic relatedness, we said, is *mutual exclusivity*. That exists when the acceptance of one investment implies the rejection of another. In that situation the two are alternatives to each other. Two pieces of equipment, either of which could be used to manufacture the same product, exhibit this type of relatedness. Less severe but equally important types of economic relatedness do not imply mutual exclusivity but do portend some cash-flow effect of one opportunity on another. A company considering the installation of a new lighting system and a new product line requiring intricate assemblies could be faced with such a decision. The lighting system and the product line could each be adopted alone. Or both could be accepted. But the two taken together would probably result in cash-flow distributions different from merely the sum of each accepted in the absence of the other.[11]

When investment opportunities are *economically independent*, it means simply that the acceptance or rejection of any one has no effect on the cash flows of the others. A corporation contemplating an investment in marketable securities and a new production facility would probably find the two economically independent.

Statistical relatedness among two investment opportunities is measured by the level of the correlation coefficient of their joint probability distribution. (You recall that a high positive coefficient, p close to $+1$, means that when one investment has a return above its expectation, the other tends to have similar outcomes, and that when one has low outcomes, the other also tends to be low; and vice versa for a p close to -1.) *Statistical relatedness implies no necessary economic or causal relationship among investments.* The correlation coefficient between the cash-flow expectations of two investments could be caused by their being economically related to each other, or to some common influence; or it might happen merely by chance alone.

In our theory, economic relatedness is the only type that matters. It should be obvious to you why corporate financial managers must be concerned about potential cash-flow causal effects of one investment on another. Pure statistical relatedness, however, is unimportant when capital-market participants can diversify their personal portfolios the way we have described. If corporate financial managers recognize and deal with economic relationships among investment opportunities, the only importance of statistical relatedness would be for corporate diversification purposes and, as we have argued, capital-market participants take care of their diversification needs themselves.[12] We shall return to this point again when we consider imperfections in the corporate investment decision.

[11]Economic relationships may, of course, affect both the expectation and risk of cash-flow distributions.

[12]Economic relatedness effects on cash-flow risks cannot be duplicated by capital-market participants, so such effects must be considered in the analysis.

ECONOMIC RELATED-NESS AND MULTIPLE INVESTMENT OPPORTU-NITIES

Since, when considering interactions among multiple investment opportunities, corporate financial managers need be concerned only about economic relatedness, we shall discuss such considerations in enough detail to give their flavor, but, as usual, leave the application specifics to texts designed for that purpose. The bibliography identifies several such references.

Mutually exclusive opportunities present no problem. Each investment is analyzed as the examples we have discussed singularly; the best alternative is accepted and the others rejected. Economically independent opportunities also are not difficult. Each investment is analyzed singularly; those with positive NPV's are accepted, those with negative NPV's rejected. In the case where a firm is faced with a number of opportunities comprising a mixture of economically independent and mutually exclusive relationships, it is most efficient first to identify and eliminate from consideration the losers in the mutual exclusivity relationships, leaving a group of economically independent opportunities which can then be judged singularly as acceptable or not, each standing on its own merit.

When multiple investment opportunities have more complex economic relationships, the analysis of the set also becomes more complex. One way to proceed would be to evaluate separately all possible combinations of investments. This would provide the correct equity-wealth-maximizing decision, but would, in the common situation of several opportunities, be very costly in time and analytical cost.[13]

A more reasonable procedure would be to group the economically related opportunities into packages of mutually exclusive alternatives, which packages are economically independent of each other. Then, the best alternative within each package is selected, and the set of "winners" is evaluated as economically independent opportunities, all, some, or none of which may finally pass the NPV ≥ 0 test.[14]

Regardless of the particular analytical procedure chosen to evaluate multiple investment opportunities, the final test is, of course, that the set of investments which are accepted provide shareholders with a greater present wealth than any other set available.

IMPERFEC-TIONS

As with the consideration of imperfections in earlier sections, we shall here point out characteristics of the theory of asset acquisition and divestment which could cause its predictions to differ in some degree from real corporations and capital markets. To begin, recall that the investment decision we have examined also required concurrent attention to financing. In other words, each investment decision a corporation faces implies a related capital acquisition/disbursement decision and a decision whether to maintain or alter capital structure. This means that the imperfections discussed in Sections

---

[13]Both the time required for and the cost of performing investment analyses are absent in our theory.

[14]This procedure is elaborated in references at the end of the section.

III and IV relating to financing also apply to the investment decision. If considerations of shareholder taxation, brokerage fees, and so forth are important, to the extent that financing decisions must take them into account, the investment decision may be affected. The simplest illustration of this would be to consider interest deductibility as an imperfection. In the presence of that imperfection, the corporation could adopt investments less profitable (because of the lower net-of-tax discount rates) than it could in the absence of deductibility.

As implied in footnote 9 to Chapter 13, another real capital-market imperfection can cause an important interaction among an investment (or divestment), its financing, and the capital structure of the with-acceptance corporation. The variability of a proposal's cash flows may be such that, when combined with an existing corporation's cash flows, the *optimal θ* of the with-acceptance corporation could differ from the without-acceptance optimal θ. Recall that, when default costs exist, optimal θ's depend not only on interest tax subsidies' values (VITS's) but also on the present value of default costs (VCD's) as we argued in Chapter 10:

$$VF = VU + VITS - VCD \qquad [10.6]$$

Should the investment's standard deviation of expected cash flows portend a higher probability of default, the with-acceptance corporation could find that a θ^w lower than θ^{wo} is optimal. Lower investment cash flow variabilities could imply higher optimal θ^w's.

Indeed, it is true, as one problem at the end of this section illustrates, that the desirability of an investment depends upon whether it can be financed at·a high enough θ^{ivs}. And the optimal θ^{ivs}, as we have just seen, may itself be affected by the investment's cash flow variability. More generally, an investment opportunity may be stochastically related to the without-acceptance corporation in such a way as to affect default probabilities and thus costs, as might multiple investments be related among themselves. The multiple interactions implied in such situations illustrate, if nothing else, why good corporate financial managers are very highly paid.

Another possible imperfection that could influence the corporate investment decision would be any effect on required rates due simply to the total number of dollars that a corporation raises for investment purposes at any time point. In the theory we have developed, our corporations can acquire capital in any amount, through a combination of internal and external sources, and the required rates will be determined only by the characteristics of the investment cash-flow probability distributions. It is possible in real capital markets, however, that small companies may not have as easy access to primary capital markets as do large, well-known corporations, regardless of the investments to be financed. In such a situation corporations with better access to capital may be able to undertake investments that other firms must forego.

The extreme example of this capital-access imperfection is something called "capital rationing," wherein only a certain number of *total dollars* are available for investment at each time point, regardless of the suitable investments that might be discovered. This situation appears most often in multidivisional enterprises where the investment decision is made at the divisional level and the financing obtained at the headquarters level of the corporation.[15] The bibliography lists several references that attempt to deal with this situation from the viewpoint of the investment decision maker.

The imperfections considered to this point (with the possible exception of default costs as discussed above and in Section III) present only minor theoretical challenges. Actually, they constitute something more akin to complexities of calculation rather than difficulties with the theory. If enough information is obtained, values and cash flows can be found in much the same way as we have done so far, but with admittedly somewhat more intricate analyses. There is another class of imperfections, however, which present more basic theoretical challenges. These have to do with the capital-market valuation mechanism that we have outlined in this section.

In the process of constructing our capital market, we made numerous assumptions about the way capital-market participants behave, and about the opportunities they have for holding and trading capital claims and portfolios. For example, one of the important characteristics of market participants is that they care only about the returns and standard deviations of return expected from their portfolios of holdings. It is possible that capital-market participants are not concerned about standard deviation at all (preferring some other risk measure), and/or are concerned about additional characteristics of their portfolios' return distributions; or it is even possible that non-wealth considerations (such as a love of gambling) affect their decisions about holding capital claims. To the extent that such concerns influence their decisions importantly, real capital markets might not be accurately represented by our theory, and the value results of corporate investment decisions would not correspond to those we have outlined.

Along similar lines, our capital-market participants hold efficiently diversified portfolios of capital claims. It follows in theory, therefore, that

[15]Another typical setting for this phenomenon is governmental institutions, activities, or programs where fixed appropriations or budgets are specified legislatively or administratively in advance for a fiscal year without reference to the possibility of a changing set of investment opportunities during the year. Care should be taken to distinguish between capital rationing arising from external capital-market imperfections and capital rationing caused by internal institutional rigidity or fiat. While the former is lamentable, the latter is inexcusable. External limits on capital are rarely absolute bars to obtaining funds; external dollars are almost always available at *some* price, however high, and while some investment proposals normally acceptable will be unattractive in the face of high capital costs, sufficiently valuable investments will be adopted. By contrast, the rigid, internally imposed budget or appropriation allows no options at all. It makes, implicitly, the economic statement that "no investment proposal is sufficiently attractive; the effective cost of the next dollar of capital is infinite."

corporations do not need to be concerned about the diversification (portfolio effect) of risk in the corporate portfolio of real assets or in the corporate investment decision. In other words, individual participant diversification is a perfect substitute for corporate diversification. If, however, participants were for some reason prohibited from diversifying well (either through ignorance or market frictions of some sort), the corporation would be forced to consider the diversification effects of its investment decisions on the returns (and therefore wealth) of its shareholders. Such corporate investment decisions would be tremendously more complex and costly than the corporate investment decisions that we have examined thus far, requiring analyses of return and cash-flow interrelationships not only with the market but with every other asset owned or potentially owned by the corporation.

In a similar vein, recall that the overall corporate required rates and capital costs with acceptance turned out to be simple weighted averages of the investment and without-acceptance corporate required rates in our examples. The economic reason for this is that *the riskiness of the corporate and investment cash flows is unaffected by their being combined or left separate.* Any statistical relatedness between the investment and corporate cash flows did not affect their risks; the only relatedness that mattered was $\rho(\text{CF}, r_m)$, the correlation with the market. Because market participants can themselves diversify well, they are not concerned with corporate diversification and therefore set required rates based on only nondiversifiable risk, $\rho(\text{CF}, r_m)\text{CV}(\text{CF})$.

If, however, participants cannot or do not themselves diversify, they *would* be concerned with diversification of real investment within the corporation whose claims they hold, and hence, they would also be interested in the relatedness of corporate and investment cash flows. Risk would then become diversifiable within the corporation and $\rho(\text{CF}, r_m)\text{CV}(\text{CF})$ would be an *inappropriate* risk measure for investments. Further, required rates for the with-acceptance corporation would no longer be simple weighted averages of the "without" and investment rates, since they would then need to recognize the risk reduction due to diversification. Again, the complexity of corporate investment analysis under such conditions would be quite awesome.

If this review of possible capital-market imperfections has shaken your confidence in the corporate investment theory we have labored so hard to develop, take heart. We have not said they *are* present, or even if they are, whether they exist in severe enough forms to invalidate the theory. To be perfectly honest, we do not know whether these are important imperfections in real capital markets or not. As we pointed out much earlier in this section, the theory of risk-altering corporate investment decision making is still very much in its infancy. This is especially true regarding empirical tests of real capital markets and their pricing processes. However, such evidence as does exist seems to be largely consistent with the general characteristics of the theory we have put forth. The references to this section include a representative sample of such studies.

Finally, recall that the SML risk–return relationship that we use in arriving at required rates of return assumes that participants can borrow and lend at the risk-free rate, *i*. In reality, we *can lend* at an essentially risk-free rate by buying and holding to maturity securities issued by a special category of institution. Specifically, risk-free securities emanate only from those institutions (usually governmental or quasi-governmental) which also have formal control over the issuance of money which can be used to fulfill the explicit promises made by the security. However, as is obvious to those who have tried, we *cannot borrow* at that rate in real capital markets. Financial theoreticians have developed a statement of capital-market equilibrium incorporating the above conditions. This alternative formulation of the theory also produces a predicted SML. Fortunately, this revised SML differs only slightly (in slope and intercept) from the original SML, and, analytically, is used in exactly the same way. The references at the end of this section list these theoretical works and empirical evidence in their support.

So things do not look so bad after all. The imperfections we know to exist (transactions costs, taxes, and so on) make the analyses somewhat more complicated, but still leave the basic economics of corporate investment theory intact. The more serious imperfections (capital-market pricing processes basically different from ours) seem to be of questionable importance; so the theory, at least at this time, survives them also.

You might reasonably ask why we go to all the trouble to elaborate the more serious imperfections if they turn out to be of no major concern at the moment. There are two reasons why studying them is worthwhile. First, it has by no means been proven that they are unimportant, and should we turn out to be wrong about their impact, ignorance of their potential implications would be inexcusable. Second, and of equal importance, we believe that studying the limitations of a theory can tell you as much about it as studying its workings directly.

CONCLUSION　Excepting the material in the appendixes to this section, we have now completed the theory of corporate asset acquisition and divestment. Although the section is a very long one, the basic idea behind the corporate investment decision is actually quite simple. When a company acquires or divests itself of an asset, it adds or subtracts present and future cash flows attributable to that asset. If shareholder present wealth, calculated in a manner consistent with our valuation formulas of Section II, is greater without the asset being considered, the asset is divested if now held, or rejected as an investment if not now held by the corporation. If shareholder wealth is greater with the asset, it is accepted as an investment, or not divested if presently held.

It took such lengthy effort to develop this simple idea because we saved until this chapter the construction of the capital-market mechanism for compensating participants' risk bearing. The capital asset pricing model (CAPM) is one of the more difficult ideas in the theory of corporate finance, but it, or something like it, is absolutely necessary for an adequate appreciation of the corporate investment decision. The CAPM gave us the appropriate risk measure for corporate cash flows and the market risk–return relationship. These, in turn, allowed us to obtain required rates of return applicable to investment and corporate cash flows. Such information was necessary in order to analyze corporate investment when the risk of the proposed asset acquisition or divestment differed from the without-proposal-acceptance corporation. Once the CAPM relationships are understood, the corporate investment decision involves little more than judicious use of the theories of corporate value, capital structure, and capital acquisition/disbursement which are by now so familiar to you.

Our most important use of the CAPM risk–return characteristics was to illustrate the correct approach to the asset acquisition/disbursement decision. As we said earlier, there really was no pressing need to develop a specific risk measure and market model until we reached this section. Earlier introduction of the model would have been both unnecessary and potentially confusing. This is not to say, however, that the market risk–return ideas we have seen in this section could not apply equally well to other aspects of corporate financial theory we have already discussed.

Consider capital structure theory, for example. We spent significant time and effort in Section III developing the notion of a relationship between required returns and capital structure based on the riskiness of the various capital claims under different θ's. These same ideas can be illustrated with the CAPM and security-market line from this section.

Look at Figure V.1. It contains the essence of capital structure theory with deductibility. Point U on the SML is the return–risk location of an unlevered corporation $[ku, \rho(\text{CAU} - \text{IVS}, r_m)\text{CV}(\text{CAU} - \text{IVS})]$. As that company substitutes debt for equity (increases θ) under conditions of interest deductibility, we know that the risk of both debt and equity claims increases, while the risk of the overall corporate cash flow, $\rho(\text{CAC} - \text{IVS}, r_m)\text{CV}(\text{CAC} - \text{IVS})$, decreases for some range of θ, and then increases again, back up to the riskiness of the unlevered cash flow when $\theta = 1$. In Figure V.1 this behavior of required rates and risk is depicted by the arrows and can be described as follows:

1. As θ increases, the risk of debt, $\rho(\text{NCDD}, r_m)\text{CV}(\text{NCDD})$, increases from zero where $kd = i$ up to debt risk of $\rho(\text{CAU} - \text{IVS}, r_m)\text{CV}(\text{CAU} - \text{IVS})$, the unlevered firm risk, when $\theta = 1$ and $kd = ku$. Point D on the SML shows the risk–return location for debt with a $\theta = 0.15$; for our initial without-acceptance corporation, $kd = 0.08$ at that capital structure.

2. As θ increases, the risk of equity, $\rho(\text{NCDE}, r_m)\text{CV}(\text{NCDE})$, also increases. Point E represents the risk–return location for equity for the $\theta = 0.15$ corporation; $ke = 0.20$ for that θ.

3. For the unlevered firm, $ku = 0.18259$. As θ increases, the risk of the overall cash flow, $\rho(\text{CAC} - \text{IVS}, r_m)\text{CV}(\text{CAC} - \text{IVS})$, decreases at

FIGURE V.1 Capital structure with interest deductibility

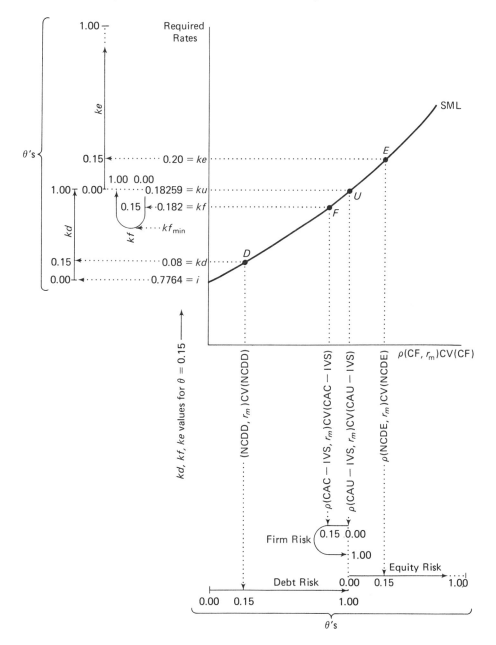

first because the ITS risk is less than the overall risk. Point F indicates a $kf = 0.182$ for $\theta = 0.15$. As θ continues to increase, however, the riskiness of the overall cash flow increases because the ITS risk is approaching the unlevered firm risk, so kf reverses its movement and returns to equal ku when $\theta = 1$.

The actual quantitative relationships between θ and the capital-market risk measures can be found, but are not really necessary for us to recognize that the capital structure decision is amenable to the same type of risk–return analysis to which we subjected the corporate investment decision.[16] The economics of capital structure, however, remains exactly the same as we saw in Section III. The CAPM–SML display in Figure V.1 is more specific about the risk/capital structure relationship and shows that capital-market equilibrium determines the resulting required rates, but it changes none of the basic economic ideas developed earlier.

It should come as no surprise that corporate financial decisions are consistent with and subject to analysis by the capital-market theory developed in this section.[17] After all, the judgmental criterion for these decisions, as we have seen time and time again, is their effect on shareholder wealth. And what better court can there be to render such judgments than the market in which equityholders' claims are traded and valued?

FINAL COMMENTS This section has presented the basic theoretical idea of corporate investment decisions which is the third of the three types of financial decisions made by corporations. We have now outlined the theories of corporate valuation, capital structure, capital acquisition/disbursement, and asset acquisition/ divestment. These constitute the basic theory of corporate finance and should provide an accurate conceptual picture of the general financial workings of corporations. We must stress, however, the adjectives "basic" and "conceptual" in this description. There are many important areas of corporate finance which have not been dealt with at all in the theory we have presented. For the most part, the dimensions we have not attempted to cover, fall into two related categories: institutional-descriptive matters and applied financial decision making. As to the first, in the interest of conceptual clarity we have dealt exclusively with the most simple corporate forms, financial instruments, real-asset characteristics, and capital-market conditions which would still allow demonstration of the basic economics of corporate finance. Financial managers in real corporations must deal continuously with complications,

[16]These quantitative capital structure risk–return relationships involve, as you might expect, the joint probability distributions for the various capital claims under different θ levels.

[17]Even in the case of capital structure alterations, researchers (see the references at the end of the section) have found that the appropriately measured risk (systematic) of common stock in real corporations tends to vary directly with θ, as our theory would predict.

such as myriad capital claim types differing widely in contractual provisions, with many different classes of capital claimants ranging from equity and debt holders to banks to leaseholders, with multiple investment proposals of intricate economic relatednesses and time patterns, and with all the empirical complexities that we have mentioned under the general rubric of imperfections.

Bearing these realities in mind, you can doubtless understand why prescriptions for financial managers in actual corporations could not play a major part in a treatment such as this. And furthermore, as we have often pointed out, the literature of corporate finance is replete with many fine references which deal with applied financial decisions as competently as is possible, given the level of comprehension of these complex phenomena.

What, then, is the value of a treatment such as ours, one that presents only the rudimentary ideas and relationships of corporate finance? Almost without exception the major theories that we have examined came into existence in the last two decades. And all too frequently these important ideas have been relegated to advanced graduate school curricula and texts and to academic journals. A major motivation for our approach has been to provide a basic, understandable, and cohesive coverage of these advances in financial thinking.

To develop expertise in corporate financial affairs requires that large amounts of time and effort be expended in studying detailed descriptions of corporations' financial environment and decision making within that environment. These efforts, however, are little more than shallow exercises without a firm appreciation of the basic economic ideas of corporate finance. The financial concepts we have studied are indeed basic and often crude abstractions of corporate reality. Nevertheless, they are the most appropriate foundation on which to build practical financial expertise.

The institutional characteristics of corporate finance can and do change rapidly. New techniques for optimal decision making also appear with encouraging regularity. The chances of successfully comprehending and profitably using these are enhanced immeasurably by understanding their stable economic underpinnings. The purpose of this text has been to provide a vehicle for that understanding.

Appendix V.A: Asset Divestment

The basic economic idea of asset *di*vestment is the mirror image of that for asset *in*vestment, with which we are now quite familiar. The only reason why the two are not completely complementary in all details is that they may be afforded different treatment under the tax laws (as they are, for example, in the United States). As with acquiring an asset in the investment decision, when divesting an asset the corporation moves from one set of future cash-flow expectations (and their risks) to another. We continue to think in terms of asset acquisition/divestment proposals which get accepted or rejected, so that the initial position of the corporation is still *without* (acceptance of the proposal to divest), and, should the proposed divestment be favorably viewed, the final cash-flow posture of the firm is then *with* (divestment proposal acceptance). Just remember that *with* and *without* refer to *proposal* acceptance, not to the physical presence of an asset.

The applicable tax rules for a divestment decision are in reality quite complex, but the actual impact of these rules is most often exactly the same as the normal corporate income tax:

1. When a corporation sells an operating asset, it receives a cash inflow net of related expenditure, in other words, a GCFO = $RCPT − $EXPT. Unless the cash a corporation receives is greater than what it originally paid for the asset (as it almost never is for operating assets), the cash flow is subject to normal corporate income tax. The excess, if any, is subject to a lower capital-gains tax rate.
2. The cash inflows from asset sales are also subject to depreciation deductibilities. The existing net book value of the asset is the deductible amount for tax purposes, and it generates a depreciation tax subsidy in exactly the same way as do regular depreciation expenses.

Thus, in divestment, there is a potential for a fairly complex cash-flow estimation situation, with a GTAX formed in two parts (income and capital gains). But that situation is quite rare in productive asset sales (with the exception of land and marketable securities), so, for practical purposes, it presents little difficulty. Actually, if the capital-gains tax rate is not applicable, the FCF statement and NPV procedures work exactly the same for divestment as for investment decisions.

As always, a numerical example is probably the best vehicle for examining the decision:

Suppose that our original two-period corporation is at time point t_1 and that someone has made an offer to purchase half of the operating assets of the corporation for $1000. It would cost the corporation $250 at t_1 to extricate the assets for sale. The result on t_2 $RCPT and $EXPT would be to cut them in half, without altering any risk. The corporate income tax rate remains at 52%, which is applied to the difference between the net cash received from a divestment (GCFO) and the book value of the assets sold; the original cost of the assets, we assume, was well in excess of $1000. The corporation would wish to maintain its capital structure were the offer to be accepted.

The analysis of a divestment decision proceeds much as any other financial decision. First, the relevant financial cash-flow effects are calculated, required rates of return or capital costs discovered, valuations made, and finally, shareholder wealth effects are judged. Table V.A.1 lists the obvious cash-flow effects of the proposed divestment. At t_1 a $1000 cash inflow occurs, which cost $250 to get. The income tax rate of 52% is applied to the $750 $GCFO_1^{divs}$, giving a $GTAX_1^{divs}$ of $390, and an $NCFO_1^{divs} = $360. The t_2 DTS^{wo} for the original corporation is $468, indicating that $468/0.52 = $900 of *book-value* assets exists at t_1. Since half of that is to be sold, the depreciation amount on which the tax is figured is $450 and $DTS_1^{divs} = $450(0.52) = $234. CAU_1^{divs} is therefore $594.

TABLE V.A.1

| | t_1 | | | t_2 | | |
	"Without" + *Divestment* =		*"With"*	*"Without"* + *Divestment* =		*"With"*
$RCPT	$6250.00	$1000.00	$7250.00	$7500.00	$-3750.00	$3750.00
$EXPT	3976.50	250.00	4226.50	4800.75	-2400.38	2400.38
GCFO	2273.50	750.00	3023.50	2699.25	-1349.63	1349.63
GTAX	1182.22	390.00	1572.22	1403.61	-701.81	701.81
NCFO	1091.28	360.00	1451.28	1295.64	-647.82	647.82
DTS	936.00	234.00	1170.00	468.00	-234.00	234.00
CAU	2027.28	594.00	2621.28	1763.64	-881.82	881.82

In terms of t_2 cash flows, since the loss of the asset will halve $RCPT_2$ and $EXPT_2$ for the corporation, the cash flows down through $NCFO_2$ are also halved. Also, since the depreciable assets remaining now have a book value of $450.00, the $DTS_2 = $450.00(0.52) = $234.00, and $CAU_2 = $881.82 for the corporation if it divests the asset.

Since operating risk has not changed and capital structure is to be constant, kf^* remains as 0.17576, and

$$VF_1^w = \frac{CAU_2^w - IVS_2^w}{1 + kf^{*w}}$$

$$= \frac{\$881.82}{1.17576}$$

$$= \$750.00$$

and

$$VD_1^w = VF_1^w(\theta)$$

$$= \$750.00(0.15)$$

$$= \$112.50$$

and

$$VE_1^w = VF_1^w - VD_1^w$$

$$= \$750.00 - \$112.50$$

$$= \$637.50$$

Remembering that the original $VE_1^{wo} = $1275.00, equityholders have experienced a $1275.00 - $637.50 = $637.50 decrease in share values at t_1 because of the divestment.

That, of course, is not the full wealth effect, because the cash inflow from the sale of the asset has not been accounted for yet. That, you recall, is $CAU_1^{divs} = \$594.00$. How is the $594.00 distributed? Note that $VD_1^w = \$112.50$ if the divestment is accepted. $VD_1^{wo} = \$225.00$ originally, so $112.50 of the $225.00 original debt value is liquidated at t_1 with a $PP_1^{divs} = \$112.50$ in order to maintain the original capital structure. This leaves $594.00 − $112.50 = $481.50 to be distributed to equity at t_1 as the proceeds of the divestment.

Equity therefore experiences a $637.50 decrease in value and a $481.50 cash inflow at t_1 due to the divestment. The wealth effect is thus $−637.50 + $481.50 = $−156.00. Equityholders would be $156.00 less well off at t_1 if the divestment were to be accepted.

Completing the t_2 cash flows, the new $VD_1^w = \$112.50$ at $kd = 8\%$ means that I_2^w becomes $9.00 and $ITS_2^w = \$4.68$. The remaining calculations are our standard financial cash-flow relationships and are shown with the value and wealth effects of the divestment in Table V.A.2.

TABLE V.A.2 Divestment

| | \multicolumn{3}{c}{t_1} | | | \multicolumn{3}{c}{t_2} | | |
	wo	+	divs	=	w	wo	+	divs	=	w
$RCPT	$6250.00		$1000.00		$7250.00	$7500.00		$−3750.00		$3750.00
$EXPT	3976.50		250.00		4226.50	4800.75		−2400.38		2400.38
GCFO	2273.50		750.00		3023.50	2699.25		−1349.63		1349.63
GTAX	1182.50		390.00		1572.22	1403.61		−701.81		701.81
NCFO	1091.28		360.00		1451.28	1295.64		−647.82		647.82
DTS	936.00		234.00		1170.00	468.00		−234.00		234.00
CAU	2027.28		594.00		2621.28	1763.64		−881.82		881.82
ITS	18.72		0.00		18.72	9.36		−4.68		4.68
CAC	2046.00		594.00		2640.00	1773.00		−886.50		886.50
I	36.00		0.00		36.00	18.00		−9.00		9.00
PP	225.00		112.50		237.50	225.00		−112.50		112.50
CDD	261.00		112.50		373.50	243.00		−121.50		121.50
NDC	0.00		0.00		0.00	0.00		0.00		0.00
NCDD	261.00		112.50		373.50	243.00		−121.50		121.50
CAE	1785.00		481.50		2266.50	1530.00		−765.00		765.00
CRF	0.00		0.00		0.00	0.00		0.00		0.00
CDE	1785.00		481.50		2266.50	1530.00		−765.00		765.00
NEC	0.00		0.00		0.00	0.00		0.00		0.00
NCDE	1785.00		481.50		2266.50	1530.00		−765.00		765.00
TCC ≡ IVS	0.00		0.00		0.00	0.00		0.00		0.00

k's: wo, divs, w

$ke = 0.2$

$kd = 0.08$

$kf = 0.182$

$kd^* = 0.0384$

$kf^* = 0.17576$

$VE_1^{wo} = \$1275.00$ $\qquad$ $VE_1^{divs} = \$−637.50$

$VD_1^{wo} = \quad225.00$ $\qquad$ $VD_1^{divs} = \quad−112.50$

$VF_1^{wo} = \quad1500.00$ $\qquad$ $VF_1^{divs} = \quad−750.00$

$VE_1^w = \$637.50$

$VD_1^w = \quad112.50$

$VF_1^w = \quad750.00$

$NPV_1^{divs} = VF_1^{divs} + (CAU_1^{divs} − IVS_1^{divs}) = \$−750.00 + (\$594.00 − \$0.00) = \$−156.00$

$\Delta PWE_1 = VE_1^{divs} + NCDE_1^{divs} = \$−637.50 + \$481.50 = \$−156.00$

In this situation the offer for the assets would be rejected because equity-holder wealth is greater with the assets operating than with the cash they would bring if sold. Note also in Table V.A.2 that the NPV of the divestment is also $\$-156.00$ at t_1, and it is calculated exactly the same way as the NPV of an investment.

Appendix V.B: Future Investment Decisions

The numerical examples of investment decisions illustrated in Section V have cash investment outlays now and inflows one period later. There are, however, several other time patterns of investment cash flows possible. One of the more interesting of these is a decision now to undertake an investment sometime in the future; that is, both the outlays and inflows of an investment are to happen at future time points, but the decision to invest is made at the present.

We can use the risk-constant example from Chapter 13 to illustrate such a situation. There, you recall, "now" was t_1, when the investment outlay occurred. Let us leave the investment expectations as they are and merely switch "now" from t_1 to t_0. This means that the investment decision is made at t_0 but the assets are not actually acquired until t_1. To retain the risk-constant characteristic we, of course, must assume that the required rates for the "without" and "with" corporate cash flows are the same in each period.

Applying an appropriate valuation formula to the information in Table 16.1,

$$\text{VF}_0^w = \frac{\text{CAU}_1^w - \text{IVS}_1^w}{1 + kf^*} + \frac{\text{CAU}_2^w - \text{IVS}_2^w}{(1 + kf^*)^2}$$

(since kf^* is constant for this two-period firm), we get

$$\text{VF}_0^w = \frac{\$2027.28 - \$1274.25}{1.17576} + \frac{\$3674.25 - \$0.00}{(1.17576)^2}$$
$$= \$3298.32$$

The *without* value of the firm at t_0 as originally shown is $\$3000.00$, so the increase due to the investment is $\$3298.32 - \$3000.00 = \$298.32$. You may wish to verify this by calculating VF_0^{ivs} directly from Table 13.6 using $kf^{*ivs} = 0.17576$. Note that this also is the t_0 net present value of the investment, since all future inflows and outflows are included in the calculation.

Continuing the analysis,

$$\text{VD}_0^w = \text{VF}_0^w(\theta)$$

and with θ constant at 0.15,

$$\text{VD}_0^w = \$3298.32(0.15)$$
$$= \$494.75$$

and hence,

$$VE_0^w = VF_0^w - VD_0^w$$
$$= \$3298.32 - \$494.75$$
$$= \$2803.57$$

The original "without" t_0 debt value is \$450.00, so VD_0^w is greater than VD_0^{wo} by \$44.75. $VE_0^{wo} = \$2550.00$, so VE_0^w has increased by \$253.57. The equity value increase is less than the \$298.32 NPV of the investment at t_0, yet we know that the present wealth of equityholders must increase by the NPV of the investment. It does this by the receipt of an extra \$44.75 cash dividend (\$253.57 + \$44.75 = \$298.32 = NPV = equity wealth increase) at t_0, due to that amount of new debt capital, $VD_0^w - VD_0^{wo}$ (\$494.75 − \$450.00 = \$44.75), being raised, and the proceeds being immediately distributed to equity suppliers, all at t_0. The cash flows and values of the corporation making this t_0 investment decision to take effect at t_1 illustrate this. These are shown in Table V.B.1.

TABLE V.B.1

Cash Flows	t_0 Investment	t_1 wo	+	ivs	=	w	t_2 wo	+	ivs	=	w
$RCPT	$ 0.00	$6,250.00	$	0.00		$6,250.00	$7,500.00		$5,000.00		$12,500.00
$EXPT	0.00	3,976.50		0.00		3,976.50	4,800.75		2,400.00		7,200.75
GCFO	0.00	2,273.50		0.00		2,273.50	2,699.25		2,600.00		5,299.25
GTAX	0.00	1,182.22		0.00		1,182.22	1,403.61		1,352.00		2,755.61
NCFO	0.00	1,091.28		0.00		1,091.28	1,295.64		1,248.00		2,543.64
DTS	0.00	936.00		0.00		936.00	468.00		662.61		1,130.61
CAU	0.00	2,027.28		0.00		2,027.28	1,763.64		1,910.61		3,674.25
ITS	0.00	18.72		1.86		20.58	9.36		10.14		19.50
CAC	0.00	2,046.00		1.86		2,047.86	1,773.00		1,920.75		3,693.75
I	0.00	36.00		3.58		39.58	18.00		19.50		37.50
PP	0.00	225.00		269.75		494.75	225.00		243.75		468.75
CDD	0.00	261.00		273.33		534.33	243.00		263.25		506.25
NDC	44.75	0.00		468.75		468.75	0.00		0.00		0.00
NCDD	−44.75	261.00		−195.42		65.58	243.00		263.25		506.25
CAE	44.75	1,785.00		−271.47		1,513.53	1,530.00		1,657.50		3,187.50
CRF	0.00	0.00		805.50		805.50	0.00		0.00		0.00
CDE	44.75	1,785.00		−1,076.97		708.03	1,530.00		1,657.50		3,187.50
NEC	0.00	0.00		0.00		0.00	0.00		0.00		0.00
NCDE	44.75	1,785.00		−1,076.97		708.03	1,530.00		1,657.50		3,187.50
TCC ≡ IVS	0.00	0.00		1,274.25		1,274.25	0.00		0.00		0.00

k's with $\theta = 0.15$, $\tau = 0.52$: w, wo, ivs

$ke = 0.2$
$kd = 0.08$
$kf = 0.182$
$kd^* = 0.0384$
$kf^* = 0.17576$

Values: $(V^{wo} + V^{ivs} = V^w)$

$VE_0^{wo} = \$2550.00$ $VE_0^{ivs} = \$253.57$
$VD_0^{wo} = 450.00$ $VD_0^{ivs} = 44.75$
$VF_0^{wo} = 3000.00$ $VF_0^{ivs} = 298.32$
$VE_0^w = \$2803.57$
$VD_0^w = 494.75$
$VF_0^w = 3298.32$

$NPV_0^{ivs} = VF_0^{ivs} + (CAU_0^{ivs} - IVS_0^{ivs}) = \$298.32 + \$0.00 - \$0.00 = \$298.32$
$\Delta PWE = VE_0^{ivs} + NCDE_0^{ivs} = \$253.57 + \$44.75 = \$298.32$

This example contains a few interesting points. The most obvious is that *the wealth effects (appropriately discounted) and market valuations implied by an investment decision occur as soon as the capital market realizes that the decision has been made, regardless of when the actual cash flows (both inflows and outflows) are expected to take place.* Here, equity suppliers got their wealth increase at t_0, even though the investment itself was not to begin until t_1. The *information* about the decision was enough for the capital market to revalue the expectations of the corporation.

Note also that, in order to maintain its capital structure at t_0 ($\theta = 0.15$), the corporation issued some debt a full period before the investment outlay. This again points out that in our capital market the important financing decision is capital structure, not capital acquisition/disbursement.[18]

Finally, it is interesting to note that a capital-market participant who wishes to share in the wealth increase of this investment must acquire equity shares of the company before the market discovers that an investment decision has been made. For example, buying equity at the VE_0^w price would return 20% per period, which is merely compensation for the risk being borne and includes no wealth change.

Appendix V.C: Investment and Capital Structure

This appendix shows the calculations for determining the appropriate required rates for a risk-altering investment, given its ku and capital structure, assuming interest deductibility. The first necessity is the market relationship between kd and θ. We shall assume, as we did in Section III for our two-period corporation, the following relationship, the reasonableness of which was demonstrated in Appendix III.C:

$$kd = i + (ku - i)\theta^2 \qquad \text{[V.C.1]}$$

Using the existing firm's p_2 rates and structure, we can solve for the risk-free rate implied thereby by restating formula V.C.1 as:

$$i = \frac{kd - \theta^2 ku}{1 - \theta^2} \qquad \text{[V.C.2]}$$

$$= \frac{0.08 - (0.15)^2(0.1826)}{1 - 0.0225}$$

$$= 0.07764$$

Hence, from formula V.C.1 we have

$$kd = 0.07764 + (ku - 0.07764)\theta^2$$

---

[18]The t_1 cash flows of the corporation are different from the previous risk-constant example because of the debt issue at t_0. You might find it instructive to review these flows. The t_1 values and t_2 cash flows remain as previously.

With the investment's $ku = 12\frac{1}{2}\%$ and $\theta = 0.15$:

$$kd^{ivs} = 0.07764 + (0.125 - 0.07764)(0.15)^2$$
$$= 0.07870$$

Formula III.C.13a indicates that for single-period situations,

$$kf = ku - \tau(ku - kd)\theta \frac{kd}{1 + kd}$$

Substituting appropriately,

$$kf^{ivs} = 0.125 - (0.52)(0.125 - 0.0787)(0.15)\frac{0.0787}{1.0787}$$
$$= 0.12474$$

and from the general relationships,

$$kf^* = kf - \tau\theta kd$$
$$kf^{*ivs} = 0.11860$$

and

$$kf = kd(\theta) + ke(1 - \theta)$$
$$ke = \frac{kf - kd\theta}{1 - \theta}$$
$$ke^{ivs} = 0.13286$$

Appendix V.D: Discount Rates for Multiperiod Investment Cash Flows

In Section V we stated that the model of capital-market equilibrium, the CAPM, being a single-period model was at this writing not yet well enough developed to give easily understood discount rates for use in multiperiod non-risk-constant corporate investment decisions. There are, however, some valuable observations we can make about such required rates. The multiperiod valuation discussion in Appendix II.C, in conjunction with the CAPM and investment ideas of Section V, is useful here.

First, we must be clear as to exactly what a future period's discount rate does conceptually within the theory, and specifically in valuing investment cash flows. From Section II and its appendixes we know that, when $P = T$

$$value_{T-1} = \frac{net\ cash\ flow_T + value_T}{1 + discount\ rate_P} \qquad \textbf{[V.D.1]}$$

Solving this for the discount rate,

$$discount\ rate_P = \frac{net\ cash\ flow_T + (value_T - value_{T-1})}{value_{T-1}} \qquad \textbf{[V.D.2]}$$

In general, any period's discount rate is the rate that equates value at the beginning of the period to value plus net cash flow at the end of the period. Computationally, that rate equals the net cash flow at the end of the period plus the value change during the period, all divided by the value at the beginning of the period.

For corporate investment decisions we are most interested in the ku_P^{ivs} rates (from which come kf_P^{*ivs} rates). Using the relationships above,

$$ku_P^{ivs} = \frac{(CAU_T^{ivs} - IVS_T^{ivs}) + (VU_T^{ivs} - VU_{T-1}^{ivs})}{VU_{T-1}^{ivs}} \qquad \text{[V.D.3]}$$

or

$$VU_{T-1}^{ivs} = \frac{(CAU_T^{ivs} - IVS_T^{ivs}) + VU_T^{ivs}}{1 + ku_P^{ivs}} \qquad \text{[V.D.4]}$$

and similarly for kf_P^{*}:

$$kf_P^{*ivs} = \frac{(CAU_T^{ivs} - IVS_T^{ivs}) + (VF_T^{ivs} - VF_{T-1}^{ivs})}{VF_{T-1}^{ivs}} \qquad \text{[V.D.5]}$$

or

$$VF_{T-1}^{ivs} = \frac{(CAU_T^{ivs} - IVS_T^{ivs}) + VF_T^{ivs}}{1 + kf_P^{*ivs}} \qquad \text{[V.D.6]}$$

For a multiperiod investment, each period's discount rate equates the end-of-period net investment cash flows $(CAU_T^{ivs} - IVS_T^{ivs})$ *plus the end-of-period value to the beginning-of-period value for the investment.*

Now consider either formula V.D.4 or V.D.6. They indicate that the investment discount rates are applicable to both time T's cash flow and investment value. Similarly, V.D.3 and V.D.4 show the investment rates being defined by both cash flows *and* values at T. *Since discount rates are determined by risk, the investment rates for each period must be a function not only of that period's cash-flow risk, but also those for all subsequent cash flows, because end-of-period value is itself dependent on all subsequent cash flows and their risks.*

We can illustrate this point by expanding formula V.D.4 or V.D.6. Consider a two-period investment, with cash flows at t_1 and t_2. Its t_0 value (from V.D.6) is

$$VF_0^{ivs} = \frac{(CAU_1^{ivs} - IVS_1^{ivs}) + VF_1^{ivs}}{1 + kf_1^{*ivs}}$$

but VF_1^{ivs} also has a cash-flow-determined value, so

$$VF_0^{ivs} = \frac{(CAU_1^{ivs} - IVS_1^{ivs}) + \dfrac{(CAU_2^{ivs} - IVS_2^{ivs}) + VF_2^{ivs}}{1 + kf_2^{*ivs}}}{1 + kf_1^{*ivs}}$$

Since this is a two-period situation, $VF_2^{ivs} = \$0.00$, and the above reduces to

$$VF_0^{ivs} = \frac{CAU_1^{ivs} - IVS_1^{ivs}}{1 + kf_1^{*ivs}} + \frac{CAU_2^{ivs} - IVS_2^{ivs}}{(1 + kf_1^{*ivs})(1 + kf_2^{*ivs})}$$

which itself is nothing more than our general multiple-period discount formula, here used with two-period investment cash flows.[19] The important thing to recognize is that kf_1^{*ivs} operates upon both the t_1 and t_2 cash flows in calculating value, and this is determined by the risks of both cash flows.

The discussion above should help in understanding why the one-period CAPM is not directly usable in discovering required rates for multiperiod investments. Specifically, formula 15.6 yields the risk-adjusted capital-market rate appropriate for discounting a single end-of-period cash flow to a beginning-of-period value; what is really needed in our multiperiod formulas is a rate determined by the riskinesses of *all* future cash flows.

With these observations in mind, what can actually be said about the determination of multiple-period discount rates in our theory of corporate finance? Such formulas as V.D.3 and V.D.5 are accurate but they are merely definitional, in that they themselves require end-of-period valuations and are therefore little more than single-period statements. But two considerations deserve deeper attention. First and most important is the fact that complex multiperiod capital claims *do* somehow or other get priced in real capital markets. And second, the CAPM, although single-period in construction, contains the basic economic ideas that seem to be appropriate for pricing (and therefore for finding appropriate discount rates applicable to) future cash flows and their risks.

In conjunction, these two ideas indicate that the future one-period rates necessary for discounting multiple-period cash flows within the theory are doubtless expectational functions of:

1. Future risk-free rates.
2. Future returns on the market portfolio.
3. Risks of the market portfolio in future periods.
4. The amount of the cash flows' risks which are not diversified away when held in participants' portfolios.

These four components are, of course, the same ones that appear in the single-period CAPM–SML relationship determining required rates for risky cash flows. There is no reason why these same factors would not also be the determinants of rates for multiple-period cash flows. The basic economics are no different.

Unfortunately, however, the theory of multiple-period portfolio holding has not progressed to the point where we can easily describe the specific way that the four elements listed above combine to produce the rates for discounting multiple-period cash flows. We are nearly certain that real capital markets

[19]The shorthand form of this is, of course,

$$VF_0^{ivs} = \sum_{T=1}^{2} \frac{CAU_T^{ivs} - IVS_T^{ivs}}{\prod_{P=1}^{T} (1 + kf_P^{*ivs})}$$

are pricing claims consistent with the general ideas developed in Section V and in this appendix, even for those with multiperiod, complex cash-flow expectations. All that remains to be done is a specification of the exact theoretical relationship.

In terms of real-world corporate financial decision making, this present theoretical frontier may not even be terribly constraining. As is argued in Section V, when dealing with multiple-period risk-constant investments or even with risk-altering investments whose cash-flow risks are not expected to change across time, the CAPM–SML relationship already developed is a good estimator of the needed rate(s). These two applications probably cover a substantial portion of all investment decisions that corporations must make.

Appendix V.E: The FCF Statement and Estimation of Investment Proposal Cash Flows

Perhaps the most difficult single aspect of real-asset investment decision making is the estimation of the cash flows associated with investment proposals. The examples treated in the text of Section V were purposefully simplistic so that only the important basic concepts would appear. The actual decisions faced by real corporations, however, usually are replete with considerations such as more complex tax effects, working capital changes, replacement of existing assets, and other complications. Although the theoretical issues involved are not difficult, merely keeping track of all relevant cash flows associated with a proposal becomes a significant task, and many opportunities for error and omissions exist. In these complex situations, the financial cash-flow statement can be a substantial aid to the correct estimation of such cash flows.

This appendix illustrates the use of the FCF statement for investment proposal cash-flow estimation. The example is a somewhat complex proposal to replace an existing asset with a new one. The situation and proposal are as follows:

> The existing corporation makes and sells cigars. One of its cigars is currently being produced and sold at the rate of 1 million per year. That rate is expected to be maintained in future years also. A proposal is under consideration to replace the existing production process with a new one. The new process also has a capacity to produce 1 million cigars per year, but the cigars would have an unusual shape, which marketing analysis indicates could be expected to sell for 5 cents more per cigar. In addition, the new process is expected to result in production cash expenditures of 3 cents less per cigar (because of lower electricity and labor expenditures). The new process is also expected, however,

to require an additional tobacco inventory, costing $20,000, to be maintained at all times. This tobacco inventory can be sold at any time for its original cost.

The new process would cost $200,000 for the new machines involved, and it would require a $20,000 outlay to have them installed. In addition, $30,000 would need to be spent immediately to retrain labor for the operation of the new process. The new process is expected to be operational for four years and then become obsolete. At that time the machines are expected to have a market value of $31,000 but cost $2000 to remove. For tax purposes the new machines carry a salvage value of $5500 when they are fully depreciated four years from now. The sum-of-the-years'-digits depreciation technique is allowed for income tax purposes.

The new process would need more floor space than the old process and would use an area of the plant that at present is rented to a concessionaire for $1500 per year. Were it not for the new process, the concessionaire would expect to continue renting permanently. Corporate accountants have decided that the additional floor space used by the new process would require an increased overhead allocation of $2650 per year over and above what the old machines now receive. The new process is not expected to require any other alterations in corporate expenditures.

The old process was bought six years ago for $75,000. Its remaining productive and accounting lives are four years. The assets carry a book salvage value of $1500 for tax purposes, but the machines could actually be sold immediately for $38,000 and would cost $1000 to extricate. Four years from now the existing machines would probably sell for $6500 and also require a $1000 expenditure for removal. The old assets are being depreciated on a straight-line basis.

The corporation regards the new process as a risk-constant investment; it would be financed so as to maintain the present corporate capital structure; the corporation's kf^* is 9%; its income tax rate is 52% (capital gains rate = 25%); and the employee training would be accomplished so quickly that the new process could begin operating immediately.

Although the solution to problems such as this can often be quite intricate, they are conceptually straightforward. The necessity is to estimate the cash flows associated exclusively with the investment proposal. From Section V you recall that a proposal's cash flows are defined as *the change in the existing corporation's cash-flow expectations were the proposal to be accepted.* In other words, to estimate proposal cash flows we must isolate all the cash-flow effects that the acceptance of the proposal implies, and no more.

The FCF statement can be a significant aid in accomplishing this. The above proposal has implications for every item used in figuring the CAU_T^{ics} − IVS_T^{ics} cash flows at each time point. Table V.E.1 lists some of the major cash-flow effects of replacement proposals such as the one that we have described. Read Table V.E.1 carefully. It can be a helpful guide in many investment–divestment situations. Generally, each of the items in the FCF statement is reviewed thoroughly for cash-flow effects. For example, under the $RCPT^{ivs} section, note that acceptance of the proposal can imply (1) the addition of productive cash inflows of the new assets, (2) opportunity costs, (3) inflow from the sale of old assets, (4) loss of productive cash receipts of the old assets, and (5) receipts from the sale of the new assets, when liquidated. Similar cash-flow effects are listed under $EXPT^{ivs}, DTS^{ivs}, and IVS^{ivs}.

The $+$ or $-$ signs in Table V.E.1 signify an increase or decrease in the *without* corporation's FCF item, were the proposal to be accepted. The time-point indications at the end of each cash-flow description signify:

1. T as the initial time point (when new assets replace old).
2. T $+$ 1, T $+$ 2, and so on, as the operating life of the assets.
3. *T* as the terminal or liquidation time point of the assets.

TABLE V.E.1 Estimating replacement proposal cash flows

$RCPT^{ivs}	$+$ (1)	Operational receipts (cash) from sale of the output from new assets at T $+$ 1, T $+$ 2, etc.
	$-$ (2)	As a negative, the opportunity cost of other assets of the firm now claimed by the investment, which would have generated cash elsewhere at T, T $+$ 1, T $+$ 2, etc.
	$+$ (3)	Inflow from sale of replaced asset at T.
	$-$ (4)	As a negative, the loss of operational cash receipts of replaced asset at T $+$ 1, T $+$ 2, etc.
	$+$ (5)	Receipts from the sale of asset(s), as, for example, liquidation of work in process, finished goods, raw materials, or released cash at *T*, plus sale of acquired asset at *T*. (*Note:* Since $RCPT^{ivs} is a cash amount, changes in accounts receivable are irrelevant.)
	$-$ (6)	Foregone sale of replaced asset at *T*.
$EXPT^{ivs}	$+$ (1)	Operational expenditures during the life of the investment, i.e., at T $+$ 1, T $+$ 2, etc.
	$+$ (2)	Cash outlays for the investment which can be expensed (e.g., training costs) at T.
	$-$ (3)	Replaced asset expenditures foregone at T $+$ 1, T $+$ 2, etc.
	$+$ (4)	Expenditures in salvaging replaced asset at T.
	$+$ (5)	$ costs of liquidating acquired asset at *T*.
	$-$ (6)	Foregone expenditures of salvaging replaced asset at *T*.
GTAX^{ivs}		Remember to distinguish between the portion of GCFO subject to regular income tax rates versus that portion, if any, subject to capital gains rates.
DTS^{ivs}	$+$ (1)	Operating DTS's of acquired asset at T $+$ 1, T $+$ 2, etc.
	$+$ (2)	DTS's from sale of replaced asset (undepreciated value, including salvage value on books times τ) at T.
	$-$ (3)	Lost DTS's of replaced asset at T $+$ 1, T $+$ 2, etc.
	$+$ (4)	Any book value of the acquired asset still existing at *T*, times τ.
	$+$ (5)	Any write-offs of working capital due to sale of replaced assets at T (negative at *T* if foregone), times τ.
	$+$ (6)	Any write-offs of working capital due to sale of acquired assets at *T*, times τ.
IVS^{ivs}	$+$ (1)	Cash cost of asset acquisition at T which must be capitalized.
	$+$ (2)	Freight, installation, etc., for (1) at T.
	$+$ (3)	Site preparation, construction, land, etc., at T.
	$+$ (4)	Increases in working capital other than accounts receivable (work in process, finished goods, raw materials, cash on hand) at T, T $+$ 1, T $+$ 2, etc.
	$-$ (5)	Foregone renewal outlays for replaced asset at T, T $+$ 1, T $+$ 2, etc.
	$+$ (6)	Renewal outlays for acquired asset itself at T $+$ 1, T $+$ 2, etc.

The procedure for using Table V.E.1 is to estimate each cash flow separately, combine those within FCF items at each time point (for example, combine all the $\$EXPT_2^{ivs}$ effects, and so on); find CAU^{ivs} and IVS^{ivs} for each time point, working with the standard FCF relationships; and, finally, calculate the proposal's NPV with the appropriate discount rate in formula 13.3a (p. 303).

To illustrate the workings of this techinque, the following is the solution to the replacement problem presented earlier:

t_0 cash flows

$\$RCPT_0^{ivs}$ + $38,000	sale of old machines	
$\$EXPT_0^{ivs}$ + 1,000	removal of old machines	
+ 30,000	expenditures for retraining employees to operate new machines	
+ $31,000		
$GCFO_0^{ivs}$ + 7,000		
$GTAX_0^{ivs}$ + 3,640	(at $\tau = 0.52$; capital-gains rate not applicable).	
$NCFO_0^{ivs}$ + 3,360		

$$DTS_0^{ivs} + 16,068 \begin{cases} \begin{array}{ll} \$75,000 & \text{original cost of old machine} \\ - 1,500 & \text{book salvage value} \\ \hline \$73,500 & \text{depreciation value of old machine} \\ \$ 7,350 & \text{depreciation/year, 10 years, straight line} \\ 6 \times \$7,350 = \$44,100 & \text{depreciation to date} \\ \$73,500 - \$44,100 = \$29,400 & \text{depreciable value at } t_0 \\ \$29,400 \times 0.52 = \$15,288 & \text{addition to } DTS_0^{ivs} \text{ due to depreciable value of old assets} \\ \$ 1,500 \times 0.52 = \$780 & \text{book salvage value} \times 0.52 \text{ equals addition to } DTS_0^{ivs} \text{ due to salvage value on books} \\ \$15,288 + \$780 = \$16,068 & \text{total } DTS_0^{ivs} \text{ due to sale of old assets} \end{array} \end{cases}$$

CAU_0^{ivs} + $19,428		
IVS_0^{ivs} + $200,000	cost of new assets	
+ 20,000	installation of new machines	
+ 20,000	increase in tobacco inventory	
$240,000		

t_{1-4} cash flows

$\$RCPT_{1-4}^{ivs}$ + $50,000	increase in cigar receipts at 5 cents per cigar	
- 1,500	opportunity cost of rent from concessionaire	
+ $48,500		
$\$EXPT_{1-4}^{ivs}$ - $30,000	lower cost of 3 cents per cigar (note that the increased overhead allocation is irrelevant)	
$GCFO_{1-4}^{ivs}$ + $78,500		
$GTAX_{1-4}^{ivs}$ + $40,820		
$NCFO_{1-4}^{ivs}$ + $37,680		

New asset DTS

	S.Y.D. factor	×	New asset gross amount depreciable	=	DEPR			
					DEPR	× 0.52 =	DTS	
t_1:	0.4	×	\$214,500	=	\$85,800	× 0.52 =	\$44,616	
t_2:	0.3	×	214,500	=	64,350	× 0.52 =	33,462	
t_3:	0.2	×	214,500	=	42,900	× 0.52 =	22,308	
t_4:	0.1	×	214,500	=	21,450	× 0.52 =	11,154	

\$7,350 lost depreciation per year on old asset results in lost DTS per year of \$3,822 (= \$7,350 × 0.52)

DTS_1^{ivs} + \$40,794

DTS_2^{ivs} + \$29,640

DTS_3^{ivs} + \$18,486

DTS_4^{ivs} + \$7,332

CAU_1^{ivs} + \$78,474

CAU_2^{ivs} + \$67,320

CAU_3^{ivs} + \$56,166

CAU_4^{ivs} + \$45,012

IVS_{1-4}^{ivs} \$0

$t_4 = T$ cash flows (terminal)

$\$RCPT_4^{ivs}$ + \$31,000		sale of new assets
+ 20,000		sale of unneeded tobacco inventory
− 6,500		foregone sale of old assets
+ \$44,500		
$\$EXPT_4^{ivs}$ + \$ 2,000		removal of new assets
− 1,000		foregone removal of old assets
+ \$ 1,000		
$GCFO_4^{ivs}$ + \$43,500		
$GTAX_4^{ivs}$ + \$22,620		
$NCFO_4^{ivs}$ + \$20,880		
DTS_4^{ivs} + \$ 2,860		salvage (book value) \$5,500 of new assets × 0.52
− 780		foregone (book value) salvage of old assets, \$1,500 × 0.52
+ 10,400		write-off against \$20,000 tobacco inventory × 0.52
\$12,480		
CAU_4^{ivs} \$33,360		
IVS_4^{ivs} \$0		

$$NPV^{ivs} = CAU_0^{ivs} - IVS_0^{ivs} + \sum_{T=1}^{4} \frac{CAU_T^{ivs} - IVS_T^{ivs}}{\prod_{P=1}^{T}(1 + kf_P^{*ivs})} = \sum_{T=0}^{4} \frac{CAU_T^{ivs} - IVS_T^{ivs}}{(1 + kf^{*ivs})^T}$$

$$= \$19,428 - \$240,000 + \frac{\$78,474 - \$0}{1.09} + \frac{\$67,320 - \$0}{(1.09)^2} + \frac{\$56,166 - \$0}{(1.09)^3}$$

$$+ \frac{\$45,012 + \$33,360 - \$0}{(1.09)^4}$$

$$= +\$6,975.55$$

The NPV of this particular replacement proposal is a positive \$6975.55. More important than that, however, is the demonstrated usefulness of the

FCF statement in keeping track of the various cash flows associated with the proposal. The major purpose of this example has been to show that, without some formal design for estimating cash flows, the complexities of such realistic decisions will almost assure the analyst of at least some errors and/or omissions.

We have used a replacement proposal because it contains several interesting complexities and also because it is a very common type of investment decision. The FCF statement can also be a most useful vehicle for other types of decisions, including those for competing proposals of differing lifetimes, economically dependent proposals, divestments, and straightforward asset acquisitions.

Problems for Section V

1. Suppose that the five-period corporation (Chapter 7, pp. 107-110; Appendix IV.A) were considering an investment proposal with the following characteristics:

1. An investment cash outlay of $2316.76 at t_0 would be required to produce additions to corporate operating cash-flow expectations (CAU's) of $1748.20 at t_1 and $5714.39 at t_2. Beyond time-point t_2, no cash flows are expected to be associated with the investment.
2. The company regards the operational aspects of the proposal as having risks identical to those of the existing corporation; and the proposal is to be financed so as to hold corporate capital structure constant.

Please answer:

(a) Should the investment be accepted, or not? If it is accepted, how can it be financed so as to hold corporate capital structure constant?
(b) Demonstrate what the effect on current equityholders' present wealth would be if the investment is accepted.
(c) Show the effect on corporate cash-flow expectations (wo, ivs, and w) of the financing and investment decisions implied by the acceptance of the proposal.
(d) Calculate the new corporate values (w) for each time point, and verify the calculations in part (a) above, using these new corporate values.

2. Suppose a corporation were considering an investment opportunity now (at t_0). The opportunity is expected to have operating cash-flows at t_1 and then cease to exist. The corporation feels that the opportunity's cash-flow joint probability distribution with overall capital-market returns is:

Possible CAU$_1$ dollar outcomes

		−1200	1500	2500	6000
Possible	−.05	.04	.03	.00	.00
r_{m_1}	.00	.01	.09	.07	.03
Outcomes	.10	.00	.07	.26	.17
	.20	.00	.01	.12	.10

The corporation can invest at a 5% risk-free rate during p_1; the capital market is composed of risk-averse portfolio analysts, and is efficient. Please answer:

(a) What is the rate of return that would be required by the capital market on the operational cash flows from this opportunity?

(b) At what t_0 price would the opportunity (to receive the t_1 operational cash flows) be acceptable?

(c) Assuming the price is known, does the corporation have enough information to decide whether to accept the opportunity? If not, what further information must be discovered?

(d) Are there capital-market and/or taxation conditions under which the company could decide about the opportunity without further information?

(e) Outline the process the company would use to make a decision about the opportunity using the information mentioned in (c) above, assuming the capital market is as described in Sections I–V of the text, and that interest payments are deductible for corporate income tax purposes.

3. An investment opportunity is available to the two-period firm in Chapter 16 (the firm "without acceptance). The opportunity has the following characteristics:

1. It requires an investment cash outlay of $1075.00 at t_1, and is expected to add $1416.29 to the corporation's operating cash flow (CAU) at t_2.

2. The opportunity's operating cash-flow carries a standard deviation, $\sigma(CAU_2^{ivs})$, of $2565.706, and is correlated with the market portfolio's returns to the extent of $\rho(CAU_2^{ivs}, r_m) = .82$.

3. The expected return on the market portfolio, its standard deviation, and the risk-free rate are as specified previously (Chapter 16) for p_2, of the two-period firm:

$$E(r_m) = .09$$
$$\rho(r_m) = .10$$
$$i = .07764$$

4. The corporation intends to maintain its capital structure in financing this proposal, if accepted.

Please answer:

(a) Should the proposal be accepted by the two-period firm (assuming t_1 is "now")? What would be the wealth effect on equity suppliers, if accepted? (Note: You may find it beneficial to refer to Appendixes III.C and V.C. in solving this problem.)

(b) Calculate the required rates and capital costs associated with the investment proposal, were it to be financed as suggested. Why do these rates differ from those of the two-period corporation which is financed identically?

(c) Calculate the cash-flow expectations for the investment proposal, and for the corporation "with acceptance" for t_1 and t_2. (Assume a reasonable capital acquisition/disbursement strategy, say, a preference for retention.)

(d) Calculate the required rates and capital costs for the corporation "with acceptance," and use these to verify corporate and investment values implied earlier in this problem.

(e) Suppose the corporation chose to finance this proposal purely by equity. Would the decision be altered? If so, explain why, both verbally and quantitatively.

(f) Suppose, at t_0 the capital market believed that the corporation would undertake the proposal at t_1, maintaining its original capital structure. Would there be any t_0 effect perceivable? If so, illustrate quantitatively. If any *corporate* decision is required at t_0 because of this, illustrate it also.

4. Suppose that the corporation in Chapter 16 contemplates financing (remembering the correct definition of that term) the original investment proposal, if accepted, with a $\theta^{ivs} = .50$.

(a) Calculate the NPV of the investment. (Note: Appendixes III.C and V.C will aid you in doing this.)

(b) Calculate the rates, capital costs, cash flows, and values of the investment proposal and with-acceptance corporation.

(c) Verify the wealth change for the company's equityholders through the resulting dividend and/or price changes.

(d) Why is this NPV different from that observed in Chapter 16? Account for the difference quantitatively.

(e) How much of a change in the investment's t_1 outlay would have been necessary before the proposal would have been *unacceptable* at a $\theta^{ivs} = 0$, but still *acceptable* at a $\theta^{ivs} = .15$? How much of an outlay alteration would cause acceptability at $\theta^{ivs} = .50$, but unacceptability at $\theta^{ivs} = .15$? What does this tell you about the interaction of investment and financing decisions?

(f) Suppose that this were a real capital market. Are there any other interactions now possible between this investment and the way it could be financed which can be important? (Hint: Could default likelihoods and, hence, the present value of future default costs be involved?)

5. The Planetary Encyclopedia Corporation is in the business of selling encyclopedias in Ida Grove, Iowa. Having lost a court case (for deceptive sales practices), the management feels it has two more time periods to sell encyclopedias in Ida Grove before Mayor Murphy runs them out of town.

Planetary's ace salesman has been doing well, but it has recently been discovered that he drives the company's flashy Zipmobile around town. A psychological profile of the average Ida Grove citizen indicates that drivers of flashy Zipmobiles are looked upon with some suspicion in this heartland community. Planetary is therefore considering replacement of its Zipmobile with a more conservative, civically respectable 1948 Henry J. This, it is felt, will help encyclopedia sales.

The Zipmobile was bought by Planetary several years ago for $1000. It carries a $50 accounting salvage value and has two remaining depreciation expenses of $150 at t_1 and $50 at t_2. Now (at t_0) it could be sold for $500, but a $200 fee to the selling agent would also be required. The Henry J. costs $1500 at t_0. In addition, since the Henry J. is a more complex auto, Planetary would need to enroll its ace salesman in a quickie driver-education course at a cost of $550 at t_0 and $75 at t_1. The Zipmobile and the Henry J. cost the same to run and maintain. The Henry J. would carry no accounting salvage value. However, Planetary foresees the need to install anti-pollution devices costing $200 on the car at t_1; this outlay would be capitalized. The Henry J. will be depreciated over two periods on the straight-line basis. At t_2, Planetary plans to sell the Henry J. for $1000 with an attached seller's fee of $150. Should the Zipmobile be kept, it could probably be sold at t_2 for $100 with only a $50 fee.

Planetary's marketing analysis staff believes that switching from the Zipmobile to the Henry J. will result in $2000 more encyclopedia cash sales at t_1 and $2100 at t_2. The ace salesman gets 55% of his sales as commission. Planetary's overall cost of capital is 10% per period, the corporate income tax rate is 52%, and the capital gains rate is 20%. The Henry J. is considered a risk-constant investment and will be financed so that Planetary's capital structure is held constant.

(a) Please advise Planetary as to whether the Zipmobile should be replaced with the Henry J. Provide all the necessary analysis to convince Planetary your recommendation is correct.

(b) Planetary's capital acquisition/disbursement policy is to finance as much as possible through internally generated cash. When it is not possible to finance completely through internal means, Planetary prefers to first issue new debt, rather than equity claims. As of t_0, Planetary's present and future cash-flow expectations without the proposal's acceptance are:

	t_0	t_1	t_2
$RCPT	$7191.90	$11144.77	$4318.47
$EXPT	3955.55	6129.62	2375.16
GCFO	3236.35	5015.15	1943.31
GTAX	1682.90	2607.88	1010.52
NCFO	1553.45	2407.27	932.79
DTS	260.00	156.00	104.00
CAU	1813.45	2563.27	1036.79
ITS	141.18	115.09	34.04
CAC	1954.63	2679.36	1070.83
I	271.50	221.33	65.45
PP	401.38	1246.98	523.63
CDD	672.88	1468.31	589.08
NDC	0.00	0.00	0.00
NCDD	672.88	1468.31	589.08
CAE	1281.75	1210.05	481.75
CRF	700.00	0.00	0.00
CDE	581.75	1210.05	481.75
NEC	0.00	0.00	0.00
NCDE	581.75	1210.05	481.75
TCC $\equiv$ IVS	700.00	0.00	0.00

The capital market is requiring a per-period equity return of 15% and a debt rate of 12.5%. The debt suppliers of Planetary allow no early or late principal payments. Please illustrate Planetary's financing if it accepts the Henry J. project. (Remember that capital structure is to be unaltered.)

(c) Prepare a FCF statement for the with-acceptance cash-flow expectations and determine the with-acceptance values.

(d) Illustrate the effect on shareholder present wealth should the Henry J. be purchased, based on your with-acceptance FCF statement.

(e) When (at t_0) should Planetary announce the decision to the capital market, *before* or *after* any new equity capital is raised? Show why, quantitatively.

References for Section V

It is most unusual when a single researcher can be identified as being solely responsible for the genesis of a particular theory. In the case of the theory of how portfolio-holding, risk-averse investors may be expected to behave, however, this is precisely the situation. The inventor was Harry M. Markowitz, "Portfolio Selection," *Journal of Finance* (March 1952). The theory of capital-market equilibrium, based on Markowitz's participants' behavior, was later proposed almost simultaneously in: William F. Sharpe, "Capital Asset Prices: A Theory of Market Equilibrium Under Conditions of Risk," *Journal of Finance* (September 1964); and John Lintner, "Security Prices, Risk, and Maximal Gains from Diversification," *Journal of Finance*

(December 1965), and "The Valuation of Risk Assets and the Selection of Risky Investments in Stock Portfolio and Capital Budgets," *Review of Economics and Statistics* (February 1965).

For a good discussion of the as-yet-unresolved theoretical issues of capital-market equilibrium, especially alternative specifications of the SML, see: Michael C. Jensen, "Capital Markets: Theory and Evidence," *The Bell Journal of Economics and Management Science* (December 1972). Some widely used empirical estimates of capital-market risk–return relationships and pricing processes appear in: Eugene F. Fama and James McBeth, "Risk, Return and Equilibrium: Empirical Tests," *Journal of the Political Economy* (May-June 1973), and James Lorie and Richard Brealey, *Modern Developments in Investment Management* (New York: Praeger Publishers, Inc., 1972). For more intensive theoretical discussions of corporate investment strategy under conditions of uncertainty, see: Charles W. Haley and Lawrence D. Schall, *The Theory of Financial Decisions* (New York: McGraw-Hill Book Company 1973), and Eugene F. Fama and Merton H. Miller, *The Theory of Finance* (New York: Holt, Rinehart and Winston, Inc., 1972).

Some evidence on the effects that corporate financial decision making has on the capital market's view of corporate risk (especially the capital structure decision) can be found in: R. Hamada, "The Effect of the Firm's Capital Structure on the Systematic Risk of Common Stocks," *Journal of Finance* (May 1972), the reading of which should be followed by reading James A. Boness, Andrew H. Chen, and Som Jatusipitak, "Investigations of Non-stationarity in Prices," *Journal of Business* (October 1974).

For illustrations of CAPM applications to the corporate investment decision, see: J. Fred Weston, "Investment Decisions Using the Capital Asset Pricing Model," *Financial Management* (Spring 1973), and James C. Van Horne, *Financial Management and Policy*, 4th ed. (Englewood Cliffs, N.J.: Prentice-Hall, Inc., 1977).

Index